THEY'RE NEVER TOO YOUNG FOR BOOKS
LITERATURE FOR PRE-SCHOOLERS

by
Edythe M. McGovern

Mar Vista Publishing, Los Angeles
1980

Copyright © 1980 by Edythe M. McGovern

All rights reserved. No part of this book may be reproduced in any form or by any electronic or mechanical means including information storage and retrieval systems without permission from the publisher, except by a reviewer who may quote brief passages in a review.

Library of Congress Catalog Card No. 80-80216

ISBN 0-9604064-0-9

First Printing 1980

Mar Vista Publishing Company
11917 Westminster Place
Los Angeles, California 90066

Printed and Bound in the United States of America

Preface

With a growing recognition that the pre-school years are the critical period in a child's sensory and intellectual development has come an awareness of the importance of books and reading in nurturing learning and the imagination.

Today, virtually every genre of the literary mainstream can be found in children's picture books. Yet, relatively little has been written exclusively about this multifaceted world of pre-school literature. Edythe McGovern's treatment of the subject is indeed a welcome aid to students of children's literature and to teachers of pre-schoolers, as well as to parents eager to introduce their children to the shared pleasures of reading.

How does one launch the lifelong adventure which literature offers? Even those adults convinced of the benefits of early exposure to books are often understandably baffled by the task of choosing and using them most effectively.

For them, this volume presents a knowledgeable, succinct and highly practical guide to the selection and use of hundreds of books to satisfy the expanding interests and developmental needs of pre-schoolers. The information is well and thoughtfully organized to provide easy access to different types of books and to specific titles, authors and illustrators.

For those already familiar with many of the books cited, the author has added another dimension, in the section on reinforcing children's experience of literature. Her techniques for reading aloud and for involving children in creative dramatics and puppetry incorporate those practical details so essential to building the adult's confidence in these areas.

Clearly, then, this is a book with a broad appeal and a variety of uses—academic, professional, and personal. For each of these audiences it will prove enlightening. However, it does more than inform; it also invites . . . invites adults to savor the enjoyment of books with children and to augment the text with their own new discoveries and delights, as their knowledge and appreciation of children's literature deepen. It says, "Happy reading!"

> Priscilla Moxom, Coordinator
> Children's Services
> Los Angeles Public Library

Acknowledgments

This book is a response to the needs of my students in pre-school children's literature classes at Los Angeles Valley College and my many friends among children's librarians, and I am sincerely grateful to both groups for their invaluable assistance in shaping the final product. In one sense, it has been a labor of love, since all of us share a deep conviction and an almost missionary zeal about the value of introducing children to books at the earliest age possible. In another way, it is designed as a tool to assist those involved with pre-schoolers as professional providers and/or parents to sift through the enormous quantity of material produced for youngsters and find "the perfect book" for each use. Therefore, the suggested book lists and extensive bibliography.

Throughout the project I have had encouragement from many individuals, among whom I would particularly like to thank David Moody, Consultants for Educational Intercommunications (CEI, Inc.), without whose computer assistance the lists would have been an impossibility; Teresa Wilcomb, who patiently typed disks; Eddie Irwin, Publication Arts Service, who designed the book's final format; Lila Chan, who conceived the cover design, using a picture by Wendy Alberts on the title page; Ruth Robinson, children's librarian emeritus, Los Angeles Public Library, who provided extensive research assistance; Serena Day, Priscilla Moxom, and Helen Muller, dedicated librarians all, who read the manuscript at various stages and made valuable suggestions, especially about the utility of the various booklists; Armida Bolton, my peerless editor, who acted as a resonant sounding-board from the beginning; her husband, Donald Bolton, who read proofs, and, finally, the many pre-school children—especially Staci Hoglund, Kim McGovern, Tori St. Clair, and Justin Alberts—who have let me practice reading to them over the years.

Table of Contents

INTRODUCTION xi
PART ONE—POSITIVE RESULTS OF READING TO
  PRE-SCHOOLERS 1
  Meeting Immediate Needs: Material Security, Safety,
    Emotional Security, Competence, Belonging,
    Acceptance of Uniqueness, Need to Play, Aesthetic
    Satisfaction, Intellectual Stimulation 2
  Future Effects: Literacy, Language Development,
    Attitude Change, Development of Imagination,
    Specific Problems, Insight Through Vicarious
    Experience, Television 4
PART TWO—BOOK SELECTION 13
  An Overview 13
  General Expectations by Age Levels 15
  Inappropriate Materials: Condensations, Bowdlerized
    Versions, Readers, Books in Series, Stereotypes,
    Sexist Books 18
  A Very Special Consideration—Illustrations 22
  Some Specifics of Selection 25
  Fiction 25
  A Check List for Excellence 29
  Fictional Book Lists (by Approximate Age Levels)
    First Books 31
    Bilingual (English-Spanish) 35
    Bilingual (English-Other Languages) 37
    Wordless Books 38
    Folk and Fairy Tales 39
    Stress on Physical Safety 50
    Age Identity 52
    Family Relationships (Siblings, Parent-Child,
      Divorce, Single Parents) 53
    Competence "I Can" 59
    The Unique Self 62
    Need to Belong 63
    Friendship 65
    Problem Solving 68

Illness, War, Death 73
Old-Age and Grandparents 74
The Need to Play 76
Humorous Books 78
Monster Stories 84
Pets as Protagonists 85
Other Animals as Protagonists 88
Sexual Identity 103
Occupational Opportunities 104
Rural Settings 105
Urban Settings 108
The Weather 109
Seasons 110
Holidays—Including Birthdays 112
Group Emphases 116
   Black Americans 116
   Blacks Outside United States 118
   Asians/Orientals 119
   Hispanic 120
   American Indian 121
   Others (Eskimo, Canadian, Cajun) 121

Informational Books 122
Informational Book Lists (by Approximate Age Level)
  Books to Learn More About
    General Information 124
    Geography 129
    History 129
    Animals 130
    Plants 135
    Environment/Ecology 136
    Other Nature 137
    Human Biology 138
    Other Science 139
  Books to Emphasize Skills
    Alphabet 140
    Numbers 141
    Pictures/Shapes/Colors 143
    Music 143
    Verbal Skills 144
    Concepts 144
    Miscellaneous 145

    Poetry Books—Lists with Types Designated (Serious, Nonsense, etc.) 146
PART THREE—READING ALOUD 153
    Some General Hints 153
    Some Rules for Successful Read Alouds 154
        Creative Dramatics 156
        The Story Board 160
        Puppets 162
IN CONCLUSION 165
    Footnotes 167
COMPLETE BIBLIOGRAPHY by Author, Title, Illustrator, Publisher, Date 169
    Names and Addresses of Publishers 279

Introduction

No one who has any contact, permanent or transitory, with pre-school children denies that exposure to books is beneficial to youngsters. It is almost a subconscious feeling, substantiated by formal research, that when literature in the broadest sense of that term is made part of a child's life from the onset, positive results are predictable. However reassuring and pleasant this assertion may be, it does seem to be something of a broad generalization. Therefore, the first purpose of this book will be to delineate these "positive results" as precisely as possible.

Once adults involved with small children have been convinced of the value of reading to those not yet able to read to themselves, these adults need to become aware of how to select books appropriate to each age level within the pre-school range. If we consider that over 2,000 new titles for children come onto the market every year and add to this the number of worthwhile old favorites, it is clear that some attempt at establishing criteria for selection can be valuable and, indeed, may be almost mandatory.

Children's librarians can and do give expert assistance, of course, but having some basic idea of what books to select without professional advice is important, particularly since many libraries do not stock a "complete collection," especially of new books or of those produced by minor publishing houses. Additionally, parents and teachers will want to know how to differentiate between books of high calibre and those so readily available in supermarkets, drug and variety stores. The second purpose of this book, therefore, will be to assist the reader in establishing his or her own guidelines for wise selection.

Next, convinced that exposure has specific positive value and that there are some objective standards for book choice, the adult will be concerned with the presentation of the material: the best times and places to read aloud, the differences between reading to one or two children and reading to a group, the actual techniques involved in presenting picture-books to small children, and the use of certain reinforcement aids, such as creative dramatics, story boards, and puppets.

And finally, there is the matter of specific titles—guideposts, really—which the adult may find useful as he expands his familiarity with children's books. For this purpose there is a complete formal bibliography at the back of the book, followed by a list of publishers' names and addresses for convenience in ordering titles not found in the local library or bookstore.

In addition, there are extensive book lists incorporated into the body of the text, each arranged according to *approximate age level* (very young, middle, and older pre-schoolers), *various emphases*, and *possible uses*. A title may be found on more than one list—sometimes on three or four—because it fits into more than a single category. For example, a book might involve a numerical concept, give information about animals, and be printed in English and a second language, in which case it would appear on three lists.

To facilitate their use, the lists which appear throughout the book have been done by book title and first author only. For complete information regarding additional authors, if any, illustrator, publisher, and date of publication, the reader must consult the bibliography. On the other hand, there are many titles included in the complete listing which do not appear on any individual list because they do not feature an emphasis which is stressed, but which are simply good stories to read to small children, stories which they will enjoy hearing.

In any case, these lists must all be individually amended and updated according to personal preference and experience, since with the proliferation of books and their ever-widening areas of focus, children's literature as a genre is apt to grow as rapidly as pre-schoolers themselves, so that the "best" book in any group may be published tomorrow.

Part One

Positive Results

If there were no discernible benefit of reading to pre-schoolers except the opportunity for the warm interaction which takes place between the adult reader and the child or children, exposing them to literature would still remain a very important activity, unique and satisfying. However, since there are quite a number of "positive results" which can be specifically identified, we need to examine them in some detail. They may be roughly divided into two categories: outcomes in terms of meeting immediate needs, and salutary effects in terms of future requirements. As we shall see, there will be some overlap here, since, to paraphrase Wordsworth, "The child is parent to the adult."

One word of caution. No thinking person would claim that "meeting needs" of small children through exposure to literature is in any sense a complete program for their development. What most emphatically is asserted is that reading aloud can reasonably be expected to add dimension to that program in a way which cannot be fulfilled as well by any other activity.

Immediate Needs of Pre-School Children

Although they are stated and explicated in various ways and in differing orders of importance by experts in the field of child development, a consensus regarding the requirements of a healthy, happy child would include the following:

1. Material Security
2. Safety
3. Emotional Security
4. Competence or Self-Actualization
5. A Need to Belong
6. A Need to Accept One's Uniqueness
7. A Need to Play and Escape
8. Aesthetic Satisfaction
9. Intellectual Stimulation

Along with a brief explanation of each of these categories, we shall investigate the connection between reading to pre-schoolers and meeting these needs.

1. Material Security

Obviously, every child requires at least a minimum of material security in his "real world" in order to survive. A hungry child cannot be expected to pay much attention to anything which does not satisfy his immediate appetite for food. Recognition of this truism, of course, has led to many programs for amelioration, such as providing breakfast for pre-schoolers and so on. But what of the child who is literally deprived in the socio-economic sense, lacking even some necessities? Can books make up in any way for indigence? Probably not. But this child has other needs, common to all children, and meeting these may help to make his material lack more bearable. Also, pragmatically, a broad exposure to the written word from a very early stage of intellectual development may well prepare that child for a more materially secure adulthood in terms of future requirements, such as literacy, for example.

2. Safety

Child psychologists stress the small child's need for a predictable somewhat proscribed world up to a point, a world which, as the toddler grows, includes to a greater and greater degree a need for new experience, excitement, and exploration, always with the knowledge that there is a home base to which he may return. As we shall see, there are a number of books which have this concept as their main idea or theme.

3. Emotional Security

Closely tied in with safety is the notion of emotional security, which means quite simply that no matter how far afield a child may wander—actually or in terms of his behavior—that child is still accepted and loved, usually by a parent. Later, he needs to become aware of the mutual trust which underlies secure relationships with his peers and/or with adults outside the immediate family circle.

4. Competence or Self-Actualization

To a small child this means that he/she *can* do it, whatever "it" may be, sometimes against great odds. Since we recognize that even adults utilize role models in this way, albeit unconsciously, it is easy to recognize the function of books which picture examples for effectively interacting with one's environment to gain, first, self-esteem, and then, the respect of others.

5. A Need to Belong

The first evidence of this need can be seen in the very young child's relationship with those who minister to his initial demands for the provision of his physical comforts. As he becomes less egocentric, he wants to feel a part of a close group, his family, and in this sense the "need to belong" is very much tied in with the desire for emotional security. However, there is a broader concept here as well; as the child matures and his world expands, he requires reassurance that he belongs in his neighborhood, is part of his ethnic/racial group, and ultimately assumes membership in the human race in the total sense.

6. A Need to Accept One's Uniqueness

Although he needs to belong to a group, the small child also needs to accept himself as a unique individual and to be reassured that being one's own self does not preclude acceptance by others who may be quite unique also.

7. A Need to Play and Escape

Books which can be included in this category may be equated with "escape" literature for adults. Even the most thoughtful grown-up enjoys humor for its own sake, amusement per se, without any intent beyond momentary pleasure, "recreation" in its original sense. Not surprisingly, even the youngest child has this same desire, which may be satisfied by nonsense words, rhyming jingles, humorous pictures, and preposterous exaggeration within a story.

8. Aesthetic Satisfaction

If we agree that "taste," particularly in the area of graphic art, is developed through repeated exposure to superior work, we have to look at picture-books for pre-schoolers in a very special way. In no other category of literature is there as great an opportunity for consistent presentation of the best as there is in books illustrated in many styles by artists of note. We are not going to attempt to sub-divide picture books, except as 1) fiction, 2) non-fiction or informational, and 3) poetry, since there seems no valid reason to attempt classifications such as picture book, picture-book story, and so on. Suffice to realize that for youngsters under the age of six or seven, books not copiously illustrated are not favored. However, we need not choose books for their aesthetic quality in terms of art work alone; on the contrary, for the most part, superior choices *incorporate outstanding illustration* which simplifies matters.

Since it is so significant, the topic of illustration will be dealt with in great depth in the section on Book Selection.

9. Intellectual Stimulation

At first glance, this may seem a low priority need for very young pre-schoolers, but many psychologists have concluded that curiosity itself is almost "inborn," and certainly the need to know and then to understand is generally evident from the time a toddler begins to investigate the kitchen cupboards. To meet this need may mean giving a city child his first (and perhaps his only) view of farm animals; it may entail reinforcing numerical concepts; it could include showing a five-year-old how to look for a word in his first picture dictionary. In short, what is involved here is both the stimulation and the satisfaction of areas which can be primarily designated as intellectual, rather than aesthetic or emotional.

Future Effects

To examine needs which are not immediately apparent is not as simple a matter as looking at those which present themselves on a day-to-day basis when one has contact with pre-schoolers. Nevertheless, certain topics clamor for consideration because they have application not only to the far-distant period of adulthood, but also because they have pertinence to the not-so-far-away times of later childhood and adolescence. In terms of long-range needs and results, what are the potentially "positive effects" of reading to children under the age of six? Let us consider seven categories.

1. Literacy

For at least the last twenty years there has been an alarming increase in illiteracy among school-age children and young adults who somehow have not mastered the basic skills involved in reading—and consequently, writing—even by the time of their graduation from high school. We do not need to search out scholarly articles in professional journals to become aware of this problem. It is brought to our attention daily in news articles, in popular magazines, and whenever education is the subject of a radio or television broadcast. We are told, "Johnny—and his sister, Mary—can't read!" and along with a statement of the problem, we are offered a plethora of solutions. Teach reading by this or that method; hire more dedicated teachers; hold them accountable; teach bilingually; decrease the number of students in each classroom; get back to "basics"; provide special services for remediation even through the college level. None of these suggestions is in itself without merit; no one would dispute the contention that if a person has not learned to read by the time he or she is in the upper grades or even ready to undertake post-secondary work, something must be done.

However, there may be an even simpler response than remediation, one which becomes quite obvious if we look back to a time when this condition (euphemistically called "functional illiteracy") did not exist or at least was not so widespread. The answer may lie in the reply to the question of why it is that people who grew up in an era when "reading aloud" was a fairly common family activity could usually master this somewhat complicated process quite easily. It is ironic that with all of the progress we have made during the last quarter century in diagnosing the "illness," with all of our attempts to "cure the patient," and with the ever-increasing need to make him "well," that is, literate, we are more and more frequently having to admit that he died! Could it be that in our very efficient and fast-paced world, we have overlooked one possible remedy? Again and again, formal studies show that children who can read are children who have been exposed to books almost from infancy, and adults who enjoy reading are adults who have been exposed to the printed word from early childhood.

It would seem, then, that there is a very practical purpose involved in presenting literature to pre-schoolers. Reading to them will obviously not obliterate completely the problem of illiteracy. But it might well prove a less expensive and frustrating solution than any other proposal meant to stem the tide in a society which requires that more and more people read well.

2. Language Development

Closely tied to the actual process of reading is the area of language development, which may be further sub-divided as a) the acquisition of vocabulary, b) a feeling for syntactical structure, c) an appreciation of underlying meanings—implicit as contrasted with explicit—and, d) a sensitivity to one's mother tongue in an overall way.

a) Vocabulary

We are all aware that we have a vocabulary much more extensive than we use in daily conversation. For example, most adults probably have not used the word "moat" once this week; yet they do not require a dictionary to understand that term. Few adults have thought specifically about a lion's "mane" or "curds and whey" in the past few days; still, there is no need to consult a dictionary to know what these words mean. But the acquisition of this non-working vocabulary is no mystery. We all learned the meanings of a great many words by hearing them and/or reading them within the context of a story, and even if we do not have occasion to use them in everyday conversation, they are safely stored in the "computer" of our minds, to be recalled at will. To understand the significance of this process, try to think in a foreign language, in which even the simplest words are not "available for retrieval" and the handicap becomes clear.

In the same way, children who have not been given the opportunity to hear words which are not used in the ordinary circumstances of their lives cannot hope to fill these gaps in their understanding. What is really alarming about this paucity of vocabulary is that this lack can never be completely made up, even with remediation, since, as research shows, almost half of one's adult language skill is dependent upon what has been "learned" before the age of five!

b) Syntactical Structure

Here we are talking at the simplest level about the way words are put together, the types and lengths of word groups or sentences.

A more complicated view of syntax involves the notion of *style* too. Think how boring it would be if every sentence in the world were either a simple declarative statement or a simple interrogative sentence. Again, to grasp this concept we need only consider a beginning class in a foreign language, where all the verbs are conjugated in the present tense and there is little possibility of constructing sentences above the first-grade level even if the student is a doctoral candidate.

By exposure to an almost boundless variety of syntactical constructions as he is being read to, even the small child subconsciously becomes aware of the many, many ways in which language can be ordered to best express shades of meaning. These diversities are also stored in the computer of the mind to be savored, retrieved at will, and perhaps used later in his own writing, whether it is in an essay for a tenth grade English class or in a letter of condolence to a friend whose mother has died.

c) Implicit Meaning

To discuss the understanding of what is not explicitly written on the page, but is merely meant or implied, we really have to consider another literary term, *tone.* Is the author serious, or does he mean for us to chuckle with recognition and understanding? As a test for sensitivity to this aspect of the printed word, discuss with any secondary school teacher what happens when an Art Buchwald column or a piece from a Richard Armour book is assigned to a class of high school seniors. Without an instructor's interpretation, few students realize the author's mode of getting the point across. Few will recognize the sly comic mode, and therefore most of the students may well misinterpret completely what has been written. It then becomes apparent that even when they have mastered the mechanics of deciphering words on a page, many young people are not able to recognize or assess underlying meaning. And this is not the case for the comic mode alone.

To further validate this hypothesis, ask the same high school English teacher what happens when the group is faced with a passage from Mark Twain's *Huckleberry Finn* or John Steinbeck's *The Pearl.* Without direction from the instructor, few teenagers understand the criticism of unfair social systems implied by these authors and instead, tend to read only the literal stories, thereby missing the point entirely. It might be a possibility that had they been exposed to literature as three-year-olds, the notion of tone might have been imbibed effortlessly with a carryover at a later time. For example, a child may never be made aware of the political implications of *Mother Goose,* and "Humpty-Dumpty" may be taken at face value by a toddler, but he will store the jingle in his mind without consciously thinking about it until finally the idea comes clear that if one "sits on a wall," falls off, and damages his "wholeness," nothing can ever put him together again—not even "all the king's horses and all the king's men." With maturation, the child might well consider less obvious interpretations.

d) Sensitivity to the Mother Tongue

This concept, of course, involves a number of ideas, such as idiomatic speech, cliches, catch phrases as opposed to thoughtful prose, and nuances of expression. When we discuss this area of language development we cannot ignore the preceding divisions of vocabulary and diction, syntax or style, and awareness of tone. Actually, an overall sense of language is a totality; those who are most literate as adults have without question acquired and enlarged this competence by early, frequent, and continued exposure to the printed word.

If we agree that the reading process itself with all that is implied—from word recognition to a sensitivity to language—is increased by exposing very young children to literature, we may count language development as a second positive result for the future.

3. Attitude Change

Undeniably, there are many factors involved in determining the way children perceive the universe, other people, behavioral standards, and so on. Indeed, it would be simplistic to ignore the major stimulus of the toddler's home environment—taken as a totality to include socio-economics, race, parental example, and the many other elements which help shape each person's world. Also, we must consider what surrounds the child when he goes outside his immediate family circle to interact with the community in the broadest sense of that term. How, then, can exposure to books alter attitudes which may be considered "undesirable"? For example, if the child is growing up in an environment where violence is more acceptable than gentleness, can exposure to a book wherein nonviolent behavior is rewarded change his attitude? Of course, there is no simple answer possible. What we do know is that books offer a great potential for enlarging the child's horizons so that he may realize that there are alternatives to violence, choices to be made.

An interesting study done by Dr. Mark Taylor at the University of Southern California in 1976 attempted to determine the efficacy of literature in this regard by presenting three books to 600 first-grade children of the Montebello, California, School District, pre-testing and then post-testing for attitude change (and also for vocabulary acquisition).[1] After exposure to these books, the children showed most encouraging changes in attitude about an important social behavior, sharing. Admittedly, no one can be certain how long-lasting these changes were, but at least there were new insights gained by the children, and once any person has looked at a situation from a fresh angle, it is improbable that he will revert completely to a less desirable attitude, at least as far as that particular area of behavior is concerned.

In effecting this kind of change, we must consider the development of empathy as a primary tool. How can books assist here? If we assume that even sophisticated adults need exposure to the lives of others before they can truly empathize with them, how much truer it must be for small children whose worlds are necessarily circumscribed. We have all heard that children can be very cruel to their peers, tending, for instance, to make fun of those who seem "different" in some way. But if they have met other children through books, vicariously experiencing some of these "differences," there is some chance that whether the problem is inconsequential—such as wearing glasses or being unusually short—or serious—such as being mentally or physically handicapped—the child may have begun to develop enough feeling for "otherness" to behave with empathy.

In regard to attitudinal change also we must consider role models in books and the effect they can have in shaping future life goal expectancy. For example, if little girls see female characters in books pictured as women engaged in activities other than homemaking, they may begin to think of themselves in terms of Doctor Nancy rather than Nurse Nancy. And in the same way, if little boys see male characters in books working in fields not traditionally considered "masculine," they may begin to consider becoming nursery school teachers or ballet dancers without feeling strange about those choices.

When we discuss attitude, we should also consider such a prosaic matter as the attitude toward books themselves as primary learning tools. If the small child is encouraged to seek information at the very simplest level by looking at a picture dictionary or encyclopedia, this behavior might well illustrate the notion that "we look things up" if we're not sure about them, which is certainly a useful habit to acquire for future academic achievement.

4. Development of Imagination

We have spoken of empathy as part of attitudinal modification, but feeling as others feel relates also to the idea of developing the imagination. If a child is encouraged to formulate mental images, unreal as well as literal, stimulated by the books which are read to him, and at this stage of development particularly the illustrations which are part of those books, it is reasonable to expect that he will enlarge the ability to "put himself in another's shoes," and, of course, to escape from the mundane world as well, when that is his primary need.

Furthermore, genuinely creative thinking generally involves being able to synthesize extant ideas imaginatively, so that it is mandatory that a small child's powers of imagination be encouraged in preparation for learning to think creatively.

5. Specific Problems

Even when a small child's world is quite secure in regard to basic necessities, he may still have "problems," some transitory, some more serious. For instance, many small children have very real fears about the dark; many are jealous of siblings (younger or older); some are afraid of animals. Other children have to come to terms with adoption, divorce, even death itself. Now books in which the characters deal successfully with these matters may not help a three or four-year old to attack the issue directly, as those who are enthusiastic about bibliotherapy sometimes assert. However, what they can do for the youngster is to substantiate the fact that other people have these problems too—thereby fostering a sense of community with others which can be an important step toward the birth of awareness. Also, dealing with some of these areas obviously connects to empathy and attitudinal changes referred to above. For instance, reading a story about a child who is the tallest in the group may help the tallest child to deal with his or her uniqueness at the same time that it may help other children to be more sympathetic toward an unusual appearance.

6. Gaining Insight Through Vicarious Experience

This positive result of reading to young children is closely related to both the development of imagination and the ability to empathize with others. When presented with a great variety of books, the child must see a concomitant variety of options open to those who face identical or similar situations. Even a very young child can assimilate (again at this age through illustrations) that in parts of the world he has never seen people may live in surroundings totally different from his own, while at the same time sharing experiences common to all. Children in Alaska or Japan or Africa also feel loneliness or jealousy or happiness, but the only way a child living in today's America can ever realize such commonality is through exposure to books. It may be obvious—perhaps too obvious to notice—but to a child who has never seen snow, even the simple antics of a toddler playing solitary games in that cold, white stuff may provide a broadening experience. Such insight is surely valuable.

7. Television

Closely connected to all we have said about "positive results" to be gained by reading to children is television watching, which unfortunately has become in some homes a substitute for reading. Realistically, the tube is such a convenient "baby sitter" that the temptation is great to use it that way. But the best that can be said of the "one-eyed monster," regardless of programming and advertising (with which we may be concerned as well), is that even at its least offensive, television engenders *mental passivity.*

There have been several excellent books, such as Marie Winn's *The Plug-In Drug*[2] and Jerry Mander's *Four Arguments for the Elimination of Television*[3] that deal most convincingly with this aspect of media watching. And there have also been a great many articles written that present scientific data in support of the hypothesis that watching television produces an "alpha" state in the viewer, which in common terms means a semi-comatose condition, regardless of the program being viewed. While this may seem desirable to some adults who choose to "unwind" after a hard day by turning off their minds—especially for people who do not enjoy reading—it is certainly not advisable as an activity for young children who have so much of the world to absorb and are so eager to participate in experience. It is charitable to label television watching for these youngsters only as a "waste of time." That this activity —or really lack of activity—literally teaches inattentiveness, that it fosters dependence on "being entertained," that it dulls emotional perception, and that it quite possibly plays a greater role in our current state of illiteracy than we will admit have become subjects on which most experienced school teachers could dwell at length. Certainly, when accused of "not teaching" properly in our schools, teachers might well cite the fact that by the time the average young person completes twelve grades of formal education, he or she will have spent 11,000 hours in classrooms and over 15,000 hours watching television. The fact that many high school graduates cannot read may well be more than coincidental.

Of course, with careful monitoring by adults, in regard to both programs viewed and time spent in front of the set, some of the negative aspects can be minimized, but it is incontrovertible that the key word in television viewing is *passivity* as contrasted with the *interaction* which occurs when the child is being read to. Coming full circle, this interaction with a caring adult may be the most significant result of all.

Part Two

Book Selection

An Overview

Definitions

Before beginning a detailed discussion of books for children in terms of specific criteria for selection, let us first define some basic terms. *Webster's Third International Unabridged Dictionary* reads: "*Literature:* writings in prose or verse; especially writings having excellence of form or expression and expressing ideas of permanent or universal interest," which seems acceptable for pre-schoolers if we emphasize the first clause—that is, [All] "writings in prose or verse," and add, "specifically designed for small children." Realistically, we must recognize that not all of the books under consideration will be of "permanent or universal interest," and unfortunately some of them may not even meet completely the criterion of "excellence of form or expression." Nevertheless, we will want to formulate some standards for evaluation in order to make the best choices from available materials.

Other terms which will be used throughout the rest of this book include:

Fiction: a made-up story, usually written in prose.

Non-fiction: works offering facts or theories, usually written in prose.

Note: In some books there may be an overlap in modes, such as informational books which also tell a "fictional" story.

Poetry: a work in metrical form.

Plot: events arranged in a particular order; what "happens" in a work of fiction.

Climax: the high point in the story; in books for small children this is commonly near the end.

Characters: creations in fiction through which the author "works out" the story; in children's books, these may be human beings, animals, or inanimate objects, such as dolls, toys, articles in the environment, or those which do not exist in reality but are purely imaginative.

Note: in juvenile fiction particularly, animals are frequently anthropomorphized (given the attributes of human beings so that they can talk and so on) and frequently inanimate objects are presented in this way as well.

Conflict: the struggle taking place between a character and an obstacle in the environment; the struggle taking place between two or more characters; or the struggle taking place between two opposing forces within a single character.

Theme: the main idea of a work.

Style: the mode of expression in terms of vocabulary, syntax, and so on; in books for pre-schoolers this must be expanded to include illustration.

Setting: the time or period in which the story takes place and the place in which it happens.

Tone: the writer's attitude toward his subject.

Point of View: the "voice" in which the fiction is written. Varieties would include the first-person storyteller, or most often utilized in books for small children, the omniscient viewpoint wherein the storyteller (author) knows and reveals what every character is thinking at all times.

Rhythm: a uniform or patterned recurrence of a beat or accent.
Rhyme: identity of sound, especially used with the ends of words or lines of verse.
Motif: a theme, character, or verbal pattern which recurs.

General Expectations

Keeping in mind that each child is a unique individual, it is still possible to schematize in a general way what may be expected of most children from birth to the time they are of school age. In this way, we can formulate an overall view of what kinds of materials should be of interest to them at each stage of development.

AGE	CHARACTERISTICS	TYPES OF MATERIAL
0–1 year	Gradually becomes aware of environment and people from first eye-focusing to overt reactions.	May begin to show interest in large, brightly colored pictures. By end of first year should enjoy some simple *Mother Goose* rhymes, such as "patty cake."
1–2 years	Begins to understand constancy of objects; starts to grasp idea of "cause and effect." May begin to use words, connecting them to objects or people.	By eighteen months should be interested in books picturing familiar objects (such as ball, dog, doll, etc.) — one or two on a page. Heavy cardboard or washable cloth books best at this age. By age two should enjoy tactile books in which he can actually "touch" objects pictured and get sense of texture. Should enjoy simple rhymes, especially accompanied by actions.
2 years	Verbal fluency shows marked increase.	Likes books with repetitions, cumulative stories with simple plot-lines. May enjoy books requiring response and involvement.

AGE	CHARACTERISTICS	TYPES OF MATERIAL
2–2½ years	Further verbal fluency develops; may talk to himself, repeating phrases from books.	Enjoys "funny" books; simple nonsense verse. May pretend characters in books are alive (pat dog, kiss doll, and so on). Wants same book repeated again and again. Begins to examine books independently.
2½–3 years	Begins to talk in phrases and even sentences. May make up stories; may "read" to others; some memorization evident.	Books can be longer, more complex. Child can now listen in "group." Enjoys verbal humor and imaginative stories about "real" people. Begins to show interest in simple informational books, such as alphabet or concept books.
3½–4 years	Imagination develops; language becomes more sophisticated. May ask for explanations. Wants to be independent; sometimes explores outside immediate environment. Plays more with others in group, rather than in parallel play. May become aware of problems, such as illness, divorce, death. May show definite preferences about what he wants to hear.	Longer stories with more plot involvement become popular toward end of period. Enjoys folk tales and fairy tales. Enjoys books with explanations of how things work, natural phenomena, and so on. Likes exaggeration and understands difference between reality and fantasy. Begins to enjoy unrhymed verse.

AGE	CHARACTERISTICS	TYPES OF MATERIAL
4–5 years	May have imaginary playmates. Shows interest in other children's activities. Interest in puppets, felt-board pieces, and so on grows. May begin to recognize words in books and on signs. Can usually count aloud. Interested in animals, wild and domestic.	Enjoys a wide variety of books. Tends to "study" illustrations carefully and critically. Enjoys books about unfamiliar people and places. By age of five may show "reading readiness" through voluntary recognition of words and numerals. May like wordless picture books that "tell a story," which child may then "read" to other, younger children.
5–6 years	Depending on school experience, may be very social. Shows growing interest in world outside the immediate environment. May memorize story and repeat as though "reading." Enjoys participatory activities, such as making puppets, doing creative dramatics, and so on.	Likes old favorites, but may readily accept new books. May enjoy books in series, if the first one has been especially enjoyable. May accept "chapter" concept — progressing from one chapter (or story) to next after a time lapse. Likes to make personal choices in library, for instance. May actually begin to read books independently.

As a glance at these very general schemata will show, there is an entirely logical rule applicable to selecting books appropriate to the age of the child or children being read to. This may be condensed to: "The younger the child, the simpler and more literal the material should be." However, we must allow for variations from child to child, and from group to group, depending on past experience with books. It is to be expected that a pre-schooler who has been exposed to books from infancy, for example, will be interested in more complicated plots and be ready to spend longer periods of time being read to at age three than a child to whom read-alouds are a totally new experience. However, even within individual families with identical exposure patterns, there may be discernible differences from child to child and strong preferences without apparent cause. The task of the concerned adult is to make appropriate materials available and enjoy them with the developing pre-schooler at each level.

Inappropriate Materials

1. Condensations

In an effort to give children "the best," at the earliest possible time, we are sometimes tempted to offer "condensed versions" of classics which seem too complicated in their original form. However, this should be avoided, since if we give youngsters the opportunity to enjoy being read to from their earliest years, they will in all probability grow into appreciation of more complex works as they mature. Watered-down versions have the same relationship to the originals as one-page plot summaries have to complete works in adult literature, with even less reason for their use.

2. Bowdlerized Versions

As to simplified or bowdlerized editions of stories which are suitable for the pre-schooler, presentations of anything short of the original version is not a good idea. If the hard-back version costs too much, the book may, of course, be borrowed from the library. As a matter of fact, it is a good idea to begin taking toddlers to the public library on a regularly scheduled basis so that the widest possible choice is made available to them from the beginning. Unfortunately, some adults hesitate to make use of this facility because they fear embarrassment when the two- or three-year-old behaves in a normally "noisy" manner. Be assured that children's sections do not require the solemn quiet of adult reading rooms, and, in fact, most public libraries plan story hours, puppet shows, and other activities specifically designed to involve small children in the world of literature as soon as possible.

A child should have his own personal library too, made up first of baby books, not available from libraries, and then augmented by those titles which the individual child has chosen repeatedly when presented with a broad selection. Many of the very best books have been reproduced in paperback also, and some excellent titles are published as inexpensive paperback editions from the first—particularly those from some of the small, specialized publishers. These books are less durable than the cloth-bound editions, of course, but less costly and quite satisfactory for ordinary home use. The same standards for book selection should be applied to the paperbacks, however, as to all other books, so that they are not chosen for price alone. Since illustration is a very significant factor in pre-school literature, we shall touch on this topic in more detail later.

3. Readers

In discussing inappropriate materials, we must mention the understandable temptation, especially toward the end of the pre-school years, when a child seems ready to read, and may in fact actually *be* reading at a very simple level, to use "beginning readers" for read-alouds. However, in general, it is wise to avoid these "I Can Read" books for a very logical reason. Even the best of them have been created for a very specific purpose, one quite different from literary goals. These readers are primarily designed for reinforcement of word recognition; many of them feature lists of words at the end, showing the exact number of times a given word has been repeated in the text. And there is nothing wrong with this format—*for the practice of reading skills*. However, the vocabulary in such books must be kept within the grasp of a young child reading to himself, so the words used are not chosen to enrich his stock of more complicated expressions, but to reinforce instead what he already knows. This same appropriate simplicity applies to sentence structure, style, and other literary elements as well. Granted we have come a long way from "See Spot run. Spot is running. See." Nevertheless, books classed as beginning readers should not be placed in competition with those written to be read *to children* not yet able to read them independently, but entirely able to understand, appreciate, and enjoy more advanced materials.

There is one notable exception to the suggestion that "readers" not be used as books to read aloud, and that is in the area of certain non-fictional books, particularly those dealing with aspects of scientific information. In order to keep the level of material simple enough for a four- or five-year-old child to understand—say, *Where does the rain come from?* or *What makes a seed grow into a flower?* —and still keep it entirely accurate, it is necessary to turn to books which are written rather simply, planned for first or second graders to read independently.

4. Books in Series

Sometimes a character is created (such as Harry the Dirty Dog, or Babar the Elephant) which is so appealing to children that the author continues to use him as protagonist in additional books. Many of these are a source of continued delight as the child looks forward to adventure after adventure in which his familiar friend is pictured. One note of caution, however, is in order. If after reading two or three books in such a series, it seems to the discerning adult that the books no longer meet the standards of the original in terms of other literary elements—plot, theme, and so on—it might be wise to suspect that it is only commercialism at work, not literature. Unfortunately, some very well known "characters" have been vulgarized in certain modern series so that even though the original was delightful, the current renditions are not the same calibre although at first sight this may not be apparent. As always, it is necessary to check carefully before making assumptions about quality.

5. What About Stereotypes?

Without going deeply into the negative aspects of stereotypes as a means of setting up "standardized conceptions" of various groups, ideas which are frequently erroneous and often denigrating, we will want to avoid stereotypes if only to give children the widest view possible, allowing maximum opportunity for choices and options. Therefore, it is incumbent on the adults who select books for and with youngsters to exercise judgment about and avoidance of books which disparage any group—racial, ethnic, religious, or sexual. The label "censorship" has little meaning when we are talking about books for pre-schoolers, unless we want to consider the elimination of some material, usually published before our society was sensitized to racism, for example, as censorship. Few adults today would want to read aloud from such a piece as *Stories of Little Brown Koko*, published in 1940, which begins:

> Once there was a little brown boy named Little Brown Koko. He was the shortest, fattest little Negro you could ever imagine. He had the blackest, little woolly head and great big round eyes, and he was the prettiest brown color, just like a bar of chocolate candy. Little Koko's Mammy thought him the most beautiful little boy in the whole wide world. Oh, he was a beautiful little brown boy, all right, but he had one bad habit.

He was greedy. Why, compared to Little Brown Koko, a pig should be called a well-mannered gentleman. One day Little Brown Koko's nice, good, ole, big, black Mammy made a big seven-layer cake...[4]

This example and others equally blatant seem to leap out from the page. However, sometimes more subtle writing may make it a little more difficult to recognize prejudice. We must, therefore, be constantly aware of the possibility even by inference of stereotypes since a small child with limited experience may well accept what is presented to him as "the way things/people are." Certainly we must avoid didacticism too because books written primarily to "teach" a particular point of view or to illustrate a principle of "correct" behavior may have little literary value. It would seem that the wisest course is to select books which do not covertly or overtly attempt to make statements about groups of people, but instead meet other criteria for excellence.

6. Sexist Books

Much more widespread than the pejorative views of races, ethnic groups, or religions, and also crossing all lines, we find what we may label "sexism," meaning the arbitrary assignment of lifelong roles based on reproductive organs alone.

During the past two decades particularly there has been a growing awareness of women's rights and with it an emphasis on girls participating in sports traditionally reserved for boys, of girls and women engaged in activities formerly assumed to be exclusively masculine, and so on. There is little doubt that even our language, which calls for the masculine to be used as the third person singular pronoun, has tended to make females seem the *other* sex. Unfortunately, in an effort to ameliorate the situation, some of the books which came on the scene in the early years of the women's movement tended to emphasize sexual equality at the expense of literary quality, and some still do. Also, significantly, these books omitted for the most part one of the most repugnant results of sexual stereotyping—its effect on boys and men. Many writers were so busy declaring that girls and women did not have to accept their customary "feminine" roles that they failed to make an equally strong case for boys and men who chose to behave in ways not traditionally designated as "masculine." What about boys who like to play with dolls? What about boys who enjoy cooking or doing macrame? What about boys who cry when they are hurt (just as girls do!), or those who prefer ballet to football? The point, of course, is that in order to combat sexism for both girls and boys we must emphasize general human characteristics, common to males and females alike, while refusing steadfastly to accept pre-determined stereotypes as though they were immutable, confusing physiological differences with role determination.

Through literature we have a unique opportunity to present non-sexist role models to children to reinforce what they should be learning in their homes and preschools regarding choices open to both sexes. We must recognize, however, the unhappy fact that many of our best titles in every other respect can be considered sexist in that the male characters dominate numerically, that female characters are frequently minor and/or passive, and that even adults as pictured in these books reinforce somewhat unrealistic stereotyped views of modern men and women. Since it is impractical to eliminate every book which with careful scrutiny could be considered somewhat sexist, the next best solution seems to be the cultivation of *awareness* concerning the problem, so that as new titles which eschew all traces of covert sexism appear, we choose those books, provided, of course, that they meet other criteria for high quality. Meanwhile, frank discussion with the children themselves can help clarify the situation for them. As one four-year-old boy said after hearing a story which involved a girl playing baseball, "My brother's team has won more games since my cousin Barbara pitches for them."

A Very Special Consideration—Illustration

As indicated previously, all books which are useful for preschoolers must be profusely illustrated, and so it is pointless to designate them as anything but picture books. In this sense they are quite different from books meant for older children or adults, books which may or may not have pictures, but which (except for particular titles, such as *Life's Book of World War II*, for example) in no way depend on illustration to tell a story or clarify a concept. Therefore, for young children's books, we should consider the illustrations as intrinsic and carefully judge the art work along with the other elements of style. And let us state quite frankly that *art* is the correct term here, since some of the foremost graphic artists create their work for superior children's books.

It is a very purposeful creation too since young children themselves in an unhampered environment show a wide range of responses to the elements of art and demonstrate wide acceptance of various "styles," showing great aesthetic sensitivity. By the same token, if they are presented with a preponderance of inferior visual impressions, a negative effect upon the development of taste and aesthetic enjoyment may result. It is once more a matter of standards. We must know what constitutes superior work in order to recognize it and to avoid inferior varieties.

Possibly the most prevalent characteristic of poor art work is the stereotyped illustration. McCann and Richard in *The Child's First Books* describe it vividly:

> The illustrator is usually conforming to derivative criteria. He duplicates a formula already known and familiar to himself and to the consumer.... Animals are either anthropomorphized or drawn so that they resemble their stuffed-toy counterparts. Children and adults are drawn in costumes designed to defy period labeling; little girls have very full skirts and boys have short pants or are schematized in some similar fashion. The individualization of characters is accomplished by a cartoon-like overstatement of features.[5]

Further, they quote illustrator Nicholas Mordinoff, who says, "... sweetness has often been used as a substitute for feeling and intelligence."[6]

In stereotyped illustration, outlining is usually done in uniform black (like a coloring book), there is very little attention paid to spatial relationships, and blatant color is used to indicate the "center of interest." However, as McCann and Richard point out, this stereotyped illustration has the broadest public acceptance since it is "familiar."

To comprehend the difference between inferior and superior illustration, one need only look at a scene showing Snow White and the seven dwarfs in a Walt Disney version of that story and then look at the edition which features illustrations done by Nancy Ekholm Burkert. In the first, Snow White bears more than a faint resemblance to Cinderella in another Disney book, whereas in Burkert's picture we have not only a more aesthetically pleasing illustration, but also one evocative of the individual characters in *this* story, set in *this* unique time and place. It is no wonder that this is so—since the Burkert illustrations are based on authenticity of detail, even down to the embroidery on Snow White's apron and the patterns of crockery on the table, whereas the Disney version merely reproduces the cartoon-like characters and setting from the movie.

If we reject the stereotype, how shall we judge what may be unfamiliar and unique? First, we must realize that each artist has his/her own highly individual view of reality, his own interpretation, as it were, and by objectifying for us his most subjective feelings, he creates a work which is truly non-repeatable. It may be done in many colors, shades of one color, black and white, or sepia tones; it may be objective, nonobjective, or abstract; it may use light and shadow in completely realistic or entirely unrealistic ways. In short, the artist may use color, shape, line, texture, and the arrangement of these components in any way which seems appropriate. He may elect to use any one of the available media from wood-cuts to pastels, from collage to gouache, or any combination of these. And he may even prefer to use creative photography or to combine that mode with drawings or paintings. Whatever the style utilized, the test for superior illustration must hinge on the question of whether or not the pictures are *complementary to the other elements of composition.*

What does this concept imply? First, the total "feeling" of the work must be considered. If the book has as its basic purpose the setting forth of concepts, such as "above-below" or "empty-full," realistic portrayals would be appropriate. If the book has as its core humor for its own sake, the drawings might well be more fanciful. If the story is set in a fairy-tale world, inhabited by princesses and fairy godmothers, the illustrations should give the reader a sense of that world. If, on the other hand, it is set in Harlem, where children play in the streets outside tenements, a very different style would seem more in order.

Next, since we know that children pay very close attention to pictures in their books, we need to make sure that if the illustrations are supposed to be "realistic," they represent reality accurately. For example, if a text reads that a character is wearing a "red dress,"the dress had better be red and not orange! This does not mean, however, that illustrations need represent reality at all. What it does suggest is that illustrations must be consistent and accurate within their own frame of reference.

Finally, young children seem to prefer pictures which are integrated into the page design so that they appear above or alongside the written text which is being illustrated, not on the page following.

The same rules apply to illustration as to other matters of style in regard to differences within the two to six age range. In general, very small children may not be able to appreciate illustrations which are abstract or those which are too "busy." Most youngsters below two and a half may be puzzled by the notion of perspective, since they need experience to acquire visual literacy, in order to "understand" that a small tree in the distance is supposed to be farther away than a larger one in the foreground. However, with exposure and perhaps explication by the adult, they catch on rather quickly. What we want to look for in picture-books, then, are illustrations which are not stereotyped, which vary according to the demands of each individual book, and which provide a galaxy of fresh and original artwork for the child's enjoyment and aesthetic development. Beni Montresor defines a picture-book as "A book whose content is expressed through its images,"[7] and this rule-of-thumb seems applicable to all books for pre-schoolers. Exposure to superior imagery seems a sensible way to reinforce verbal content as the adult presents books to small children.

Closely related to this subject of illustration is the topic of the format of books for pre-schoolers. Title pages are important, as they frequently give an idea of the book's subject. Generally, large type, widely spaced, with generous margins on all sides are inviting, and double-page spreads are popular. Sometimes a particular book will lend itself to an unusual treatment, as in Virginia Lee Burton's *The Little House*, where the type follows the winding road described in the text, or the very special calligraphy so effectively used in the Babar books. Small children do like very small sized books, such as those by Beatrix Potter, and they enjoy some novel shapes, such as the very "tall" books or those which are contoured to illustrate the subject matter, such as *Book of Dogs* or *Book of Cats*, and so on—but as a rule, clarity is the major aim.

If possible, strong binding and high quality paper are desirable to insure long life, and even in paperback editions, there are differences of quality in these respects which should be noted. For the infant-toddler, cardboard or washable cloth books are a necessity, and where there are participatory activities involved, as in *Pat the Bunny*, damage can be minimized only by sturdy construction. Pop-up books, giving the effect of three dimensions can be fun too, but these and some other novel formats are less durable than more conventionally bound books, which is why libraries do not stock them. Fortunately, most books which are worth selecting are well-designed, an important consideration since small children do not have the experience to realize that "You can't tell a book by its cover."

Some Specifics of Selection

Fiction

As a first major division, let us consider the general category which would include all stories, generally written in prose, without any specific teaching goals in mind. Informational books written as "stories" for young children will be discussed separately under the general heading of non-fiction, since these books have certain characteristics different from story-books, although, as we shall see, they may share some of the same elements.

Keeping in mind the general rule about increased complexity as the child matures, let us look in some detail at the literary elements briefly defined earlier. To illustrate specifically how these "operate" we will use an old favorite, *The Story of Ferdinand* by Munro Leaf, published in 1936, as an example.

1. Plot

Just as in any good fiction, plots for children's books should be clearly arranged and come to a climax. If the book merely recounts events with no particular high point, the typical response could be, "So what?" The major difference between a story line for an adult book and a child's (in addition to intricacy and length, of course) is that in books for pre-schoolers there is no use made of flashbacks or any other literary device which interferes with the clear line from beginning through the middle to the end.

Ferdinand begins when the bull is young, growing up with his brothers, and tells of his early preference for "sitting under a cork tree and just smelling the flowers," rather than behaving as the other bulls do—butting and snorting and fighting. It explains how he grows up, still wanting only to sit under his favorite tree peacefully, then goes on to recount how the "men in funny hats" come from Madrid looking for the fiercest bull to fight in the bullfights. Not interested in the competition to be chosen, Ferdinand starts to walk toward his tree when he unknowingly sits on a bee who stings him. This leads logically to his overtly "fierce" behavior, which in turn causes the men to choose him and cart him away to Madrid. Next, the human participants at the arena are shown and briefly explained. There are "the lovely ladies with flowers in their hair," in the grandstands; there are the *Banderilleros* "with long sharp pins with ribbons on them to stick in the bull and make him mad." Then come the *Picadores* "who rode skinny horses and had long spears to stick in the bull and make him madder." And finally, the *Matador*, who "had a red cape and a sword and was supposed to stick the bull last of all."

All of the human participants are terrified of "Ferdinand the Fierce," who hesitantly comes into the ring, only to sit down and smell the ladies' flowers, refusing to fight and frustrating the bloodthirsty men who had anticipated a battle. The climactic line could be, "The *Matador* was so mad he cried because he couldn't show off with his cape and sword." Following quickly, the story's conclusion shows Ferdinand returning to his home, resuming his usual activity —just sitting under his favorite cork tree, "smelling the flowers." The final line reads, "He is very happy."

2. Characters

As the protagonist (main character), this bull is created with a distinct personality, or what we would term in adult literature, dimension. He is very briefly anthropomorphized in an early scene which shows his mother, concerned because Ferdinand is "different" from her other children, asking him, "Why don't you run and play with the other little bulls and skip and butt your head?" But because she is a wise mother, she accepts his reply, "I like it better here where I can sit just quietly and smell the flowers." Except for this short episode, Ferdinand behaves like a bull, albeit a rather unusual one, instead of like a human being.

3. Conflict

In this fairly simple tale there is an obvious difference between Ferdinand's desire for peace and tranquility and the presumptions made by those in his environment that he will welcome participating in the bullfight. He is not shown to be afraid, merely uninterested in combative behavior, as his siblings are. And, of course, he has his way in the end; in other words, he wins the conflict.

4. Theme

Without explication the average three-year-old understands quite clearly the main idea of this story; namely, that each of us is a unique individual and should be allowed to follow his own inner voice to fulfill himself. In this particular book too, the main character is a bull, commonly stereotyped as somewhat fierce, but behaving here quite differently, whereas the traditionally macho men connected with bullfighting are at one point afraid, and later frustrated because they cannot "perform" according to expectation.

5. Style

In *Ferdinand* linguistic and illustrative styles are completely integrated. For example, when the men from Madrid first come to look over the potential fighting bulls, Ferdinand is on his way to his favorite cork tree to sit down. On the following page, the text reads, "He didn't look where he was sitting and instead of sitting on the nice cool grass in the shade, he sat on a bumble bee." The accompanying picture has as its center of interest the bee sitting on a flower, looking balefully toward a view of Ferdinand's rear end, followed on the next page by text that reads,"Well, if you were a bumble bee and a bull sat on you, what would you do? You would sting him. And that is just what this bee did to Ferdinand." The illustration here shows only the startled face of the bull, a few hairs standing up on his neck, nostrils dilated, and one eye (in profile) wide open. Then Leaf writes, "Wow! Did it hurt! Ferdinand jumped up with a snort. He ran around puffing and snorting, butting and pawing the ground as if he were crazy," and the accompanying illustration shows the deflated bee at the lower left hand corner of the page with the flying hoofs of the bull *above* the cloud formation which appeared in normal position on the preceding page. While the language level is not unduly complicated, words like "puffing," "snorting," "butting," and "pawing" are very descriptive and are made meaningful to the very small child through the accompaniment of pictures which show Ferdinand in action.

6. *Setting*

The time factor is indefinite, so it is introduced in this book by the familiar phrase, "Once upon a time . . ." and continues with a statement of locale,"in Spain . . . ." Robert Lawson, the illustrator, using black India ink drawings, with plenty of white space where appropriate, creates the world of rural Spain so precisely that each picture is informative, expertly combining realistic elements with such fanciful ones as having the corks hang from the tree in bunches like fruit.

7. *Tone*

Munro Leaf, the author, tells a straightforward story in an appropriate narrative style with no overt attempt to criticize bullfighting. Still, one gets the strong impression that his sympathy does not lie with the "five men in very funny hats," and again Lawson's pictures of these characters reinforces this judgment, thus complementing the text superbly. One of the men resembles a pig; another has a black patch over one eye; a third has a trim on his hat picturing an angel ministering to a *dead* bull. Ferdinand, on the other hand, is always shown as though content—except when stung by the bee—and even then he is only startled, not belligerent.

8. *Point of View*

So that the reader (and the listener, of course) is aware at all times of what all the characters think and what motivates their action, an omniscient point of view is used throughout.

Like so many other children's stories which have become "classics" because youngsters have continued to enjoy them for a very long time, *The Story of Ferdinand* meets all of the standards for selection. It tells an exciting story; it never preaches its theme, but makes the point clear instead through context; it has a main character with whom a child can identify and empathize; and it exemplifies the principle of text and illustration perfectly blended. We can all think of many other books which have stood the test of time, noting that although Beatrix Potter's *Tale of Peter Rabbit,* Watty Piper's *The Little Engine That Could,* and Margaret Wise Brown's *Goodnight Moon,* (as examples) differ in every way from *The Story of Ferdinand* and from each other, each qualifies as a superior picture book because each in its own way meets the same criteria for excellence.

A Check List for Excellence

To test for high quality in new fictional books, we might make judgments based on answers to the following questions:

1. Does the book have an interesting plot?
2. Is that plot the correct level of complexity to match the age of the child (or children) to whom the story is being read?
3. Does the story have a clear line of development—beginning, middle, climax, then ending?
4. Is the theme or main idea made clear within the context of the book, not by didactic insistence?
5. Are the characters (or at least the main characters) well-rounded and unique?
6. Is the setting (time and place) adequately described verbally? Pictorially?
7. Is the style appropriate to this particular book both verbally and pictorially?
8. Are the illustrations complementary to the text? Are they on the same page as the verbal text, especially for very young children?
9. Are the illustrations aesthetically pleasing in themselves?
10. Does the book avoid stereotyping?

And, when all is said and done, does the child *enjoy* the book? If it is requested over and over again, the question is adequately answered. Generally, if the adult reading the book likes it and is enthusiastic, the child will take a positive view. However, if for any reason (sometimes one not known to the child himself), a youngster seems uninterested or negative even about a book beloved by the parent or teacher, it is wise to lay that book aside, at least temporarily. Conversely, if a child selects a book in the library which seems inappropriate, but to which he seems attracted, the adult should respect that choice. After all, if enough variety is presented from the beginning, children tend to develop a taste for superior works, and if one child's preference varies from another child's, that very individuality has value in itself.

In the following section, many titles are listed in various ways to fulfill specific needs. However, these are in no sense to be taken as prescriptions, only as guidelines in regard to probable age levels at which children will enjoy the books listed, particular subject emphases, and so on. These titles should be used with flexibility to allow for individual differences, keeping in mind that although human beings share a great many characteristics in common, they also present an almost infinite variety within that commonality, and that is as it should be.

Unfortunately, not all of the titles included meet every criterion for excellence either. For example, a book may meet most standards but fall short of being outstanding because the illustrations could have been more interesting. However, such a book may be included because at the moment there seems to be no better one in that particular category. Again, it needs to be stressed that any bibliography is inadequate on the day it is compiled simply because of the time factor, so it is important to update constantly, evaluating as we go.

First Books

There are some sub-divisions within the fictional group, of course. First, there are the "baby" or "first" books, which simply means that many of the titles are those which suit the one- to two-year-old and which will not be found, generally speaking, in libraries. There are a great many in this sub-group which cannot be designated as "literature" at all, but which will give toddlers an important start. At the simplest level they will serve the function of giving the small child notions which adults take for granted. For example, the child will begin to understand right side up versus upside down; he will get the idea of how to turn pages; and he will start to see the connection between pictures (even one to the page) and the real world around him. Many titles are washable cloth books; others are printed on heavy cardboard; some include tactile experiences.

For these "first" books, it seems natural to read them to toddlers as "bedtime stories," but we must be sure not to inadvertently connect the idea of reading and going to sleep. To avoid this pitfall, it is preferable to offer books to the young child—from the earliest age at which he or she will sit quietly even for five or ten minutes—at a time other than when sleep is the next order of business, as well as at bedtime.

These books are available from shops which cater to children's books or by ordering directly from the publishers.

First Books

Each Peach, Pear, Plum, Janet and Allen Ahlberg
Baby Animal Dress-Up Book, Anon.
Baby Farm Animals, Anon.
Baby's First Golden Books (4), Anon.
Baby's First Library: Counting, Anon.
Baby's First Library: ABC, Anon.
Baby's First Library (4 in Box), Anon.
Baby's First Whitman Books (3), Anon.
Board Story Books, Anon.
Board Story Books (Child's Play; My Baby Brother), Anon.
Brimax Animal Board Books, Anon.
Counting Rhymes Board Book, Anon.
Dean's Cloth Books, Anon.
Golden Photo Board Books, Anon.
Long Board Books (6), Anon.
Mother Goose Board Books, Anon.
Panorama Folding Board Books (3), Anon.
Peggy Cloth Books (5), Anon.
Perma-Life Books (3), Anon.
Wipe-Clean Books (4), Anon.
Wipe-Clean Books (5), Anon.
I Love You, Mary Jane, Lorna Balian
Would You Like a Parrot?, Frances Barberis
Willy and Nilly and the Silly Cat, Elizabeth K. Barr
Green Eyes, A. Birnbaum
Early Birds... Early Words, Ann Bonner
Hey Diddle Diddle and Other Nonsense Rhymes, Davi Botts
No School Today!, Franz Brandenberg
A Robber! A Robber!, Franz Brandenberg
My Hopping Bunny, Robert Bright
Baby Animal ABC, Robert Broomfield
Golden Egg Book, Margaret Wise Brown
Goodnight, Moon, Margaret Wise Brown
Runaway Bunny, Margaret Wise Brown
Another Story to Tell, Dick Bruna
The Apple, Dick Bruna
Dick Bruna's ABC Frieze, Dick Bruna
Dick Bruna's One-Two-Three Frieze, Dick Bruna

The Egg, Dick Bruna
I Can Count, Dick Bruna
My Shirt Is White, Dick Bruna
A Story to Tell, Dick Bruna
Grandmother and I, Helen E. Buckley
The Baby, John Burningham
The Blanket, John Burningham
The Cupboard, John Burningham
The Dog, John Burningham
Rabbit, John Burningham
The School, John Burningham
The Snow, John Burningham
My Very First Book of Colors, Eric Carle
My Very First Book of Numbers, Eric Carle
My Very First Book of Shapes, Eric Carle
The Chimp and the Clown, Ruth Carroll
Rolling Downhill, Ruth Carroll
What Whiskers Did, Ruth Carroll
Where's the Bunny?, Ruth Carroll
Be Good, Harry, Mary Chalmers
Hurray for Me!, Rene Charlip
The Baby's Lap Book, Kay Chorao
What's Good for a Three-Year-Old?, William Cole
Mother Goose in French, Illus. by Barbara Cooney
You Go Away, Dorothy Corey
Scuffy the Tugboat, Gertrude Crampton
Baby Animal Book, Daphne Davis
Book of Nursery and Mother Goose Rhymes, Marguerite De Angeli
Prancing Pony: Nursery Rhymes from Japan, Charlotte DeForest
Aunt Possum and the Pumpkin Man, Bruce Degen
Alligator's Toothache, Diane DeGroat
Flip, Wesley Dennis
The Little Red Hen, Janina Domanska
Harry: A True Story, Blanche Dorsky
Jasmine, Roger Duvoisin
Are You My Mother?, Philip D. Eastman
Big Dog, Little Dog: A Bedtime Story, Philip D. Eastman
Flap Your Wings, Philip D. Eastman
Lullabies and Night Songs, Edited by William Engvick
Danny and His Thumb, Kathryn F. Ernst
Nursery Rhymes of London Town, Eleanor Farjeon
Country Bunny and Little Golden Shoes, Marjorie Flack
Babies, Gyo Fujikawa
Board Books, Gyo Fujikawa
Mother Goose, Gyo Fujikawa
Our Best Friends, Gyo Fujikawa
Little Red Hen, Paul Galdone

The Three Bears, Paul Galdone
The Three Little Pigs, Paul Galdone
Chick and the Duckling, Mirra Ginsburg
Shape Books, Elisa Gittings
Did You Ever?, Paula Goldsmid
Sheep Book, Carmen Goodyear
Timothy Turtle, Al Graham
Animal Babies, Arthur S. Gregor
Little Elephant, Arthur S. Gregor
Teddy Bears—One to Ten, Susanna Gretz
Little Puff, Margaret Hillert
Little Brute Family, Russell Hoban
One Little Kitten, Tana Hoban
A House Is a House for Me, Mary Ann Hoberman
Come with Me to Nursery School, Edith Hurd
Bright Barnyard, Dahlov Ipcar
I Want to Be Big, Genie Iverson
Tawny Scrawny Lion, Kathryn Jackson
Big Elephant, Kathryn Jackson
Saggy Baggy Elephant, Kathryn Jackson
The Knee Baby, Mary Jarrell
Sara and the Door, Virginia Jensen
Harold and the Purple Crayon, Crockett Johnson
Harold's ABC, Crockett Johnson
Harold's Circus, Crockett Johnson
There and Back Again, Harold Jones
Blue Sea, Robert Kalan
Kitten for a Day, Ezra Jack Keats
Peter's Chair, Ezra Jack Keats
Snowy Day, Ezra Jack Keats
Mystery of the Missing Red Mitten, Steven Kellogg
Won't Somebody Play with Me?, Steven Kellogg
The Egg Book, Jack Kent
Big Red Bus, Ethel Kessler
When Shoes Eat Socks, Barbara Klimowicz
Night Before Christmas, Hilary Knight
Carrot Seed, Ruth Krauss
Little Boat Lighter Than a Cork, Ruth Krauss
Pat the Bunny, Dorothy Kunhardt
Big Little Davy, Lois Lenski
Little Blue and Little Yellow, Leo Lionni
Gregory Griggs and Other Nursery Rhyme People, Arnold Lobel
Poky Little Puppy, Janet S. Lowrey
Ten Bears in My Bed: A Goodnight Countdown, Stan Mack
Here Comes Tagalong, Ann Mallett
The Little Brown Hen, Patricia Miles Martin
Old Mother Hubbard and Her Dog, Sarah Martin
Grandma's Tiny Kitty, Minnie T. Miller

If I Were a Cricket, Kazue Mizumura
My Day on the Farm, Chiyoko Nakatani
Yeck Eck, Evelyn Ness
What's That Noise?, Carol Nicklaus
Who Took the Farmer's Hat?, Joan Nodset
I Spy, Lucille Ogle
Santa's Beard Is Soft and Warm, Bob Ottum
Smile for Auntie, Diane Paterson
The Box with Red Wheels, Maud Petersham
Circus Baby, Maud Petersham
✗*The Little Engine That Could*, Watty Piper
Baby's Song Book, Elizabeth Poston
A Book of Seasons, Alice Provensen
My Little Hen, Alice Provensen
Colors, John J. Reiss
See the Circus, H.A. Rey
What Sadie Sang, Eve Rice
My Doctor, Harlow Rockwell
My Nursery School, Harlow Rockwell
Tall Book of Mother Goose, Feodor Rojankovsky
Tall Book of Nursery Tales, Feodor Rojankovsky
It Is Night, Phyllis Rowand
Knitted Cat, Antonella Bollinger-Savelli
Mouse and the Knitted Cat, Antonella Bollinger-Savelli
Peggy's New Brother, Eleanor Schick
The Hunt for Rabbit's Galosh, Ann Schweninger
It Looked Like Spilt Milk, Charles G. Shaw
Big Book of Wild Animals, Sutton
Hello, This Is a Shape Book, John Trotta
Mother Goose, Tasha Tudor
Elephant Buttons, Noriko Ueno
One, Two, Where's My Shoe?, Tomi Ungerer
Mother Goose, Vollaud Edition
Count the Cats, Erika Weihs
My First Picture Book, Leonard Weisgard
Whose Little Bird Am I?, Leonard Weisgard
Max's First Word/Ride/New Suit/Toys, Rosemary Wells
Baby Farm Animals, Garth Williams
Little Red Hen, Herb Williams
Look Look Book, Pat Witte
Touch Me Book, Pat Witte
Who Lives Here?, Pat Witte
Betsy and the Chicken Pox, Gunilla Wolde
Betsy's First Day at Nursery School, Gunilla Wolde
Tommy Goes to the Doctor, Gunilla Wolde
Umbrella, Taro Yashima
Bears Are Sleeping, Yulya

Basil and Hillary, Jane B. Zalben
Cecilia's Older Brother, Jane B. Zalben
Baby Animals, Naoma Zimmerman
Animal Babies, Max Zoll

Bilingual Books

We have mentioned language development as a positive value of reading to pre-schoolers. However, there are several varieties of books which are unique in this respect, since all children do not have English as their native language. At present, most bilingual books are in English and Spanish. Some books are done in English and other languages, but since there are so few of these, there is a conglomerate list. Actually, there is a great need for additional titles in this area so that non-English speaking children may derive pleasure from books while becoming familiar at the same time with their second language.

Note: *Spaces between groups of titles in this and all additional lists in this portion of the book indicate approximate age levels.* The first group is for the youngest children, the second list for the next age range, and the last for the older group. In some of the lists, there may be only two groups, indicating that there is only one division feasible. Conversely, in cases where there are four sets of titles, the age levels may be more precisely delineated.

Books in English and Spanish

Leonard the Lion and Raymond the Mouse, Dorothy Bishop
Tina the Tortoise and Carlos the Rabbit, Dorothy Bishop
Case of the Hungry Stranger, Crosby Bonsall
The Day I Had to Play with My Sister, Crosby Bonsall
My Red Umbrella, Robert Bright
The King, Dick Bruna
Mochito: The Story of an Ordinary Dog, Nelly Canepari
Senora Pepino and Her Bad Luck Cats,
    Esther de Michael Cervantes
Jo, Flo and Yolanda, Carol DePoix
Hare and the Tortoise, William Pene Du Bois
Angus and the Cat, Marjorie Flack
Angus and the Ducks, Marjorie Flack
House That Jack Built: A Picture Book in Two Languages,
    Antonio Frasconi

Alberto and His Missing Sock, Barbara Ganz
Herman the Helper, Robert Kraus
Milton the Early Riser, Robert Kraus
Owliver, Robert Kraus
The Little Auto, Lois Lenski
Papa Small, Lois Lenski
Alexander and the Wind-Up Mouse, Leo Lionni
The Biggest House in the World, Leo Lionni
Fish Is Fish, Leo Lionni
Greentail Mouse, Leo Lionni
Tico and the Golden Wings, Leo Lionni
Little Bear, Else H. Minarik
A Fish Out of Water, Helen M. Palmer
The Nicest Gift, Leo Politi
I Am a Kitten, Ole Risom
Peter Pelican, Annia Roa
Sylvester and the Magic Pebble, William Steig
Albert's Toothache, Barbara Williams
Little Red Hen, Herb Williams

Maria Teresa, Mary Atkinson
Faces (Caras), Barbara Brenner
Juan Bobo and the Pig: Puerto Rican Folktale, Bernice Chardiet
No Company Was Coming to Samuel's House, Dorothy Corey
Babar's Spanish Lessons, Laurent DeBrunhoff
Snow and Sun: So. American Folk Rhyme in Two Languages, Antonio Frasconi
Peppy, Patchy and Magic Star, Thelma Galyean
Adventures of Connie and Diego, Marcia Garcia
My Aunt Otilia's Spirits, Richard Garcia
Yolanda's Hike, Tomas Rodriguez Gaspar
Straight Hair, Curly Hair, Augusta Goldin
Perico Bonito, Monica Gunning
Two Georges, Monica Gunning
The Return of Chato, Susan Lewke
Yagua Days, Cruz Martel
The Adventures of Sapo, Susan Martin
My Mother and I Are Growing Strong, Inez Maury
My Mother the Mail Carrier, Inez Maury
The Horse Book, Virginia Parsons
Curious George, H.A. Rey
The Headless Pirate: Costa Rica, Harriet Rohmer
How We Came to the Fifth World: Aztecs, Harriet Rohmer
Little Horse of Seven Colors: Nicaragua, Harriet Rohmer
The Magic Boys: Guatemala, Harriet Rohmer
The Mighty God Viracocha: Peru and Bolivia, Harriet Rohmer

Skyworld Woman: Phillipines, Harriet Rohmer
Atariba and Niguayona: Puerto Rico, Harriet Rohmer
Cuna Song: Panama, Harriet Rohmer
Treasure of Guatavita: Colombia, Harriet Rohmer
Terry and the Caterpillars, Millicent E. Selsam
Welcome Roberto!, Mary Serfozo
The Cat in the Hat, Dr. Seuss
Look at Your Eyes, Paul Showers
What Do I Do?, Norma Simon
What Do I Say?, Norma Simon
Poco, Garry Smith
The Tiger, Letty Williams
Sights and Sounds of the City, Hope Warriner

Books in English and Other Foreign Languages

Mother Goose in French, Illus. by Barbara Cooney
Babar and Father Christmas, Jean DeBrunhoff
Inch by Inch, Leo Leonni
Tailor of Gloucester, Beatrix Potter
Tale of Mrs. Tiggy-Winkle, Beatrix Potter
Laughing Camera for Children, Edited by Hanns-Reich
Cajun Alphabet, James Rice
Teaser and the Firecat, Cat Stevens
Mother Goose Abroad, Nicholas Tucker
Kids Can Count, Angela Wood

I Like Birds, Rist Arnold
Iron Moonhunter, Kathleen Chang
Babar's French Lessons, Laurent DeBrunhoff
At Home: A Visit in Four Languages, Esther Hautzig
In School: Learning in Four Languages, Esther Hautzig
Village in Normandy, Laurence
House at Pooh Corner, A.A. Milne
Winnie the Pooh, A.A. Milne
Papa Albert, Lillian Moore
Aekyung's Dream, Min Paek
Gaston Goes to Mardi Gras, James Rice
Gaston Goes to Texas, James Rice
Gaston, the Green-Nosed Alligator, James Rice
Looking for Ifuago Mountain, Al Robles
Bufo a Toad: Un Crapaud, Maria Stevenson
The Little Weaver of Thai-Yen Village, Knanh Tuyet
Don't Put the Vinegar in the Copper, Kate Wong

Wordless Books

Books which tell a story entirely through illustration constitute a special group with value different from those having text. They contribute to the development of the child's imagination, of course, and additionally, they make it possible for a youngster to increase his verbal fluency, since even shy children often volunteer to "tell" the story of such a book to an adult or a younger child.

Books Without Words

Another Story to Tell, Dick Bruna
The Chimp and the Clown, Ruth Carroll
Rolling Downhill, Ruth Carroll
What Whiskers Did, Ruth Carroll
Where's the Bunny?, Ruth Carroll
Aunt Possum and the Pumpkin Man, Bruce Degen
Alligator's Toothache, Diane DeGroat
Elephant Buttons, Noriko Ueno

Ma nDa La, Arnold Adoff
Bobo's Dream, Martha Alexander
Out! Out! Out!, Martha Alexander
Topsy-Turvies: Pictures to Stretch the Imagination, Mitsumasa Anno
Elephant, Byron Barton
Birds of a Feather, Willi Baum
The Snowman, Raymond Briggs
Seasons, John Burningham
Do You Want to Be My Friend?, Eric Carle
I See a Song, Eric Carle
Journey to the Moon, Erich Fuchs
Adventures of Paddy Pig, John S. Goodall
Creepy Castle, John S. Goodall
Paddy's Evening Out, John S. Goodall
Naughty Nancy, the Bad Bridesmaid, John S. Goodall
The Surprise Picnic, John S. Goodall
Birthday Trombone, Margaret Hartelius
The Chicken's Child, Margaret Hartelius
April Fools, Fernando Krahn
Flying Saucer Full of Spaghetti, Fernando Krahn
Little Love Story, Fernando Krahn
The Self-Made Snowman, Fernando Krahn
Agatha's Alphabet, Kathryn Lasky

Lost, Sonia Lisker
The Chicken and the Egg, Iela Mari
Ah-Choo, Mercer Mayer
Bubble Bubble, Mercer Mayer
Four Frogs in a Box, Mercer Mayer
Frog Goes to Dinner, Mercer Mayer
Frog on His Own, Mercer Mayer
Frog, Where Are You?, Mercer Mayer
Hiccup, Mercer Mayer
Oops, Mercer Mayer
Two Moral Tales, Mercer Mayer
A Boy, A Dog, A Frog and a Friend, Mercer Mayer
One Frog Too Many, Mercer Mayer
My Feet Roll, Winnie Mertens
Making Friends, Eleanor Schick
A Dance for Three, Ann Schweninger
The Foolish Frog, Pete Seeger
A Special Birthday, Symeon Shimin
Crash, Bang, Boom, Peter Spier
Gobble, Growl, Grunt, Peter Spier
My Friend Little John, Yutaka Sugita
Deep in the Forest, Brinton Turkle

Mud Time and More Nathaniel Stories, Jim Arnosky
Grey Lady and the Strawberry Snatcher, Molly Bang
The Tadpole and the Frog, Susan Knobler
Sebastian and the Mushroom, Fernando Krahn
Dandelion Year, Ron McTrusty
On the Go: A Book of Adjectives, Betsy Maestro
The Apple and the Moth, Iela Mari

Folk and Fairy Tales

In the category of fiction, there are two rather special kinds of books for children: fairy tales and folk tales. Strictly speaking, fairy stories would include characters such as elves, gnomes, witches, giants, and other supernatural figures, and would tell of all manner of impossible events and fantastic outcomes. Folk tales, on the other hand, are usually stories which have come down from the oral tradition (sometimes from several) of the common people—the folk—and have been set down on paper later. Both of these types often involve a number of motifs which are worth mentioning.

The Youngest Child

Since quite frequently the youngest child was not thought to be a valuable addition to the family, particularly in earlier societies which set great store by the tradition of the first-born being rather special (see any dictionary definition of "primogeniture"), it is understandable that stories would evolve to exalt the youngest member. Quite often he or she turns out to be the best-natured, the smartest, and the most fortunate, usually in a family of three children.

The Gullible Innocent

Closely connected to being the youngest child is the notion that a virtuous person may be temporarily outsmarted, but that he will eventually emerge victorious because he is "good." Tied into this motif also is the need which every small child has to triumph over those who rule him merely because they are the giants (adults) in his real world.

The Clever Animal

Sometimes this animal outsmarts other animals. If he is evil, he may come to a bad end; if he is good, all ends well for him. At times also he assists a human being who deserves his help.

The Evil Stepmother

Stemming from the fear of losing one's main source of protection through her death, the child projects what a substitute for his mother would be like. Unfortunately, this character never likes the stepchildren and frequently attempts to eliminate them completely from the family circle. There is an element of sexism here, too, since the father never seems to protest the ill treatment of his children, but passively accepts the situation. Then, when the evil stepmother is punished (usually through death), the father who allowed her to mistreat his children is shown reunited with them—no questions asked.

Evil Is Ugly—Good Is Beautiful

Another motif which seems negative in terms of the development of a child's value system is the equation of appearance with character. Except for *Beauty and the Beast* there is no well-known tale in which the connection is reversed, and even in this story the beast turns into a handsome prince through the use of another frequently included motif, tears.

Tears as a Way to Break a Spell

There may be a connection here to water as a means of purification, or this may be looked upon as an objectification of the idea that compassion itself can thwart evil and release beneficence, personified as a beautiful or handsome person.

The Magical Solution to a Problem

The desire to find a way out of a situation which seems hopeless has no doubt evoked this motif throughout a wide range of stories. Along with this goes the galaxy of characters from leprechauns to fairy godmothers who can call forth such "miracles."

The Pourquoi Story

In response to natural curiosity and the need to explain phenomena in terms understandable to all, these stories which border on myth or legend appear in many cultures. Since they attempt to answer questions concretely (although the explanations are usually fantastic in the literal sense of that word), they are designated "pourquoi" stories.

The Cumulative Repetitive Story

This motif is a great favorite with small children, possibly because they can feel a sense of their own ability in that they can correctly guess what will come next, even before it is read to them. Also, of course, the rhythm that is part and parcel of the repetitive mode is pleasing in itself and sometimes quite humorous.

There is always the question of violence in folk and fairy tales, and there is some concern on the part of modern adults in regard to "telling children the truth," which these stories cannot be said to do. However, according to Dr. Bruno Bettleheim, the world renowned child psychologist, and explained in detail in his book *The Uses of Enchantment*,[8] there is no need for worry on either score. In regard to violence, Dr. Bettleheim feels that these tales often meet the child's need for release of negative feelings which he is not able to express in any other way. And regarding veracity, he asserts that fairy and folk tales have a different kind of "truth" from modern, realistic books, yes, but that they meet the child's deep psychological needs better than any other type of literature.

In any case, these kinds of stories have been very popular with children for a very long time and have spawned a great number of modern-day books in the same mode. Therefore, the list which follows here includes both the old favorites and titles which can be classified as belonging to folk and fairy tales because they include some of the motifs described above and others which are closely related. Settings or places of origin have been indicated in most instances.

Folk and Fairy Tales

Little Red Hen, Paul Galdone
The Three Bears, Paul Galdone
The Three Little Pigs, Paul Galdone
Old Mother Hubbard and Her Dog, Sarah Martin
Little Red Hen, Herb Williams

King Orville and the Bullfrogs, Kathleen Abell (W. Eur.)
Town Mouse and the Country Mouse, Aesop
Three Aesop Fox Fables: Fox and Grapes, Stork, Crow, Aesop
Three Billy Goats Gruff, Peter Asbjornsen (W. Eur.)
Buzz, Buzz, Buzz, Byron Barton
Larbi and Leila: A Tale of Two Mice, Harold Berson (Africa)
Grasshopper to the Rescue, Carey Bonnie (E. Eur.)
Bun, a Tale from Russia, Marcia Brown (E. Eur.)
Stone Soup, Marcia Brown (E. Eur.)
Pied Piper of Hamelin, Robert Browning (W. Eur.)
Little Wooden Farmer, Alice Dalgliesh
Peasants' Pea Patch, Guy Daniels (W. Eur.)
Catch a Little Fox, Beatrice De Regniers
May I Bring a Friend?, Beatrice De Regniers
Turnip, Janina Domanska (E. Eur.)
William the Dragon, Polly Donnison (W. Eur.)
Seven Little Popovers, Ivy O. Eastwick (E. Eur.)
King Who Could Not Sleep, Benjamin Elkin
Loudest Noise in the World, Benjamin Elkin
Such Is the Way of the World, Benjamin Elkin (Africa)
Drummer Hoff, Barbara Emberley
House That Jack Built: A Picture Book in Two Languages, Antonio Frasconi
Millions of Cats, Wanda Gag
Henny Penny, Paul Galdone
History of Mother Twaddle and the Marvelous Achievements of Her Son Jack, Paul Galdone

Horse, Fox, and Lion, Paul Galdone (W. Eur.)
Little Red Riding Hood, Paul Galdone
Magic Porridge Pot, Paul Galdone
Monkey and the Crocodile, Paul Galdone (Asia)
Old Woman and Her Pig, Paul Galdone
Three Wishes, Paul Galdone
Omoteji's Baby Brother, Mary Joan Gerson (Africa)
Androcles and the Lion, Janusz Grabianski (W. Eur.)
The Hole in the Dike, Retold by Norma Green (W. Eur.)
Bremen Town Musicians, Grimm Brothers (W. Eur.)
Rumpelstiltskin, Grimm Brothers (W. Eur.)
Snow White and the Seven Dwarfs, Grimm Brothers (W. Eur.)
Table, Donkey and Stick, Grimm Brothers (W. Eur.)
Shoemaker and the Elves, Jacob Grimm (W. Eur.)
Froggy Went A-Courtin', Harriett
Surprise Party, Pat Hutchins
Jack and the Beanstalk, Joseph Jacobs
Jack and the Giant Killer, Joseph Jacobs
Clay Pot Boy, Cynthia Jameson (E. Eur.)
Over in the Meadow, Ezra Jack Keats
Bunya, the Witch, Robert Kraus
Hare and the Tortoise, Jean de La Fontaine
Lion and the Rat, Jean de La Fontaine
The King's Shadow, Robert Larranga
Knee-High Man, Julius Lester (U.S.)
Theodore and the Talking Mushroom, Leo Lionni
Tico and the Golden Wings, Leo Lionni
Elves and the Shoemaker, Retold by Freya Littledale
Hee Haw, Ann McGovern
Curious Cow, Esther K. Meeks
How the Rabbit Stole the Moon, Louise Moeri
The Bad Bear, Rudolph Neumann (W. Eur.)
Stone Soup, Carol Pasternack
Cat and Mouse, Rodney Peppe
Cinderella, Charles Perrault
Little Red Riding Hood, Charles Perrault
Rooster Crows, Maud Petersham
Bubba and Babba, Maria Polushkin (E. Eur.)
The Little Hen and the Giant, Maria Polushkin
The Stolen Mirror, Lidia Postma
Old MacDonald Had a Farm, Robert Quackenbush (U.S.)
One Monday Morning, Uri Shulevitz
Caps for Sale, Esphyr Slobodkina
Tattercoats, Flora Annie Steel
Great Big Enormous Turnip, Alexei Tolstoy (E. Eur.)
Mitten, Alvin R. Tresselt (E. Eur.)
Pigs and Pirates: A Greek Tale, Barbara K. Walker (W. Eur.)

✗ *Lazy Jack*, Kurt Werth
The Cap That Mother Made, Christine Westerberg (W. Eur.)
Turnabout, William Wiesner
The Simple Prince, Jane Yolen
Mommy, Buy Me a China Doll, Harve Zemach (U.S.)
Hush, Little Baby, Margot Zemach (U.S.)

Brave Soldier Janosh, Victor Ambrus (E. Eur.)
✗ *Emperor's New Clothes*, Hans C. Andersen (W. Eur.)
✗ *Princess and the Pea*, Hans C. Andersen (W. Eur.)
Thumbelina, Hans C. Andersen (W. Eur.)
✗ *Ugly Duckling*, Hans C. Andersen (W. Eur.)
Red Fox and the Hungry Tiger, Paul Anderson (Asia)
Mud Time and More Nathaniel Stories, Jim Arnosky
Squire's Bride, Peter Asbjornsen (W. Eur.)
Sweet Touch, Lorna Balian
The Boy, the Baker, the Miller and More, Harold Berson
Hungry Leprechaun, Mary Calhoun
Picture That!, Bernice Carlson
In My Mother's House, Ann Clark (U.S.)
Why the Sun and the Moon Live in the Sky,
    Elphinstone Dayrell (Africa)
King Krakus and the Dragon, Janina Domanska (E. Eur.)
A Gift, Claudia Fregosi (U.S.)
Puss in Boots, Paul Galdone
Once Upon a Dinkelsbuhl, Patricia Gauch (W. Eur.)
Bembel Man's Bakery, Melinda Green (E. Eur.)
Hansel and Gretel, Grimm Brothers (W. Eur.)
Frog Prince, Jacob Grimm (W. Eur.)
We Came A-Marching One, Two, Three,
    Mildred Hobzek (E. Eur.)
The Leprechaun's Story, Richard Kennedy (W. Eur.)
Jack Kent's Book of Nursery Tales, Jack Kent
The Cow Who Fell in the Canal, Phyllis Krasilovsky (W. Eur.)
A Single Speckled Egg, Sonia Levitan
A Birthday for the Princess, Anita Lobel
A Treeful of Pigs, Arnold Lobel
The Queen Who Always Wanted to Dance, Mercer Mayer
Terrible Troll, Mercer Mayer
The Little Giant Girl and the Elf Boy, Else H. Minarik
Tikki Tikki Tembo, Arlene Mosel (Asia)
Tom Tit Tot, Eveline Ness (W. Eur.)
Poor Goose, Anne Rockwell (W. Eur.)
Of Cobblers and Kings, Aure Sheldon
The Queen Who Couldn't Bake Gingerbread,
    Dorothy Van Woerkom
← *Little Tiny Woman*, **Margot Zemach**

Book Selection / 45

Half-a-Ball-of-Kenki, Verna Aardema (Africa)
Riddle of the Drum, Verna Aardema (Hispanic America)
Who's in Rabbit's House: A Masai Tale, Verna Aardema (Africa)
Why Mosquitoes Buzz in People's Ears, Verna Aardema (Africa)
Coll and His White Pig, Lloyd Alexander (W. Eur.)
Twelve Months, Aliki (W. Eur.)
Snow Queen, Hans C. Andersen (W.Eur.)
Princess and the Unicorn, Lily Arbore
Joanjo, a Portuguese Tale, Jan Balet (W. Eur.)
Old Woman and the Red Pumpkin, Molly G. Bang (Asia)
Wind Thief, Judi Barrett
Those Foolish Molboes!, Lillian Bason
Hare's Race, Hans Baumann (W. Eur.)
Ote: A Puerto Rican Folk Tale, Pura Belpre (Hispanic America)
Rainbow Colored Horse, Pura Belpre (Hispanic America)
Balarin's Goat, Harold Berson (W. Eur.)
How the Devil Gets His Due, Harold Berson (W. Eur.)
Kassim's Shoes, Harold Berson (Middle East)
Why Jackal Won't Speak to Hedgehog, Harold Berson (Africa)
Peter's Adventures in Blueberry Land, Elsa Beskow (W. Eur.)
Ring in the Prairie, John Bierhorst (U.S.)
Woman of the Wood, Algernon Black (E. Eur.)
Ivanko and the Dragon, Marie Bloch (E. Eur.)
Field of Buttercups, Alice Boden (W. Eur.)
Small Deer's Magic Tricks, Betty Boegehold (Asia)
Wooden Man, Max Bolliger (W. Eur.)
Little One Inch, Barbara Brenner (Asia)
Mythical Adventures of Kraken, the Sea Monster, Beverly Brown
Dick Whittington and His Cat, Marcia Brown (W. Eur.)
Once a Mouse, Marcia Brown (Asia)
Puss in Boots, Marcia Brown (W. Eur.)
Wheel on the Chimney, Margaret Brown
Stone Giants and Flying Heads,Told by
  Joseph Bruchac (U.S. Ind.)
Turkey Brothers and Other Iroquois Tales, Told by Joseph
  Bruchac (U.S. Ind.)
Dancing Granny, Ashley Bryan (Asia)
New Boy in Dublin: Story of Ireland, Clyde R. Bulla (W. Eur.)
Tigger: Story of a Mayan Ocelot, Bunny (Hispanic America)
Runaway Brownie, Mary Calhoun (W. Eur.)
The Third Gift, Jan Carew (Africa)
I Can Squash Elephants: A Masai Tale About Monsters,
  Malcolm Carrick (Africa)
Tot Botot and His Little Flute, Laura Cathon (Asia)
Contrary Jenkins, Rebecca Caudill (U.S.)
Juan Bobo and the Pig: A Puerto Rican Folktale, Bernice
  Chardiet (Hispanic America)
Harlequin and the Gift of Many Colors, Remy Charlip

It Could Be Worse, Eleanor Chroman (E. Eur.)
The King at the Door, Brock Cole
Tops and Bottoms, Lesley Conger (W. Eur.)
The Magic Pot, Patricia Combs (W. Eur.)
Little Oleg, Margaret Cort
Fairy Tales, E.E. Cummings
Andy and the Lion, James Daugherty
Terrible Troll-Bird, Ingri D'Aulaire (W. Eur.)
Earth and Sky, Mona Dayton
Big Anthony and the Magic Ring, Tomie De Paola
Strega Nona, Tomie De Paola (W. Eur.)
Little Sister and Month Brothers, Beatrice DeRegniers (E. Eur.)
Wise Man on the Mountain, Ellis Dillon (W. Eur.)
Gilly Gilhooley: A Tale of Ireland, Arnold Dobrin (W. Eur.)
Little Monk and the Tiger: A Tale of Thailand,
    Arnold Dobrin (Asia)
Look, There's a Flying Turtle, Janina Domanska
Tobei: A Japanese Tale, Retold by Mae Durham (Asia)
Story of Paul Bunyan, Barbara Emberley (U.S.)
Great Green Turkey Creek Monster, James Flora (U.S.)
Sir Ribbeck of Ribbeck of Havilland, Theodore Fontaine
Coconut Thieves, Edited by Catherine Fournier (Africa)
Natasha's New Doll, Frank Francis (E. Eur.)
Snow and Sun: South American Folk Rhyme in Two Languages,
    Antonio Frasconi (Hispanic America)
Crackle Gluck and the Sleeping Toad, Dick Gackenbach
Adventures of Connie and Diego, Marcia Garcia
The Wentletrap, Jean C. George (Hispanic America)
Why the Sky Is Far Away, Mary-Joan Gerson (Africa)
How the Sun Was Brought Back to the Sky,
    Mirra Ginsburg (E. Eur.)
Proud Maiden Tungak and the Sun,
    Mirra Ginsburg (Canad. Ind.)
Two Greedy Bears, Mirra Ginsburg (E. Eur.)
Which Is the Best Place?, Mirra Ginsburg (E. Eur.)
Legend of the Orange Princess, Mehlli Gobhai (Asia)
Across the Sea, M.B. Goffstein
The Golden Lamb, Irene Gough
Bigger Giant, Nancy Green (W. Eur.)
The Bear and the Kingbird, Grimm Brothers (W. Eur.)
Briar Rose: Story of Sleeping Beauty, Grimm Brothers (W. Eur.)
Hans In Luck, Grimm Brothers (W. Eur.)
Seven Ravens, Grimm Brothers (W. Eur.)
Thorn Rose, Grimm Brothers (W. Eur.)
Wolf and the Seven Little Kids, Grimm Brothers (W. Eur.)
The Fable of the Fig Tree, Michael Gross
A Story, A Story, Gail Haley (Africa)
Gunniwolf, Wilhelmina Harper (U.S.)

The Forest Princess, Harriet Herman
Could Anything Be Worse?, Marilyn Hirsch (E. Eur.)
Potato Pancakes All Around, Marilyn Hirsch (E. Eur.)
The Rabbi and the Twenty-Nine Witches,
    Marilyn Hirsch (E. Eur.)
Ugly Bird, Russell Hoban
Wave, Margaret Hodges (Asia)
The Contest, Nonny Hogrogian (E. Eur.)
Tom and Sam, Pat Hutchins (W. Eur.)
In the Village, Hilde Heyduck-Huth (W. Eur.)
One for the Price of Two, Cynthia Jameson (Asia)
Thieves and the Raven, Janosch
How Do You Hide a Monster?, Virginia Kahl
Little White Hen, Hajime Kijima (Asia)
Lum Foo and the Golden Mountain, Hisako Kimishima (Asia)
The Princess of the Rice Fields, Hisako Kimishima (Asia)
Magic in the Mist, Margaret M. Kimmel (W. Eur.)
To Your Good Health, Andrew Lang (E. Eur.)
Go and Shut the Door, Nola Langner
Rafiki, Nola Langner (Africa)
Wa O'Ka, Jean Latham
Turnabout, Munro Leaf
Crocodile and the Hen, Joan Lexau (Africa)
Mud Snail Son, Betty Lifton (Asia)
One-Legged Ghost, Betty Lifton (Asia)
Sticks, Stones, Carlos A. Llerena (Hispanic America)
Seamstress of Salzburg, Anita Lobel (W. Eur.)
Sven's Bridge, Anita Lobel
Giant John, Arnold Lobel
Prince Bertram the Bad, Arnold Lobel
Crystal Apple: A Russian Tale, Beverly McDermott
An Eskimo Myth, Beverly McDermott (Canada)
Anansi the Spider: A Tale from Ashanti,
    Gerald McDermott (Africa)
Arrow to the Sun: A Pueblo Indian Tale,
    Gerald McDermott (U.S.)
Magic Tree: A Tale from the Congo, Gerald McDermott (Africa)
The Stonecutter: A Japanese Folktale, Gerald McDermott (Asia)
Half a Kingdom, Ann McGovern (Canada)
The Mermaid and the Whale, Georgess McHargue (U.S.)
The Man Who Was Going to Mind the House,
    David McKee (W. Eur.)
Rakoto and the Drongo Bird, Robin McKown
Tortoise's Tug of War, Guilio Maestro
Wish Again, Big Bear, Richard Margolis
Taro and the Bamboo Shoot, Masako Matsuno (Asia)
Crane Maiden, Miyoko Matsutani (Asia)
That Noodle-Headed Epaminondas, Eve Merriam

Funny Little Woman, Arlene Mosel (Asia)
Adventures of Muku, Geraldine Nicholson
The Great Fish, Peter Parnell
King of the Fish, Marian Parry (Asia)
Cowardly Clyde, Bill Peet
Amy and the Cloud Basket, Ellen Pratt
When the Monkeys Wore Sombreros, Mariana Prieto
    (Hispanic America)
Clementine, Robert Quackenbush (U.S.)
Blind Men and the Elephant, Lillian Quigley (Asia)
Fool of the World and the Flying Ship,
    Arthur Ransome (E. Eur.)
My Mother Is the Most Beautiful Woman in the World,
    Becky Reyther (E. Eur.)
Babushka and the Three Kings, Ruth Robbins (E. Eur.)
Femi and the Old Grandaddie, Adjai Robinson (Africa)
Clever Turtle, A.K. Roche (Africa)
Dancing Stars: An Iroquois Legend, Anne Rockwell (U.S.)
Monkey's Whiskers: A Brazilian Folktale, Anne Rockwell
    (Hispanic America)
When the Drum Sang, Anne Rockwell (Africa)
The Wolf Who Had a Wonderful Dream: A French Folktale,
    Anne Rockwell (W. Eur.)
The Headless Pirate: Costa Rica, Harriet Rohmer
    (Hispanic America)
How We Came to the Fifth World: Aztecs, Harriet Rohmer
    (Hispanic America)
The Little Horse of Seven Colors: Nicaragua, Harriet Rohmer
    (Hispanic America)
The Magic Boys: Guatemala, Harriet Rohmer
    (Hispanic America)
The Mighty God Viracocha: Peru and Bolivia, Harriet Rohmer
    (Hispanic America)
Skyworld Woman: Phillipines, Harriet Rohmer
    (Hispanic America)
Atariba and Niguayona: Puerto Rico, Harriet Rohmer
    (Hispanic America)
Cuna Song: Panama, Harriet Rohmer (Hispanic America)
Land of Icy Death: Chile, Harriet Rohmer (Hispanic America)
The Treasure of Guatavita: Colombia, Harriet Rohmer
    (Hispanic America)
Akimba and the Magic Cow, Retold by Anne Rose (Africa)
How Does a Czar Eat Potatoes?, Anne Rose (E. Eur.)
Giant Devil-Dingo, Dick Roughsey (Australia)
Japanese Children's Favorite Stories, Edited by Florence Sakade
    (Asia)
Twelve Years, Twelve Animals, Yoshiko Samuel (Asia)

Wedding Procession of the Rag Doll and the Broom Handle,
    Carl Sandburg
The Golden Thread: Japanese Stories for Children,
    Tazu Sasaki (Asia)
Journey Cake, Ho, Ruth Sawyer (U.S.)
Feast of Lanterns, Allen Say (Asia)
The Wee, Wee Mannie and the Big, Big Coo,
    Marcia Sewall (W. Eur.)
Hester the Jester, Ben Shecter
The Magician, Uri Shulevitz
The Soldier and the Tsar in the Forest, Uri Shulevitz (E. Eur.)
The Treasure, Uri Shulevitz (E. Eur.)
Two Fools and a Faker, Gloria Skurzynski (Middle East)
The Angry Moon, William Sleator (U.S.)
Baba Yaga, Ernest Small (E. Eur.)
The Amazing Bone, William Steig
Caleb and Kate, William Steig
Ballad of Penelope Lou ... and Me, Drew Stevenson
Simon Boom Gives a Wedding, Yuri Suhl
What Kind of Bird Is That?, Vladimir Suteyev (E. Eur.)
Hulda, Carol Svendsen (W. Eur.)
The Clever Princess, Ann Tompert
Magic Cooking Pot, Faith M. Towle (Asia)
How Summer Came to Canada, William Toye (Canada)
Mountain Goats of Temlaham, William Toye
Frog in the Well, Alvin R. Tresselt
Babushka and the Pig, Ann Trofimuk (E. Eur.)
Magician of Cracow, Krystyna Turksa (E. Eur.)
The Woodcutter's Duck, Krystyna Turksa (E. Eur.)
Alumette, Tomi Ungerer
Zeralda's Ogre, Tomi Ungerer
How a Shirt Grew in the Field, Constantin Ushinsky (E. Eur.)
The Rat, the Ox and the Zodiac, Dorothy Van Woerkom (Asia)
The Battle of the Wind Gods, Judy Varga
Janko's Wish, Judy Varga (E. Eur.)
Magic Wall, Judy Varga (E. Eur.)
The Woman with Eggs, Jan Wahl
Father Fox's Pennyrhymes, Clyde Watson
Golden Spinning Wheel, Lisl Weil (E. Eur.)
Small Boy Chuku, Alice K. Wellman (Africa)
Molly and the Giant, Kurt Werth
Daxius, Dante Westbrook (Africa)
Vasilisa the Beautiful, Thomas Whitney (E. Eur.)
Little Sarah and Her Johnny Cake, William Wiesner
Everyone Knows What a Dragon Looks Like, Jay Williams (Asia)
Forgetful Fred, Jay Williams
Petronella, Jay Williams

Practical Princess, Jay Williams
Silver Whistle, Jay Williams
The Surprising Things Maui Did, Jay Williams
A Cool Ride in the Sky, Diane Wolkstein
The Magic Orange Tree and Other Haitian Folktales, Diane Wolkstein (Hispanic America)
Squirrel's Song, Diane Wolkstein
Cornrows, Camille Yarbrough (Africa)
Tusya and the Pot of Gold, Yaraslava (E. Eur.)
Seashore Story, Taro Yashima (Asia)
Tonweya and the Eagles and Other Lakota Indian Tales by Rosebud, Retold by Yellow Robe (U.S.)
Little Spotted Fish, Jane Yolen (W. Eur.)
The Seeing Stick, Jane Yolen
Two Korean Brothers: A Story of Hungbu and Nolbu, Grace Yoo (Asia)
Rosachok: A Russian Story, Boris Zakhoder (E. Eur.)
Salt: A Russian Tale, Harve Zemach (E. Eur.)
The Beautiful Rat, Kathe Zemach (Asia)
It Could Always Be Worse: A Yiddish Folktale, Margot Zemach
Benny and His Goose, or the Royal Game of the Goose, Tjerk Ziljlstra (W. Eur.)
Troll Island, Arnold Zimmerman

Physical Safety

In the original list of children's "needs" this aspect of security was cited, and the following list includes titles which emphasize this area, whether in regard to getting lost, fearing the dark, or crossing streets safely. We must keep in mind that children identify with characters in their books (even the non-human ones), so that when Mother Rabbit talks to her baby about safety in Margaret Wise Brown's *The Runaway Bunny*, the theme comes across clearly. In the same way, vague nameless fears are speedily defused when the small hero in Mercer Mayer's *There's a Nightmare in My Closet* takes complete charge of the terrified and comical creatures who beg him for mercy.

Books About Physical Safety

Goodnight Moon, Margaret Wise Brown
Runaway Bunny, Margaret Wise Brown
Grandmother and I, Helen E. Buckley
The Blanket, John Burningham

Be Good, Harry, Mary Chalmers
You Go Away, Dorothy Corey
Scuffy the Tugboat, Gertrude Crampton
Are You My Mother?, Philip E. Eastman

Town Mouse and Country Mouse, Aesop
And My Mean Old Mother Will Be Sorry, Blackboard Bear,
   Martha Alexander
I'll Protect You from the Jungle Beasts, Martha Alexander
Three Billy Goats Gruff, Peter Asbjornsen
Something, Natalie Babbitt
Little Pig in the Cupboard, Helen E. Buckley
After Dark, Blossom Budney
Lester's Overnight, Kay Chorao
Clyde Monster, Robert L. Crowe
Your Owl Friend, Crescent Dragonwagon
Angus and the Ducks, Marjorie Flack
Angus Lost, Marjorie Flack
Story About Ping, Marjorie Flack
Chalk Box Story, Don Freeman
First Pink Light, Eloise Greenfield
Hi, Cat, Ezra Jack Keats
The King's Shadow, Robert Larranga
The Other Side of the Mountain, Robert Leydenfrost
There's a Nightmare in My Closet, Mercer Mayer
What's in the Dark?, Carl Memling
The Little Raccoon and No Trouble at All, Lilian Moore
My House, Miriam Schlein
Where the Wild Things Are, Maurice Sendak
Rex, Marjorie W. Sharmot
Sylvester and the Magic Pebble, William Steig
Little Fox Goes to the End of the World, Ann Tompert
Try It Again, Sam: Safety When You Walk, Judith Viorst
The Funny Old Bag, Lisl Weil
Harry by the Sea, Gene Zion
Harry the Dirty Dog, Gene Zion

Plink, Plink, Plink, Peter Baylor
Witch Next Door, Norman Bridwell
Molly's Moe, Kay Chorao
Fight the Night, Tomie De Paola
Quicksand Book, Tomic De Paola
When Everyone Was Fast Asleep, Tomie De Paola
Magic Wallpaper, Frank Francis
Poor Goose, Anne Rockwell

Hildilid's Night, Cheli D. Ryan
Outside My Window, Liesel M. Skorpen

The Day the Hurricane Happened, Lonzo Anderson
Joseph, the Border Guard, Kurt Baumann
A Moose Is Not a Mouse, Harold Berson
Switch on the Night, Ray Bradbury
Cross-Country Cat, Mary Calhoun
When Light Turns into Night, Crescent Dragonwagon
Will I Be Okay?, Crescent Dragonwagon
In the Middle of the Night, Aileen Fisher
Yolanda's Hike, Tomas Rodriguez Gaspar
Dreams, Ezra Jack Keats
Five Little Monkeys, Juliet Kepes
Runaway John, Leonore Klein
Noel the Coward, Robert Kraus
The Drinking Gourd, F.N. Monjo
Cowardly Clyde, Bill Peet
Harriet and the Promised Land, Jacob Lawrence
No Pushing, No Ducking: Safety in the Water, Barbara Rinkoff
When the Drum Sang, Anne Rockwell
The Tiger-Skin Rug, Gerald Rose
One Way: A Trip with Traffic Signs, Leonard Shortall
About Phobias, Sara Bonnett Stein
Ellie to the Rescue, Beth Weiner Woldin
Beatrice and Vanessa, John Yeoman

Age Identity

The realm of emotional security, of course, is much broader than that which deals with material security or physical safety, and it includes many sub-categories. First, there is the matter of age identity. It is quite probable that every child has at some time wondered if the world of giants—as adults must seem to a toddler—will ever accept him as an equal, and before that, if all the demi-giants (older children) can be "conquered."

Books About Age Identity

I Want to Be Big, Genie Iverson
Snowy Day, Ezra Jack Keats
Big Little Davy, Lois Lenski
Here Comes Tagalong, Anne Mallett

Little Gorilla, Ruth Bornstein
Impossible Possum, Ellen Conford
Don't Worry, Dear, Joan Fassler
Happy Birthday, Sam, Pat Hutchins
Titch, Pat Hutchins
Big Brother, Robert Kraus
Littlest Rabbit, Robert Kraus
Tiny Little Rooster, William Lipkind
Little Though I Be, Joseph Low
House So Big, Joan Lexau
Jane's Blanket, Arthur Miller
Wait, Says His Father, Jane B. Moncure
Great Big Enormous Turnip, Alexei Tolstoy
I'll Fix Anthony, Judith Viorst
Goodbye, Hello, Robert Welber
Someday, Said Mitchell, Barbara Williams
Big Brother, Charlotte Zolotow
Big Sister and Little Sister, Charlotte Zolotow

Tom in the Middle, Berthe Amoss
Rosa-Too-Little, Sue Felt
My Brother Never Feeds the Cat, Reynold Ruffins
Ralphi Rhino, Lisl Weil

Crackle Gluck and the Sleeping Toad,
 Dick Gackenbach
Much Bigger Than Martin, Steven Kellogg
Andy the Dog Walker, Leonard Shortall
Obadiah, the Bold, Brinton Turkle
Someone New, Charlotte Zolotow

Family Relationships of Various Kinds

Next, since the typical pre-schooler's world is centered in the family, we must consider a number of relationships with siblings and parents. There is the two- or three-year-old faced with a new baby who seems suddenly to have usurped center stage. There are the everyday interactions among all siblings. There are the unusual brothers and sisters, perhaps with a handicap which requires special care. Finally, there is the parental relationship to the child or children, including "special" cases involving the single parent family.

Books About the New Baby

The Baby, John Burningham
The Knee Baby, Mary Jarrell
Peter's Chair, Ezra Jack Keats
Peggy's New Brother, Eleanor Schick
On Mother's Lap, Ann Herbert Scott

Nobody Asked Me If I Wanted a Baby Sister, Martha Alexander
New Baby, Andrew C. Andry
Families Grow in Different Ways, Barbara Parrish-Benson
Go and Hush the Baby, Betty Byers
Tommy's Big Problem, Lilli D. Chaffin
Everett Anderson's Nine Month Long, Lucille Clifton
Just Momma and Me, Christine Engla Eber
She Come Bringing Me That Little Baby Girl, Eloise Greenfield
My Name Is Emily, Norse Hamilton
Monster's Nose Was Cold, Joan Hanson
We're Going to Have a Baby, Vicki Holland
A New Baby Is Coming to My House, Chihiro Iwasaki
David's Waiting Day, Bernadette Watts
Betsy's Baby Brother, Gunilla Wolde

Billy and Our New Baby, Helene S. Arnstein
New Baby, Terry Berger
We Want a Little Sister, Felix Mattmuller
My Brother Never Feeds the Cat, Reynold Ruffins
That New Baby, Sara Bonnett Stein
Amanda the Panda and the Redhead, Susan Terris

Books About Other Kinds of Sibling Rivalry

Grouchy Uncle Otto, Alice Bach
Millicent the Magnificent, Alice Bach
Smartest Bear and His Brother Oliver, Alice Bach
Baby Sister for Frances, Russell Hoban
Free as a Frog, Elizabeth Hodges
Big Brother, Robert Kraus
I'll Fix Anthony, Judith Viorst

Tom in the Middle, Berthe Amoss
Nicky's Sister, Barbara Brenner
My Brother Fine with Me, Lucille Clifton

The Eleven Steps, Lucy Freeman
Much Bigger Than Martin, Steven Kellogg
Ha, Ha, Ha, Henrietta, Barbara Klimowicz
Monnie Hates Lydia, Susan Pearson
Panda Cake, Rosalie Sander
I Was So Mad!, Norma Simon
It's Not Fair!, Robin Supraner

Additional Books About Siblings, Including Exceptional Children (Marked EC)

I'll Be the Horse If You'll Play with Me, Martha Alexander
The Day I Had to Play with My Sister, Crosby Bonsall
Piggle, Crosby Bonsall
Who's a Pest?, Crosby Bonsall
I Wish I Was Sick Too, Franz Brandenberg
Abby, Jeanette Caines
Good News, Eloise Greenfield
We're Very Good Friends, My Brother and I, P.K. Hallinan
Why Couldn't I Be an Only Child Like You, Wigger?, Barbara Shook Hazen
Here Comes Tagalong, Anne Mallett
Just One More Block, Patrick Mayers
Feeling Angry, Sylvia R. Tester
Too Hot for Ice Cream, Jean Van Leeuwen
Alexander and the Terrible . . . Very Bad Day, Judith Viorst
If He's My Brother, Barbara Williams
Betsy and the Chicken Pox, Gunilla Wolde
Cecilia's Older Brother, Jane Zalben
Big Brother, Charlotte Zolotow
Big Sister and Little Sister, Charlotte Zolotow
If It Weren't for You, Charlotte Zolotow

My Sister's Silent World, Catherine Arthur (EC)
Wish for Little Sister, Jacqueline Ayer
Real Hole, Beverly Cleary
More Time to Grow, Sharon Grollman (EC)
My Sister, Karen Hirsch (EC)
He's My Brother, Joe Lasker (EC)
Bright Fawn and Me, Jay Leech
Brothers Are All the Same, Mary Milgram
I Have a Sister; My Sister Is Deaf, Jeanne Peterson (EC)
A Special Kind of Sister, Lucia B. Smith (EC)
My Special Best Words, John Steptoe
Walk Home Tired, Billy Jenkins, Ianthe Thomas

When Is Tomorrow?, Nancy D. Watson
Don't Spill It Again, James, Rosemary Wells
Noisy Nora, Rosemary Wells

Parent-Child Relationships

The Snow, John Burningham
Be Good, Harry, Mary Chalmers
You Go Away, Dorothy Corey
Are You My Mother?, Philip D. Eastman

Mushy Eggs, Adrienne Adams
And My Mean Old Mother Will Be Sorry, Blackboard Bear, Martha Alexander
We Never Get to Do Anything, Martha Alexander
Sand Cake, Frank Asch
Peter's Pocket, Judith Barrett
Families Grow in Different Ways, Barbara Parrish-Benson
Joey's Cat, Robert Burch
Go and Hush the Baby, Betty Byars
Trixie and the Tiger, Victoria Cabassa
Abby, Jeanette Caines
Daddy, Jeanette Caines
Clearing in the Forest, Carol Carrick
Awful Alexander, Judith Choate
Lester's Overnight, Kay Chorao
Two Dog Biscuits, Beverly Cleary
Amifika, Lucille Clifton
Everett Anderson's Nine Month Long, Lucille Clifton
Everett Anderson's One-Two-Three, Lucille Clifton
Minoo's Family, Sue Heffernan Crawford
Jo, Flo and Yolanda, Carol DePoix
Just Momma and Me, Christine Engla Eber
Martin's Father, Margrit Eichler
First Pink Light, Eloise Greenfield
My Name Is Emily, Norse Hamilton
Crybaby, Jacquie Hamm
The Gorilla Did It, Barbara Shook Hazen
Bedtime for Frances, Russell Hoban
Peter's Chair, Ezra Jack Keats
Is There a Lion in the House?, Ruth Krauss
I Am Adopted, Susan Lapsley
Nice Little Girls, Elizabeth Levy
Papa Small, Lois Lenski
Little Though I Be, Joseph Low

In My Boat, Betty Maestro
Lion in the Meadow, Margaret Mahy
The Chosen Baby, Valentina Nasson
The Biggest Snowstorm Ever, Diane Paterson
The Littles, John Peterson
On Mother's Lap, Ann Herbert Scott
Sam, N. H. Scott
Where the Wild Things Are, Maurice Sendak
Mooch the Messy, Marjorie W. Sharmot
Friday Night Is Papa Night, Ruth A. Sonneborn
The Daddy Book, R. Stewart
Andy and the Wild Worm, Jane Thayer
The Quitting Deal, Tobi Tobias
Alexander and the Terrible . . . Very Bad Day, Judith Viorst
My Mama Says, Judith Viorst
Lyle Finds His Mother, Bernard Waber
Curl Up Small, Sandol S. Warburg
Goodbye, Hello, Robert Welber
Papa's Panda, Nancy Willard
Someday, Said Mitchell, Barbara Williams
To Hilda for Helping, Margot Zemach
A Father Like That, Charlotte Zolotow
My Grandson Lew, Charlotte Zolotow
William's Doll, Charlotte Zolotow

Black Is Brown Is Tan, Arnold Adoff
Horse for Sherry, Catherine Barr
The Sand Lot, Mary Blount Christian
Gabrielle and Selena, Peter Desbarats
Do Bears Have Mothers Too?, Aileen Fisher
Bembel Man's Bakery, Melinda Green
Mittens in May, Maxine Kumin
A Birthday for the Princess, Arnold Lobel
Mommy and Daddy Are Divorced, Patricia Perry
The Awful Mess, Anne Rockwell
The Flower Family, Yutaka Sugita
Days with Daddy, Pauline Watson
Bag Full of Nothing, Jay Williams
Saturday Walk, Ethel Wright

Sarah and Simon and No Red Paint, Edward Ardizzone
An Apple a Day, Judith Barrett
Eli Lives in Israel, Anna R. Brick
Andrew Henry's Meadow, Doris Burn
Watch That Watch, Hila Colman
Thalia Brown and the Blue Jug, Michelle Dionetti

Wind Rose, Crescent Dragonwagon
All Alone with Daddy, Joan Fassler
The Man of the House, Joan Fassler
Best Little House, Aileen Fisher
A New Mother for Martha, Phyllis Green
You and Your Child Measuring Things, Iris Grender
If I Had My Way, Norma Klein
Big World and Little House, Ruth Krauss
The Sunshine Family and the Pony, Sharron Loree
Please, Michael, That's My Daddy's Chair, Susan E. Mark
My Mother and I Are Growing Strong, Inez Maury
Brothers Are All the Same, Mary Milgram
My Daddy Don't Go to Work, Madeena Spray Nolan
Rainy Day Together, Ellen Parsons
When the Drum Sang, Anne Rockwell
Come On Out, Daddy, Inger Sandberg
City in the Summer, Eleanor Schick
City in the Winter, Eleanor Schick
Tell Me a Mitzi, Lore Segal
Tell Me a Trudy, Lore Segal
I Was So Mad!, Norma Simon
The Adopted One, Sara Bonnett Stein
Simon Boom Gives a Wedding, Yuri Suhl
Forever Christmas Tree, Yoshiko Uchida
The Summer Night, Charlotte Zolotow
When I Have a Little Girl, Charlotte Zolotow
When I Have a Son, Charlotte Zolotow

Single Parent Families

Mushy Eggs, Adrienne Adams
Daddy, Jeanette Caines
Minoo's Family, Sue Heffernan Crawford
Just Momma and Me, Christine Engla Eber
Where's Daddy? A Story of Divorce, Beth Goff
Joshua's Day, Sandra Lucas Surowiecki
I Love My Mother, Paul Zindel
A Father Like That, Charlotte Zolotow

A Friend Can Help, Terry Berger
How Does It Feel When Your Parents Get Divorced?,
   Terry Berger
All Alone with Daddy, Joan Fassler
The Man of the House, Joan Fassler
Two Homes to Live In, Barbara Shook Hazen

Lucky Wilma, Wendy Kindred
Emily and the Clunky Baby and the Next-Door Dog, Joan Lexau
Two Special Cards, Sonia Lisker
Please, Michael, That's My Daddy's Chair, Susan E. Mark
My Mother the Mail Carrier, Inez Maury
My Mommy and Daddy Are Divorced, Patricia Perry
This Is That, Jeanne Whitehouse Peterson
Morris and His Brave Lion, Helen Spelman Rogers
Two Places to Sleep, Joan Schuchman
Martin by Himself, Gloria Skurzynski
On Divorce, Sara Bonnett Stein

Competence: I Can

Another requirement of a happy child usually involves a feeling of self-worth achieved through mastery or competence. The list of books exemplifying that even the least likely to succeed can emerge triumphant with sufficient perseverance is headed "I Can" in honor of one of the very early books in this vein, the still-popular *Little Engine That Could* by Watty Piper.

I Can

Baby Animal Dress-up Book, Joan Allen
Another Story to Tell, Dick Bruna
A Story to Tell, Dick Bruna
Little Red Hen, Janina Domanska
Jasmine, Roger Duvoisin
I Want to Be Big, Genie Iverson
When Shoes Eat Socks, Barbara Klimowicz
The Little Brown Hen, Patricia Miles Martin
The Little Engine That Could, Watty Piper

Things We Like to Do, Evelyn M. Andre
Look What I Can Do, Jose Aruego
Sand Cake, Frank Asch
Sunflowers for Tina, Anne Baldwin
Sammy Seal of the Circus, Cathrine Barr
Harry Is a Scaredy Cat, Byron Barton
Fireflies, Max Bolliger
Katy and the Big Snow, Virginia Lee Burton
Euphonia and the Flood, Mary Calhoun
Clearing in the Forest, Carol Carrick

Busy Beaver's Day, Donald Charles
Three Wishes, Lucille Clifton
Impossible Possum, Ellen Conford
Tootle, Gertrude Crampton
Six Special Places, Monica De Bruyn
Hare and the Tortoise, Jean de La Fontaine
Lion and the Rat, Jean de La Fontaine
Jo, Flo and Yolanda, Carol DePoix
Little Duck, Judy Dunn
Just Me, Marie Hall Ets
Small One, Zhenya Gay
The Hole in the Dike, Retold by Norma Green
Boy with a Drum, David Harrison
Free as a Frog, Elizabeth Hodges
Jasper Makes Music, Betty Horvath
Titch, Pat Hutchins
Jack the Giant Killer, Joseph Jacobs
Bus Ride, Nancy Jewell
Peter Learns to Crochet, Irene Levinson
Frederick, Leo Lionni
Swimmy, Leo Lionni
I Can Be, Sonia Lisker
Zoo, Where Are You?, Ann McGovern
Just for You, Mercer Mayer
Hooray for Captain Jane, Sam Reavin
Billy's Picture, Margaret Rey
Oh, Lewis!, Eve Rice
Alec's Sand Castle, Lavinia Russ
Say Hello, Vanessa, Marjorie W. Sharmot
Partouche Plants a Seed, Ben Shecter
I Am a Giant, Ivan Sherman
Roland the Minstrel Pig, William Steig
Chasing the Goblins Away, Tobi Tobias
Great Big Enormous Turnip, Alexei Tolstoy
Benny's Magic Baking Pan, Kenneth Truse
Doctor Rabbit's Foundling, Jan Wahl
Lollipop, Wendy Watson
Goodbye, Hello, Robert Welber
Noisy Nora, Rosemary Wells
Unfortunately Harriet, Rosemary Wells
Someday, Said Mitchell, Barbara Williams
Edith and the Little Bear Lend a Hand, Dare Wright
Miss Susy's Easter Surprise, Miriam Young

Mandy and the Flying Map, Beverley Allinson
A Moose Is Not a Mouse, Harold Berson
Pelle's New Suit, Elsa Beskow

Pantaloni, Bettina
Miguel's Mountain, Bill Binzen
Shawn's Red Bike, Petronella Breinberg
Come Away from the Water, Shirley, John Burningham
Time to Get Out of the Bath, Shirley, John Burningham
Maybelle the Cable Car, Virginia Lee Burton
The Milkmaid, Randolph Caldecott
Pancakes! Pancakes!, Eric Carle
Picture That!, Bernice Carlson
A Rabbit for Easter, Carol Carrick
Hullabaloo: The Elephant Dog, Ruth Carroll
Pickles and Jake, Janet Chenery
Good, Says Jerome, Lucille Clifton
Cranberry Mystery, Harry Devlin
Another Day, Marie Hall Ets
Rosa-Too-Little, Sue Felt
Bembel Man's Bakery, Melinda Green
Little Stone House, Berta Hader
A Lion Under Her Bed, Mark Hawkins
Emmet Otter's Jug-Band Christmas, Russell Hoban
Carlotta and the Scientist, Patricia Riley Lenthall
Benjie, Joan Lexau
Benjie on His Own, Joan Lexau
Right Thumb, Left Thumb, Osmond Molarsky
That's Enough for One Day, J.P., Susan Pearson
Poor Goose, Anne Rockwell
Outside My Window, Liesel M. Skorpen
Hooray for Pig!, Carla Stevens
I Climb Mountains, Barbara Taylor
The Queen Who Couldn't Bake Gingerbread, Dorothy Van Woerkom
Train, Robert Welber
Bag Full of Nothing, Jay Williams
The Young Performing Horse, John Yeoman

Do You Know What Time It Is?, Roz Abisch
Waymond the Whale, Caroline Aimar
Six Days from Sunday, Betty Biesterveld
Andrew Henry's Meadow, Doris Burn
Cross-Country Cat, Mary Calhoun
Real Hole, Beverly Cleary
Michael Bird-Boy, Tomie De Paola
Howie Helps Himself, Joan Fassler
Crackle Gluck and the Sleeping Toad, Dick Gackenbach
Send Wendell, Genevieve Gray
Bubbles, Eloise Greenwald
Thieves and the Raven, Janosch

Mog, the Forgetful Cat, Judith Kerr
Clever Coot, Alfred Konner
Leo the Late Bloomer, Robert Kraus
Wee Gillis, Munro Leaf
Half a Kingdom, Ann McGovern
Hans and Peter, Heindrun Petrides
No Trespassing, Ray Prather
Pirates in the Dark, Thom Roberts
Akimba and the Magic Cow, Retold by Anne Rose
Bird, Liesel M. Skorpen
Michael, Liesel M. Skorpen
Moon Blossom and the Golden Penny, Louis Slobodkin
Scuttle, the Stowaway Mouse, Jean C. Soule
Blackie, the Bird Who Could, Yutaka Sugita
Free to Be You and Me, Marlo Thomas
The Clever Princess, Ann Tompert
Bonnie Bess, the Weathervane Horse, Alvin R. Tresselt
Mary Jo's Grandmother, Janice Udry
Zeralda's Ogre, Tomi Ungerer
Tatu and the Honey Bird, Alice W. Wellman
Forgetful Fred, Jay Williams
Ellie to the Rescue, Beth Weiner Woldin
Crow Boy, Taro Yashima

The Unique Self

The second group which deals with competence frequently involves a connected topic, the acceptance of oneself even if one is different. It also may mean overcoming obstacles and achieving a sense of satisfaction through the knowledge that a handicap has been worked through.

Books That Emphasize Acceptance of Being Unique

Rachel, Elizabeth Fanshawe
Color of His Own, Leo Lionni
Tico and the Golden Wings, Leo Lionni
My Feet Roll, Winnie Mertens
Moose, Goose and Nobody, Ellen Raskin
If He's My Brother, Barbara Williams

The Ugly Duckling, Hans C. Andersen
Princess and the Unicorn, Lily Arbore

Sweetheart for Valentine, Lorna Balian
Like Me, Alan Brightman
Howie Helps Himself, Joan Fassler
One Little Girl, Joan Fassler
More Time to Grow, Sharon Grollman
To Be Me, Barbara Shook Hazen
Sound of Sunshine, Sound of Rain, Florence Heide
Lisa and Her Soundless World, Edna Levine
Spectacles, Ellen Raskin
My Mother Is Blind, Margaret Reuter
About Handicaps, Sara Bonnett Stein
The Bear Who Wanted to Be a Bear, Jorg Steiner
Everyone Knows What a Dragon Looks Like, Jay Williams
Crow Boy, Taro Yashima

Socialization Outside the Home

After the toddler has begun to attend nursery school or at least has begun to go beyond his immediate family circle, other needs begin to become evident. There is the question of belonging to a group, and as the child begins to engage in play with other children (rather than in parallel play), the topic of friendship becomes important. The child may consider what can happen if he "fights" with his friend, or what will happen when a friend moves away. Certain books may prove helpful in assuaging some of these concerns.

Books That Emphasize the Need to Belong

Ma nDa La, Arnold Adoff
Jenny's Birthday, Esther Averill
Secret Hiding Place, Rainey Bennett
Families Grow in Different Ways, Barbara Parrish-Benson
Amifika, Lucille Clifton
Watch Out for the Chicken Feet in Your Soup, Tomie De Paola
Just Momma and Me, Christine Engla Eber
Story About Ping, Marjorie Flack
Rotten Ralph, Jack Gantos
Irene's Idea, Bernice Geoffrey
Goodbye Kitchen, Mildred Kantrowitz
I Am Adopted, Susan Lapsley
Tico and the Golden Wings, Leo Lionni
Little Tiny Rooster, William Lipkind
That New Boy, Mary Lystad
Jesse's Dream Skirt, Bruce Mack

Silly Story, Mercer Mayer
Maggie and the Goodbye Gift, Sue Milord
My Teddy Bear, Chiyoko Nakatani
The Chosen Baby, Valentina Nasson
Sam, N.H. Scott
Welcome, Roberto!, Mary Serfozo
Say Hello, Vanessa, Marjorie W. Sharmot
Friday Night Is Papa Night, Ruth A. Sonneborn
Betsy's First Day at Nursery School, Gunilla Wolde
Harry by the Sea, Gene Zion

Carlos Goes to School, Eloise Anderson
Maria Teresa, Mary Atkinson
Shawn Goes to School, Petronella Breinberg
Will I Have a Friend?, Miriam Cohen
Pepe's Private Christmas, Dorothy Corey
Missing Milkman, Roger Duvoisin
Rosa-Too-Little, Sue Felt
Pet of the Met, Lydia Freeman
Me and Nessie, Eloise Greenfield
I'm Moving, Martha Whitmore Hickman
My Friend William Moved Away, Martha Whitmore Hickman
Go Away, Dog, Joan Nodset
Sad Day, Glad Day, Vivian Thompson

Big Sister Tells Me That I'm Black, Arnold Adoff
Little Brother, No More, Robert Benton
Being Alone, Being Together, Terry Berger
Six Days from Sunday, Betty Biesterveld
Wagon Wheels, Barbara Brenner
All Us Come Cross the Water, Lucille Clifton
Thalia Brown and the Blue Jug, Thelma Dionetti
Will I Be Okay?, Crescent Dragonwagon
Best Little House, Aileen Fisher
Neighbors, M.B. Goffstein
Willy Bear, Mildred Kantrowitz
Five Little Monkeys, Juliet Kepes
Runaway John, Leonore Klein
Scaredy Cat, Phyllis Krasilovsky
Just Like Everyone Else, Karla Kuskin
This Is That, Jeanne Whitehouse Peterson
New Neighbors, Ray Prather
Hug Me, Patti Stren
Moving Day, Tobi Tobias
Bonnie Bess, the Weathervane Horse, Alvin R. Tresselt

Magic Wall, Judy Varga
May I Visit?, Charlotte Zolotow

Books That Emphasize Friendship

The Golden Egg Book, Margaret Wise Brown
Our Best Friends, Gyo Fujikawa
The Chick and the Duckling, Mirra Ginsburg
Little Blue and Little Yellow, Leo Lionni
Basil and Hillary, Jane Zalben

Jenny's Birthday Book, Esther Averill
Oscar the Selfish Octopus, John M. Barrett
One to Teeter-Totter, Edith Battles
There Is Someone Standing on My Head, Elizabeth Bram
The Friend, John Burningham
Mary Louise and Christophe, Natalie Savage Carlson
Everett Anderson's Friend, Lucille Clifton
Three Wishes, Lucille Clifton
Best Friends, Miriam Cohen
Two Is Company, Judy Delton
How Joe Bear and Sam Mouse Got Together,
    Beatrice DeRegniers
Snow Party, Beatrice DeRegniers
Snowy and Woody, Roger Duvoisin
Robbie's Friend George, Shirley Estes
Elephant in a Well, Marie Hall Ets
Play with Me, Marie Hall Ets
We'll Have a Friend for Lunch, Jane Flory
Corduroy, Don Freeman
That's What a Friend Is, P.K. Hallinan
We're Very Good Friends, My Brother and I, P.K. Hallinan
Monster's Nose Was Cold, Joan Hanson
That's What Friends Are For, Florence Heide
The Cat and the Mouse Who Shared a House, Ruth Hurlimann
Friends, Satomi Ichikawa
Snuggle Bunny, Nancy Jewell
Three Friends, Robert Kraus
Trouble with Spider, Robert Kraus
Toss and Catch, Anne Lewis
Frog and Toad Together, Arnold Lobel
I'm Not Going, Nancy Mack
The Guest, James Marshall
Willis, James Marshall

A Boy, a Frog, a Dog and a Friend, Mercer Mayer
Small Rabbit, Miska Miles
Maggie and the Goodbye Gift, Sue Milord
The Little Raccoon and No Trouble at All, Lilian Moore
The Bad Bear, Rudolph Neumann
Marshmallow, Claire T. Newberry
The Stolen Mirror, Lidia Postma
Making Friends, Eleanor Schick
Peter and Mr. Brandon, Eleanor Schick
The Great Big Elephant and the Very Small Elephant, Barbara Seuling
Burton and Dudley, Marjorie W. Sharmot
Goodnight Andrew, Goodnight Craig, Marjorie W. Sharmot
I'm Not Oscar's Friend Anymore, Majorie W. Sharmot
I Do Not Like It When My Friend Comes to Visit, Ivan Sherman
Let's Be Enemies, Janice Udry
What Mary Jo Shared, Janice Udry
The Checker Players, Alan Venable
Ira Sleeps Over, Bernard Waber
Walt and Pepper, Lisl Weil
Benjamin and Tulip, Rosemary Wells
Potbellied Possums, Elizabeth Winthrop
My Friend John, Charlotte Zolotow
The Hating Book, Charlotte Zolotow
Hold My Hand, Charlotte Zolotow
Janey, Charlotte Zolotow
The Quarreling Book, Charlotte Zolotow
Three Funny Friends, Charlotte Zolotow
The Unfriendly Book, Charlotte Zolotow

Carlos Goes to School, Eloise Anderson
Rebecka, Frank Asch
Maria Teresa, Mary Atkinson
Mr. Tall and Mr. Small, Barbara Brenner
The Magic Hat, Kim Westsmith Chapman
Will I Have a Friend?, Miriam Cohen
Two Good Friends, Judy Delton
Gabrielle and Selena, Peter Desbarats
Owl's New Cards, Kathryn Ernst
Two Giants, Michael Foreman
Turtle and the Dove, Don Freeman
Green Hornet Lunchbox, Shirley Gordon
Me and Nessie, Eloise Greenfield
I'm Moving, Martha Whitmore Hickman
My Friend William Moved Away, Martha Whitmore Hickman
Moving Molly, Shirley Hughes
I Wonder If Herbie's Home Yet, Mildred Kantrowitz

Simon's Soup, Beverly Komoda
Shy Little Girl, Phyllis Krasilovsky
A Letter Goes to Sea, Lore Leher
A Birthday for the Princess, Anita Lobel
Erik and the Christmas Horse, Hans Peterson
Old Tiger, New Tiger, Ron Roy
Sad Day, Glad Day, Vivian Thompson
The Painter and the Bird, Max Velthuijs
A Special Trade, Sally Wittman

Hotel Cat, Esther Averill
Are We Still Best Friends?, Carol Barkin
Together, June Behrens
Swimming Hole, Jerrold Beim
Two Is a Team, Lorraine Beim
Being Alone, Being Together, Terry Berger
A Friend Can Help, Terry Berger
Muffin, Judith Brown
Harlequin and the Gift of Many Colors, Remy Charlip
Tiny Little House, Eleanor Clymer
Lonely Maria, Elizabeth Coatsworth
No Company Was Coming to Samuel's House, Dorothy Corey
The Boy with a Problem, Joan Fassler
Neighbors, M.B. Goffstein
Crystal Is the New Girl, Shirley Gordon
The River Bank (from *Wind in the Willows*), Kenneth Grahame
Best Friends for Frances, Russell Hoban
Madeline and Ermadello, Tim Wynne-Jones
Nothing But a Dog, Bobbi Katz
Visiting Pamela, Norma Klein
On the Other Side of the River, Joanne Oppenheim
New Neighbors, Ray Prather
Franklin Stein, Ellen Raskin
One Small Blue Bead, Byrd Schweitzer
Gladys Told Me to Meet Her Here, Marjorie W. Sharmot
Octavia Told Me a Secret, Marjorie W. Sharmot
Sophie and Gussie, Marjorie W. Sharmot
The Toughest and Meanest Kid on the Block, Ben Shecter
Not Here and Never Was, Virginia Smith
The Bridge, Ralph Steadman
Amos and Boris, William Steig
Wilfred the Rat, James Stevenson
Hello, I'm Karen, Margaret Sutherland
The Woodcutter's Duck, Krystyna Turksa
Magic Wall, Judy Varga
Nobody Is Perfick, Bernard Waber
A Promise Is for Keeping, Anne Wade

Beatrice and Vanessa, John Yeoman
The Rainbow Rider, Jane Yolen
May I Visit?, Charlotte Zolotow
New Friend, Charlotte Zolotow
When I Have a Son, Charlotte Zolotow

Problem Solving

We have mentioned the possibility that books may function as aids in ameliorating particular problems simply by making it clear to the child that his or her difficulty has been experienced by others. In this general category there are stories which deal with a wide variety of perplexities, from learning Rumpelstiltskin's name (so that the princess doesn't lose her child to the evil dwarf) to finding a toy bear lost in the laundromat, as in *Pocket for Corduroy.* Some of these titles will therefore be found in other lists; all, however, do deal with finding solutions or learning to deal with difficulties or immutable situations.

Books That Deal With Problems of Various Kinds

Baby Animal Dress-Up Book, Joan Allen
Hooray for Me!, Remy Charlip
Danny and His Thumb, Kathryn Ernst
Three Little Pigs, Paul Galdone
Mystery of the Missing Red Mitten, Steven Kellogg

Mushy Eggs, Adrienne Adams
Harold, the Happy Handyman, Gareth Adamson
Blackboard Bear, Martha Alexander
Sabrina, Martha Alexander
King's Flower, Mitsumasa Anno
Monkey Face, Frank Asch
Case of the Scaredy Cats, Crosby Bonsall
Mine's the Best, Crosby Bonsall
Piggle, Crosby Bonsall
Who's a Pest?, Crosby Bonsall
Runaway Flying Horse, Paul J. Bonzen
Fresh Cider and Pie, Franz Brandenberg
I Wish I Was Sick Too, Franz Brandenberg
Stone Soup, Marcia Brown
Pied Piper of Hamelin, Robert Browning
Angelique, Alice Brustlein

Joey's Cat, Robert Burch
Mike Mulligan and His Steam Shovel, Virginia Lee Burton
Trixie and the Tiger, Victoria Cabassa
Abby, Jeanette Caines
Houn' Dog, Mary Calhoun
Mochito: Story of an Ordinary Dog, Nelly Canepari
Do You Want to Be My Friend?, Eric Carle
Lost in the Storm, Carol Carrick
The Foundling, Carol Carrick
Senora Pepino and Her Bad Luck Cats,
    Esther de Michael Cervantes
Awful Alexander, Judith Choate
New Teacher, Miriam Cohen
Lobo and Brewster, Gladys Cretan
Messy Sally, Gladys Cretan
The Enormous Crocodile, Roald Dahl
My Friend Jasper Jones, Rosamond Dauer
Just Momma and Me, Christine Engla Eber
Rachel, Elizabeth Fanshawe
Don't Worry, Dear, Joan Fassler
Angus and the Cat, Marjorie Flack
Dandelion, Don Freeman
A Pocket for Corduroy, Don Freeman
Happy Dromedary, Berniece Freschet
Monkey and the Crocodile, Paul Galdone
Christina Katerina and the Box, Patricia Gauch
Irene's Idea, Bernice Geoffrey
Bremen Town Musicians, Grimm Brothers
Rumpelstiltskin, Grimm Brothers
Snow White and the Seven Dwarfs, Grimm Brothers
Lost in the Zoo, Bertha Hader
Martha's Mad Day, Miranda Hapgood
Bear by Himself, Geoffrey Hayes
The Gorilla Did It, Barbara Shook Hazen
Why Couldn't I Be an Only Kid Like You, Wigger?,
    Barbara Shook Hazen
Grownups Cry Too, Nancy Hazen
Boy, Was I Mad!, Kathryn Hitte
Bread and Jam for Frances, Russell Hoban
Saggy, Baggy Elephant, Kathryn Jackson
Biggest Fish in the Sea, Dahlov Ipcar
Jack and the Beanstalk, Joseph Jacobs
Clay Pot Boy, Cynthia Jameson
Cheer Up, Pig, Nancy Jewell
Snuggle Bunny, Nancy Jewell
Maxie, Mildred Kantrowitz
Louie, Ezra Jack Keats
The Fat Cat, Jack Kent

Floyd, the Tiniest Elephant, Jack Kent
Run, Little Monkeys, Run, Run, Run, Juliet Kepes
The Family Minus, Fernando Krahn
The Story of Ferdinand, Munro Leaf
Wishing Pool, Munro Leaf
Alexander and the Wind-up Mouse, Leo Lionni
Fish Is Fish, Leo Lionni
Frederick, Leo Lionni
On My Beach There Are Many Pebbles, Leo Lionni
Pezzetino, Leo Lionni
Finders Keepers, William Lipkind
Mouse Soup, Arnold Lobel
You Ought to See Herbert's House, Doris Lund
A Wise Monkey Tale, Betsy Maestro
Mine, Mercer Mayer
One Frog Too Many, Mercer Mayer
Cat and Dog, Else H. Minarik
Theodore's Rival, Edward Ormondroyd
Stone Soup, Carol Pasternak
Katy-No-Pocket, Emmy Payne
Cinderella, Charles Perrault
Circus Baby, Maud Petersham
Temper Tantrum Book, Edna Mitchell Preston
Squawk to the Moon, Little Goose, Edna Mitchell Preston
And It Rained, Ellen Raskin
Moose, Goose and Little Nobody, Ellen Raskin
Billy's Picture, Margaret Rey
Pretzel, Margaret Rey
New Blue Shoes, Eve Rice
Peter and Mr. Brandon, Eleanor Schick
On Mother's Lap, Ann Herbert Scott
Sam, N.H. Scott
Mooch the Messy, Marjorie W. Sharmot
I Do Not Like It When My Friend Comes to Visit, Ivan Sherman
The Dog Who Insisted He Wasn't, Marilyn Singer
Sometimes I Like to Cry, Elizabeth Stanton
Smart Bear, Tom Tichenor
Alexander and the Terrible, Horrible ... Very Bad Day, Judith Viorst
Ira Sleeps Over, Bernard Waber
Rich Cat, Poor Cat, Bernard Waber
Grandmother Told Me, Jan Wahl
Tom Fox and the Apple Pie, Clyde Watson
Just Awful, Alma Whitney
That's Mine, Elizabeth Winthrop
Benjamin's Perfect Solution, Beth Weiner Woldin
Dear Garbage Man, Gene Zion
Meanest Squirrel I Ever Met, Gene Zion
No Roses for Harry, Gene Zion

Plant Sitter, Gene Zion
Unfriendly Book, Charlotte Zolotow

It's Mine!, Crosby Bonsall
The Magic Hat, Kim Westsmith Chapman
Tootle, Gertrude Crampton
Fight the Night, Tomie De Paola
Cranberry Mystery, Harry Devlin
King Krakus and the Dragon, Janina Domanska
Another Day, Marie Hall Ets
Puss in Boots, Paul Galdone
Boy with the Special Face, Barbara Girion
Katie's Magic Glasses, Jane Goodsell
Me and Nessie, Eloise Greenfield
Hansel and Gretel, Grimm Brothers
I Won't Be Afraid, Joan Hanson
Evan's Corner, Elizabeth S. Hill
Emmet Otter's Jug-Band Christmas, Russell Hoban
I Wonder If Herbie's Home Yet, Mildred Kantrowitz
My Dog Is Lost, Ezra Jack Keats
Nancy's Backyard, Eros Keith
Lucky Wilma, Wendy Kindred
Simon's Soup, Beverly Komoda
Too Much Noise, Ann McGovern
The Awful Mess, Anne Rockwell
Morris and His Brave Lion, Helen Spelman Rogers
Panda Cake, Rosalie Seidler
I'm Going to Run Away, Jean Thompson
No Bath Tonight, Jane Yolen

Diogenes: The Story of the Greek Philosopher, Aliki
Miss Nelson Is Missing, Harry Allard
Billy and Our New Baby, Helene S. Arnstein
Humbug Witch, Lorna Balian
Little Brother, No More, Robert Benton
Felix in the Attic, Larry Bogard
Do You Know What I Know?, Helen Borten
Emilio's Summer Day, Miriam Bourne
Wagon Wheels, Barbara Brenner
Milly-Molly-Mandy Stories, Joyce Lankester Brisley
Once a Mouse, Marcia Brown
Puss in Boots, Marcia Brown
Barney the Beard, Eve Bunting
Haunted Churchbell, Barbara Byfield
Tiny Little House, Eleanor Clymer
The King at the Door, Brock Cole
No Company Was Coming to Samuel's House, Dorothy Corey

Little Oleg, Margaret Cort
The Boy with a Problem, Joan Fassler
Howie Helps Himself, Joan Fassler
The Man of the House, Joan Fassler
The Unexpected Grandchildren, Jane Flory
Dinosaurs and All That Rubbish, Michael Foreman
Two Giants, Michael Foreman
The Eleven Steps, Lucy Freeman
Yolanda's Hike, Tomas Rodriguez Gaspar
Beginning Search-A-Word Shapes, Dawn Gerger
Two Greedy Bears, Mirra Ginsburg
A New Mother for Martha, Phyllis Green
Hans in Luck, Grimm Brothers
Just Being Alone, P.K. Hallinan
Two Homes to Live In, Barbara Shook Hazen
Tom and Sam, Pat Hutchins
Max, Rachel Isadora
Willaby, Rachel Isadora
Learning About Love, Jordan Jenkins
Pet Show!, Ezra Jack Keats
Pimm's Place, Beverly Keller
The Lost Kingdom of Karnica, Richard Kennedy
Lum Fu and the Golden Mountain, Hisako Kimishima
What Is a Man?, Fernando Krahn
Leo the Late Bloomer, Robert Kraus
I'll Tell on You, Joan Lexau
The Story of the Little Round Man, Alice Lindley
Sven's Bridge, Anita Lobel
The Man Who Was Going to Mind the House, David McKee
The Mouse and the Mirage, Janet McNeill
King Lawrence, the Alarm Clock, Peggy Mann
Wish Again, Big Bear, Richard Margolis
Please, Michael, That's My Daddy's Chair, Susan E. Mark
Do You Have Time, Lydia?, Evaline Ness
Sam Bangs and Moonshine, Evaline Ness
Big Orange Splot, Manus Pinkwater
The Three Big Hogs, Manus Pinkwater
Along Came the Model T, Robert Quackenbush
Dudley Pippin, Philip Ressner
Femie and Old Grandaddie, Adjai Robinson
Clever Turtle, A.K. Roche
Monkey's Whiskers: A Brazilian Folktale, Anne Rockwell
Akimba and His Magic Cow, Retold by Anne Rose
Fanshen, the Magic Bear, Becky Sarah
Robert and the Magic String, Ivan Sherman
The Giving Tree, Shel Silverstein
Martin by Himself, Gloria Skurzynski
On Divorce, Sara Bonnett Stein

Free to Be You and Me, Marlo Thomas
Easy or Hard? That's a Good Question, Tobi Tobias
The Clever Princess, Ann Tompert
The Smallest Pirate, Denise Trez
Corgiville Fair, Tasha Tudor
Nobody Is Perfick, Bernard Waber
A Promise Is for Keeping, Anne Wade
The Woman with Eggs, Jan Wahl
Biggest Bear, Lynd Ward
Two Korean Brothers: A Story of Hungbu and Nolbu, Grace Yoo
New Friend, Charlotte Zolotow

Some Serious Subjects

Closely tied in with problem books are those which deal with illness, war, and death. For young children, of course, these topics are dealt with in a positive way, truthfully but without morbidity. For instance, those who are ill recover; war is shown as unspeakably stupid; and death, although very sad, is typically shown as an event which leaves the living with happy memories of the beloved person or pet who has died. Many of these titles are meant to be used on appropriate occasions with one child, not in a group reading; most are best used with the upper end of the age range.

Books About Illness

A Visit to the Hospital, Francine Chase
Dear Little Mumps Child, Marguerite Rush Lerner, M.D.
Michael Gets the Measles, Marguerite Rush Lerner, M.D.
I Want Mama, Marjorie W. Sharmot
Emergency Room: An ABC Tour, Julie Steedman
The Day the Zoo Caught the Flu, Jean Van Tuyle
Elizabeth Gets Well, Alfons Weber, M.D.
Just Awful, Alma Whitney
Betsy and the Chicken Pox, Gunilla Wolde
Tommy Goes to the Doctor, Gunilla Wolde

Mother, Mother, I Feel Sick; Send for the Doctor Quick, Quick, Quick, Remy Charlip
Muffin, Judith Brown
The Sick Story, Linda Hirsch
I Love Gram, Ruth A. Sonneborn

A Hospital Story, Sara Bonnett Stein
Little Weaver of Thai-Yen Village, Knanh Tuyet
Mary Jo's Grandmother, Janice Udry
Crocodile Medicine, Marjorie-Ann Watts

Books About War

Brave Soldier Janosh, Victor Ambrus
Battle of Reuben Robin and Kite Uncle John, Mary Calhoun
Drummer Hoff, Ed Emberley
War and Peas, Michael Foreman
Millions of Cats, Wanda Gag
The Bear and the Kingbird, Grimm Brothers
Noel the Coward, Robert Kraus
Potatoes, Potatoes, Anita Lobel
Apple War, Bernice Myers
On the Other Side of the River, Joanne Oppenheim

Books About Death

The Dead Bird, Margaret Wise Brown
The Accident, Carol Carrick
The Tenth Good Thing About Barney, Judith Viorst
My Grandson Lew, Charlotte Zolotow

Nona, Jennifer Bartoli
Someone Small, Barbara Borack
Nana Up and Nana Down, Tomie De Paola
Grandpa Died Today, Joan Fassler
A New Mother for Martha, Phyllis Green
The Last Visit, Doug Jamieson
When Violet Died, Mildred Kantrowitz
About Dying, Sara Bonnett Stein
When Grandpa Died, Margaret Stevens
Growing Time, Sandol S. Warburg

Grandparents and Old Age

Somewhat related to the serious subjects treated above is the topic of old age. However, there are a great many books which deal with older people, especially grandparents, in a most positive manner. This is understandable since in "real life" there is usually a very special relationship between pre-schoolers and their grandparents.

Books About Children and the Older Generation

A Little at a Time, David Adler
Grandpa, Barbara Borack
Secret for Grandmother's Birthday, Fritz Brandenberg
Grandmother and I, Helen E. Buckley
Wonderful Little Boy, Helen E. Buckley
Watch Out for the Chicken Feet in Your Soup, Tomie De Paola
Fish for Supper, M.B. Goffstein
Grandma Is Somebody Special, Susan Goldman
Grandma and the Genji, Susan Jeschke
Maxie, Mildred Kantrowitz
Bunya and the Witch, Robert Kraus
I Have Four Names for My Grandfather, Kathryn Lasky
David and His Grandfather, Pamela Rogers
Dodo Every Day, Margret-Ilse Vogel
Grandmother Told Me, Jan Wahl
Kevin's Grandma, Barbara Williams
My Grandson Lew, Charlotte Zolotow
William's Doll, Charlotte Zolotow

Carrie Hepple's Garden, Ruth Craft
Devil Did It, Susan Jeschke
Lion and the Bird's Nest, Eriko Kishida
My Island Grandma, Kathryn Lasky
Benjie on His Own, Joan Lexau
David's Windows, Alice Low
A Special Trade, Sally Wittman

Hotel Cat, Esther Averill
Nonna, Jennifer Bartoli
Mr. Kelso's Lion, Arna Bontemps
Shopping Bag Lady, Robert Censori
Grandmother's Pictures, Sam Cornish
Fourteen Rats and a Rat Catcher, James Cressey
Nana Upstairs and Nana Downstairs, Tomie De Paola
The Unexpected Grandchildren, Jane Flory
Grandpa and Me, Patricia Gauch
The Piano Tuners, M.S. Goffstein
The River That Gave Gifts, Margo Humphrey
The Last Visit, Doug Jamieson

Apt. 3, Ezra Jack Keats
Pet Show!, Ezra Jack Keats
Big World and the Little House, Ruth Krauss
Freddy, My Grandfather, Nola Langner
Grandma's Beach Surprise, Ilka List
The Hundred Penny Box, Sharon Mathis
Monster Night at Grandma's House, Richard Peck
Jumping Jackdaws! Here Comes Simon, Elizabeth Roberts
Femi and Old Grandaddie, Adjai Robinson
Grandparents Around the World, Edited by Caroline Rubin
City in the Summer, Eleanor Schick
City in the Winter, Eleanor Schick
Mandy's Grandmother, Liesel M. Skorpen
Old Arthur, Liesel M. Skorpen
I Love Gram, Ruth A. Sonneborn
About Dying, Sara Bonnett Stein
When Grandpa Died, Margaret Stevens
Could Be Worse!, James Stevenson
Hi, Mrs. Mallory, Ianthe Thomas
Mary Jo's Grandmother, Janice Udry
All of Grandmother's Clocks: About Time, Sandra Ziegler

The Lighter Side of Life

As an antidote to the more serious aspect of life, every child has a need to "escape," and, of course, the fairy and folk tales listed earlier can draw the youngster into a never-never world to fulfill this desire. However, there are several other kinds of books which also meet this need. As a special category, there are stories which emphasize the act of playing itself, and there are also books designated as humorous. Adults do not always recognize the extent to which children relish the absurd, whether it is a matter of a character who behaves ridiculously or only a repetition of silly sounds. This innate love of fun accounts for the continued popularity of *Mother Goose*, the early Dr. Seuss books, and the cumulative tale, as well as many nonsense rhymes listed later in the poetry section.

Books That Deal with Playing

Wipe-Clean Books, Anon.
The Dog, John Burningham
The Snow, John Burningham
Tommy and Sarah Dress Up, Gunilla Wolde
Basil and Hillary, Jane B. Zalben

I'll Be the Horse If You'll Play with Me, Martha Alexander
Sand Cake, Frank Asch
One to Teeter-Totter, Edith Battles
Monroe's Island, Gregory Brooks
Josie and the Snow, Helen E. Buckley
Jo, Flo and Yolanda, Carol DePoix
Catch a Little Fox, Beatrice DeRegniers
May I Bring a Friend?, Beatrice DeRegniers
Your Owl Friend, Crescent Dragonwagon
Snowy and Woody, Roger Duvoisin
Play with Me, Marie Hall Ets
Come Again, Pelican, Don Freeman
Noisy Nancy Norris, Lou Ann Gaeddert
Noisy Nancy and Nick, Lou Ann Gaeddert
House Mouse, Dorothy J. Harris
The Wonderful Pumpkin, Lennart Helsing
Last One Home Is a Green Pig, Edith Hurd
Won't Somebody Play with Me?, Steven Kellogg
Very Special House, Ruth Krauss
Martha, the Movie Mouse, Arnold Lobel
The Private Zoo, Georgess McHargue
Swinging and Swinging, Fran Manushkin
Just One More Block, Patrick Mayers
Hooray for Captain Jane!, Sam Reavin
Let's Play Desert, Inger Sandberg
A Dance for Three, Ann Schweninger
Where the Wild Things Are, Maurice Sendak
I Am a Giant, Ivan Sherman
Good Place to Hide, Louis Slobodkin
Monkeys and the Pedlar, Susanne Suba
At the Beach, Tobi Tobias
Mary Ann's Mud Day, Janice Udry
Moon Jumpers, Janice Udry
Too Hot for Ice Cream, Jean Van Leeuwen
The Marvelous Mud Washing Machine, Patty Wolcott
Harry and the Lady Next Door, Gene Zion
Harry by the Sea, Gene Zion

Miguel's Mountain, Bill Binzen
Come Away from the Water, Shirley, John Burningham
The Sand Lot, Mary Blount Christian
Carrie Hepple's Garden, Ruth Craft
Boffo: The Great Motorcycle Race, Frank Dickens
Easter Treat, Roger Duvoisin
Magic Wallpaper, Frank Francis
Bertie's Escapade, Kenneth Grahame
Bembel Man's Bakery, Melinda Green

Stone Doll of Sister Brute, Russell Hoban
We Came A-Marching One, Two, Three, Mildred Hobzek
Shy Little Girl, Phyllis Krasilovsky
My Island Grandma, Kathryn Lasky
I'm Hiding, Myra C. Livingston
Scram, Kid!, Ann McGovern
The Tallest Tree, George Overlie
Frederick's Alligator, Esther Allen Peterson
A Wet and Sandy Day, Joanne Ryder
Sign on Rosie's Door, Maurice Sendak
I'm Going on a Bear Hunt, Sandra Sivulich
Oh, Were They Ever Happy!, Peter Spier
Someday, Charlotte Zolotow

Humbug Witch, Lorna Balian
Sometimes I Dance Mountains, Byrd Baylor
Big Yellow Balloon, Edward Fenton
Yolanda's Hike, Tomas Rodriguez Gaspar
The Pirate Book, Lennart Helsing
Just Like Everyone Else, Karla Kuskin
The Blue Marble, Hans Lenzen
A Ride on High, Candida Palmer
Rainy Day Together, Ellen Parsons
Fun for Chris, Blossom E. Randall
Don't Open This Box!, James Razzi
Curious George, Hans Rey
Pirates in the Dark, Thom Roberts
Conrad's Castle, Ben Shecter
We Were Tired of Living in a House, Liesel M. Skorpen
The Princess and the Giants, Zilpha K. Snyder
Minnie Maloney and the Macaroni, Mark Stamaty
Henry the Castaway, Mark Taylor
World in the Candy Egg, Alvin R. Tresselt
Moon Man, Tomi Ungerer
I Wish, Lisl Weil
Amanda Dreaming, Barbara Wersba
Beatrice and Vanessa, John Yeoman
Jellybeans for Breakfast, Miriam Young
I Have a Horse of My Own, Charlotte Zolotow

Books with an Emphasis on Humor

Would You Like a Parrot?, France Barberis
Willy and Nilly and the Silly Cat, Elizabeth K. Barr
My Hopping Bunny, Robert Bright

Whose Mouse Are You?, Robert Kraus
Smile for Auntie, Diane Paterson

I Will Not Go to Market Today, Harry Allard
Topsy-Turvies: Pictures to Stretch the Imagination,
    Mitsumasa Anno
Aminal, Lorna Balian
I Hate to Take a Bath, Judi Barrett
Madeline, Ludwig Bemelmans
Madeline and the Bad Hat, Ludwig Bemelmans
Madeline in London, Ludwig Bemelmans
Madeline's Rescue, Ludwig Bemelmans
Case of the Hungry Stranger, Crosby Bonsall
Mother Goose Treasury, Edited by Raymond Briggs
The Snowman, Raymond Briggs
Ring O'Roses, Leslie Brooke
Monroe's Island, Gregory Brooks
Stone Soup, Marcia Brown
Mr. Gumpy's Outing, John Burningham
Clyde Monster, Robert L. Crowe
Elephant Girl, Ivor Cutler
The Enormous Crocodile, Roald Dahl
Veronica, Roger Duvoisin
Six Foolish Fishermen, Benjamin Elkin
Wing on a Flea: A Book About Shapes, Ed Emberley
Story About Ping, Marjorie Flack
Three Wishes, Paul Galdone
Alberto and His Missing Sock, Barbara Ganz
*What If a Lion Eats Me and I Fall into a Hippopotamus'
    Mudhole?*, Emily Hanlon
Froggie Went A-Courtin', Harriett
Rosie's Walk, Pat Hutchins
Wind Blew, Pat Hutchins
Giants Indeed!, Virginia Kahl
D Is for Rover, Leonore Klein
Flying Saucer Full of Spaghetti, Fernando Krahn
The Man Who Tried to Save Time, Phyllis Krasilovsky
Trouble with Spider, Robert Kraus
Is Milton Missing?, Steven Kroll
The Tyrannosaurus Game, Steven Kroll
A Boy Had a Mother Who Bought Him a Hat, Karla Kuskin
Roar and More, Karla Kuskin
Did Anyone See My Elephant?, Robert Leydenfrost
Giant Jam Sandwich, John V. Lord
Witches' Holiday, Alice Low
Hello, Mrs. Piggle-Wiggle, Betty MacDonald

Lentil, Robert McCloskey
Art, the Altogether Aged Aardvark, Joan Mahon
How to Make Elephant Bread, Kathy Mandry
Ah-Choo, Mercer Mayer
Bubble Bubble, Mercer Mayer
Four Frogs in a Box, Mercer Mayer
Frog Goes to Dinner, Mercer Mayer
Frog on His Own, Mercer Mayer
Frog, Where Are You?, Mercer Mayer
Hiccup, Mercer Mayer
If I Had..., Mercer Mayer
There's a Nightmare in My Closet, Mercer Mayer
Two Moral Tales, Mercer Mayer
What Do You Do with a Kangaroo?, Mercer Mayer
Arthur's Artichoke, Geoffrey Moss
The Littles' Surprise Party, John Peterson
Popcorn and Ma Goodness, Edna Mitchell Preston
Nothing Ever Happens on My Block, Ellen Raskin
Very Far Away, Maurice Sendak
And to Think That I Saw It on Mulberry Street, Dr. Seuss
Farmer Palmer's Wagon Ride, William Steig
Monkeys and the Pedlar, Susanne Suba
Stand Back, Said the Elephant, I'm Going to Sneeze,
  Patricia Thomas
There Are Rocks in My Socks, Said the Ox to the Fox,
  Patricia Thomas
I'd Like to Try a Monster's Eye, Judith Thurman
Deep in the Forest, Brinton Turkle
The Don't Be Scared Book: Scares, Remedies and Pictures,
  Ilse-Margret Vogel
I Was All Thumbs, Bernard Waber
You Look Ridiculous, Said the Rhino to the Hippo,
  Bernard Waber
From Amblebee to Zumblebee, Sandol S. Warburg

Stupids Step Out, Harry Allard
Dr. Anno's Magical Midnight Circus, Mitsumasa Anno
Mud Time and More Nathaniel Stories, Jim Arnosky
Pilyo the Piranha, Jose Aruego
Squire's Bride, Peter Asbjornsen
Turtle Tale, Frank Asch
Sometimes It's Turkey, Sometimes It's Feathers, Lorna Balian
Sweet Touch, Lorna Balian
A Sweetheart for Valentine, Lorna Balian
Grey Lady and the Strawberry Snatcher, Molly Bang
Animals Should Definitely Not Wear Clothing, Judith Barrett
Nine Hundred Buckets of Paint, Edna Becker

1000 Monsters, Alan Benjamin
Ethel's Exceptional Egg, Linda Bourke
Mr. Tall and Mr. Small, Barbara Brenner
Clifford's Good Deeds, Norman Bridwell
Georgie, Robert Bright
Mr. Gumpy's Motor Car, John Burningham
The Witch Who Forgot, Wayne Carley
Cat's Whiskers, Bill Charmatz
The Sand Lot, Mary Blount Christian
Boffo: The Great Motorcycle Race, Frank Dickens
Do Bears Have Mothers Too?, Aileen Fisher
Harry and the Terrible Whatzit, Dick Gackenbach
The Perfect Pal, Jack Gantos
How We Live, Anita Harper
How We Work, Anita Harper
Devil Did It, Susan Jeschke
The Duchess Bakes a Cake, Virginia Kahl
Whose Cat Is That?, Virginia Kahl
The Man Who Didn't Do His Dishes, Phyllis Krasilovsky
Have You Ever Seen a Monster?, John McInnes
The Remarkable Plant in Apartment 4, Guilio Maestro
Portly McSwine, James Marshall
Chameleon Was a Spy, Diane Redfield Massie
I Know a Monster, Amy Myers
Amelia Bedelia, Peggy Parish
The Awful Mess, Anne Rockwell
Everything About Easter Rabbits, Wiltrud Roser
Pierre, Maurice Sendak
Of Cobblers and Kings, Aure Sheldon
A Yellow Elephant Called Trunk, Barbara Softly
Never Tease a Weasel, Jean C. Soule
Don't Put the Vinegar in the Copper, Kate Wong

Cops and Robbers, Allan Ahlberg
Mary Alice, Operator Number Nine, Jeffrey Allen
Green Harpy at the Corner Store, Rosemary Allison
Fresh Fish... and Chips, Jan Andrews
Upside-Downers: More Pictures to Stretch the Imagination, Mitsumasa Anno
Dozen Dinosaurs, Richard Armour
Sea Full of Whales, Richard Armour
Humbug Witch, Lorna Balian
Old MacDonald Had an Apartment House, Judith Barrett
Slightly Irregular Fire Engine or the Hithering, Thithering Djinn, Donald Barthelme
Applebet Story, Byron Barton
Buzz, Buzz, Buzz, Byron Barton

Bad Child's Book of Beasts, Hilaire Belloc
Little Brother, No More, Robert Benton
Joseph and the Snake, Harold Berson
Georgette, Claire H. Bishop
Know What? No, What?, Arlene Blum
Felix in the Attic, Larry Bograd
Fun House, B. Bottner
Jonathan Bing, Beatrice C. Brown
Time for the White Egret, Natalie Savage Carlson
Contrary Jenkins, Rebecca Caudill
It Could Be Worse, Eleanor Chroman
Carp in the Bathtub, Barbara Cohen
The King at the Door, Brock Cole
Paulus and the Dragon, Jean Dulieu
The Tiger's Spots, Harley Elliott
My Aunt Otilia's Spirit, Richard Garcia
Chocolate Moose for Dinner, Fred Gwynne
The Sick Story, Linda Hirsch
Don't Forget the Bacon, Pat Hutchins
Gunhilde and the Halloween Spell, Virginia Kahl
Habits of the Rabbits, Virginia Kahl
Pip Squeak, Mouse in Shining Armor, Robert Kraus
Gobbledy Gook, Steven Kroll
Go and Shut the Door, Nola Langner
The Dong with the Luminous Nose, Edward Lear
On the Day Peter Stuyvesant Sailed into Town, Arnold Lobel
The Adventures of Sapo, Susan Martin
Dazzle, Diane Redfield Massie
That Noodle-Head Epaminondas, Eve Merriam
Tooley! Tooley!, Frank Modell
Squeeze a Sneeze, Bill Morrison
Animal Garden, Ogden Nash
The Cruise of the Aardvark, Ogden Nash
Custard the Dragon and the Wicked Knight, Ogden Nash
The Church Cat Abroad, Graham Oakley
The Church Mice Adrift, Graham Oakley
The Church Mice and the Moon, Graham Oakley
The Church Mice at Bay, Graham Oakley
The Church Mice Spread Their Wings, Graham Oakley
The Church Mouse, Graham Oakley
Merry Merry Fibruary, Doris Orgel
Amelia Bedelia and the Surprise Shower, Peggy Parish
Thank You, Amelia Bedelia, Peggy Parish
Love from Uncle Clyde, Nancy W. Parker
Cowardly Clyde, Bill Peet
Red Raspberry Crunch, Charles Fox Phillips
Big Orange Splot, Manus Pinkwater
Wuggie Norple Story, Manus Pinkwater

Ballad of the Long-Tailed Rat, Charlotte Pomerantz
The Piggy in the Puddle, Charlotte Pomerantz
Terrible Tiger, Jack Prelutsky
Gollywhopper Egg, Anne Rockwell
How to Eat Fried Worms, Thomas Rockwell
Hucket-A-Bucket Down the Street, Sara Rush
Conrad's Castle, Ben Shecter
A Book of Scary Things, Paul Showers
Where the Sidewalk Ends, Shel Silverstein
Whistling Teakettle and Other Stories About Hannah,
 Mindy W. Skolsky
The Hungry Thing, Jan Slepian
Magic Michael, Louis Slobodkin
Only Silly People Waste, Nora Smaridge
Laughing Time, William J. Smith
Minnie Maloney and Macaroni, Mark Stamaty
Ballad of Penelope Lou and Me, Drew Stevenson
It Could Be Worse!, James Stevenson
Simon Boom Gives a Wedding, Yuri Suhl
Zoophabet, Robert Tallon
Amanda the Panda and the Redhead, Susan Terris
There's a Hippopotamus Under My Bed, Mike Thaler
What Can a Hippopotamus Be?, Mike Thaler
Granfa' Grig Had a Pig... New from Mother Goose,
 Wallace Tripp
A Great Big Ugly Man Came Up and Tied His Horse to Me,
 Wallace Tripp
The Camel Who Took a Walk, Jack Tworkov
Zeralda's Ogre, Tomi Ungerer
The Queen Who Couldn't Bake Gingerbread,
 Dorothy Van Woerkom
A Box to Begin With, Greg Walter
A Spider Might, Tom Walther
Hopping Knapsack, Lisl Weil

Sometimes It's Fun to be Scared

As we can see in any amusement park, human beings seem to get a sense of escape and enjoyment through being frightened when they know that there is no real danger. In terms of children's literature this tendency can be seen by the increasing popularity of books about monsters. It is interesting to note that when Maurice Sendak's *Where the Wild Things Are* first appeared, adults were almost uniformly of the opinion that it would be "too scary" for pre-schoolers. However, "child pressure" soon changed their minds.

As Sendak has said, the children send him pictures of the monsters they have drawn which make his look pale by comparison.

Monster Stories

Something, Natalie Babbitt
Clyde Monster, Robert L. Crowe
William the Dragon, Polly Donnison
Two Monsters, Lucretia Fisher
Little Brute Family, Russell Hoban
Favorite Tales of Trolls and Monsters, George Jonsen
How Many Dragons Are Behind the Door?, Virginia Kahl
The King's Shadow, Robert Larranga
Cora Copycat, Helen Lester
There's a Nightmare in My Closet, Mercer Mayer
You're the Scaredy-Cat, Mercer Mayer
Around Fred's Bed, Manus Pinkwater
Where the Wild Things Are, Maurice Sendak
The Monster at the End of the Book, Jon Stone
Mary Monster, Mischief Maker, Kazuko Taniguchi
The Popcorn Dragon, Jane Thayer
Twitchtoe the Beastfinder, William Van Horn
My Mama Says..., Judith Viorst
Frankenstein's Dog, Jan Wahl
Judge: An Untrue Tale, Harve Zemach

Left-Over Dragon, Claire Boiko
Monster Den or Look What Happened at My House, John Ciardi
King Krakus and the Dragon, Janina Domanska
Harry and the Terrible Whatzit, Dick Gackenbach
Stone Doll of Sister Brute, Russell Hoban
Fergus and the Sea Monster, Yasuko Kimura
Have You Ever Seen a Monster?, John McInnes
Monstrous Glisson Glop, Diane R. Massie
The Terrible Troll, Mercer Mayer
I Know a Monster, Amy Myers
ABC of Monsters, Deborah Niland
Buster and the Bogeyman, Anne Rockwell
Dunmousie Monster, Robin Wild
Gary and the Very Terrible Monster, Barbara Williams

Myth Adventures of Kraken, the Sea Monster, Beverly Brown
I Can Squash Elephants: A Masai Tale, Malcolm Carrick
Bonhomme and the Huge Monster, Laurent DeBrunhoff

Paulus and the Dragon, Jean Dulieu
Great Green Turkey Creek Monster, James Flora
Jimmy and Joe See a Monster, Sally Glendenning
The Abominable Swampman, Gail E. Haley
Monster! Monster!, David Harrison
Nessie the Monster, Ted Hughes
How Do You Hide a Monster?, Virginia Kahl
Mystery Beast of Ostergeest, Steven Kellogg
Pip Squeak, Mouse in Shining Armor, Robert Kraus
Goodnight, Orange Monster, Betty Lifton
Troll Music, Anita Lobel
Under a Mushroom, Anita Lobel
Prince Bertram the Bad, Arnold Lobel
Great Monster Contest, Ruthanna Long
Custard the Dragon and the Wicked Knight, Ogden Nash
Monster Night at Grandma's House, Richard Peck
Cowardly Clyde, Bill Peet
Pea Soup and Sea Serpents, William Schroder
The Hungry Thing, Jan Slepian
Not Here and Never Was, Virginia Smith
Bad Island, William Steig
Zeralda's Ogre, Tomi Ungerer
Alexandra, the Rock Eater, Dorothy Van Woerkom
Monster Poems, Edited by Daisy Wallace
Practical Princess, Jay Williams
Monsters of the Middle Ages, William Wise
Fafnerl, the Ice Dragon, Arnold Zimmerman
Troll Island, Arnold Zimmerman

Leading Characters

In defining literary elements, we stressed the importance of presenting children with stories in which the characters are fully developed and dimensional in the sense that they belong in *that* story and in no other. Since children so readily identify with pets, and to an even greater extent with animals outside that category, two lists follow: the first group features pets as protagonists; the second features other animals in those roles.

Books Which Emphasize Pets as Protagonists

I Love You, Mary Jane, Lorna Balian
Would You Like a Parrot?, France Barberis
Green Eyes, A. Birnbaum

No School Today, Franz Brandenberg
A Robber! A Robber!, Franz Brandenberg
The Dog, John Burningham
Rabbit, John Burningham
What Whiskers Did, Ruth Carroll
Where's the Bunny?, Ruth Carroll
Be Good, Harry, Mary Chalmers
One Little Kitten, Tana Hoban
Kitten for a Day, Ezra Jack Keats
Old Mother Hubbard and Her Dog, Sarah Martin
Grandma's Tiny Kitten, Minnie T. Miller

The Old Dog, Sarah Abbott
Easter Egg Artists, Adrienne Adams
Bobo's Dream, Martha Alexander
Jenny's Birthday Book, Esther Averill
Where's Al?, Byron Barton
One to Teeter-Totter, Edith Battles
Underground Cats, Susan Bennett
Hark, Hark, the Dogs Do Bark, Lenore Blegvad
Mittens for Kittens and Other Rhymes About Cats, edited by Lenore Blegvad
Secret for Grandmother's Birthday, Franz Brandenberg
Felice, Marcia Brown
Josie and the Snow, Helen E. Buckley
Joey's Cat, Robert Burch
Trixie and the Tiger, Victoria Cabassa
Houn' Dog, Mary Calhoun
Mochito: Story of an Ordinary Dog, Nelly Canepari
Have You Seen My Cat?, Eric Carle
Secret Birthday Message, Eric Carle
The Accident, Carol Carrick
The Foundling, Carol Carrick
Lost in the Storm, Carol Carrick
Pocketful of Cricket, Rebecca Caudill
Senora Pepino and Her Bad Luck Cats, Esther de Michael Cervantes
Scrappy the Pup, John Ciardi
Horatio, Eleanor Clymer
Leave Horatio Alone, Eleanor Clymer
My Puppy Is Born, Joanna Cole
Lobo and Brewster, Gladys Cretan
Kat: The Tale of a Calico Cat, Velma Seawell Daniels
Spring Is, Janina Domanska
Angus and the Cat, Marjorie Flack
Angus and the Ducks, Marjorie Flack
Angus Lost, Marjorie Flack

Minou, Francoise
Millions of Cats, Wanda Gag
Life of Jack Sprat, His Wife and His Cat, Paul Galdone
Rotten Ralph, Jack Gantos
Where's Daddy? A Story of Divorce, Beth Goff
Benjy and the Barking Bird, Margaret Graham
Benjy's Boat Trip, Margaret Graham
Benjy's Dog House, Margaret Graham
Eric Gurney's Pop-Up Book of Dogs, Eric Gurney
Looking Book, Mary Ann Hoberman
The Christmas Cat, Tudor Holmes
Catfish and the Kidnapped Cat, Edith Hurd
The Cat and the Mouse Who Shared a House, Ruth Hurlimann
Hi, Cat, Ezra Jack Keats
Pssst! Doggie, Ezra Jack Keats
Whistle for Willie, Ezra Jack Keats
The Mouse God, Richard Kennedy
Fat Cat, Jack Kent
Winter Cat, Howard Knotts
Piebald Pup, Irina Korschunow
Gustavus and Stop, Fernando Krahn

Stupids Step Out, Harry Allard
Dog Who Thought He Was a Boy, Cora Annett
Rebecka, Frank Asch
Little Rabbit's Loose Tooth, Lucy Bate
Pantaloni, Bettina
Dogs Don't Belong on Beds, Enid P. Bloome
And I Mean It, Stanley, Crosby Bonsall
Clifford's Good Deeds, Norman Bridwell
Percy the Parrot Yelled Quiet!, Wayne Carley
Rabbit for Easter, Carol Carrick
Hullabaloo, the Elephant Dog, Ruth Carroll
Pickles and Jake, Janet Chenery
No Dogs Allowed, Jonathan, Mary Blount Christian
Missing Milkman, Roger Duvoisin
Marc and Pixie and the Walls in Mrs. Jones' Garden,
    Louise Fatio
Flash the Dash, Don Freeman
The Boy and the Bird, Tamao Fujita
Puss in Boots, Paul Galdone
Me I See, Barbara Shook Hazen
Whose Cat Is That?, Virginia Kahl
When Violet Died, Mildred Kantrowitz
My Dog Is Lost!, Ezra Jack Keats
Fergus, Yasuko Kimura
Rice Bowl Pet, Patricia Miles Martin

Go Away, Dog, Joan Nodset
Taxi Dog, Svend Otto
Mice on My Mind, Bernard Waber
Rich Cat, Poor Cat, Bernard Waber

Hotel Cat, Esther Averill
Muffin, Judith Brown
Valentine Cat, Clyde R. Bulla
Boomer, the $3.00 Dog: A Puppy Tale, Marilyn Caines
Cross-Country Cat, Mary Calhoun
Managing Hen and the Floppy Hound, Ruth Carroll
Horatio's Birthday, Eleanor Clymer
Po'nya, Her Story, Helen Cole
Kim Soo and His Tortoise, David Collins
I Like Weather, Aileen Fisher
My Cat Has Eyes of Sapphire Blue, Aileen Fisher
Do You Love Me?, Dick Gackenbush
Barry: The Story of a Brave St. Bernard, Bettina Hurlimann
Rima and Zeppo, Susan Jeschke
Dreams, Ezra Jack Keats
Pet Show, Ezra Jack Keats
Mog, the Forgetful Cat, Judith Kerr
Peter's Long Walk, Lee Kingman
Scaredy Cat, Phyllis Krasilovsky
The Magician and the Petnapping, David McKee
A Puppy Named Gih, Sarah Machetanz
The Dog and the Boat Boy, Patricia Miles Martin
Nobody's Cat, Miska Miles
Animal for Alan, Edward Ricciuti
Some Swell Pup, Maurice Sendak
All the Lassies, Liesel M. Skorpen
Poco, Garry Smith
Caleb and Kate, William Steig
About Dying, Sara Bonnett Stein
Hi, Mrs. Mallory, Ianthe Thomas
Growing Time, Sandol S. Warburg
The Silver Pony, Lynn Ward
The Tiger, Letty Williams
The Trouble with Alark, Jane Williamson

Books Which Emphasize Other Animals as Protagonists

Half-a-Ball-of-Kenki, Verna Aardema
Willy-Nilly and the Silly Cat, Elizabeth K. Barr
Baby Animal ABC, Robert Broomfield

The Golden Egg Book, Margaret Wise Brown
Alligator's Toothache, Diane DeGroat
Flip, Wesley Dennis
Little Red Hen, Janina Domanska
Harry: A True Story, Blanche Dorsky
Jasmine, Roger Duvoisin
Country Bunny and the Little Golden Shoes, Marjorie Flack
Little Red Hen, Paul Galdone
The Three Bears, Paul Galdone
Three Little Pigs, Paul Galdone
Animal Babies, Arthur S. Gregor
Little Elephant, Arthur S. Gregor
Little Brute Family, Russell Hoban
Bright Barnyard, Dahlov Ipcar
Tawny, Scrawny Lion, Kathryn Jackson
Big Elephant, Kathryn Jackson
Saggy Baggy Elephant, Kathryn Jackson
Whose Mouse Are You?, Robert Kraus
Who Took the Farmer's Hat?, Joan Nodset
The Box with the Red Wheels, Maud Petersham.
Circus Baby, Maud Petersham
Mouse and the Knitted Cat, Antonella Bollinger-Savelli
The Hunt for Rabbit's Galosh, Ann Schweninger
Little Red Hen, Herb Williams
Basil and Hilary, Jane B. Zalben

King Orville and the Bullfrogs, Kathleen Abell
Smallest Brownie and the Flying Squirrel, Gladys Adshead
Town Mouse and the Country Mouse, Aesop
Three Aesop Fox Fables: Fox and Grapes, Stork, and Crow, Aesop
Who's Zoo?, Conrad Aiken
And My Mean Old Mother Will Be Sorry, Blackboard Bear, Martha Alexander
Out! Out! Out!, Martha Alexander
At Mary Bloom's, Aliki
Little Goat in the Mountains, Pascale Allamand
I Will Not Go to Market Today, Harry Allard
Little Hippo, Frances Allen
Travels of Ms. Beaver, Rosemary Allison
Acorn Tree, Valenti Angelo
Mother Goose Board Book, Anon.
Brown Mouse and Vole, Vicki Kimmel Artis
Look What I Can Do, Jose Aruego
Three Billy Goats Gruff, P.C. Asbjornsen
Moon Bear, Frank Asch
Sand Cake, Frank Asch

Grouchy Uncle Otto, Alice Bach
Millicent the Magnificent, Alice Bach
Most Delicious Camping Trip Ever, Alice Bach
Smartest Bear and His Brother Oliver, Alice Bach
Humbug Rabbit, Lorna Balian
Bears in—Bears Out, Cathrine Barr
Littlest Mule, John Barrett
Oscar, the Selfish Octopus, John Barrett
Hester, Byron Barton
Birds of a Feather, Willi Baum
Good Morning, Sun's Up, Stewart Beach
Looking for Lucas, Per. Beckman
Secret Hiding Place, Rainey Bennett
Berenstain Bears' Counting Book, Stan Berenstain
He Bear, She Bear, Stan Berenstain
There's Nothing to Do, So Let Me Be You, Jean Berg
I'm Bored, Ma, Harold Berson
Larbi and Leila: A Tale of Two Mice, Harold Berson
Leonard the Lion and Raymond the Mouse, Dorothy Bishop
Tina the Tortoise and Carlos the Rabbit, Dorothy Bishop
Fireflies, Max Bolliger
Golden Apple, Max Bolliger
Grasshopper to the Rescue, Carey Bonnie
Piggle, Crosby Bonsall
What Spot?, Crosby Bonsall
Who's a Pest?, Crosby Bonsall
Runaway Flying Horse, Paul J. Bonzen
Little Gorilla, Ruth Bornstein
Fresh Cider and Pie, Franz Brandenberg
Friendly Bear, Robert Bright
My Red Umbrella, Robert Bright
Gordon's House, Julie Brinckloe
Tim Mouse Visits the Farm, Judy Brook
Ring O'Roses, Leslie Brooke
Bun, A Tale from Russia, Marcia Brown
How, Hippo!, Marcia Brown
Once a Mouse, Marcia Brown
Puss in Boots, Marcia Brown
Little Fur Family, Margaret Wise Brown
Sleepy Little Lion, Margaret Wise Brown
Wait Till the Moon Is Full, Margaret Wise Brown
Pied Piper of Hamelin, Robert Browning
Miffy, Dick Bruna
Angelique, Janice Brustlein
Lace Snail, Betsy Byars
Euphonia and the Flood, Mary Calhoun
Do You Want to Be My Friend?, Eric Carle
The Mixed-Up Chameleon, Eric Carle

The Rooster Who Set Out to See the World, Eric Carle
The Very Hungry Caterpillar, Eric Carle
Very Long Tail: A Folding Book, Eric Carle
Mary Louise and Christophe, Natalie Savage Carlson
Where's the Bunny?, Ruth Carroll
Bear Weather, Lillie D. Chaffin
Maudie's Umbrella, Kay Chorao
Impossible Possum, Ellen Conford
Winter Bear, Ruth Craft
The Enormous Crocodile, Roald Dahl
Little Wooden Farmer, Alice Dalgleish
Mrs. Piggery Snout, Rosamond Dauer
Babar and Zephir, Jean DeBrunhoff
Babar the King, Jean DeBrunhoff
Meet Babar and His Family, Jean DeBrunhoff
Babar's Birthday Surprise, Laurent DeBrunhoff
Babar's Castle, Laurent DeBrunhoff
Babar's Cousin, Laurent DeBrunhoff
Two Strikes, Four Eyes, Ned Delaney
Penny Wise, Fun Foolish, Judy Delton
Rabbit Finds a Way, Judy Delton
Three Friends Find Spring, Judy Delton
Two Good Friends, Judy Delton
Two Is Company, Judy Delton
Catch a Little Fox, Beatrice DeRegniers
How Joe Bear and Sam Mouse Got Together, Beatrice DeRegniers
May I Bring a Friend?, Beatrice DeRegniers
When the Snow Is Blue, Marguerite Dorian
Your Owl Friend, Crescent Dragonwagon
Bear Circus, William Pene Du Bois
Bear Party, William Pene Du Bois
Hare and the Tortoise, William Pene Du Bois
Lion, William Pene Du Bois
Little Duck, Judy Dunn
Our Veronica Goes to Petunia's Farm, Roger Duvoisin
Petunia, Roger Duvoisin
Snowy and Woody, Roger Duvoisin
Two Lonely Ducks: A Counting Book, Roger Duvoisin
Veronica, Roger Duvoisin
Veronica and the Birthday Present, Roger Duvoisin
Are You My Mother?, Philip D. Eastman
Such Is the Way of the World, Benjamin Elkin
Klippity Klop, Ed Emberley
Robbie's Friend George, Shirley Estes
Elephant in a Well, Marie Hall Ets
In the Forest, Marie Hall Ets
Just Me, Marie Hall Ets

Play with Me, Marie Hall Ets
Sleepy Time, Eva Evans
Happy Lion, Louise Fatio
Red Bantam, Louise Fatio
Three Happy Lions, Louise Fatio
Sing, Little Mouse, Aileen Fisher
Ask Mr. Bear, Marjorie Flack
Story About Ping, Marjorie Flack
A Big Surprise, Terry Flanagan
Stewed Goose, James Flora
We'll Have a Friend for Lunch, Jane Flory
Chou Chou, Francoise
Bearymore, Don Freeman
Dandelion, Don Freeman
Guard Mouse, Don Freeman
Inspector Peckit, Don Freeman
Norman the Doorman, Don Freeman
Penguins of All People, Don Freeman
Happy Dromedary, Berniece Freschet
The Owl and the Prairie Dog, Berniece Freschet
The Easter Bunny That Overslept, Priscilla Friedrich
Betty Bear's Birthday, Gyo Fujikawa
ABC Bunny, Wanda Gag
Gertrude, the Goose Who Forgot, Joanna Galdone
Henny Penny, Paul Galdone
Horse, Fox and Lion, Paul Galdone
Little Red Riding Hood, Paul Galdone
Monkey and the Crocodile, Paul Galdone
Old Woman and Her Pig, Paul Galdone
Sleepy Ronald, John B. Gantos
Small One, Zhenya Gay
The Nest, Constantin Georgiou
Adventures of Paddy Pig, John S. Goodall
Paddy's Evening Out, John S. Goodall
Androcles and the Lion, Janusz Grabianski
Be Nice to Spiders, Margaret Graham
Bolivar, Hardie Gramatky
Bremen Town Musicians, Grimm Brothers
The Table, the Donkey and the Stick, Grimm Brothers
Froggie Went A-Courtin', Harriett
House Mouse, Dorothy J. Harris
Boy with a Drum, David Harrison
Little Turtle's Big Adventure, David Harrison
Birthday Trombone, Margaret Hartelius
The Chicken's Child, Margaret Hartelius
That's What Friends Are For, Florence Heide
The Wonderful Pumpkin, Lennart Helsing
Mr. Pig and Sonny Too, Lillian Hoban

Baby Sister for Frances, Russell Hoban
A Bargain for Frances, Russell Hoban
Bedtime for Frances, Russell Hoban
Birthday for Frances, Russell Hoban
Bread and Jam for Frances, Russell Hoban
Egg Thoughts and Other Frances Songs, Russell Hoban
Harvey's Hideout, Russell Hoban
Letitia Rabbit's String Song, Russell Hoban
Nothing to Do, Russell Hoban
Little Book of Beasts, Mary Ann Hoberman
Carrot Cake, Nonny Hogrogian
One Fine Day, Nonny Hogrogian
Rain Puddle, Adelaide Holl
Remarkable Egg, Adelaide Holl
Rosie's Walk, Pat Hutchins
Surprise Party, Pat Hutchins
Land of Flowers, Dahlov Ipcar
One Horse Farm, Dahlov Ipcar
Clay Pot Boy, Cynthia Jameson
Calf, Goodnight, Nancy Jewell
Cheer Up, Pig, Nancy Jewell
Snuggle Bunny, Nancy Jewell
Will Spring Be Early or Will Spring Be Late?, Crockett Johnson
Penelope the Tortoise, Sylvia A. Johnson
Penny and Pete, the Lambs, Sylvia A. Johnson
Moll and Troll Trim the Tree, Tony Johnston
I Didn't Want to Be Nice, Penelope Jones
Nanny Goat and the Fierce Dog, Charles Keeping
The Mouse God, Richard Kennedy
Floyd, the Tiniest Elephant, Jack Kent
Run, Little Monkeys, Run, Run, Run, Juliet Kepes
Jolli, Alfred Konner
Big Brother, Robert Kraus
Daddy Long Ears, Robert Kraus
Herman the Helper, Robert Kraus
How Spider Saved Halloween, Robert Kraus
Littlest Rabbit, Robert Kraus
Milton the Early Riser, Robert Kraus
Owliver, Robert Kraus
Happy Day, Ruth Krauss
Roar and More, Karla Kuskin
Hare and Tortoise, Jean de La Fontaine
Frog Went A-Courtin', John Langstaff
Over in the Meadow, John Langstaff
The Story of Ferdinand, Munro Leaf
The Hungry Fox and Foxy Duck, Kathleen Leverich
The Other Side of the Mountain, Robert Leydenfrost
Alexander and the Wind-Up Mouse, Leo Lionni

Biggest House in the World, Leo Lionni
Fish Is Fish, Leo Lionni
Frederick, Leo Lionni
Greentail Mouse, Leo Lionni
Inch by Inch, Leo Lionni
Swimmy, Leo Lionni
Tico and the Golden Wings, Leo Lionni
Little Tiny Rooster, William Lipkind
New at the Zoo, Peter Lippman
Days with Frog and Toad, Arnold Lobel
Frog and Toad Together, Arnold Lobel
Holiday for Mister Muster, Arnold Lobel
Martha, the Movie Mouse, Arnold Lobel
Mouse Soup, Arnold Lobel
Owl at Home, Arnold Lobel
Boo to a Goose, Joseph Low
Blueberries for Sal, Robert McCloskey
Make Way for Ducklings, Robert McCloskey
Hee Haw, Ann McGovern
Leo Lion Paints It Red, John McInnes
Bear's Toothache, David McPhail
A Wise Monkey Tale, Betsy Maestro
George and Martha, James Marshall
The Guest, James Marshall
Willis, James Marshall
Walter Was a Frog, Diane R. Massie
Ah-Choo, Mercer Mayer
Four Frogs in a Box, Mercer Mayer
Frog Goes to Dinner, Mercer Mayer
Frog on His Own, Mercer Mayer
Frog, Where Are You?, Mercer Mayer
Hiccup, Mercer Mayer
Just for You, Mercer Mayer
Oops, Mercer Mayer
Two Moral Tales, Mercer Mayer
What Do You Do with a Kangaroo?, Mercer Mayer
A Boy, a Dog, a Frog and a Friend, Mercer Mayer
One Frog Too Many, Mercer Mayer
Curious Cow, Esther H. Meeks
Goodnight to Annie, Eve Merriam
Blue China Pitcher, Elizabeth C. Meyer
Small Rabbit, Miska Miles
Mousekin's Woodland Sleepers, Edna Miller
Little Bear, Else H. Minarik
If I Were a Mother, Kazue Mizumura
Patty Cake, Elizabeth Moody
The Little Raccoon and No Trouble at All, Lilian Moore

Miss Harriet Hippopotamus and the Most Wonderful,
   Nancy Moore
Mister Mole, Luis Murschetz
No! No! No!, Louis Myllar
The Bad Bear, Rudolph Neumann
Marshmallow, Claire T. Newberry
Pig Tale, Helen Oxenbury
A Fish Out of Water, Helen M. Palmer
Snapping Turtle's All Wrong Day, Peggy Parish
Katy No-Pocket, Emmy Payne
Huge Harold, Bill Peet
Cat and Mouse, Rodney Peppe
Happy Owls, Celestino Piatti
Terrible Roar, Manus Pinkwater
Bubba and Babba, Maria Polushkin
The Little Hen and the Giant, Maria Polushkin
Tailor of Gloucester, Beatrix Potter
Tale of Johnny Townmouse, Beatrix Potter
Tale of Mrs. Tiggy-Winkle, Beatrix Potter
Tale of Mrs. Tittlemouse, Beatrix Potter
Tale of Peter Rabbit, Beatrix Potter
Tale of Timmy Tiptoes, Beatrix Potter
Tale of Tupenny, Beatrix Potter
Tale of Two Bad Mice, Beatrix Potter
Squawk to the Moon, Little Goose, Edna Mitchell Preston
Temper Tantrum Book, Edna Mitchell Preston
And It Rained, Ellen Raskin
Moose, Goose and Little Nobody, Ellen Raskin
Twenty-Two, Twenty-Three, Ellen Raskin
Where's My Baby?, H.A. Rey
Billy's Picture, Margaret Rey
Laughing Camera for Children, Edited by Hanns-Reich
August Explains, Phil Ressner
Peter Pelican, Annia Roa
Animals in the Zoo, Feodor Rojankovsky
Animals on the Farm, Feodor Rojankovsky
The Great Big Wild Animal Book, Feodor Rojankovsky
The Too-Long Trunk, Regina Sauro
I'm Going to the Ocean, Eleanor Schick
Jeannie Goes Riding, Eleanor Schick
Heavy Is a Hippopotamus, Miriam Schlein
The Great Big Elephant and the Very Small Elephant,
   Barbara Seuling
Burton and Dudley, Marjorie W. Sharmot
I'm Terrific, Marjorie W. Sharmot
Mooch the Messy, Marjorie W. Sharmot
Say Hello, Vanessa, Marjorie W. Sharmot

Molly Patch and Her Animal Friends, Ben Shecter
Partouche Plants a Seed, Ben Shecter
Caps for Sale, Esphyr Slobodkina
Farmer Palmer's Wagon Ride, William Steig
Roland, the Minstrel Pig, William Steig
Sylvester and the Magic Pebble, William Steig
Ten in a Family, Charlotte Steiner
Monkeys and the Pedlar, Susanne Suba
Mushroom in the Rain, A. Suteyev
What Happened to Hector?, Kathleen Teague
Stand Back, Said the Elephant, I'm Going to Sneeze, Patricia Thomas
Smart Bear, Tom Tichenor
Little Fox Goes to the End of the World, Ann Tompert
Arthur and Clementine, Adela Turin
Deep in the Forest, Brinton Turkle
Crictor, Tomi Ungerer
The Checker Players, Alan Venable
The Don't Be Scared Book: Scares, Remedies and Pictures, Ilse-Margret Vogel
Anteater Named Arthur, Bernard Waber
Firefly Named Torchy, Bernard Waber
House on East Eighty-eighth Street, Bernard Waber
Lovable Lyle, Bernard Waber
Lyle and the Birthday Party, Bernard Waber
Lyle Finds His Mother, Bernard Waber
You Look Ridiculous Said the Rhino to the Hippo, Bernard Waber
Carrot Nose, Jan Wahl
Dr. Rabbit's Foundling, Jan Wahl
Pleasant Fieldmouse's Halloween Party, Jan Wahl
Pigs and Pirates: A Greek Tale, Barbara K. Walker
Lollipop, Wendy Watson
Candy Egg Bunny, Lisl Weil
Frog, Frog, Frog, Robert Welber
Benjamin and Tulip, Rosemary Wells
Stanley and Rhoda, Rosemary Wells
Albert's Toothache, Barbara Williams
Potbellied Possums, Elizabeth Winthrop
Little New Kangaroo, Bernard Wiseman
Benjamin's Perfect Solution, Beth Weiner Woldin
Mouse Trouble, John Yeoman
Two Little Bears, Ylla
Miss Suzy's Easter Surprise, Miriam Young
Princess and Froggie, Harve Zemach
Meanest Squirrel I Ever Met, Gene Zion
Sugar Mouse Cake, Gene Zion
Bunny Who Found Easter, Charlotte Zolotow

Mister Rabbit and the Lovely Present, Charlotte Zolotow
Three Funny Friends, Charlotte Zolotow
Tiger Called Thomas, Charlotte Zolotow

Reasons and Raisins, Josephine Aldridge
Keep Your Mouth Closed, Dear, Aliki
Izzard, Lonzo Anderson
Two Hundred Rabbits, Lonzo Anderson
Red Fox and the Hungry Tiger, Paul Anderson
Adventures of Egbert, the Easter Egg, Richard Armour
Pilyo the Piranha, Jose Aruego
Turtle Tale, Frank Asch
Where in the World Is Henry?, Lorna Balian
Horse for Sherry, Cathrine Barr
Animals Should Definitely Not Wear Clothing, Judith Barrett
Nine Hundred Buckets of Paint, Edna Becker
A Moose Is Not a Mouse, Harold Berson
Twenty-Two Bears, Claire H. Bishop
Here's Pippa Again, Betty Boegehold
Pippa Mouse, Betty Boegehold
It's Mine!, Crosby Bonsall
Someone Small, Barbara Borack
Indian Bunny, Ruth Bornstein
Mr. Tall and Mr. Small, Barbara Brenner
Mr. Gumpy's Motor Car, John Burningham
Fantastic Mr. Fox, Roald Dahl
Owl's New Cards, Kathryn Ernst
Another Day, Marie Hall Ets
Hector Penguin, Louise Fatio
Marc and Pixie and the Walls in Mrs. Jones' Garden, Louise Fatio
Do Bears Have Mothers Too?, Aileen Fisher
Listen, Rabbit, Aileen Fisher
We Went Looking, Aileen Fisher
The Seal and the Slick, Don Freeman
Turtle and the Dove, Don Freeman
Will's Quill, Don Freeman
Pet of the Met, Lydia Freeman
Old Bullfrog, Berniece Freschet
The Perfect Pal, Jack Gantos
Bertie's Escapade, Kenneth Grahame
Frog Prince, Jacob Grimm
School Mouse, Dorothy J. Harris
Emmet Otter's Jug-Band Christmas, Russell Hoban
Stone Doll of Sister Brute, Russell Hoban
Raucus Auk: A Menagerie of Poems, Mary Ann Hoberman
Anna Banana, Rosekrans Hoffman

The Nosy Colt, Nils Hogner
Lost and Found Horse, Consuelo Joerns
The Man Who Loved Birds, Ken Kenniston
Time for Jody, Wendy Kesselman
Do Bears Sit in Chairs?, Ethel Kessler
Fergus and the Sea Monster, Yasuko Kimura
Lion and the Bird's Nest, Eriko Kishida
Where's Wallace?, Hilary Knight
The Tadpole and the Frog, Susan Knobler
Simon's Soup, Beverly Komoda
Clever Coot, Alfred Konner
The Cow Who Fell in the Canal, Phyllis Krasilovsky
Mittens in May, Maxine Kumin
Carlotta and the Scientist, Patricia Riley Lenthall
Happy Birthday, Oliver!, Pierre Le-Tan
Runaway Roller Skate, John Vernon Lord
Too Much Noise, Ann McGovern
The Boy Who Was Followed Home, Margaret Mahy
Portly McSwine, James Marshall
Yummers, James Marshall
Briar Rose and the Golden Eggs, Diane R. Massie
Chameleon Was a Spy, Diane R. Massie
Hi, All You Rabbits, Carl Memling
Broderick, Edward Ormondroyd
Pinkish, Purplish, Bluish Egg, Bill Peet
Garth Pig and the Ice Cream Lady, Mary Rayner
Cecily G. and Nine Monkeys, H.A. Rey
Poor Goose, Anne Rockwell
Everything About Easter Rabbits, Wiltrud Roser
Old Tiger, New Tiger, Ron Roy
Fog in the Meadow, Joanne Ryder
Panda Cake, Rosalie Seidler
Pierre, Maurice Sendak
Edgemont, Marjorie W. Sharmot
Yellow-Lemon Elephant Called Trunk, Barbara Softly
Hooray for Pig!, Carla Stevens
Monty, James Stevenson
Helena, the Unhappy Hippopotamus, Yutaka Sugita
The Painter and the Bird, Max Velthuijs
Ralphi Rhino, Lisl Weil
The Mule Who Refused to Budge, Lionel Wilson
The Young Performing Horse, John Yeoman
Thistle, Era Zistel

Waymond the Whale, Caroline Aimar
It's So Nice to Have a Wolf Around the House, Harry Allard

Coll and His White Pig, Lloyd Alexander
Four Donkeys, Lloyd Alexander
Ponies of Mykillengi, Lonzo Anderson
I Like Birds, Rist. Arnold
Pig War, Betty Baker
Voyage of Jim, Janet Barber
Muggins' Big Balloon, Marjorie Barrows
Hare's Race, Hans Baumann
Indy and Mr. Lincoln, Natalia Belting
Rats Who Lived in the Delicatessen, Harold Berson
Why Jackal Won't Speak to Hedgehog, Harold Berson
Georgette, Claire H. Bishop
Truffle Pig, Claire H. Bishop
Mushroom Center Disaster, Niels M. Bodecker
Parrak, the White Reindeer, Inga Borg
Little Fox in the Middle, Pearl Buck
Little Pig in the Cupboard, Helen E. Buckley
Aloysius Alligator, Bunny
Tigger: Story of a Mayan Ocelot, Bunny
Trubloff, the Mouse Who Wanted to Play the Balalaika,
    John Burningham
Haunted Churchbell, Betsy Byars
Battle Reuben Robin and Kite Uncle John, Mary Calhoun
Beach Bird, Carol Carrick
Managing Hen and the Floppy Hound, Ruth Carroll
Juan Bobo and the Pig: A Puerto Rican Folktale,
    Bernice Chardiet
Real Hole, Beverly Cleary
Carp in the Bathtub, Barbara Cohen
Fourteen Rats and a Rat Catcher, James Cressey
Andy and the Lion, James Daugherty
Terrible Troll-Bird, Ingri D'Aulaire
Babar Comes to America, Laurent DeBrunhoff
Babar Visits Another Planet, Laurent DeBrunhoff
Babar's Moon Trip, Laurent DeBrunhoff
Babar's Spanish Lessons, Laurent DeBrunhoff
Tumble, The Story of a Mustang, Wesley Dennis
When Everyone Was Fast Asleep, Tomie De Paola
Little Monk and the Tiger: A Tale of Thailand, Arnold Dobrin
Taro and the Sea Turtles, Arnold Dobrin
Crocodile in the Tree, Roger Duvoisin
Goats of Agadez, Victor Engelbert
Warton and Morton, Russell Erickson
Odette, a Bird in Paris, Kay Fender
My Mother and I, Aileen Fisher
Dinosaurs and All That Rubbish, Michael Foreman
Fly High, Fly Low, Don Freeman

The Mammoth, the Owl and the Crab, Claudia Fregosi
Bernard of Scotland Yard, Berniece Freschet
Turtle Pond, Berniece Freschet
Tremendous Tree Book, May Garelick
Two Greedy Bears, Mirra Ginsburg
Honschi, Aline Glasgow
Boy Who Loved Horses, Martha Goldberg
The River Bank (from *Wind in the Willows*), Kenneth Grahame
The Bear and the Kingbird, Grimm Brothers
Wolf and the Seven Little Kids, Grimm Brothers
Slip, Slop, Gobble, Jean Hardendorff
Rebel, the Reluctant Racehorse, B. Hetty
Best Friends for Frances, Russell Hoban
Amy's Goose, Efner Tudor Holmes
Thieves and the Raven, Janosch
Muktu, the Backward Muskox, Heather Stewart-Kellerhals
Island of the Skog, Steven Kellogg
Five Little Monkeys, Juliet Kepes
Frogs Merry, Juliet Kepes
White Little Hen, Hajime Kijima
Elephant's Child, Rudyard Kipling
How the Leopard Got His Spots, Rudyard Kipling
How the Rhinoceros Got His Skin, Rudyard Kipling
Boris Bad Enough, Robert Kraus
Pip Squeak, Mouse in Shining Armor, Robert Kraus
Voices of Green Willow Pond, Carolyn Lane
Rafiki, Nola Langner
Turnabout, Munro Leaf
Leese Webster, Ursula LeGuin
Crocodile and the Hen, Joan Lexau
Cock and the Ghost Cat, Betty Lifton
Mud Snail Son, Betty Lifton
Goat in the Rug, Martin Link
Alexander, Harold Littledale
Sticks, Stones, Charles A. Llerena
Lucille, Arnold Lobel
The Sunshine Family and the Pony, Sharron Loree
Little Whale, Ann McGovern
The Mermaid and the Whale, Georgess McHargue
My Friend Mac, May McNeer
The Mouse and the Mirage, Janet McNeil
Tortoise's Tug of War, Guilio Maestro
King Lawrence, the Alarm Clock, Peggy Mann
Wish Again, Big Bear, Richard Margolis
Raccoon and Mrs. McGinnis, Patricia Miles Martin
The Adventures of Sapo, Susan Martin
Dazzle, Diane R. Massie
Travels of Marco, Jean Merrill

Wharf Rat, Miska Miles
House at Pooh Corner, A.A. Milne
Now We Are Six, A.A. Milne
When We Were Very Young, A.A. Milne
Winnie the Pooh, A.A. Milne
Bruno Munari's Zoo, Bruno Munari
Pierre the Muskrat, Jane Oliver
Too Many Rabbits, Peggy Parish
Love from Uncle Clyde, Nancy W. Parker
Hubert's Hair-Raising Adventure, Bill Peet
Merle, the High Flying Squirrel, Bill Peet
Chester, the Worldly Pig, Bill Peet
Kermit the Hermit, Bill Peet
Randy's Dandy Lions, Bill Peet
The Spooky Tail of Prewitt Peacock, Bill Peet
Wump World, Bill Peet
Salt Boy, Mary Perrine
Red Tag Comes Back, Frederick Phleger
Three Big Hogs, Manus Pinkwater
Terrible Tiger, Jack Prelutsky
When the Monkeys Wore Sombreros, Mariana Prieto
Go Tell Aunt Rhody, Robert Quackenbush
The Most Welcome Visitor, Robert Quackenbush
Blind Men and the Elephant, Lillian Quigley
The Red Horse and the Bluebird, Sandy Rabinowitz
Who, Said Sue, Said Whoo?, Ellen Raskin
Curious George, H.A. Rey
Spotty, Margaret Rey
Animal for Alan, Edward Ricciuti
Catch a Whale by the Tail, Edward Ricciuti
Sam Who Never Forgets, Eve Rice
Gaston Goes to Mardi Gras, James Rice
Gaston Goes to Texas, James Rice
Gaston, the Green-Nosed Alligator, James Rice
The Mouse and the Song, Marilynne Roach
Clever Turtle, A.K. Roche
Monkey's Whiskers: A Brazilian Folktale, Anne Rockwell
The Wolf Who Had a Wonderful Dream: A French Folktale, Anne Rockwell
The Tiger-Skin Rug, Gerald Rose
Giant Devil-Dingo, Dick Roughsey
Once We Had a Horse, Glen Rounds
Motherly Smith and Brother Bimbo, Solveig P. Russell
Bambi, Felix Salten
Twelve Years, Twelve Animals, Yoshiko Y. Samuel
Fanshen, the Magic Bear, Becky Sarah
The Gorilla in the Hall, Alice Schertle
The Rabbit's World, Miriam Schlein

What's Wrong with Being a Skunk?, Miriam Schlein
Cottontail Rabbit, Charles Schwartz
The Wee, Wee Mannie and the Big, Big Coo, Marcia Sewall
Mr. Jameson and Mr. Phillips, Marjorie W. Sharmot
Sophie and Gussie, Marjorie W. Sharmot
The 329th Friend, Marjorie W. Sharmot
Walter the Wolf, Marjorie W. Sharmot
Gregory the Terrible, Mitchell Sharmot
Robert and the Magic String, Ivan Sherman
Mary's Marvelous Mouse, Mary Shura
Bird, Liesel M. Skorpen
Scuttle, the Stowaway Mouse, Jean C. Soule
The Amazing Bone, William Steig
Amos and Boris, William Steig
The Bear Who Wanted to Be a Bear, Jorg Steiner
Wilfred the Rat, James Stevenson
Bufo: A Toad—Un Crapaud, Maria Stevenson
Hug Me, Patti Stren
Blackie, the Bird Who Could, Yutaka Sugita
Henry Explores the Jungle, Mark Taylor
What Can a Hippopotamus Be?, Mike Thaler
Anatole, Eve Titus
Corgiville Fair, Tasha Tudor
Thy Friend, Obadiah, Brinton Turkle
The Woodcutter's Duck, Krystyna Turksa
The Camel Who Took a Walk, Jack Tworkov
Snail, Where Are You?, Tomi Ungerer
The Rat, the Ox and the Zodiac, Dorothy Van Woerkom
Biggest Bear, Lynd Ward
Hickory Stick Rag, Clyde Watson
Animal Dictionary, Jane Watson
The Elephant That Became a Ferry Boat, Mabel Watts
Crocodile Medicine, Marjorie-Ann Watts
Lambs, Martin Weaver
Abdul, Rosemary Wells
Daxius, Dante Westbrook
Charlotte's Web, E.B. White
Stuart Little, E.B. White
Once a Bright Red Tiger, Alex Whitney
Rabbits' Wedding, Garth Williams
The Tiger, Letty Williams
Morris the Moose, Bernard Wiseman
Wild Ducks and the Goose, Carl Withers
Ellie to the Rescue, Beth Weiner Woldin
A Cool Ride in the Sky, Diane Wolkstein
Bear's Winter Picnic, John Yeoman
Beatrice and Vanessa, John Yeoman
Clumsy Octupus, Marvin Zetlin

Girls and Boys; Men and Women and Their Occupations

Because of a recent awareness of sexual roles, not only in regard to changed role models for little girls, but also in relation to less stereotyped behavior by boys, a list of books emphasizing sexual identity should be useful. Along with this, there is a short list of books in which occupational opportunities are stressed—frequently reconfirming new paths for females to follow.

Books Which Emphasize Sexual Identity

Case of the Scaredy Cats, Crosby Bonsall
Katy and the Big Snow, Virginia Lee Burton
Naptime, Gilbert Coker
Christina Katerina and the Box, Patricia Gauch
Letter to Amy, Ezra Jack Keats
A Train for Jane, Norma Klein
Mothers Can Do Anything, Joe Lasker
Peter Learns to Crochet, Irene Levinson
Nice Little Girls, Elizabeth Levy
Jesse's Dream Skirt, Bruce Mack
Boys and Girls, Girls and Boys, Eve Merriam
Mommies at Work, Eve Merriam
Strange Street, Ann Powell
The Daddy Book, R. Stewart
Ira Sleeps Over, Bernard Waber
Turnabout, William Wiesner
Tommy and Sarah Dress Up, Gunilla Wolde
William's Doll, Charlotte Zolotow

Come Away from the Water, Shirley, John Burningham
Time to Get Out of the Bath, Shirley, John Burningham
Maybelle, the Cable Car, Virginia Lee Burton
The Milkmaid, Randolph Caldecott
The Magic Hat, Kim Westsmith Chapman
Girls Can Too!, Lee Bennett Hopkins
Monkey Day, Ruth Krauss
Carlotta and the Scientist, Patricia Riley Lenthall
My Mother the Mail Carrier, Inez Maury
The Girl Who Would Rather Climb Trees, Miriam Schlein
I Climb Mountains, Barbara Taylor

Milly-Molly-Mandy Stories, Lankester Brisley
Yolanda's Hike, Tomas Rodriguez Gaspar

Hey, Wait for Me; I'm Amelia, Linda Glovach
Best Friends for Frances, Russell Hoban
Coleen, the Question Girl, Arlie Russell Hochschild
Max, Rachel Isadora
Girls Can Be Anything, Norma Klein
The Sunshine Family and the Pony, Sharron Loree
Half a Kingdom, Ann McGovern
The Man Who Was Going to Mind the House, David McKee
My Mother and I Are Growing Strong, Inez Maury
What to Be?, Meredith Powell
Amy and the Cloud Basket, Ellen Pratt
Firegirl, Gibson Rich
By George, Bloomers!, Judith St. George
Butcher, Baker, Cabinet Maker: Women at Work, Wendy Saul
Hester the Jester, Ben Shecter
Quiet on Account of the Dinosaur, Jane Thayer
Free to Be You and Me, Marlo Thomas
The Clever Princess, Ann Tompert
What Is a Girl? What Is a Boy?, Stephanie Waxman
Petronella, Jay Williams
The Beautiful Rat, Kathe Zemach

Books That Emphasize Occupational Opportunities

He Bear, She Bear, Stan Berenstain
Dig, Drill, Dump, Fill, Tana Hoban
Ten Big Farms, Dahlov Ipcar
Mothers Can Do Anything, Joe Lasker
I Can Be, Sonia Lisker
Mommies at Work, Eve Merriam

Cowboys: What Do They Do?, Carla Greene
How We Work, Anita Harper
Girls Can Too!, Lee Bennett Hopkins
Carlotta and the Scientist, Patricia Riley Lenthall
My Mother the Mail Carrier, Inez Maury

Terrible Thing That Happened at Our House, Marge Blaine
Women at Their Work, Edited by Betty English
Busy Day, Busy People, Tibor Gergely
What Can She Be? A Farmer, Gloria Goldreich
What Can She Be? A Geologist, Gloria Goldreich
What Can She Be? A Lawyer, Gloria Goldreich

What Can She Be? A Newscaster, Gloria Goldreich
What Can She Be? A Police Officer, Gloria Goldreich
What Can She Be? A Veterinarian, Gloria Goldreich
Ben Goes into Business, Marilyn Hirsch
Odd Jobs, Tony Johnston
Girls Can Be Anything, Norma Klein
The Sunshine Family and the Pony, Sharron Loree
Please, Michael, That's My Daddy's Chair, Susan E. Mark
My Mother and I Are Growing Strong, Inez Maury
What to Be?, Meredith Powell
Amy and the Cloud Basket, Ellen Pratt
Along Came the Model T, Robert Quackenbush
Firegirl, Gibson Rich
I Can Be Anything You Can Be, Joel Rothman
Butcher, Baker, Cabinet Maker: Women at Work, Wendy Saul
Hester the Jester, Ben Shecter
Quiet on Account of the Dinosaur, Jane Thayer
Free to Be You and Me, Marlo Thomas
The Man Who Made Tops: Why People Do Different Work, Marie Winn

Various Locales

Because children can learn about settings vicariously, books in which a sense of place is an important element seem to call for listings. Children who live in cities, for example, may very well never have the opportunity to see rural life first-hand, just as country-bred children may not have the chance to learn personally about city life. So, although reading about other environments is not equal in any sense to actual experience, it is certainly better than nothing. Sense of time and place are not concepts easily grasped by the young child, but illustrations can help to make a Vermont farm a reality for a child who has been raised in a Los Angeles barrio, just as they can bring into focus a street in Harlem for a youngster reared on a ranch in Wyoming.

Books with Rural Settings

Three Billy Goats Gruff, Peter Asbjornsen
Tim Mouse Visits the Farm, Judy Brooks
Country Noisy Book, Margaret Wise Brown
Mr. Gumpy's Outing, John Burningham
Houn' Dog, Mary Calhoun

Dirt Road, Carol Carrick
Pocketful of Cricket, Rebecca Caudill
Little Wooden Farmer, Alice Dalgleish
Peasants Pea Patch, Guy Daniels
Snow Party, Beatrice DeRegniers
Turnip, Janina Domanska
Jasmine, Roger Duvoisin
Our Veronica Goes to Petunia's Farm, Roger Duvoisin
Petunia, Roger Duvoisin
Gilberto and the Wind, Marie Hall Ets
Story About Ping, Marjorie Flack
Eighteen Cousins, Carol G. Hogan
One Horse Farm, Dahlov Ipcar
Ten Big Farms, Dahlov Ipcar
Try and Catch Me, Nancy Jewell
Story of Ferdinand, Munro Leaf
One Morning in Maine, Robert McCloskey
Here I Come...Ready or Not, Jean Merrill
Blue China Pitcher, Elizabeth C. Meyer
Vermont Farm and the Sun, Constance Montgomery
The Box with the Red Wheels, Maud Petersham
Rooster Crows, Maud Petersham
Popcorn and Ma Goodness, Edna Mitchell Preston
Cajun Alphabet, James Rice
Melissa, Lisl Weil
The Simple Prince, Jane Yolen
Mommy, Buy Me a China Doll, Harve Zemach

Squire's Bride, Peter Asbjornsen
Ethel's Exceptional Egg, Linda Bourke
Mr. Gumpy's Motor Car, John Burningham
Nancy's Backyard, Eros Keith
My Island Grandma, Kathryn Lasky
David's Windows, Alice Low
Poor Goose, Anne Rockwell

Penny and a Periwinkle, Josephine Aldridge
Story of Johnny Appleseed, Aliki
Day in the Country, Willis Barnstone
Balarin's Goat, Harold Berson
Raccoons Are for Loving, Miriam Bourne
Andrew Henry's Meadow, Doris Burn
Exploring as You Walk in the Meadow, Phyllis S. Busch
Managing Hen and Floppy Hound, Ruth Carroll
Contrary Jenkins, Rebecca Caudill

Motoring Millers, Alberta Constant
Grandmother's Pictures, Sam Cornish
Charlie Needs a Cloak, Tomie De Paola
Strega Nona, Tomie De Paola
Little Sister and Month Brothers, Beatrice DeRegniers
Taro and the Sea Turtles, Arnold Dobrin
Dirk's Wooden Shoes, Ilona Fennema
Best Little House, Aileen Fisher
In the Middle of the Night, Aileen Fisher
Hans in Luck, Grimm Brothers
Princess of the Rice Fields, Hisako Kimishima
Peter's Long Walk, Lee Kingman
Harriet and the Promised Land, Jacob Lawrence
A Perfect Place to Be, Bijou LeTord
One-Legged Ghost, Betty Lifton
The Mermaid and the Whale, Georgess McHargue
The Man Who Was Going to Mind the House, David McKee
Yagua Days, Cruz Martel
Vermont Road Builder, Constance Montgomery
Vermont School Bus Ride, Constance Montgomery
Chester, the Worldly Pig, Bill Peet
Our Animal Friends at Maple Hill Farm, Alice Provensen
Blind Men and the Elephant, Lillian Quigley
Two Windmills, Maryke Reesink
Gaston Goes to Texas, James Rice
Gaston, the Green-Nosed Alligator, James Rice
Femi and Old Grandaddie, Adjai Robinson
Onion Maidens, A.K. Roche
Gollywhopper Egg, Anne Rockwell
The Wolf Who Had a Wonderful Dream: A French Folktale, Anne Rockwell
Akimba and the Magic Cow, Retold by Anne Rose
Journey Cake, Ruth Sawyer
Old Arthur, Liesel M. Skorpen
Autumn Harvest, Alvin R. Tresselt
Bonnie Bess, the Weathervane Horse, Alvin R. Tresselt
Babushka and the Pig, Ann Trofimuk
Corgiville Fair, Tasha Tudor
The County Fair, Tasha Tudor
How a Shirt Grew in the Field, Constantin Ushinsky
Sugar on Snow, Nancy D. Watson
When Is Tomorrow?, Nancy D. Watson
The Elephant That Became a Ferry Boat, Mabel Watts
Tatu and the Honey Bird, Alice W. Wellman
Crow Boy, Taro Yashima
The Village Tree, Taro Yashima

Books with Urban Settings

Mushy Eggs, Adrienne Adams
Madeline, Ludwig Bemelmans
Madeline in London, Ludwig Bemelmans
Madeline's Rescue, Ludwig Bemelmans
City Noisy Book, Margaret Wise Brown
Angelique, Janice Brustlein
A Kiss Is Round, Blossom Budney
Jo, Flo and Yolanda, Carol DePoix
Happy Lion, Louise Fatio
Minou, Francoise
Jeanne-Marie in Gay Paree, Francoise
Noisy Nancy Norris, Lou Ann Gaedert
Girl on the Yellow Giraffe, Ronald Himler
Hi, Cat, Ezra Jack Keats
Make Way for Ducklings, Robert McCloskey
Strange Street, Ann Powell
Friday Night Is Papa Night, Emily A. Sonneborn
Melissa's Friend, Lisl Weil

Mandy and the Flying Map, Beverley Allinson
Maria Teresa, Mary Atkinson
No Dogs Allowed, Jonathan, Mary Blount Christian
Boy Who Didn't Believe in Spring, Lucille Clifton
King Krakus and the Dragon, Janina Domanska
Noisy Nancy and Nick, Lou Ann Gaedert
City Rhythms, Ann Grifalconi
Evan's Corner, Elizabeth S. Hill
My Dog Is Lost!, Ezra Jack Keats
Benjie, Joan Lexau
Benjie on His Own, Joan Lexau
Scram, Kid!, Ann McGovern
Rice Bowl Pet, Patricia Miles Martin
Henri Goes to the Mardi Gras, Mildred W. Wright
The Young Performing Horse, John Yeoman

Hotel Cat, Esther Averill
Kevin Cloud: Chippewa Boy in the City, Carol A. Bales
Voyage of Jim, Janet Barber
Old MacDonald Had an Apartment House, Judith Barrett
Carmen, Bill Binzen
Emilio's Summer Day, Miriam Bourne
New Boy in Dublin: A Story of Ireland, Clyde R. Bulla
Haunted Churchbell, Barbara Byfield

Odette, a Bird in Paris, Kay Fender
Hey, Wait for Me—I'm Amelia, Linda Glovach
The Hot Day, Sheila Greenwald
Big City, Francine Grossbart
Tom and Sam, Pat Hutchins
In the Village, Hilda Heyduck-Huth
Apt. 3, Ezra Jack Keats
Goggles, Ezra Jack Keats
Maggie and the Pirate, Ezra Jack Keats
Mister Chu, Norma Keating
Angelita, Wendy Kesselman
Visiting Pamela, Norma Klein
Village in Normandy, Laurence
The Park, Richard Lewis
A Week in Henry's World: El Barrio, Inger McCabe
Rolling the Cheese, Patricia Miles Martin
Don't Ride the Bus on Monday: The Rosa Parks Story,
 L. Meriwether
Travels of Marco, Jean Merrill
Papa Albert, Lilian Moore
Taxi Dog, Svend Otto
A Ride on High, Candida Palmer
Gaston Goes to the Mardi Gras, James Rice
City Green, Eleanor Schick
City in the Summer, Eleanor Schick
City in the Winter, Eleanor Schick
Sara and the Apartment Building, Yvonne Singer
Whistling Teakettle and Other Stories About Hannah,
 Mindy W. Skolsky
Moon Blossom and the Golden Penny, Louis Slobodkin
Read About the Policeman, Louis Slobodkin
My Special Best Words, John Steptoe
Stevie, John Steptoe
Little Red Lighthouse and Great Gray Bridge, Hildegarde Swift
Come to the City, Ruth Tensen
Mira! Mira!, Dawn Thomas
Anatole, Eve Titus
Obadiah the Bold, Brinton Turkle
Sumi and the Goat and the Tokyo Express, Yoshiko Uchida
Mary Jo's Grandmother, Janice Udry
The Park Book, Charlotte Zolotow

Weather and Seasons

Along the same line as locale are the matters of weather and the seasons. Books which stress these can make other places seem more "real" to children and help them to understand that youngsters who live in conditions strange to them are not really very different in terms of behavior, family life, and so on.

Books About Weather

We Never Get to Do Anything, Martha Alexander
Winter Bear, Ruth Craft
Snow Party, Beatrice DeRegniers
Gilberto and the Wind, Marie Hall Ets
Where Does the Butterfly Go When It Rains?, May Garelick
Little Pieces of the West Wind, Christian Garrison
Snowy Day, Ezra Jack Keats
And It Rained, Ellen Raskin
Little Cloud, Robert Tallon
Umbrella, Taro Yashima
Hold My Hand, Charlotte Zolotow
Storm Book, Charlotte Zolotow

The Day the Hurricane Happened, Lonzo Anderson
Mr. Gumpy's Motor Car, John Burningham
The Bravest Babysitter, Barbara Greenberg
Wild Whirlwind, Dahlov Ipcar
When It Rains, Mary Kwitz
Rainy Day Together, Ellen Parsons
Elizabeth Catches a Fish, Jane Resh Thomas
Rain Drop Splash, Alvin R. Tresselt
White Snow, Bright Snow, Alvin R. Tresselt
What Causes It?, Bruce Wannamaker
The Weather, Jean Wilson
Rain Rain Rivers, Uri Shulevitz
It Rains—It Shines, William J. Smith
When the Wind Stops, Charlotte Zolotow

Books About Spring

Easter Egg Artists, Adrienne Adams
Humbug Rabbit, Lorna Balian
Three Friends Find Spring, Judy Delton
Spring Is, Janina Domanska
Strawberry Dress Escape, Crescent Dragonwagon
Going Barefoot, Aileen Fisher

Spring Is Here, Lois Lenski
In a Spring Garden, Richard Lewis

Adventures of Egbert the Easter Egg, Richard Armour
The Boy Who Didn't Believe in Spring, Lucille Clifton
My Mother and I, Aileen Fisher
Time for Jody, Wendy Kesselman
Mittens in May, Maxine Kumin
When It Rains, Mary Kwitz
Day of Spring, Betty Miles
Really Spring, Gene Zion

Books About Summer

Sand Cake, Frank Asch
Emilio's Summer Day, Miriam Bourne
On a Summer Day, Lois Lenski
City in Summer, Eleanor Schick
Milkweed Days, Jane Yolen
Summer Snowman, Gene Zion
Summer Is, Charlotte Zolotow

Books About Autumn

Woggle of Witches, Adrienne Adams
Acorn Tree, Valenti Angelo
Humbug Witch, Lorna Balian
Down Come the Leaves, Henrietta Bancroft
When Autumn Comes, Charles P. Fox
Now It's Fall, Lois Lenski
Autumn Harvest, Alvin R. Tresselt
Emily's Autumn, Janice Udry

Books About Winter

Another Story to Tell, Dick Bruna
Josie and the Snow, Helen E. Buckley
The Snow, John Burningham
Katy and the Big Snow, Virginia Lee Burton
Bear Weather, Lillie D. Chaffin
Winter Bear, Ruth Craft
Babar and Father Christmas, Jean DeBrunhoff
Snow Party, Beatrice DeRegniers

When the Snow Is Blue, Marguerite Dorian
The Snowy Day, Ezra Jack Keats
Winter Cat, Howard Knotts
In the Flaky, Crusty Morning, Karla Kuskin
I Like Winter, Lois Lenski
Day of Winter, Betty Miles
Mousekin's Woodland Sleepers, Edna Miller
The Biggest Snowstorm Ever, Diane Paterson

Cops and Robbers, Allan Ahlberg
Animals in Winter, Henrietta Bancroft
Walk in the Snow, Phyllis S. Busch
The Snow of Ohreeganau, Russell Erickson
Prairie Boy's Winter, William Kurelick
Vermont School Bus Ride, Constance Montgomery
City in Winter, Eleanor Schick
White Snow, Bright Snow, Alvin R. Tress, elt

Books About Combinations—Seasons

Green Eyes, A. Birnbaum
Seasons, John Burningham
Everything Happens to Aaron, P.P. Eastman
Pocketful of Seasons, Doris V. Foster
Who Will Wake Up Spring?, Sharon Lerner
A Book of Seasons, Alice Provensen

Twelve Months, Aliki
Swamp Spring, Carol Carrick
Four Stories for Four Seasons, Tomie De Paola
Spring Snow, Roger Duvoisin
I Like Weather, Aileen Fisher
Listen, Rabbit, Aileen Fisher
Mouse at Home, Mary Kwitz
The Park, Richard Lewis
Bonnie Bess, the Weathervane Horse, Alvin R. Tressell
It's Time Now, Alvin R. Tressell
Fafnerl, the Ice Dragon, Arnold Zimmerman

Holidays

All children look forward to holidays; as a matter of fact, many youngsters delineate their entire lives in terms of particular days which will bring special treats. Omitting any religious connotations, holidays are listed from the beginning of the year through year's end, in sequence, and we have included what is often a " holiday" of highest importance to a pre-schooler, his birthday.

Books About the New Year

The Chinese New Year, Hou-Tien Chang
Mister Chu, Norma Keating

Books About Valentine's Day

Little Love Story, Fernando Krahn
Valentine Box, Maud Lovelace
Miss Flora McFlimsy's Valentine, Mariana
The Hunt for Rabbit's Galosh, Ann Schweninger
The Valentine Box, Marjorie Thayer

A Sweetheart for Valentine, Lorna Balian
Valentine Party, Pamela Bianco
Valentine Cat, Clyde R. Bulla
Valentine Fantasy, Carolyn Haywood

Books About Spring Holidays

Easter Egg Artists, Adrienne Adams
Humbug Rabbit, Lorna Balian
The Golden Egg Book, Margaret Wise Brown
Country Bunny and the Little Golden Shoes, Marjorie Flack
The Easter Bunny That Overslept, Priscilla Friedrich
Jennie's Hat, Ezra Jack Keats
Daddy Long Ears, Robert Kraus
Miss Flora McFlimsy's May Day, Mariana
A Tale for Easter, Tasha Tudor
Candy Easter Bunny, Lisl Weil
Miss Suzy's Easter Suprise, Miriam Young
The Bunny Who Found Easter, Charlotte Zolotow

Adventures of Egbert, the Easter Egg, Richard Armour
A Rabbit for Easter, Carol Carrick
Easter Treat, Roger Duvoisin

May Day, Dorothy Lestima
Everything About Easter Rabbits, Wiltrud Roser
Let's Find Out About Trees: Arbor Day, Charles Shapp

Books About Halloween

A Woggle of Witches, Adrienne Adams
Humbug Witch, Lorna Balian
Hester, Byron Barton
Wobble the Witch Cat, Mary Calhoun
Old Mother Witch, Carol Carrick
Aunt Possum and the Pumpkin Man, Bruce Degen
Tell Me, Mr. Owl, Doris Foster
Space Witch, Don Freeman
So-So Cat, Edith Hurd
How Spider Saved Halloween, Robert Kraus
Witches' Holiday, Alice Low
Halloween Parade, Mary Lystad
One Dark Night, Edna Mitchell Preston
Suppose You Met a Witch, Ian Serraillier
The Kitten in the Pumpkin Patch, Richard Shaw
Pleasant Fieldmouse's Halloween Party, Jan Wahl
A Tiger Called Thomas, Charlotte Zolotow

Halloween Party, Lonzo Anderson
Pumpkin Smasher, Anita Benarde
Old Witch Rescues Halloween, Wende Devlin
Tilly Witch, Don Freeman
Gunhilde and the Halloween Spell, Virginia Kahl
Candy Witch, Steven Kroll
The Ghost with Halloween Hiccups, Stephen Mooser
Teeny Tiny Woman: An Old English Ghost Tale,
    Barbara Seuling
Trick or Treat, Louis Slobodkin
Ghost Poems, Edited by Daisy Wallace
Monster Poems, Edited by Daisy Wallace
Witch Poems, Edited by Daisy Wallace

Books About Fall Harvest Season—Thanksgiving

Sometimes It's Turkey, Sometimes It's Feathers,
    Lorna Balian
Thanksgiving Story, Alice Dalgleish

Books About Year-End—Including Christmas

Brownies—It's Christmas, Gladys Adshead
Bah, Humbug!, Lorna Balian
Twelve Bells for Santa, Crosby Bonsall
Babar and Father Christmas, Jean DeBrunhoff
Din, Dan, Don: It's Christmas, Janina Domanska
The Christmas Cat, Efner Tudor Holmes
Plum Pudding for Christmas, Virginia Kahl
Little Drummer Boy, Ezra Jack Keats
A Train for Jane, Norma Klein
Night Before Christmas, Hilary Knight
The Self-Made Snowman, Fernando Krahn
Small Sheep in a Pear Tree, Adrianne Lobel
Santa's Beard Is Soft and Warm, Bob Ottum
The Nicest Gift, Leo Politi
Twenty-Two, Twenty-Three, Ellen Raskin
Elizabeth, Liesel M. Skorpen
The Dolls' Christmas, Tasha Tudor

Cops and Robbers, Allan Ahlberg
Pepe's Private Christmas, Dorothy Corey
Firefly in a Fir Tree, Hilary Knight
Erik and the Christmas Horse, Hans Peterson
The Most Welcome Visitor, Robert Quackenbush
Babushka and the Three Kings, Ruth Robbins
Forever Christmas Tree, Yoshiko Uchida

Books About Birthdays

I Love You, Mary Jane, Lorna Balian
Secret for Grandmother's Birthday, Franz Brandenberg
Secret Birthday Message, Eric Carle
Don't You Remember?, Lucille Clifton
Babar's Birthday Surprise, Laurent DeBrunhoff
Veronica and the Birthday Present, Roger Duvoisin
Loudest Noise in the World, Benjamin Elkin
Ask Mr. Bear, Marjorie Flack
Dandelion, Don Freeman
Betty Bear's Birthday, Gyo Fujikawa
Birthday Trombone, Margaret Hartelius
Birthday for Frances, Russell Hoban
Happy Birthday, Sam, Pat Hutchins
The Birthday Wish, Chihiro Iwasaki
Letter to Amy, Ezra Jack Keats

Won't Somebody Play with Me?, Steven Kellogg
Birthday Party, Ruth Krauss
Suprise for Davy, Lois Lenski
Snapping Turtle's All Wrong Day, Peggy Parish
Lyle and the Birthday Party, Bernard Waber
Margaret's Birthday, Jan Wahl
Papa's Panda, Nancy Willard
Mister Rabbit and the Lovely Present, Charlotte Zolotow

Benjamin's 365 Birthdays, Judith Barrett
Amy's Doll, Barbara Brenner
Little Boy and the Birthdays, Helen E. Buckley
Horatio's Birthday, Eleanor Clymer
Monster! Monster!, David Harrison
Little Owl, Keeper of the Trees, Ronald Himler
Peter's Long Walk, Lee Kingman
Happy Birthday, Oliver, Pierre Le-Tan
Me Day, Joan Lexau
A Birthday for the Princess, Anita Lobel
Portly McSwine, James Marshall
Go Away, Dog, Joan Nodset
Love from Uncle Clyde, Nancy W. Parker
Ronnie, Eileen Rosenbaum
Big Cowboy Western, Ann Herbert Scott
Birthday, John Steptoe
The Birthday Visitor, Yoshiko Uchida
Over and Over, Charlotte Zolotow

Group Emphases

Because we should stress commonality rather than differences, citing titles by various ethnic groups might seem something of a contradiction. However, for the convenience of those who might want to use books for special purposes, such as Black Awareness Week or a unit on Hispanic heritage, a few specialized lists are included below.

Books About Black Americans

Case of the Scaredy Cats, Crosby Bonsall
The Day I Had to Play with My Sister, Crosby Bonsall
Doctor Shawn, Petronella Breinberg
Joey's Cat, Robert Burch

Abby, Jeanette Caines
Daddy, Jeanette Caines
Amifika, Lucille Clifton
Don't You Remember?, Lucille Clifton
Everett Anderson's Friend, Lucille Clifton
Everett Anderson's Nine Month Long, Lucille Clifton
Everett Anderson's 1-2-3, Lucille Clifton
Three Wishes, Lucille Clifton
Corduroy, Don Freeman
A Pocket for Corduroy, Don Freeman
First Pink Light, Eloise Greenfield
Good News, Eloise Greenfield
She Come Bringing Me That Little Baby Girl, Eloise Greenfield
Free as a Frog, Elizabeth Hodges
Jasper Makes Music, Betty Horvath
Sara and the Door, Virginia Jensen
Hi, Cat, Ezra Jack Keats
Letter to Amy, Ezra Jack Keats
Peter's Chair, Ezra Jack Keats
Snowy Day, Ezra Jack Keats
Whistle for Willie, Ezra Jack Keats
Knee-High Man, Julius Lester
Valentine Day, Maud Lovelace
The Little Brown Hen, Patricia Miles Martin
Sam, N.H. Scott
What Mary Jo Shared, Janice Udry

Black Is Brown Is Tan, Arnold Adoff
Shawn Goes to School, Petronella Breinberg
Shawn's Red Bike, Petronella Breinberg
The Boy Who Didn't Believe in Spring, Lucille Clifton
My Brother Fine with Me, Lucille Clifton
Gabrielle and Selena, Peter Desbarats
Me and Nessie, Eloise Greenfield
City Rhythms, Ann Grifalconi
Evan's Corner, Elizabeth S. Hill
Benjie, Joan Lexau
Benjie on His Own, Joan Lexau

Big Sister Tells Me That I'm Black, Arnold Adoff
Swimming Hole, Jerrold Beim
Two Is a Team, Lorraine Beim
Mr. Kelso's Lion, Arna Bontemps
Raccoons Are for Loving, Miriam Bourne
Wagon Wheels, Barbara Brenner
All Us Come Cross the Water, Lucille Clifton

Good, Says Jerome, Lucille Clifton
Thalia Brown and the Blue Jug, Michelle Dionetti
Send Wendell, Genevieve Gray
Bubbles, Eloise Greenfield
Sound of Sunshine, Sound of Rain, Florence Heide
Apt. 3, Ezra Jack Keats
Dreams, Ezra Jack Keats
Goggles, Ezra Jack Keats
Maggie and the Pirate, Ezra Jack Keats
Pet Show!, Ezra Jack Keats
Harriet and the Promised Land, Jacob Lawrence
Me Day, Joan Lexau
The Hundred Penny Box, Sharon Mathis
Don't Ride the Bus on Monday: The Rosa Parks Story, L. Meriwether
The Drinking Gourd, F.N. Monjo
My Daddy Don't Go to Work, Madeena Spray Nolan
A Ride on High, Candida Palmer
No Trespassing, Ray Prather
Fun for Chris, Blossom E. Randall
Ronnie, Eileen Rosenbaum
Big Cowboy Western, Ann Herbert Scott
I Love Gram, Ruth A. Sonneborn
Birthday, John Steptoe
My Special Best Words, John Steptoe
Stevie, John Steptoe
Bonnie Bess, the Weathervane Horse, Alvin R. Tresselt
Mary Jo's Grandmother, Janice Udry
A Cool Ride in the Sky, Diane Wolkstein

Books About Blacks Outside United States

Why Mosquitos Buzz in People's Ears, Verna Aardema
Such Is the Way of the World, Benjamin Elkin
Omoteji's Baby Brother, Mary-Joan Gerson

Half-a-Ball-of-Kenki, Verna Aardema
Who's in Rabbit's House: A Masai Tale, Verna Aardema
The Third Gift, Jan Carew
I Can Squash Elephants: A Masai Tale About Monsters, Malcolm Carrick
Jambo Means Hello: Swahili Alphabet Book, Muriel Feelings
Moja Means One: Swahili Counting Book, Muriel Feelings
Coconut Thieves, Edited by Catherine Fournier
Why the Sky Is Far Away, Mary-Joan Gerson

A Story, A Story, Gail Haley
Goats Who Killed the Leopard, Judy Hawes
The River That Gave Gifts, Margo Humphrey
Rafiki, Nola Langner
Anansi the Spider: A Tale from Ashanti, Gerald McDermott
Magic Tree: A Tale from the Congo, Gerald McDermott
Femi and Old Grandaddie, Adjai Robinson
Clever Turtle, A.K. Roche
When the Drum Sang, Anne Rockwell
Akimba and the Magic Cow, Retold by Anne Rose
Small Boy Chuku, Alice W. Wellman
Tatu and the Honey Bird, Alice W. Wellman
Abdul, Rosemary Wells
The Magic Orange Tree and Other Haitian Tales, Diane Wolkstein
Cornrows, Camille Yarbrough

Books About Asians/Orientals

Chinese Mother Goose Rhymes, Edited by Robert Wyndam
Momo's Kitten, Taro Yashima
Umbrella, Taro Yashima

Wish for Little Sister, Jacqueline Ayer
The Boy and the Bird, Tamao Fujita
Rice Bowl Pet, Patricia Miles Martin
Aekyung's Dream, Min Paek
Don't Put the Vinegar in the Copper, Kate Wong

Old Woman and the Red Pumpkin, Molly G. Bang
Little One Inch, Barbara Brenner
Iron Moonhunter, Kathleen Chang
Chinese New Year, Hou-Tien Cheng
Little Monk and the Tiger: A Tale of Thailand, Arnold Dobrin
Moke and Poki in the Rain Forest, Mamoru Funai
Legend of the Orange Princess, Mehlli Boghai
Dance, Dance, Amy Chan, Lucy Hawkinson
Favorite Children's Stories of China and Tibet, Lotta Carswell Hume
Mr. Chu, Norma Keating
The Princess of the Rice Fields, Hisako Kimishima
Dragon Kite, Thomas P. Lewis
The Dog and the Boat Boy, Patricia Miles Martin
I Have a Sister: My Sister Is Deaf, Jeanne Peterson

Moy Moy, Leo Politi
Moon Blossom and the Golden Penny, Louis Slobodkin
Japan: A Week in Daisuke's World, Martha Sternberg
Little Weaver of Thai-Yen Village, Khanh Tuyet
The Birthday Visitor, Yoshiko Uchida
Sumi and the Goat and the Tokyo Express,
   Yoshiko Uchida
Crow Boy, Taro Yashima
Seashore Story, Taro Yashima
The Village Tree, Taro Yashima

Books About Hispanic People

Jo, Flo and Yolanda, Carol DePoix
Martin's Father, Margrit Eichler
Gilberto and the Wind, Marie Hall Ets
Angelo, the Naughty One, Helen Garrett
The Nicest Gift, Leo Politi
Pedro, Angel of Olvera Street, Leo Politi
Friday Night Is Papa Night, Ruth A. Sonneborn

Riddle of the Drum: A Tale from Tizapan, Mexico,
   Verna Aardema
Maria Teresa, Mary Atkinson
Raymond and the Pirate Gull, Robert Barry
Emilio's Summer Day, Miriam Bourne
Juan Bobo and the Pig: A Puerto Rican Folktale,
   Bernice Chardiet
Pepe's Private Christmas, Dorothy Corey
Yolanda's Hike, Tomas Rodriguez Gaspar
The Wentletrap, Jean C. George
My Dog Is Lost, Ezra Jack Keats
The Return of Chato, Susan Lewke
A Week in Henry's World: El Barrio, Inger McCabe
Yagua Days, Cruz Martel
The Incas Knew, Tillie Pine
Atariba and Niguayona: Puerto Rico, Harriet Rohmer
Cuna Song: Panama, Harriet Rohmer
The Headless Pirate: Costa Rica, Harriet Rohmer
How We Came to the Fifth World: Aztecs, Harriet Rohmer
Land of Icy Death: Chile, Harriet Rohmer
The Little Horse of Seven Colors: Nicaragua,
   Harriet Rohmer
The Magic Boys: Guatemala, Harriet Rohmer
The Mighty God Viracocha: Peru, Harriet Rohmer

Skyworld Woman: The Philippines, Harriet Rohmer
The Treasure of Guatavita: Colombia, Harriet Rohmer
Poco, Garry Smith

Books About American Indians

Corn Is Maize: The Gift of the Indians, Aliki
Little Runner of the Longhouse, Betty Baker
They Put on Masks, Byrd Baylor
Red Fox and His Canoe, Nathaniel Benchley
Small Wolf, Nathaniel Benchley
Ring in the Prairie, John Bierhorst
Six Days from Sunday, Betty Biestervelt
Stone Giants and Flying Heads, Told by Joseph Bruchac
Turkey Brothers and Other Tales of Iroquois,
　Told by Joseph Bruchac
In My Mother's House, Ann Clark
A Gift, Claudia Fregosi
Trees Stand Shining: Poetry of American Indians, Hettie Jones
Wa O'Ka, Jean Latham
Little Indians' ABC, Faustina H. Lucero
Goat in the Rug, Martin Link
Arrow to the Sun: A Pueblo Indian Tale, Gerald McDermott
Little Indian, Peggy Parish
The Great Fish, Peter Parnall
Salt Boy, Mary Perrine
Dancing Stars: An Iroquois Legend, Anne Rockwell
The Angry Moon, William Sleator
Mountain Goats of Temlaham, William Toye
The Battle of the Wind Gods, Judy Varga
Squirrel's Song, Diane Wolkstein
*Tonweya and the Eagles and Other Lakota Indian Tales by
　Rosebud,* Retold by Yellow Robe

Books About Eskimos and Canadian Indians

Matuk, Eskimo Boy, Vee Crawston
Proud Maiden, Tungak and the Sun, Mirra Ginsburg
Three Visitors, Marjorie Hopkins
Adventures of Muku, Geraldine Nicholson
Ootah's Lucky Day, Peggy Parish
On Mother's Lap, Ann Herbert Scott
Muktu, the Backward Muskox, Heather Kellerhals-Stewart
How Summer Came to Canada, William Toye
Let's Find Out About Eskimos, Eleanor Wiesenthal

Books About Cajuns

Cajun Columbus, Alice Durio
Cajun Alphabet, James Rice
Gaston Goes to Mardi Gras, James Rice
Gaston Goes to Texas, James Rice
Gaston, the Green-Nosed Alligator, James Rice

Informational Books

In this category there is a great range of subject matter, and in order to find material written at a level comprehensible to pre-schoolers, some titles designated "I Can Read" or "Let's Read and Find Out" have been included. This does not mean that these can be called literature in the strict sense. It signifies only that in order to satisfy the curiosity of a four-year-old about the natural sciences or geography, for instance, it is sometimes necessary to choose books written to be read silently by children in an older age range.

The general heading "Informational" refers to the main object of certain books; that is, the imparting of factual material, but in this category too there will be some titles which could be called "fiction" where the author has constructed a "story" in the traditional sense, with plot, characters, and setting, in order to catch and hold the interest of the average pre-schooler. Where the book has this format, the same rules about a straightforward, exciting story, vividly drawn characters, and a clear sense of time and place characteristic of any superior fictional work, hold true, and, of course, the illustrations must be both literally accurate and aesthetically pleasing. Furthermore, whether an informational book is done as a story or as what we might call straight non-fiction, it must meet one more criterion, perhaps the most significant one for this kind of book—it must be *factually accurate at whatever level it is written.*

What do we mean by "whatever level it is written"?

Informational books in almost all categories can be individually designed so that they are appropriate for different age levels. For instance, alphabet books all have a single subject—the twenty-six letters in the English alphabet—but they range widely in complexity. For the youngest child, we might want a single capital letter presented on each page, with a clear and literal rendition of an object which is spelled beginning with that letter, say an "A" and an apple. For a child nearing school age, however, we might prefer an alphabet book which shows both the upper and lower case letters with a less obvious example, such as "aardvark," perhaps modified by adjectives. The point is that whatever is presented as factual may be simple or quite complex, but it must never be incorrect.

There is also an opportunity in this area to consider concepts of a more philosophical nature, but again, adherence to fact is imperative. For instance, the book *What Is a Girl? What Is a Boy?* explains with tastefully done photographs that it is not the length of one's hair (a boy is shown with long hair), the clothes he or she wears (a girl is shown in slacks), or the sports in which a child participates (a girl is shown playing basketball) that makes the youngster male or female, but that it is the physiological difference —having a vagina or a penis—that designates one's sex. And it goes on to say and show that a girl grows into a woman and a boy grows into a man. Suitable for five or six-year-olds, the idea of non-sexism is very clear, but at the same time the book imparts information about the human body in a wholesome fashion. It does not attempt to appeal to the more sophisticated child of ten or twelve who is seeking "sex education," but simply gives *accurate information* within a particular and limited frame of biological reference.

As a further example, we might look at an all-time favorite, *The Very Hungry Caterpillar*, which combines successfully some fictional elements with factual information. There is very little plot, per se, and the only "character" is the very tiny egg which turns into a caterpillar and then into a butterfly.

Without doubt, a great part of this book's attractiveness is due to the magnificent illustrations which combine stylization of the sun and the moon, for example, with pictures of edibles that capture the essence of each item. There is some fantasy here too, since the "very hungry caterpillar" eats through "one apple on Monday, two pears on Tuesday," and so on, and he finally ends up with a stomach ache on Saturday after he's eaten through everything from "one piece of chocolate cake" to one "slice of watermelon," tasting everything in between from a pickle to an ice-cream cone! Nevertheless, the days of the week are correctly ordered; and the way in which the egg progresses from a tiny caterpillar to a "big, fat caterpillar," and then "builds a small house around himself," finally pushing his way out of the cocoon at the end of the story is a completely factual account of the process involved in the "birth" of a butterfly.

In the lists which follow, every effort has been made to cover books which can be considered "informational," whether or not the manner of presentation is "fictional." Titles are listed in two general categories: first, those which merely inform about particular subjects, such as animals, plants, and the environment; and, secondly, those which involve particular skills, such as color recognition, counting, and concept books. All have been chosen to expand the youngster's knowledge of himself, the world in which he lives, and the animate and inanimate objects with which he shares that world. As explained in the introduction, a title may well appear in more than one list if its content fits into more than a single category.

Once more, we must keep in mind that no list is really "complete," nor can we assume that every possible category has been taken into account. Readers are strongly urged to add titles as the need arises.

Informational Books—General

Baby's First Golden Books, Anon.
Baby's First Library—Counting, Anon.
Baby's First Library—ABC, Anon.
The Very First Book of Colors, Eric Carle
Shape Books, Elisa Gittings
A House Is a House for Me, Mary Ann Hoberman
Come with Me to Nursery School, Edith Hurd
Big Red Bus, Ethel Kessler
Pat the Bunny, Dorothy Kunhardt
What's That Noise?, Carol Nicklaus
I Spy, Lucille Ogle
Santa's Beard Is Soft and Warm, Bob Ottum
My Doctor, Harlow Rockwell
My Nursery School, Harlow Rockwell
It Looked Like Spilt Milk, Charles G. Shaw
My First Picture Book, Leonard Weisgard
Betsy's First Day at Nursery School, Gunilla Wolde
Tommy Goes to the Doctor, Gunilla Wolde

I Hate to Take a Bath, Judi Barrett
Tell Me Some More, Crosby Bonsall
A Kiss Is Round, Blossom Budney
The School, John Burningham
Choo Choo, Virginia Lee Burton
The Mixed-Up Chameleon, Eric Carle
Visit to the Hospital, Francine Chase
Messy Sally, Gladys Cretan
Freight Train, Donald Crews
The Everyday Train, Amy Ehrlich
Green Says Go, Ed Emberley
Hey, Look at Me: A City ABC, Sandy Grant
Mommy Works on Dresses, Louise De Grosbois

Handful of Surprises, Anne Heathers
Eighteen Cousins, Carol G. Hogan
You Can Be Taller, Axel Horn
Changes, Changes, Pat Hutchins
Clocks and More Clocks, Pat Hutchins
Ten Big Farms, Dahlov Ipcar
Only One Ant, Leonore Klein
What Is an Inch?, Leonore Klein
Firemen, William Kotzwinkle
One Dancing Drum, Gail Kredenser
Policeman Small, Lois Lenski
The Pop-Up Book of Trucks, Loretta Lustig
Red Light, Green Light, Golden MacDonald
What's in the Dark?, Carl Memling
Kittens' ABC, Claire T. Newberry
Can You Find What's Missing?, Carol Nicklaus
I Hear Sounds in a Children's World, Lucille Ogle
Colors, Jan Pienkowski
Little Red Caboose, Marian Potter
Listen! Listen!, Ann Rand
This Is My Father and Me, Dorka Raynor
My Dentist, Anne Rockwell
Head to Toe, Anne Rockwell
Apples to Zippers: An Alphabet Book, Patricia Ruben
The Magic Pencil, Scapa
I Know What I Like, Norma Simon
The See and Hear and Smell and Taste and Touch Book,
    Elwood Smith
Crash, Bang, Boom, Peter Spier
Emergency Room: An ABC Tour, Julie Steedman
The Daddy Book, R. Stewart
My Toolbox Book, Jan Sukus
Giggly-Wiggly Snicketty-Snick, Robin Supraner
Elizabeth Gets Well, Alfons Weber, M.D.
Melissa, Lisl Weil
Big Book of Fire Engines, George Zaffo
Big Book of Real Boats and Ships, George Zaffo

My Hands, Aliki
Anno's Alphabet: An Adventure in Imagination,
    Mitsumasa Anno
Little People of the Night, Laura Bannon
Who Built the Bridge?, Norman Bate
Pelle's New Suit, Elsa Beskow
Pancakes! Pancakes!, Eric Carle
Thanksgiving Story, Alice Dalgliesh
Sign Book, William Dugan

Hold Everything, Sam Epstein
X Marks the Spot, Eleanor Felder
Cowboys, What Do They Do?, Carla Greene
City Rhythms, Ann Grifalconi
How We Live, Anita Harper
How We Work, Anita Harper
Things That Go, Richard Hefter
ABC of Cars, Trucks and Machines, Adelaide Holl
Boats, Ruth Lachman
The Truck Book, Harry McNaught
Easy Book of Grand Prix Racing, Ross
All Kinds of Families, Norma Simon
Left, Right, Left, Right, Muriel Stanek
What Is a Girl? What Is a Boy?, Stephanie Waxman
Saturday Walk, Ethel Wright

Do You Know What Time It Is?, Roz Abisch
Waymond the Whale, Caroline Aimar
Sometimes I Dance Mountains, Byrd Baylor
They Put on Masks, Byrd Baylor
Together, June Behrens
Being Alone, Being Together, Terry Berger
A Friend Can Help, Terry Berger
How Does It Feel When Your Parents Get Divorced?, Terry Berger
I Have Feelings, Terry Berger
New Baby, Terry Berger
Do You Know What I Know?, Helen Borten
Do You See What I See?, Helen Borten
Someone Always Needs a Policeman, David Brown
The Chinese New Year, Hou-Tien Cheng
Matuk, the Eskimo Boy, Vee Crawston
What Makes a Telephone Work?, Leonard Darwin
Babar's French Lessons, Laurent DeBrunhoff
Babar's Spanish Lessons, Laurent DeBrunhoff
Charlie Needs a Cloak, Tomie De Paola
Women at Their Work, Edited by Betty English
Pick It Up, Sam Epstein
Where's Gomer?, Norma Farber
Rosa-Too-Little, Sue Felt
Dirk's Wooden Shoes, Ilona Fennema
Chalk Box Story, Don Freeman
Will's Quill, Don Freeman
The Clock, Constantine Georgiou
What Can She Be? A Farmer, Gloria Goldreich
What Can She Be? A Lawyer, Gloria Goldreich
What Can She Be? A Newscaster, Gloria Goldreich

What Can She Be? A Police Officer, Gloria Goldreich
What Can She Be? A Veterinarian, Gloria Goldreich
Keep an Eye on Kevin: Safety Begins at Home, Genevieve Gray
Everybody Has a House and Everybody Eats, Mary M. Green
You and Your Child Measuring Things, Iris Grender
The Two Georges, Monica Gunning
Riddle Rat, Donald Hall
At Home: A Visit in Four Languages, Esther Hautzig
In School: Learning in Four Languages, Esther Hautzig
Dance, Dance, Amy Chan, Lucy Hawkinson
What's Inside?, Barbara Shook Hazen
Yes and No: A Book of Opposites, Richard Hefter
Nock Family Circus, Ursula Huber
Learning About Love, Jordan Jenkins
Upstairs and Downstairs, Ryerson Johnson
Odd Jobs, Tony Johnston
Baseball Book, Joe Kaufman
Just a Minute: A Book About Time, Leonore Klein
Just Like You, Leonore Klein
Girls Can Be Anything, Norma Klein
Big Book of Helicopters, Clayton Knight
The Life of Numbers, Fernando Krahn
Open House for Butterflies, Ruth Krauss
Safety Can Be Fun, Munro Leaf
Taking Pictures, Nina Leen
More Tell Me Why, Arkady Leokum
Picking and Weaving, Bijou LeTord
The Dentist and Me, Joy Schalaben-Lewis
Goat in the Rug, Martin Link
Days of the Week, Beman Lord
Black Is Beautiful, Ann McGovern
What Can You Do With a Pocket?, Eve Merriam
A House for Everyone, Betty Miles
Ashanti to Zulu: African Traditions, Margaret W. Musgrove
What Time Is It?, John Peter
I Have a Sister: My Sister Is Deaf, Jeanne Peterson
Measurements and How We Use Them, Tillie Pine
Let's Find Out About Streets, Valerie Pitt
Let's Build a House, Billy Pope
Let's Go to the Supermarket, Billy Pope
Let's Visit a Rubber Company, Billy Pope
Let's Visit a Silver Company, Billy Pope
Let's Visit the Newspaper, Billy Pope
Let's Visit the Railroad, Billy Pope
Along Came the Model T, Robert Quackenbush
I Know a Lot of Things, Ann Rand
No Pushing, No Ducking: Safety in the Water, Barbara Rinkoff
Machines, Anne Rockwell

Tool Box, Anne Rockwell
Thru Way, Anne Rockwell
Night Lights, Joel Rothman
Size, Distance, Weight: A First Look at Measuring,
　Solveig P. Russell
Train Whistles: A Language in Code, Helen R. Sattler
Richard Scarry's Hop Aboard, Here We Go, Richard Scarry
How Do You Travel?, Miriam Schlein
One Small Blue Bead, Byrd Schweitzer
More Potatoes!, Millicent E. Selsam
Chicken Soup with Rice: A Book of Months, Maurice Sendak
What Happens When You Go to the Hospital, Arthur Shay
One Way: A Trip with Traffic Signs, Leonard Shortall
Sleep Is for Everyone, Paul Showers
Oh, What a Noise!, Uri Shulevitz
I Was So Mad!, Norma Simon
Read About the Policeman, Louis Slobodkin
Jeff's Hospital Book, Harriet Sobol
About Handicaps, Sara Bonnett Stein
About Phobias, Sara Bonnett Stein
The Adopted One, Sara Bonnett Stein
The Trucks That Haul by Night, Leonard Stevens
Let's Catch a Fish, Jack Stokes
Cars, Trucks and Trains, Su Swallow
Little Red Lighthouse and Great Gray Bridge,
　Hildegarde Swift
Come to the City, Ruth Tensen
Easy or Hard? That's a Good Question, Tobi Tobias
Quiet or Noisy? That's a Good Question, Tobi Tobias
Where Does It Come From? That's a Good Question,
　Tobi Tobias
Around the Year, Tasha Tudor
The Rat, the Ox and the Zodiac, Dorothy Van Woerkom
One Is No Fun, But Twenty Is Plenty, Ilse-Margret Vogel
Sights and Sounds of the City, Hope Warriner
Animal Dictionary, Jane Watson
Sugar on Snow, Nancy D. Watson
Let's Find Out About Eskimos, Eleanor Wiesenthal
Fisherman Who Needed a Knife: Why People Need Money,
　Marie Winn
Man Who Made Tops: Why People Do Different Work,
　Marie Winn
I Like Trains, Catherine Wooley
Beware the Polar Bear: Safety on the Ice, Miriam Young
If I Drove a Tractor, Miriam Young
If I Drove A Train, Miriam Young
If I Drove a Truck, Miriam Young
All of Grandmother's Clocks: About Time, Sandra Ziegler
All Falling Down, Gene Zion

The Park Book, Charlotte Zolotow
The Sky Was Blue, Charlotte Zolotow

Informational Books—Geography

Around the World With Ant and Bee, Angela Banner
Ship in the Field, Henry Boschini
Scuffy the Tugboat, Gertrude Crampton
Babar Comes to America, Laurent DeBrunhoff
Island of Hawaii, Louise Floethe
Turkey: A Week in Samil's World, Louis Goldman
A Week in Hagar's World: Israel, Louis Goldman
Supreme, Superb, Exalted . . . One and Only Magic Building, William Kotzwinkle
Kuma Is a Maori Girl, Pat Lawson
Travels of Marco, Jean Merrill
Grandparents Around the World, Edited by Caroline Rubin
Islands, William M. Stephens
Japan: A Week in Daisuke's World, Martha Sternberg
Little Fox Goes to the End of the World, Ann Tompert

Informational Books—History

Ox-Cart Man, Donald Hall
The Tyrannosaurus Game, Steven Kroll
Before the Indians, Julian May
Taxi Dog, Svend Otto

Diogenes: The Story of the Greek Philosopher, Aliki
Fossils Tell of Long Ago, Aliki
My Visit to the Dinosaurs, Aliki
Small Wolf, Nathaniel Benchley
Tigger: Story of a Mayan Ocelot, Bunny
Life Story, Virginia Lee Burton
Cajun Columbus, Alice Durio
El Circo Magico: Finding Magic Circus, MacDuff Everton
Danbury's Burning, Anne Grant
Ben Goes into Business, Marilyn Hirsch
I Like Old Clothes, Mary Ann Hoberman
Flying Reptiles in the Age of Dinosaurs, John Kaufman
Elephant Boy, William Kotzwinkle
When Grandmother Was Young, Maxine Kumin
Harriet and the Promised Land, Jacob Lawrence
Bright Fawn and Me, Jay Leech

A Perfect Place to Be, Bijou LeTord
On the Day Peter Stuyvesant Sailed into Town, Arnold Lobel
Six Silver Spoons, Janette S. Lowrey
Rolling the Cheese, Patricia Martin
Drinking Gourd, F.N. Monjo
Looking for Ifuago Mountain, Al Robles
Onion Maidens, A.K. Roche
Pumpkin Heads, A.K. Roche
The Surprising Things Maui Did, Jay Williams
Martin Luther King, Jr., Beth Williams
Monsters of the Middle Ages, William Wise

Informational Books—Animals

Baby's Farm Animals, Anon.
Brimax Animal Board Books, Anon.
Green Eyes, A. Birnbaum
Baby Animal Book, Daphne Davis
Sheep Book, Carmen Goodyear
Animal Babies, Arthur S. Gregor
Little Elephant, Arthur S. Gregor
Bright Barnyard, Dahlov Ipcar
See the Circus, H.A. Rey
Big Book of Wild Animals, Sutton
Baby Farm Animals, Garth Williams
Baby Animals, Naoma Zimmerman
Animal Babies, Max Zoll

Let's Find Out About Butterflies, Roz Abisch
Bears In—Bears Out, Catherine Barr
Littlest Mule, John Barrett
Bath Time, Jean Bethell
If You Were an Ant, Barbara Brenner
Caterpillar's Story, Achim Breoger
The Very Hungry Caterpillar, Eric Carle
Very Long Tail: A Folding Book, Eric Carle
Clearing in the Forest, Carol Carrick
Bear Weather, Lillie D. Chaffin
A Chick Hatches, Joanna Cole
My Puppy Is Born, Joanna Cole
The Most Amazing Hide and Seek Alphabet Book, Robert Crowther
Little Duck, Judy Dunn
Sleepy Time, Eva Evans
As I Was Crossing Boston Common, Norma Farber

Happy Dromedary, Berniece Freschet
Be Nice to Spiders, Margaret Graham
Eric Gurney's Pop-Up Book of Dogs, Eric Gurney
What If the Lion Eats Me and I Fall into a Hippopotamus' Mud Hole?, Emily Hanlon
Ladybug, Ladybug, Fly Away Home, Judy Hawes
My Daddy Longlegs, Judy Hawes
Nanny Goat and the Fierce Dog, Charles Keeping
Piebald Pup, Irina Korschunow
Roar and More, Karla Kuskin
Inch by Inch, Leo Lionni
The Chicken and the Egg, Iela Mari
Mousekin's Woodland Sleepers, Edna Miller
Patty Cake, Elizabeth Moody
Celestino Piatti's Animal ABC, Celestino Piatti
Anybody at Home?, H.A. Rey
Feed the Animals, H.A. Rey
Animals in the Zoo, Feodor Rojankovsky
Animals on the Farm, Feodor Rojankovsky
Great Big Wild Animal Book, Feodor Rojankovsky
What Do the Animals Say?, Grace Skaar
Gobble, Growl, Grunt, Peter Spier
I Was All Thumbs, Bernard Waber
Frog, Frog, Frog, Robert Welber
Brian Wildsmith's Birds, Brian Wildsmith
Brian Wildsmith's Fishes, Brian Wildsmith
Python's Party, Brian Wildsmith
Little New Kangaroo, Bernard Wiseman

Whiskers, the Rabbit, Rebecca Anders
Why Can't I?, Jeanne Bendick
I Caught a Lizard, Gladys Conklin
We Went Looking, Aileen Fisher
Web in the Grass, Berniece Freschet
The Man Who Loved Birds, Ken Kenniston
The Tadpole and the Frog, Susan Knobler
Koalas, Bernice Kohn
Hi, All You Rabbits, Carl Memling
Butterfly Book, Cynthia Overbeck
Curly the Piglet, Cynthia Overbeck
Fish Book, Cynthia Overbeck
Did a Bear Just Walk There?, Ann Rand

Green Grass and White Milk, Aliki
Long Lost Coelacanth and Other Living Fossils, Aliki
Wild and Woolly Mammoths, Aliki

Everyday Birds, Gertrude E. Allen
Everyday Insects, Gertrude E. Allen
Everyday Turtles, Toads and Their Kin, Gertrude E. Allen
I Like Birds, Rist. Arnold
True Book of Reptiles, Lois Ballard
Animals in Winter, Henrietta Bancroft
Hosie's Aviary, Tobias Baskin
In the Jungle, Eugene Booth
Under the Ground, Eugene Booth
Is It Bigger Than a Sparrow: A Box for Young Birdwatchers, Barbara Brenner
Lion Island, William Bridges
Puddles and Ponds—Living Things in Watery Places, Phyllis S. Busch
Skunk for a Day, Roger A. Caras
The Blue Lobster, Carol Carrick
A Rabbit for Easter, Carol Carrick
Toad Hunt, Janet Chenery
Little Apes, Gladys Conklin
Lucky Ladybugs, Gladys Conklin
Tarantula, the Giant Spider, Gladys Conklin
We Like Bugs, Gladys Conklin
When Insects Are Babies, Gladys Conklin
Big Book of Cats, Gladys Cook
Giraffes at Home, Ann Cooke
Fish from Japan, Elizabeth Cooper
Steven and the Green Turtle, William J. Cromie
A Child's Book of Birds, Kathleen Daly
Worms, Lois Darling
Animals Everywhere, Ingri D'Aulaire
What Is a Mammal?, Jennifer W. Day
Emperor Penguins, Jean-Claude Deguine
One Dragon to Another, Ned Delaney
Fawn in the Woods, Irmegarde Eberle
Robins on the Windowsill, Irmegarde Eberle
Goats of Agadez, Victor Engelbert
The Amazing Bee, William W. Fox
Turtle Pond, Berniece Freschet
The Eel's Strange Journey, Joy T. Friedman
Birds at Night, Roma Gans
Bird Talk, Roma Gans
Humming Birds in the Garden, Roma Gans
About Owls, May Garelick
The Parrot Book, Tibor Gergely
Rosy: The Oldest Horse in St. Augustine, Miriam Gilbert
Long Winter's Sleep: Story of Animal Hibernation, Ellen H. Goins

Sunlit Sea, Augusta Goldin
Dinosaurs and Prehistoric Animals, Simon Goodenough
A Book About Pandas, Ruth Belov Gross
Snakes, Ruth Belov Gross
What Is That Alligator Saying?, Ruth Belov Gross
Bees and Beelines, Judy Hawes
Shrimps, Judy Hawes
Spring Peepers, Judy Hawes
Watch Honeybees with Me, Judy Hawes
What I Like About Toads, Judy Hawes
Why Frogs Are Wet, Judy Hawes
Shetland Ponies, Lilo Hess
Carab: The Trapdoor Spider, Alice Hopf
Let's Look at Insects, Harriet E. Huntington
Look for a Bird, Edith Hurd
The Mother Beaver, Edith Hurd
The Mother Whale, Edith Hurd
Sandpipers, Edith Hurd
Starfish, Edith Hurd
A Foal Is Born, Hans-Heinrich Isenbart
Moon Jelly, Marie Jenkins
Nothing But a Dog, Bobbi Katz
Bats in the Dark, John Kaufman
A Day in the Life of a Baby Gibbon, Helen Kay
Rrra-a-h, Eros Keith
Frogs Merry, Juliet Kepes
Raccoons, Bernice Kohn
The Spider Makes a Web, Joan Lexau
Horseshoe Crab, Robert McClung
Ladybug, Robert McClung
Sea Star, Robert McClung
Little Whale, Ann McGovern
Sharks, Ann McGovern
Woodchuck, Faith McNulty
The Apple and the Moth, Iela Mari
Horses: How They Came to Be, Julian May
Gaggle of Geese, Eve Merriam
Wharf Rat, Miska Miles
Blue Whale, Kizue Mizumura
Opossum, Kizue Mizumura
Seahorse, Robert Morris
The Biggest and Littlest Animals, Tony Palazzo
The Horse Book, Virginia Parsons
Penguins Are Coming, Richard L. Penney
Hand, Hand, Fingers, Thumb, Al Perkins
Billions of Bugs, Haris Petie
Red Tag Comes Back, Frederick Phleger

Our Animal Friends at Maple Hill Farm, Alice Provensen
Polly, the Guinea Pig, Margaret Sanford Pursell
What's Happening to Daisy?, Sandy Rabinowitz
Laughing Camera for Children, Edited by Hanns Reich
Animal for Alan, Edward Ricciuti
Catch a Whale by the Tail, Edward Ricciuti
The Life Cycle Book of Frogs, Ronald Ridout
Toad, Anne Rockwell
The Crusty Ones: A First Look at Crustaceans, Solveig P. Russell
What Good Is a Tail?, Solveig P. Russell
Cottontail Rabbit, Charles Schwartz
When Water Animals Are Babies, Charles Schwartz
Downey Woodpecker, Paul McCutcheon Sears
Animals of the Sea, Millicent E. Selsam
Benny's Animals and How He Put Them in Order, Millicent E. Selsam
Egg to Chick, Millicent E. Selsam
How Animals Sleep, Millicent E. Selsam
How Puppies Grow, Millicent E. Selsam
Let's Get Turtles, Millicent E. Selsam
When an Animal Grows, Millicent E. Selsam
A First Look at Mammals, Millicent E. Selsam
First Look at Snakes, Lizards and Other Reptiles, Millicent E. Selsam
Some Swell Pup, Maurice Sendak
Let's Find Out About Snakes, Charles Shapp
A Fish Out of School, Evelyn Shaw
Octopus, Evelyn Shaw
Flamingo: Bird of Flame, William M. Stephens
Hermit Crab, William M. Stephens
Octupus, William M. Stephens
Beaver Pond, Alvin R. Tresselt
Fish and Mammals, Jennifer Vaughan
A Spider Might, Tom Walther
Lambs, Martin Weaver
Let's Find Out About Mosquitos, David Webster
Brian Wildsmith's Wild Animals, Brian Wildsmith
Squirrels, Brian Wildsmith
Animals of Warmer Lands, Jean Wilson
Giant Snakes and Other Amazing Reptiles, William Wise
Monsters of North America, William Wise
Gorilla Baby: The Story of Patty Cake, Pearl Wolf
My Goldfish, Herbert Wong
My Lady Bug, Herbert Wong
Bony, Frances W. Zweifel

Informational Books—Plants

Acorn Tree, Valenti Angelo
Apples, Nonny Hogrogian
The Garden Book, Marilyn Kratz
A Tree Is Nice, Janice Udry
Plant Sitter, Gene Zion

Cocoa Beans and Daisies: How Swiss Chocolate Is Made,
    Pascale Allamand
A Tree Is a Plant, Clyde R. Bulla
Hungry Leprechaun, Mary Calhoun
Tiny Seed, Eric Carle
How to Grow a Jelly Glass Farm, Kathy Mandry
Flower Book, Anne Orange
Leaf Book, Anne Orange
Fruit Book, Cynthia Overbeck
Vegetable Book, Cynthia Overbeck

Corn Is Maize: The Gift of the Indians, Aliki
Story of Johnny Appleseed, Aliki
Everyday Trees, Gertrude E. Allen
Everyday Wildflowers, Gertrude E. Allen
Down Come the Leaves, Henrietta Bancroft
Roots Are Food Finders, Franklyn M. Branley
Green Machine, Polly Cameron
Plants in Winter, Joanna Cole
My Sea, Herman Fay
Mushrooms and Molds, Robert Froman
Tremendous Tree Book, May Garelick
Where Does Your Garden Grow?, Augusta Goldin
From Apple Seed to Applesauce, Hannah L. Johnson
From Seed to Jack-O-Lantern, Hannah L. Johnson
How a Seed Grows, Helene Jordan
Seeds by Wind and Water, Helene Jordan
Wonderful Tree, Ulf Lofgren
Have You Seen Trees?, Joanne Oppenheim
Water Plants, Laurence Pringle
Guess What Trees Do, Barbara Rinkoff
Little Sponge Fisherman, Florence W. Rowland
Popcorn, Millicent E. Selsam
Seeds and More Seeds, Millicent E. Selsam
Let's Find Out About Trees: Arbor Day, Charles Shapp
A Tree on Your Street, Seymour Simon

Plants to Grow Indoors, George Sullivan
The Dead Tree, Alvin R. Tresselt
My Garden Grows, Aldren A. Watson
Up Above and Down Below, Irma Webber
From One Seed, Vera Webster
Our Tree, Herbert Wong

Informational Books—Environment and Ecology

The Little House, Virginia Lee Burton
Where Does the Butterfly Go When It Rains?, May Garelick
Wilson's World, Edith Hurd
Vermont Farm and the Sun, Constance Montgomery
The Lorax, Dr. Seuss

Walk, Bill Binzen
Left-Over Dragon, Claire Boiko
Who Likes the Sun?, Beatrice DeRegniers
Seal and the Slick, Don Freeman
World, World, What Can I Do?, Barbara Shook Hazen

Around the House That Jack Built, Roz Abisch
Clean Brook, Margaret Bartlett
Where the Brook Begins, Margaret Bartlett
Energy from the Sun, Melvin Berger
Storms, Melvin Berger
Mushroom Center Disaster, Niels M. Bodecker
Wind Is Air, Mary Brewer
Aloysius Alligator, Bunny
Haunted Ghost, Barbara Byfield
Swamp Spring, Carol Carrick
The Tree, Donald Carrick
Run, Zebra, Run, Tony Chen
Earth and Sky, Mona Dayton
Dinosaurs and All That Rubbish, Michael Foreman
Once There Was a Passenger Pigeon, Bernard Gordon
There Really Was a Dodo, Esther Gordon
Why Does It Rain?, Fran Harvey
Wind Is to Feel, Shirley Hatch
Splash and Flow, Ruth Ann Howell
Who Cares? I Do, Munro Leaf
Swamp Witch, Janet McCaffery
If I Built a Village, Kazue Mizumura
Rain, Rain, Don't Go Away, Shirley Morgan
Farewell to Shady Glade, Bill Peet

Wump World, Bill Peet
What's the Time, Starling? . . . Nature's Clocks,
 Solveig P. Russell
About Garbage and Stuff, Ann Z. Shanks
Where Does the Garbage Go?, Paul Showers
Only Silly People Waste, Norah Smaridge
Not Here and Never Was, Virginia Smith
It Rains—It Shines, William J. Smith
Someone Is Eating the Sun, Ruth A. Sonneborn
Let's Be Nature's Friend, Jack Stokes
Last Free Bird, A. Harris Stone
Follow the Wind, Alvin R. Tresselt
The Basket That Flew Over the Mountain, Mabel Watts
Summer Is, Charlotte Zolotow

Informational Books—Other Nature

Who Has Seen the Wind?, Marion Conger
What Do You See?, Janina Domanska
A Rainbow of My Own, Don Freeman
Pocketful of Seasons, Doris V. Foster
Down to the Beach, May Garelick
Pails and Snails, Kate Loree
My Day on the Farm, Chiyoko Nakatani
A Book of Seasons, Alice Provensen
Dawn, Uri Shulevitz

Drip Drop, Donald Carrick
Once We Went on a Picnic, Aileen Fisher
Turtle and the Dove, Don Freeman
The Day the Sun Danced, Edith Hurd
Rain, Robert Kalan
Mouse at Home, Mary Kwitz
How to Dig a Hole to the Other Side of the World,
 Faith McNulty
The Zoo in My Garden, Chiyoko Nakatani
Drop of Water, Sam Rosenfeld

Everybody Needs a Rock, Byrd Baylor
Baltimore Orioles, Barbara Brenner
Spider Web, Julie Brinckloe
Walk in the Snow, Phyllis S. Busch
Brook, Carol Carrick
The Pond, Carol Carrick

Spring Snow, Roger Duvoisin
Water Come, Water Go, Mary Elting
Best Little House, Aileen Fisher
When Autumn Comes, Charles P. Fox
Boat That Mooed, C. Fry
Caves, Roma Gans
Icebergs, Roma Gans
Oil: The Buried Treasure, Roma Gans
Wonder of Stones, Roma Gans
All Upon a Sidewalk, Jean George
Salt, Augusta Goldin
What Can She Be? A Geologist, Gloria Goldreich
The Day We Saw the Sun Come Up, Alice Goudey
Walk When the Moon Is Full, Frances Hamerstrom
When the Sky Is Like Lace, Elinor L. Horwitz
Wild Whirlwind, Dahlov Ipcar
Legs of the Moon, Francine Jacobs
Watch My Tracks, Bob Kaufman
The Lost Kingdom of Karnica, Richard Kennedy
What Does the Tide Do?, Jean Kinney
Paint-Box Sea, Doris Lund
The Underwater World of the Coral Reef, Ann McGovern
Day of Spring, Betty Miles
Animal Garden, Ogden Nash
Guess What Rocks Do, Barbara Rinkoff
Let's Find Out About the Moon, Charles Shapp
Let's Find Out About the Sun, Charles Shapp
Let's Find Out About Water, Charles Shapp
Rain Rain Rivers, Uri Shulevitz
Listen to My Seashell, Charlotte Steiner
Raindrop Splash, Alvin R. Tresselt
White Snow, Bright Snow, Alvin R. Tresselt
What Causes It?, Bruce Wannamaker
Overhead the Sun, Lines from Walt Whitman, Walt Whitman
Let's Find Out About Rivers, Eleanor Wiesenthal
The Weather, Jean Wilson

Informational Books—Human Biology

Bodies, Barbara Brenner
We Are Having a Baby, Vicki Holland
My Feet Do, Jean Holzenthaler
My Hands Can, Jean Holzenthaler
Dear Little Mumps Child, Marguerite Rush Lerner, M.D.
Michael Gets the Measles, Marguerite Rush Lerner, M.D.
The See and Hear and Taste and Touch Book, Elwood Smith

My Five Senses, Aliki
My Hands, Aliki
Listen, Listen, Crosby Bonsall
Becoming, Eleanor Faison

Fat and Skinny, Phillip Balestrino
Skeleton Inside You, Phillip Balestrino
Faces, Barbara Brenner
Wind Rose, Crescent Dragonwagon
Straight Hair, Curly Hair, Augusta Goldin
More Time to Grow, Sharon Grollman
Sometimes I Worry, Alan Gross
A Book About Your Skeleton, Ruth Belov Gross
Twins, Marguerite Rush Lerner, M.D.
Lisa and Her Soundless World, Edna Levine
Ear Book, Al Perkins
Nose Book, Al Perkins
A Baby Starts to Grow, Paul Showers
Drop of Blood, Paul Showers
Find Out by Touching, Paul Showers
Follow Your Nose, Paul Showers
Hear Your Heart, Paul Showers
How Many Teeth?, Paul Showers
How You Talk, Paul Showers
In the Night, Paul Showers
Listening Walk, Paul Showers
Look at Your Eyes, Paul Showers
Your Skin and Mine, Paul Showers
About Your Heart, Seymour Simon
Finding Out with Your Senses, Seymour Simon
Look! How Your Eyes See, Marcel Sislowitz
Jeff's Hospital Book, Harriet Sobol
A Hospital Story, Sara Bonnett Stein
Bones and Skeletons, Brenda Thompson
What Is a Girl? What Is a Boy?, Stephanie Waxman
Mom, I Broke My Arm, Angelicka Wolff
Mom, I Need Glasses, Angelicka Wolff
What's Inside of Me?, Herbert Zim

Informational Books—Other Science

My Five Senses, Aliki
I Feel: A Picture Book of Emotions, George Ancona
Whose Eye Am I?, Crosby Bonsall
I See a Song, Eric Carle

Becoming, Eleanora Faison
Journey to the Moon, Erich Fuchs

Prove It!, Gerald Ames
Other Way to Listen, Byrd Baylor
What Floats?, Mary Brewer
Eli Lives in Israel, Anna R. Brick
What Makes a Shadow?, Clyde R. Bulla
Take Another Look, R. Carini
Crystal Magic, Eugene David
Babar Visits Another Planet, Laurent DeBrunhoff
I Am Happy, Maryann Dotts
Penny, the Medicine Maker: The Story of Penicillin,
 Sherrie S. Epstein
Goats Who Killed the Leopard, Judy Hawes
Easy Answers to Hard Questions, Susanne Kirtland
Let's Find Out About Mars, David C. Knight
Let's Find Out About Sound, David C. Knight
Let's Find Out About Telephones, David C. Knight
Walk the Mouse Girls Took, Karla Kuskin
Dandelion Year, Ron McTrusty
Why People Are Different Colors, Julian May
What Is a Shadow?, Bob Ridiman
This Is a Baby Dinosaur? . . . Science Picture Puzzles,
 Millicent E. Selsam
Let's Find Out What Electricity Does, Charles Shapp
Liquid or Solid? . . . That's a Good Question, Tobi Tobias
Let's Find Out About Milk, David Whitney

Informational Books—The Alphabet

Baby's First Library: ABC, Anon.
Baby Animal ABC, Robert Broomfield
Dick Bruna's ABC Frieze, Dick Bruna
A B C, John Burningham
C Is for Circus, Berniece Chardiet
The Most Amazing Hide and Seek Alphabet Book,
 Robert Crowther
Ape in a Cape, Fritz Eichenberg
As I Was Crossing Boston Common, Norma Farber
Gyo Fujikawa's A—Z Picture Book, Gyo Fujikawa
ABC Bunny, Wanda Gag
Hey! Look at Me: A City ABC, Sandy Grant
Great Big Alphabet Picture Book, Richard Hefter

D Is for Rover, Leonore Klein
Agatha's Alphabet, Kathryn Lasky
Little Indians' ABC, Faustana H. Lucero
Good Night to Annie, Eve Merriam
Apricot ABC, Miska Miles
Kittens' ABC, Claire T. Newberry
Celestino Piatti's Animal ABC, Celestino Piatti
Apples to Zippers: An Alphabet Book, Patricia Ruben
Alligators All Around, Maurice Sendak
Emergency Room: An ABC Tour, Julie Steedman
A Is for Annabelle, Tasha Tudor
From Ambledee to Zumbledee, Sandol S. Warburg
Brian Wildsmith's ABC, Brian Wildsmith

Anno's Alphabet: An Adventure in Imagination,
    Mitsumasa Anno
Jambo Means Hello: Swahili Alphabet Book, Muriel Feelings
X Marks the Spot, Eleanor Felder
Nuts to You and Nuts to Me: An Alphabet of Poems,
    Mary Ann Hoberman
Harold's ABC, Crockett Johnson
ABC, Bruno Munari
ABC of Monsters, Deborah Niland

Applebet Story, Byron Barton
Sonia Delaunay's Alphabet, Sonia Delaunay
I Found Them in the Yellow Pages, Norma Farber
Big City, Francine Grossbart
The Two Georges, Monica Gunning
Alphabet Tree, Leo Lionni
Helen Oxenbury's ABC of Things, Helen Oxenbury
Zoophabets, Robert Tallon

Informational Books—Numbers

Baby's First Library: Counting, Anon.
Dick Bruna's One-Two-Three Frieze, Dick Bruna
I Can Count, Dick Bruna
My Very First Book of Numbers, Eric Carle
Teddy Bears One to Ten, Susanna Gretz
Ten Bears in My Bed: A Goodnight Countdown, Stan Mack
One, Two, Where's My Shoe?, Tomi Ungerer
Count the Cats, Erika Weihs

Seven Little Rabbits, John Becker
Berenstain Bears' Counting Book, Stan Berenstain
Rooster Who Set Out to See the World, Eric Carle
Very Hungry Caterpillar, Eric Carle
Very Long Train: A Folding Book, Eric Carle
Freight Train, Donald Crews
Two Lonely Ducks: A Counting Book,
 Roger Duvoisin
Dancing in the Moon: Counting Rhymes,
 Fritz Eichenberg
Chicken Little Count to Ten, Margaret Friskey
Let's Count and Count Out, Marion F. Grayson
Ten What? A Mystery Counting Book, Russell Hoban
Count and See, Tana Hoban
How Many Dragons Are Behind the Door?,
 Virginia Kahl
One Dancing Drum, Gail Kredenser
James and the Rain, Karla Kuskin
Ten Little Elephants, Robert Leydenfrost
One Snail and Me, Emilie McLeod
Pop-Up Hide and Seek: A Child's First Counting Book,
 Albert G. Miller
Monster Bubbles: A Counting Book, Dennis Nolan
Numbers, John J. Reiss
Richard Scarry's Best Counting Book Ever,
 Richard Scarry
Ten in a Family, Charlotte Steiner
One Is No Fun, But Twenty Is Plenty, Ilse-Margret Vogel
Brian Wildsmith's One, Two, Three, Brian Wildsmith
Sixes and Sevens, John Yeoman
Counting Carnival, Feenie Ziner

Twenty-two Bears, Claire H. Bishop
All the Little Bunnies, Elizabeth Bridgman
I Can Count More, Dick Bruna
Moja Means One: Swahili Counting Book, Muriel Feelings
Three by Three, James Kruss

Anno's Counting Book, Mitsumasa Anno
One Wide River to Cross, Barbara Emberley
The Life of Numbers, Fernando Krahn
One to Ten, Count Again, Elaine Livermore
All in the Morning Early, Sorche Nic Leodhas
Numbers of Things, Helen Oxenbury
Numbers, Jan Pienkowski
One Was Johnny, Maurice Sendak

Informational Books—Pictures, Shapes and Colors

My Shirt Is White, Dick Bruna
My Very First Book of Colors, Eric Carle
My Very First Book of Shapes, Eric Carle
Little Yellow and Little Blue, Leo Lionni
It Looked Like Spilt Milk, Charles G. Shaw
Hello, This Is a Shape book, John Trotta

The Mixed-Up Chameleon, Eric Carle
Secret Birthday Message, Eric Carle
Wing on a Flea: A Book About Shapes, Ed Emberley
Chalk Box Story, Don Freeman
Is It Red? Is It Yellow? Is It Blue?, Tana Hoban
Red Is for Apples, Beth G. Hoffman
Colors, Jan Pienkowski
Colors, John J. Reiss
Shapes, John J. Reiss
Poems Make Pictures; Pictures Make Poems, Giose Rimanelli
The Magic Pencil, Scapa
Tale of the Black Cat, Carl A. Withers

Picture That!, Bernice Carlson
Picture for the Palace, Flora Fifield
Beginning Search-A-Word Shapes, Dawn Gerger
Everything Has a Shape and Everything Has a Size, Bernice Kohn
Lines and Shapes, Solveig P. Russell
Shapes, Miriam Schlein

Informational Books—Music

Din, Dan, Don— It's Christmas, Janina Domanska
Lullabies and Night Songs, Edited by William Engvick
Froggie Went A-Courtin', Harriett
Frog Went A-Courtin', John Langstaff
Over in the Meadow, John Langstaff
Small Sheep in a Pear Tree, Adrianne Lobel
Baby's Song Book, Elizabeth Poston
Old MacDonald Had a Farm, Robert Quackenbush
Pop Goes the Weasel!...New York in 1776 and Today, Robert Quackenbush
The Foolish Frog, Pete Seeger
Fox Went Out on a Chilly Night, Peter Spier

Mother Goose Abroad, Nicholas Tucker
Mommy, Buy Me a China Doll, Harve Zemach
Hush Little Baby, Margot Zemach

Six Little Ducks, Chris Conover
We Came A-Marching One, Two, Three, Mildred Hobzeck
Firefly in a Fir Tree, Hilary Knight
Ol' Dan Tucker, John Langstaff
Soldier, Soldier, Won't You Marry Me?, John Langstaff
Always Room for One More, Sorche Nic Leodhas
Clementine, Robert Quackenbush
Father Fox's Pennyrhymes, Clyde Watson
Little Sarah and Her Johnny-Cake, William Wiesner
Cornrows, Camille Yarbrough

Informational Books—Verbal Skills

Early Birds...Early Words, Ann Bonner
My Very First Book of Words, Eric Carle
A Hole Is to Dig: First Book of Definitions, Ruth Krauss
Richard Scarry's Best Word Book Ever, Richard Scarry

Nailheads and Potato Eyes, Cynthia Basil
Know What? No, What?, Arlene Baum
Chocolate Moose for Dinner, Fred Gwynne
Strawberry Word Book, Richard Hefter
Yes and No: A Book of Opposites, Richard Hefter
One Day It Rained Cats and Dogs, Bernice Kohn
Open House for Butterflies, Ruth Krauss
Five Hundred Words to Grow On, Harry McNaught
On the Go: A Book of Adjectives, Betty Maestro
Where Is My Friend? A Word Concept Book, Betty Maestro
The Hungry Thing, Jan Slepian
Animal Dictionary, Jane Watson

Informational Books—Concepts

Look Around and Listen, Joy T. Friedman
Dig, Drill, Dump, Fill, Tana Hoban
Look Again, Tana Hoban
Over, Under, Through and Other Spatial Concepts, Tana Hoban

Push-Pull, Empty-Full: A Book of Opposites, Tana Hoban
What Is an Inch?, Leonore Klein
A Flower Pot Is Not a Hat, Martha Moffett
I Spy, Lucille Ogle
Odd One Out, Rodney Peppe
Head to Toe, Anne Rockwell
Look Look Book, Pat Witte

Where in the World Is Henry?, Lorna Balian
Take Another Look, E. Carini
Hold Everything, Sam Epstein
Pick It Up, Sam Epstein
Upstairs and Downstairs, Ryerson Johnson
Just a Minute: A Book About Time, Leonore Klein
Rain, Robert Kalan
Size, Distance, Weight: A First Look at Measuring, Solveig Russell
Fast-Slow, High-Low: A Book of Opposites, Peter Spier

Informational Books—Miscellaneous

Baby Animal Dress-Up Book, Joan Allen
The Apple, Dick Bruna
See the Circus, Hans A. Rey
Elephant Buttons, Noriko Ueno
Touch Me Book, Pat Witte
Who Lives Here?, Pat Witte

Whose Eye Am I?, Crosby Bonsall
I See a Song, Eric Carle
It Does Not Say Meow, Beatrice DeRegniers
Adventures of Paddy Pig, John S. Goodall
Creepy Castle, John S. Goodall
Jacko, John S. Goodall
Paddy's Evening Out, John S. Goodall
Midnight Adventures of Kelly, Dot and Esmeralda, John S. Goodall
Naughty Nancy, the Bad Bridesmaid, John S. Goodall
The Surprise Picnic, John S. Goodall
Where Is It?, Tana Hoban
Anybody at Home?, Hans A. Rey
Feed the Animals, Hans A. Rey
Where's My Baby?, Hans A. Rey

Giggly-Wiggly, Snicketty-Snick, Robyn Supraner
But Where Is the Green Parrot?, Thomas Zacharias

1000 Monsters, Alan Benjamin
Do You See What I See?, Helen Borton
A Pack of Riddles, Compiled by William Gerler
Riddle Rat, Donald Hall
Harriet Goes to the Circus, Betsy Maestro
Hailstones and Halibut Bones, Mary O'Neill
Chicken Soup with Rice: A Book of Months, Maurice Sendak
Around the Year, Tasha Tudor

Poetry

When dealing with pre-schoolers, it is acceptable to interpret broadly the definition of poetry as "a work in metrical form," so that we may include the simplest nursery rhymes for the diaper set and go on to unrhymed verse for the older child. Perhaps the most important point to keep in mind when dealing with this form is to include poetry as an integral part of literature, rather than setting it apart as something "special" or different, once the patty-cake period has passed. The negative attitudes so commonly encountered when poetry is mentioned to elementary or secondary school children may be forestalled if a pre-school child has been presented with sufficient poetic expression without comment, simply as a book to hear read. A very useful technique in this regard is to tie a poem into a prose selection, subject-wise, with animals or weather or seasons of the year, in such a way as to make it seem less extraordinary.

One of the main features of this kind of writing is its potential for lyrical expression, so that even adults may enjoy the musical aspects of poetry, sometimes without full intellectual comprehension. Therefore, if the reader chooses well and prepares carefully, he should be able to stress this aspect, resulting in the child's enjoyment of poetic form along with prose at each level of his development.

Another mark of good poetry is strong use of imagery, which is helped along for pre-schoolers by copious illustration in their books. Especially after the age of four, many youngsters appreciate humor, and compressed language which is so often a part of poetic expression can easily come into play here. While on the subject of "play," let us keep in mind the games which children play as accompaniment to simple rhymes, all the way from *This Little Piggy Went to Market* to David McCord's *The Pickety Fence* or *The Farmer in the Dell*, and other natural bridges to poetry.

As in all literature, in choosing poetry we must select the best available, taking special care in this form to avoid sentimentalism, a pitfall into which it seems particularly easy to fall when dealing with verses written especially for children. We will also want to avoid didacticism, common prior to the period of William Blake's *Songs of Innocence* (first published in 1789) and continuing well into the modern era. It is obvious that not only are such pieces poor poetry, but also that their purpose—to teach proper behavior—might quite possibly have the opposite effect on a youngster today. As an example, consider two poems on the same subject. First, a poem called *Dreams*, from the Victorian period:

> If children have been good all day,
>   And kept their tongues and lips quite clean,
> They dream of flowers that nod and play,
>   And fairies dancing on the green.
> But if they've spoken naughty words,
>   Or told a lie, they dream of rats,
> Of crawling snakes, and ugly birds,
>   Of centipedes and vampire bats.[9]

Then, contrast it with a piece by Louise Driscoll called *Hold Fast Your Dreams*.

> Hold fast your dreams!
> Within your heart
> Keep one still, secret spot
> Where dreams may go,
> And sheltered so,
> May thrive and grow—
> Where doubt and fear are not.
> Oh, keep a place apart
> Within your heart,
> For little dreams to go.[10]

In terms of imagery alone, it is not difficult to understand the difference between these two, and the response each would be likely to get from a pre-schooler.

The same format has been used in this section as that found in the fiction and informational sections in regard to suggested materials. The type of poem appears next to each title: (S) = Serious; (Non-S) = Non-Serious; Verse and Nonsense are self-explanatory.

148 / They're Never Too Young for Books

Poetry

Early Birds...Early Words, Ann Bonner (Verse)
Hey Diddle and Other Rhymes, Davi Botts (Nonsense)
My Hopping Bunny, Robert Bright (Nonsense)
The Baby's Lap Book, Kay Chorao (Non-S)
Mother Goose in French, Illustrated by Barbara Cooney (Verse)
Book of Nursery and Mother Goose Rhymes,
    Marguerite De Angeli (Non-S)
Prancing Pony: Nursery Rhymes from Japan,
    Charlotte B. DeForest (Non-S)
Nursery Rhymes of London Town, Eleanor Farjeon (Verse)
Mother Goose, Gyo Fujikawa (Verse)
Did You Ever?, Paula Goldsmid (Verse)
Little Boat Lighter Than a Cork, Ruth Krauss (Non-S)
Gregory Griggs and Other Nursery Rhyme People,
    Arnold Lobel (Verse)
Baby's Song Book, Elizabeth Poston (Non-S)
Tall Book of Mother Goose, Feodor Rojankovsky (Verse)
Mother Goose, Tasha Tudor (Verse)
Mother Goose, Vollaud Edition (Verse)
Bears Are Sleeping, Yulya (S)

Make a Circle, Keep Us In: Poems for a Good Day,
    Arnold Adoff (S)
Who's Zoo?, Conrad Aiken (Nonsense)
Things We Like to Do, Evelyn M. Andre (Verse)
Hark, Hark, the Dogs Do Bark, Lenore Blegvad (Non-S)
Mittens for Kittens and Other Rhymes About Cats,
    Lenore Blegvad (Non-S)
Mother Goose Treasury, Edited by Raymond Briggs (Non-S)
Johnny Crow's Garden, Leslie Brooke (Non-S)
Ring O'Roses, Leslie Brooke (Non-S)
I Can't, Said the Ant, Polly Cameron (Nonsense)
I Went to the Animal Fair, William Cole (Non-S)
Catch a Little Fox, Beatrice DeRegniers (Non-S)
Din, Dan, Don—It's Christmas, Janina Domanska (Non-S)
Did You Ever See?, Walter Einsel (Nonsense)
Wing on a Flea: Book About Shapes, Ed Emberley (Nonsense)
Winken, Blinken and Nod, Eugene Field (Non-S)
Going Barefoot, Aileen Fisher (Verse)
Sing, Little Mouse, Aileen Fisher (Non-S)
Snow and Sun: South American Folk Rhymes in Two
    Languages, Antonio Frasconi (Verse)
Gertrude, the Goose Who Forgot, Joanna Galdone (Verse)

*History of Mother Twaddle and the Marvelous Achievements of
  Her Son Jack,* Paul Galdone (Verse)
Egg Thoughts and Other Frances Songs, Russell Hoban (Verse)
The Foolish Frog, Pete Seeger (Non-S)
Dawn, Uri Shulevitz (S)
Fox Went Out on a Chilly Night, Peter Spier (Non-S)
A Frog He Would A-Wooing Go, Henry Louis Stephens (Non-S)
There Are Rocks in My Sox, Said the Ox to the Fox,
  Patricia Thomas (Nonsense)
Mother Goose Abroad, Nicholas Tucker (Non-S)
From, Ambledee to Zumbledee, Sandol S. Warburg (Nonsense)
Brian Wildsmith's Mother Goose, Brian Wildsmith (Non-S)
The Real Mother Goose, Blanche Fisher Wright (Non-S)
Chinese Mother Goose Rhymes,
  Edited by Robert Wyndham (Non-S)

Day in the Country, Willis Barnstone (S)
Muggins' Big Balloon, Marjorie Barrows (Non-S)
They Put on Masks, Byrd Baylor (Verse)
Bad Child's Book of Beasts, Hillaire Belloc (Nonsense)
Fun House, Barbara Bottner (Nonsense)
Jonathan Bing, Beatrice C. Brown (Nonsense)
Green Machine, Polly Cameron (Nonsense)
Around and About, Marchette Chute (S)
You Know Who, John Ciardi (Nonsense)
Oh, What Nonsense, Edited by William Cole (Nonsense)
The Sand, the Sea and Me, M. Jean Craig (S)
Warmint, Walter De LaMare (Non-S)
Sonia Delaunay's Alphabet, Sonia Delaunay (Verse)
Cricket in a Thicket, Aileen Fisher (S)
I Like Weather, Aileen Fisher (Non-S)
In the Middle of the Night, Aileen Fisher (S)
My Cat Has Eyes of Sapphire Blue, Aileen Fisher (Verse)
My Mother and I, Aileen Fisher (S)
Sir Ribbeck of Ribbeck of Havelland, Theodore Fontaine (Verse)
The Blue Horse and Other Night Poems, Siv Cedering Fox (S)
A Bat Is Born, Randall Jarrell (S)
Bugs: Poems, Mary Ann Hoberman (Non-S)
A Little Book of Beasts, Mary Ann Hoberman (Verse)
Looking Book, Mary Ann Hoberman (Verse)
Red Is for Apples, Beth G. Hoffman (Non-S)
Go to Bed!, Edited by Lee Bennett Hopkins (Non-S)
Wonky Donkey, Charlotte Hough (Nonsense)
Wind Blew, Pat Hutchins (Non-S)
All the Pretty Horses, Susan Jeffers (S)
Giants Indeed!, Virginia Kahl (Nonsense)

Perfect Pancake, Virginia Kahl (Nonsense)
Plum Pudding for Christmas, Virginia Kahl (Nonsense)
Little Drummer Boy, Ezra Jack Keats (S)
Over in the Meadow, Ezra Jack Keats (Non-S)
All for Fall, Ethel Kessler (Non-S)
Frog Went A-Courtin', John Langstaff (Verse)
In a Spring Garden, Richard Lewis (S)
Small Sheep in a Pear Tree, Adrianne Lobel (Verse)
Witches' Holiday, Alice Low (Verse)
How to Make Elephant Bread, Kathy Mandry (Nonsense)
The Night Before Christmas, Clement Moore (Non-S)
Arthur's Artichoke, Geoffrey Moss (Nonsense)
Cat and Mouse, Rodney Peppe (Verse)
Waltzing Tiger and Other Animal Verses,
    Elizabeth Perry (Non-S)
Popcorn and Ma Goodness, Edna Mitchell Preston (Nonsense)
Old MacDonald Had a Farm, Robert Quackenbush (Verse)
Pop Goes the Weasel!... New York in 1776 and Today,
    Robert Quackenbush (Verse)
Listen! Listen!, Ann Rand (Non-S)
Twenty-Two, Twenty-Three, Ellen Raskin (Nonsense)
Poems Make Pictures; Pictures Make Poems, Giose Rimanelli (S)
Rain Makes Applesauce, Julian Scheer (Nonsense)
Upside Down Day, Julian Scheer (Nonsense)
The Man in the Moon as He Sails the Sky,
    Edited by Ann Schweninger (Non-S)

Trees Stand Shining: Poetry of North American Indians,
    Hettie Jones (S)
Baron's Booty, Virginia Kahl (Verse)
The Duchess Bakes a Cake, Virginia Kahl (Nonsense)
Gunhilde and the Halloween Spell, Virginia Kahl (Non-S)
Habits of the Rabbits, Virginia Kahl (Nonsense)
How Do You Hide a Monster?, Virginia Kahl (Verse)
Gobbledy Gook, Steven Kroll (Nonsense)
Firefly in a Fir Tree, Hilary Knight (Non-S)
The Dong with the Luminous Nose, Edward Lear (Nonsense)
The Jumblies, Edward Lear (Nonsense)
Who Will Wake up Spring?, Sharon Lerner (S)
The Park, Richard Lewis (S)
Giant Jam Sandwich, John V. Lord (Nonsense)
Every Time I Climb a Tree, David McCord (S)
Feeling Mad, Sad, Bad, Glad, Ann McGovern (S)
Now We Are Six, A.A. Milne (Non-S)
When We Were Very Young, A.A. Milne (Non-S)
Flower Moon Snow: A Book of Haiku, Kazue Mizumura (S)

I See Wings, Kazue Mizumura (S)
All Along the Way, John Travers Moore (S)
Squeeze a Sneeze, Bill Morrison (Nonsense)
Animal Garden, Ogden Nash (Nonsense)
The Cruise of the Aardvark, Ogden Nash (Nonsense)
Custard the Dragon and the Wicked Knight,
    Ogden Nash (Nonsense)
Amelia Mixed the Mustard and Other Poems,
    Evaline Ness (Nonsense)
Grouch and the Tower and Other Sillies, John O'Brien (Non-S)
Hailstones and Halibut Bones, Mary O'Neill (S)
Merry Merry Fibruary, Doris Orgel (Nonsense)
Hubert's Hair Rising Adventure, Bill Peet (Non-S)
Smoky Bill, Bill Peet (Verse)
Red Raspberry Crunch, Charles Fox Phillips (Nonsense)
Ballad of the Long-Tailed Rat, Charlotte Pomerantz (Nonsense)
The Piggy in the Puddle, Charlotte Pomerantz (Nonsense)
Clementine, Robert Quackenbush (Verse)
Who, Said Sue, Said Whoo?, Ellen Raskin (Nonsense)
What Is Pink?, Christina Rossetti (S)
City Green, Eleanor Schick (Non-S)
Chicken Soup with Rice: A Book of Months,
    Maurice Sendak (Non-S)
Where the Sidewalk Ends, Shel Silverstein (Non-S)
Clear the Track, Louis Slobodkin (Non-S)
Magic Michael, Louis Slobodkin (Nonsense)
Laughing Time, William J. Smith (Nonsense)
Ballad of Penelope Lou and Me, Drew Stevenson (Non-S)
Granfa' Grig Had a Pig... New from Mother Goose,
    Wallace Tripp (Nonsense)
A Great Big Ugly Man Came up and Tied His Horse to Me,
    Wallace Tripp (Nonsense)
Ghost Poems, Edited by Daisy Wallace (Non-S)
Monster Poems, Edited by Daisy Wallace (Non-S)
Witch Poems, Edited by Daisy Wallace (S)
Father Fox's Pennyrhymes, Clyde Watson (Nonsense)
Hickory Stick Rag, Clyde Watson (Verse)
Overhead the Sun: Lines from Walt Whitman,
    Walt Whitman (S)
Little Sarah and Her Johnny-Cake, William Wiesner (Non-S)
Cornrows, Camille Yarbrough (S)
Clumsy Octupus, Marvin Zetlan (Verse)

Part Three

Reading Aloud

Some General Hints

There are some specific differences to be noted between reading to one or two children, usually in a home setting, and reading to a group of perhaps eight or ten youngsters in a more formal atmosphere of a nursery school, kindergarten, or child care center. On the other hand, some of the basic "rules" for successfully reading aloud are quite apt to be consistently applicable. First, the *differences*.

When reading to one child or to a very small number, it is practical to offer suggestions, but to allow the final decision about what book or books are to be read at a given sitting up to the child or children. When there are a greater number of children, there is apt to be a greater number of preferences, which can set up a poor initial atmosphere for a story, and may even result in a behavior problem or two with a child whose book is not the choice of the majority. Therefore, with a group, it is preferable for the adult who is reading to make the selections in advance.

Then, secondly, there is the matter of interruptions. Assuming that one or two children are being read to at home (ignoring such common nuisances as telephones and doorbells which might interrupt the reading), the adult is able to stop and explicate more often in answer to a child's questions than he/she would be able to do in a group situation. Anyone who has read to a group of three-year olds knows how easily a reading about zoo animals, for example, may be side-tracked by a child's recital about *his* trip to the zoo. Practice in incorporating such comment into the reading without allowing the discussion to become too general—with the book forgotten—is the only means of dealing with the problem.

Next, in groups there is often a wider age spread than is apt to be involved when reading in the home setting, and this may be difficult to deal with. In general, it is a good idea to read to a rather limited number of children within a similar age frame, and then go on with the next group, rather than try to interest children who range from age three to age five in the same story at one sitting.

There is also the practical matter of book size to consider. For one or two children, a very small book held in the reader's lap is quite cozy. For a group, however, it is necessary to select a book which is large enough to be easily seen by all, and it must be held so that it is facing the youngsters at all times.

Finally, although in all situations the child or children need to be comfortably settled before being read to, and extraneous noise kept at a minimum, the practice of reading *only as a prelude to rest, nap or bed time is undesirable*. Such a time slot suggests that reading is an activity meant to put one to sleep, certainly not an idea we want to promote. In the case of children who resist a cessation of physical activity, we must be careful to avoid the impression that reading is being used as though it were a sedative! Ideally, of course, an available adult should acquiesce to every child's request to be read to at any time such a request is made, and in the home this is quite possible within limits. However, in a group situation, it is less likely that at any given moment it is convenient for a teacher or aide to stop whatever activity is under way to read to one child. In any case, promising to read a story as a kind of reward for completing a task or doing a good job of tidying up after an art project, for example, sets the scene for a favorable attitude toward books and reinforces positive feelings about reading books.

Some Rules for Successful Read-Alouds

In spite of the differences in reading aloud at home or in a group situation, there are some very basic rules for success in making literature live for pre-schoolers under any circumstances:

1. Choose a book that you like, one appropriate to the age of the child/children. Your enthusiasm will be contagious.
2. Handle the book carefully, as an example to your listener(s).
3. Be *absolutely familiar* with the book beforehand—especially with what are called the "hinges" of the plot, the points at which the story progresses from one situation to the next. This will help with point 4.
4. If reading to more than three children, seat them in a semicircle in front of you and sit on a very low chair, facing them. Then hold the book *toward* the children at all times. Practice beforehand so that you can read "upside down" or by glancing sideways at the text.
5. Make as much eye contact with your listeners as possible.
6. If there are any explanations necessary before starting to read, make them. For instance, if you are reading a folktale from faraway Indonesia, you might want to mention this, calling attention to the illustrations.
7. In the same way, if there is an unfamiliar word which is not made self-explanatory through context or illustration, stop and paraphrase it. However, do not "read down" or change words to simplify the material since this would preclude the acquisition of new vocabulary words. For example, in Leo Lionni's book *Frederick* the word *granary* is used, but not pictured. Read the word as written; then explain its meaning very simply, as "A granary is like a barn, a big building on a farm, but the animals stay in the barn and the grain is put in the granary."
8. Make certain that you are reading at an appropriate speed, taking time to show the illustrations and varying the tempo as the story calls for such variation.
9. Make sure that you are audible at all times.
10. Possibly the most important point in an effective read-aloud may be termed "animation," or what might loosely approximate "acting."
    a. Be sure that your voice and tone are appropriate to the story; if it is a serious story, be serious; if it is a funny story, take a light tone, and so on.
    b. If there are several characters, try to differentiate among them by using different voices, if possible. For example, if there is a small mouse speaking, make your voice a bit "squeaky"; if the character is a huge troll,

make your voice loud and booming. One word of caution: do not attempt a book with too many characters at first.
   c. Make good use of the built-in stylistic devices provided by the author. For instance, if a character is running quickly, try to simulate some sense of breathlessness and speed; if a character is described as a "teeny, tiny" person, emphasize the words *teeny* and *tiny*.
11. Remember that what you may consider somewhat "hammy" behavior while reading will probably delight your audience. Nothing fails as completely or quickly as a drab rendition.
12. Certain stories lend themselves well to oral participation by children, which increases their sense of immediate involvement. A book such as *The Very Hungry Caterpillar*, mentioned above, will on repeat readings elicit spontaneous group recitation of numerical sequence, the days of the week, and items of food consumed by the protagonist.
13. Individual books adapt well as bases for creative dramatics, a topic discussed separately in the following section.
14. Particular books lend themselves to the use of story boards and/or simple hand puppets as visual reinforcements. The use of these will also be discussed in the following section.
15. Be prepared for success, which means that you will have requests to read and reread the same books to the same child or children. As anyone who has read to youngsters knows, this is the highest form of praise both for the material and for its interpreter. If you have chosen a book you like in the first place, you will still enjoy it when asked for repeat performances. But remember, even if you are bored by the fifth repetition, don't let down on your "performance." Suggest another book tactfully, for a change of pace, and then cheerfully do all the encores of the original book requested by your listeners. The child or children may have a special reason for wanting a particular story, even though that reason is never verbalized.

Creative Dramatics

Before beginning a detailed discussion of this mode of reinforcing literary values, we must first be aware that this activity bears little resemblance to the presentation of "plays," in the usual sense. No sets are used, except as informal arrangements may occur to the children themselves; no costumes or makeup are involved; no audience of doting adults is allowed; and there are no speeches or lines to be learned. Actually, Creative Dramatics parallels what in adult theatre would be called "improvisation," with the concomitant benefits of that form and the necessity of introducing certain "performance techniques" to the children before any reference is made to literature.

If we examine these "techniques," the advantages of participation will become clear. First, for youngsters to whom playing and making believe are such common activities, impromptu responses to imagined situations seem a natural kind of behavior. For example, children will listen to music and "act out" a march of elephants or a circle of merry-go-round horses at the slightest suggestion, and pre-training can be begun with simple movements like these. Then, gradually, additional games can be added to stimulate imaginative thinking. For instance, if the youngsters are seated in a circle, told to close their eyes, and then to put their hands on the floor next to them, they will respond to suggestions regarding supposed changes in that floor. If the adult now says that it has become sticky, so that they cannot pick up their hands without tremendous effort, they will enter into the game and do some very realistic tugging and pulling. If the floor is then supposed to become a pool of ice water, the children will react appropriately, and so on. Obviously, there is no limit to the kinds of situations which the teacher might want to suggest.

Going from group activity to individual children, the teacher could then pretend to put something into each child's mouth, varying the item with each one. As one child blows an imaginary bubble with his "bubble gum," another will realistically react with a puckered mouth while "eating" a sour dill pickle. All of these exercises are done without any props at all, of course, so that the activities may vary according to the adult's imagination and stimulate without limit the imaginative faculties of the children.

Returning to the group, the children may be given a "make-believe" situation, such as getting ready to go to the beach for a day's outing or packing to move to a new house, with the adult briefly suggesting progressive activities in the pretended situations. As anyone who has worked with groups of children knows, they will assign roles to each other, pantomime behavior, and interact freely, with a minimum of direction from the sidelines. This kind of "performance" again stimulates formation of original mental images, and, in addition, sharpens listening skills. After the children have mastered a number of these "situation" scenes, they can be directed toward characterization.

This is easily done by instructing individuals to enact various tasks, as the rest of the group watches. For instance, one child may be told to "walk like an old person going outside in the rain," or another may be told to "walk like a princess going to your throne," while a third may be directed to "walk in a dark woods, trying to find the way home." After they have mastered to some degree the idea of acting out individual roles, they can work together in pairs in similar kinds of scenes. For example, a child could play the dog who doesn't want to come into the house for the old person going out in the rain to fetch him. Or in the second situation, a child could pick up the princess's train as she walked toward her throne, while in the third scene, a second "actor" could become an owl in the dark woods where his partner is "lost." After a few sessions, sometimes with children suggesting roles for themselves, most youngsters over age four should be ready for Creative Dramatics in the more formal sense.

At this juncture particularly, the books chosen must have specific qualities. First, they should be stories with rather simple plot lines—even some already familiar to the youngsters. Secondly, the "characters" in the books should be equal in number to the participants, since young children find it difficult to sit as "audience" while others in their group "perform." In regard to this, certain flexibility may be derived by choosing stories in which some "characters" may or may not be used—trees, for example, can be "acted out" or not, depending on the number of children in the group. Next, stories which have action, but which do not require forceful physical contact between characters are literally the safest, since small children may become so involved that their interactions become dangerous to other participants. Finally, stories with a variety of characterizations will provide the broadest scope for the youngsters. As a footnote, it may be noticed that children who have watched a lot of television will tend at first to imitate cliches they've seen, but as they become more familiar with this form, they will learn to draw more and more on their own creativity in regard to both action and dialogue.

As an introduction to children who have been doing the kinds of improvisations suggested above, it is usually enough to merely announce that a story will now be the basis for their "play." It is important that the children be seated in a semicircle and told that they will resume the same seats when the activity is completed; we shall see the reason for this shortly. At this point, the teacher reads the story in the usual way, with the book held toward the children so that they can see the illustrations. When the story is over, the adult reviews the "hinges" so that they are kept in the correct order when being dramatized. This may be done by asking the children to retell the plot, point by point; then, if any important action is left out, the teacher can gently remind the group of the omission. After the story line is firmly set in the minds of the youngsters, the characters should be reviewed in the same way, and beginning from the left side of the semicircle, each child asked to say what "part" he or she would like to try. If there is a shy child in the group, the teacher may want to assign a role which does not require more than a minimum of effort, perhaps a part which does not call for any speaking lines at all. When all roles have been assigned, the next item is the "setting." If more than one locale is called for, the children may need a little prompting before they can decide which part of the space will be designated as one place, which another. When all is ready, the adult need only coach from the sidelines, and the rule of "the less, the better" should apply.

The first time a story is done this way, whole sections may be inadvertently omitted and the characterizations may not be too well done. But no matter. After the action has been completed, the children take their same places in the semicircle and an informal critique is initiated. Questions such as, "Did we forget any parts of the story?" or "Did the lion sound really fierce when she roared?" will elicit responses, and then, beginning from the other side (the right-hand side) of the semicircle parts are again assigned—this time to different children, of course—and the whole story is acted out again. Usually, a group will want to do the play at least three times in succession, so that after the second "critique" the teacher can assign parts beginning with the middle child and going toward each end alternately. This may seem picayune, but the repeat performances make it mandatory that the children resume their original seats after each time through to avoid having the same child ask to play a major role each time.

When children become familiar with this kind of activity, they not only grow to appreciate the literature involved, but also they learn to speak extemporaneously, to listen to each other, and to answer appropriately (since they make up all the dialogue as they go along), and to objectively criticize performance. Additionally, the youngsters who are very shy in the beginning frequently gain in self-confidence as they go along, while those who customarily expect to be the center of attention come to understand the value of being a supporting player, so to speak. Consistently including Creative Dramatics in the literature program for pre-schoolers is worthwhile then as a painless way to modify behavior as well as to reinforce literary values.

Some stories which are particularly suitable for this activity follow:

>*Nobody Asked Me If I Wanted a Baby Sister,* Martha Alexander
>*Angus and the Ducks,* Marjorie Flack
>*Dandelion,* Don Freeman
>*The Three Bears,* Paul Galdone
>*Nice Little Girls,* Elizabeth Levy
>*Tico and tbe Golden Wings,* Leo Lionni
>*Stone Soup,* Carol Pasternak
>*Caps for Sale,* Esphyr Slobodkina
>*Sylvester and the Magic Pebble,* William Steig
>*Ira Sleeps Over,* Bernard Waber
>*The Little Red Hen,* Herb Williams

Many of these books have animals as characters, frequently of an indeterminate number, which makes casting less of a problem. The more familiar the story (*The Little Red Hen,* for instance), the easier it will be to get started with children under four. Some of the more complex stories (such as *Nice Little Girls* or *Tico and the Golden Wings*) might best be used with five-year-olds. Any book with a fairly simple plot line and some action involving a number of interesting characters can be used, of course, depending on the children to be involved. What is important to keep in mind is that if a story doesn't work well for any reason, it should simply be dropped from the repertoire. There will be many books asked for repeatedly so that a "favorites" list can easily be compiled; then, with a new story added from time to time, Creative Dramatics can be a popular reinforcement tool in the presentation of pre-school literature.

The Story Board

Another reinforcement tool is the Story Board, which can be used even with a few children in a home situation. Once the board has been constructed, youngsters themselves can often do the "art work" necessary to add to the enjoyment of stories illustrated in this way.

First, using a piece of 1/4-inch thick plywood, cut (or have the lumber yard cut) the board to a suitable size: two by one and a half feet for home use, three feet by two feet for use with a larger group. Then, using a staple gun, cover the board with black or white felt, securing the material firmly to the plywood all around the edges, after covering both sides. This is easily done, since felt is commonly available in 72-inch width at most fabric stores. This material has no right/wrong side, no "straight of the goods" to complicate its handling. There are several alternatives, however. Flannel may be substituted for felt, but it is less durable, wrinkles easily, and has less surface nap on which to make the cut-outs stick. One may also use an inexpensive indoor-outdoor carpeting and glue it to the board. If the larger size board is used, a strap handle (a piece of a discarded belt will do) should then be attached to the middle of the top edge to make the board portable. At any rate, there is little difficulty involved in making this "background" ready for use.

From this point on, the procedure can be extremely simple or, if one is an artist, it can become quite complex. Assuming no particular artistic ability at all, let us illustrate how to use the Story Board for an uncomplicated book, such as *It Looked Like Spilt Milk*, which features royal blue pages, each with a white shape in outline form. These shapes (one to the page) resemble single objects, such as a mitten, an ice-cream cone, a woolly lamb, and so on. Each of these can easily be traced onto white felt, cut out, and used "as is," since the felt pieces will adhere to the board's covering material. As the adult reads the book, each piece can then be "placed" by a child, insuring immediate involvement. In this particular book the questions are repeatedly asked, such as, "Is it a mitten?" or "Is it a rabbit?" and so on, as each page is turned, and each time, of course, the answer is negative. Finally, we learn that each shaped white blob only *seems* to be a particular object, but that they are all really just white cloud shapes in a blue sky.

Many activities may well follow such a reading. For instance, the children could go outside and make up their own items by looking at real white clouds in a blue sky; then they might attempt outline drawings of their own to be translated into additional felt pieces. In any case, this sort of book stretches the child's imagination while still remaining a suitable choice for those who are at a very literal level of understanding in regard to illustration.

With a more complicated book, such as *What Is a Man?*, there will be some drawing necessary as each individual piece is cut out, since more than silhouettes are used in the illustrations. By tracing, if one cannot draw freehand, it is not too difficult to do such drawing with a felt-tip pen which works well directly on the felt.

Figures may also be made by simply cutting out the pictures from books and stiffening them with pelon, which will adhere well to the felt or carpet covered board. However, it is necessary to have two books to cut up, plus a third one to read from, so that unless funds are no concern, it is necessary to look for good inexpensive paperback reproductions to use in this way. Even so, this method is still not as costly as purchasing commercially produced sets, and has the added advantage of a much wider choice of books, since only the "classics" are generally available to buy as complete sets.

With the simpler books, four- and five-year-olds can participate in making many of the pieces to be used, which is an art project in itself, and with the more complex productions, children can often make some of the background objects, such as the green pasture to which the goats go in *Three Billy Goats Gruff*. The possibilities are almost limitless for using this tactile aid to appreciating books. In *The Storyteller, 2nd edition*,[7] Ramon Ross has a fine chapter entitled "The Flannel Board," in which he gives the reader many ideas about the use of materials for backgrounds as well as for characters, storing the ready-to-use stories, and so on. Although the emphasis in this book is on telling stories, rather than reading them, there is the tacit assumption that the storyteller has memorized his tale from a book before doing the three-dimensional presentation, and, of course, a taped recording of the text could be substituted for direct story-telling. Ramon Ross's assertion that certain kinds of stories work best is certainly valid (he cites the folk tale, the scientific account, and the accumulative tale), and he goes through one story of each category with full illustrations and instructions.

In terms of the age group dealt with in this book, the reader is advised to consult the lists entitled *Folk and Fairy* and several of the *Informational* lists for some specific suggested titles which are not too complicated. The same general rule applies here, of course, as for all other areas: the younger the child, the simpler should be the material chosen.

Puppets

We know that children relate very well to puppets, sometimes holding conversations with them when talking to real live people seems threatening. Puppets can therefore often provide a bridge over which real communication can take place between an adult and a child or between one child and another. For example, a child whose native language is not English may be shy about speaking to others, but that same child will frequently "talk" to a puppet, particularly if it "answers" through the ingenuity of a sensitive adult.

There is then no limit to the use of puppets with pre-school children's books. Almost any story can be enhanced by the use of a single puppet, perhaps "turning the pages" of the book, or just "listening" to the story, and, of course, complete sets of characters may be used as well. In the latter case, the story chosen (particularly by beginning puppeteers) should have a limited number of characters in order to facilitate using a different voice with each one. Books which lend themselves to this form of reinforcement usually have a great deal of action, just as would be required in any stage presentation. If a number of puppets are used, the story should be told, rather than read, so that the adult can concentrate completely on working the puppets without having to juggle a book at the same time, and with this format pre-recording the story on tape usually works best.

No attempt will be made here to discuss details of the art of puppetry itself, since that is quite beyond the scope of this book. Several basics, however, should be kept in mind. First, hand puppets are not the same as marionettes, and so there is no need to fear using them because of difficulty in manipulation. Secondly, puppets should be kept simple and be durable so that they do not become show pieces which children cannot touch and use at will. Next, we should remember that while puppets are available commercially, they are quite easy to construct with a basic "body" pattern, some styrofoam balls and a little imagination. Equally easy to create are puppets made from gloves, socks, discarded stuffed animals (with the stuffing removed), and even paper bags. Some can be made and manipulated by the children themselves. Finally, in order to make the best use of puppets, interested adults might find it useful—and great fun—to enroll in a course in beginning puppetry, or, if that is not possible, to read a few basic books on the subject and then experiment with various materials which can be used.

Because their use is dependent only on the desire of the teacher or parent, and not based specifically on one book or another, it seems more useful to list adult self-help books in this section, rather than titles with which to use puppets. Therefore, with the expert advice of Betsy Brown George, noted puppeteer and teacher of puppetry at California State University, Northridge, and Los Angeles Valley College, the following brief bibliography was compiled. Ms. George's forthcoming book on the subject will probably serve in place of many of the following titles because it will be a copiously illustrated college-level text for beginning and advanced students of puppetry. But since it is not available yet, here are her recommendations:

Chernoff, Goldie Taub, *Puppet Party*, Published by Walker, New York, 1971.

Emberley, Ed, *Punch and Judy,* Published by Little, Brown, New York, 1965.

Hutchings, Margaret, *Making and Using Finger Puppets,* Published by Taplinger, New York, 1973.

McLaren, Esme, *Making Glove Puppets,* Published by Plays, Inc., Boston, 1973.

Paludan, Liz, *Playing with Puppets,* Published by Plays, Inc., Boston, 1972.

Philpott, Violet and Mary Jean McNeil, *The Know-How Book of Puppets,* Published by Sterling, New York, 1976.

In Conclusion

The modern world is a very busy place, and it is quite understandable that adults who interact with small children find themselves having to make choices constantly regarding the best use of time. They are urged at every turn to involve the child in play experiences so that he can "act out" his feelings; they are encouraged to provide the child with physical activities so that he can develop his musculature; and they are concerned that the child interact with other children so that he can become "socialized." Furthermore, parents find themselves with many claims on their time which have little or nothing to do with the children in their care.

And tempting them too often is the all-too-convenient electronic baby sitter, the television set, which promises to enlarge the scope of the child's learning while simultaneously providing needed free time for supervising adults.

Somewhat analogous to the expenditure of money in a limited budget, then, is the expenditure of time which is also somewhat scarce. Therefore, adults must become convinced of the benefits of exposing pre-schoolers to literature before they decide to expend the time necessary for wise book selection and for the sharing process itself. However, just reading *about* the benefits to be gained and the ways in which children can profit from exposure to literature will never convince adults as completely as experience with real live youngsters! It is earnestly hoped that this book will encourage its readers to participate with pre-schoolers in the enjoyment of literature. Remember, they're never too young for books.

Footnotes

[1] Mark Taylor, *A Study of the Effects of Presenting Literature to First-Grade Students by Means of Five Visual-Verbal Presentation Modes: A Dissertation* (Los Angeles: University of Southern California, June, 1976).

[2] Marie Winn, *The Plug-In Drug* (New York: Viking Press, 1977).

[3] Jerry Mander, *Four Arguments for the Elimination of Television* (New York: William Morrow, 1978).

[4] Blanche Seale Hunt, *Stories of Little Brown Koko* (New York: Colortype Company, 1940).

[5] Donnarae MacCann and Olga Richard, *The Child's First Books: A Critical Study of Pictures and Texts* (New York: H.W. Wilson Company, 1973).

[6] Nicholas Mordvinoff, "Caldecott Award Acceptance," *Horn Book* (August, 1952, p.222).

[7] Beni Montressor, "Caldecott Award Acceptance," *Horn Book* (August, 1965, p.371).

[8] Bruno Bettleheim, *The Uses of Enchantment* (New York: Alfred A. Knopf, 1976).

[9] "Dreams," from *The Child World* (London: John Lane, Third Edition, 1896).

[10] Louise Driscoll, "Hold Fast Your Dreams" (New York: The New York Times Company, 1916).

Bibliography

Aardema, Verna
Half-a-Ball-of-Kenki
Illustrated by Diane Stanley Zuromskis
Published by Warne, 1979
Aardema, Verna
Riddle of the Drum: A Tale from Tizapan, Mexico
Translated by Verna Aardema
Illustrated by Tony Chen
Adapted by Verna Aardema
Published by Scholastic, 1979
Aardema, Verna
Who's in Rabbit's House: A Masai Tale
Illustrated by Diane Dillon
Published by Dial, 1977
Aardema, Verna
Why Mosquitos Buzz in People's Ears
Illustrated by Leo and Diane Dillon
Published by Dial, 1975
Abbott, Sarah
The Old Dog
Illustrated by Sarah Abbott
Published by Coward, 1972
Abell, Kathleen
King Orville and the Bull Frogs
Illustrated by Erroll Le Cain
Published by Little, Brown, 1974
Abisch, Roz
Around the House That Jack Built
Illustrated by Boche Kaplan
Published by Parents Magazine Press, 1972
Abisch, Roz
Do You Know What Time It Is?
Illustrated by Boche Kaplan
Published by Prentice-Hall, 1968
Abisch, Roz
Let's Find Out About Butterflies
Illustrated by Boche Kaplan
Published by Watts, 1972
Adam, Barbara
Big, Big Box
Illustrated by Barbara Adam
Published by Doubleday, (n.d.)
Adams, Adrienne
Easter Egg Artists
Illustrated by Adrienne Adams
Published by Scribner, 1976
Adams, Adrienne
Mushy Eggs
Illustrated by Marilyn Hirsh
Published by Putnam, 1973
Adams, Adrienne
Woggle of Witches
Illustrated by Adrienne Adams
Published by Scribner, 1971
Adamson, Gareth
Harold, the Happy Handyman
Illustrated by Gareth Adamson
Published by Harvey House, 1968
Adler, David
A Little at a Time
Illustrated by N.M. Bodecker
Published by Random, 1976
Adoff, Arnold
Big Sister Tells Me That I'm Black
Illustrated by Lorenzo Lynch
Published by Holt, Rinehart and Winston, 1976
Adoff, Arnold
Black Is Brown Is Tan
Illustrated by Emily A. McCully
Published by Harper and Row, 1973
Adoff, Arnold
Make a Circle Keep Us In: Poems for a Good Day
Illustrated by Arnold Himler
Published by Delacorte, 1975
Adoff, Arnold
MA nDA LA
Illustrated by Emily A. McCully
Published by Harper and Row, 1971
Adshead, Gladys
Brownies—It's Christmas!
Illustrated by Velma Illsley
Published by Walck, 1955
Adshead, Gladys
Smallest Brownie and the Flying Squirrel
Illustrated by Richard Lebenson
Published by Walck, 1972
Aesop
Town Mouse and the Country Mouse
Illustrated by Paul Galdone
Published by McGraw-Hill, 1971
Aesop
Three Aesop Fox Fables (Fox & Grapes, Stork, Crow)
Illustrated by Paul Galdone
Published by Seabury, 1971
Ahlberg, Allan
Cops and Robbers

Illustrated by Janet Ahlberg
Published by Greenwillow, 1979
Ahlberg, Janet and Allan
Each Peach, Pear, Plum
Illustrated by Janet and Allan
  Ahlberg
Published by Viking Press, 1979
Aiken, Conrad
Cats and Bats and Things with
  Wings
Illustrated by Milton Glaser
Published by Atheneum, 1965
Aiken, Conrad and John Lord
Who's Zoo?
Illustrated
Published by Atheneum, 1977
Aimar, Caroline
Waymond the Whale
Illustrated by Martha Heath
Published by Prentice-Hall, 1975
Aldridge, Josephine
Penny and a Periwinkle
Illustrated by Ruth Robbins
Published by Parnassus Press, 1961
Aldridge, Josephine
Reasons and Raisins
Illustrated by John Larrecq
Published by Parnassus Press, 1971
Alexander, Lloyd
Coll and His White Pig
Illustrated by Evaline Ness
Published by Holt, Rinehart and
  Winston, 1965
Alexander, Lloyd
Four Donkeys
Illustrated by Lester Abrams
Published by Holt, Rinehart and
  Winston, 1972
Alexander, Martha
And My Mean Old Mother Will Be
  Sorry, Blackboard Bear
Illustrated by Martha Alexander
Published by Dial, 1972
Alexander, Martha
Blackboard Bear
Illustrated by Martha Alexander
Published by Dial, 1969
Alexander, Martha
Bobo's Dream
Illustrated by Martha Alexander
Published by Dial, 1970
Alexander, Martha
I'll Be the Horse If You'll Play
  with Me
Illustrated by Martha Alexander
Published by Dial Press, 1975
Alexander, Martha
I'll Protect You from the Jungle
  Beasts

Illustrated by Martha Alexander
Published by Dial, 1973
Alexander, Martha
Nobody Asked Me If I Wanted a Baby
  Sister
Illustrated by Martha Alexander
Published by Dial, 1971
Alexander, Martha
No Ducks in Our Bathtub
Illustrated by Martha Alexander
Published by Dial, 1973
Alexander, Martha
Out! Out! Out!
Illustrated by Martha Alexander
Published by Dial, 1968
Alexander, Martha
Sabrina
Illustrated by Martha Alexander
Published by Dial, 1971
Alexander, Martha
We Never Get to Do Anything
Illustrated by Martha Alexander
Published by Dial, 1970
Aliki
At Mary Bloom's
Illustrated by Aliki
Published by Greenwillow, 1976
Aliki
Corn Is Maize: The Gift of the Indians
Illustrated by Aliki
Published by T.Y. Crowell, 1976
Aliki
Diogenes: The Story of the Greek
  Philosopher
Illustrated by Aliki
Published by Prentice-Hall, 1968
Aliki
Fossils Tell of Long Ago
Illustrated by Aliki
Published by T.Y. Crowell, 1972
Aliki
Green Grass and White Milk
Illustrated by Aliki
Published by T.Y. Crowell, 1974
Aliki
Keep Your Mouth Closed, Dear
Illustrated by Aliki
Published by Dial, 1966
Aliki
Long Lost Coelacanth and Other
  Living Fossils
Illustrated by Aliki
Published by T.Y. Crowell, 1973
Aliki
My Five Senses
Illustrated by Aliki
Published by T.Y. Crowell, 1972
Aliki
My Hands

Aliki
Illustrated by Aliki
Published by T.Y. Crowell, 1962
Aliki
My Visit to the Dinosaurs
Illustrated by Aliki
Published by T.Y. Crowell, 1969
Aliki
Story of Johnny Appleseed
Illustrated by Aliki
Published by Prentice-Hall, 1963
Aliki
Twelve Months
Illustrated by Aliki
Published by Greenwillow, 1979
Aliki
Wild and Woolly Mammoths
Illustrated by Aliki
Published by T.Y. Crowell, 1977
Allamand, Pascale
Cocoa Beans & Daisies: How Swiss Chocolate Is Made
Illustrated by Pascale Allamand
Published by Warne, 1978
Allamand, Pascale
Little Goat in the Mountains
Illustrated by Pascale Allamand
Published by Warne, 1978
Allamand, Pascale
Pop Rooster
Illustrated by Pascale Allamand
Published by Scribner, 1975
Allard, Harry
I Will Not Go to Market Today
Illustrated by James Marshall
Published by Dial, 1979
Allard, Harry
It's So Nice to Have a Wolf Around the House
Illustrated by James Marshall
Published by Doubleday, 1977
Allard, Harry
Stupids Step Out
Illustrated by James Marshall
Published by Houghton Mifflin, 1977
Allard, Harry and James Marshall
Miss Nelson Is Missing!
Illustrated by James Marshall
Published by Houghton Mifflin, 1977
Allen, Frances
Little Hippo
Illustrated by Laura J. Allen
Published by Putnam, 1971
Allen, Gertrude E.
Everyday Birds
Illustrated by Gertrude E. Allen
Published by Houghton Mifflin, 1973
Allen, Gertrude E.
Everyday Insects
Illustrated by Gertrude E. Allen
Published by Houghton Mifflin, 1963
Allen, Gertrude E.
Everyday Trees
Illustrated by Gertrude E. Allen
Published by Houghton Mifflin, 1968
Allen, Gertrude E.
Everyday Turtles, Toads, and Their Kin
Illustrated by Gertrude E. Allen
Published by Houghton Mifflin, 1970
Allen, Gertrude E.
Everyday Wildflowers
Illustrated by Gertrude E. Allen
Published by Houghton Mifflin, 1965
Allen, Jeffrey
Mary Alice, Operator Number Nine
Illustrated by James Marshall
Published by Little, Brown, 1975
Allen, Joan
Baby Animal Dress-up Book
Illustrated by Joan Allen
Published by Platt & Munk, (n.d.)
Allinson, Beverley
Mandy and the Flying Map
Illustrated by Ann Powell
Published by Canadian Women's Educational Press, 1973
Allison, Rosemary
Green Harpy at the Corner Store
Illustrated by Claire Watson Garcia
Published by Kids Can Press (Canada), 1976
Allison, Rosemary and Ann Powell
Travels of Ms. Beaver
Illustrated by Rosemary Allison
Published by Canadian Women's Educational Press, 1973
Ambrus, Victor
Brave Soldier Janosh
Illustrated by Victor Ambrus
Published by Harcourt Brace Jovanovich, 1967
Ambrus, Victor
Mishka
Illustrated by Victor Ambrus
Published by Warne, 1978
Ambrus, Victor
Sultan's Bath
Illustrated by Victor Ambrus
Published by Harcourt Brace Jovanovich, 1972
Ambrus, Victor
Three Poor Tailors
Illustrated by Victor Ambrus
Published by Harcourt Brace Jovanovich, 1966

Ames, Gerald and Rose Wyler
Prove It!
Illustrated by Talivaldis Stubis
Published by Harper and Row, 1963
Amoss, Berthe
Tom in the Middle
Illustrated by Berthe Amoss
Published by Harper and Row, 1968
Ancona, George
I Feel: A Picture Book of Emotions
Illustrated by George Ancona
Published by Dutton, 1977
Anders, Rebecca
Whiskers the Rabbit
Translated by Diane Hammarberg
Illustrated by Rebecca Anders
Published by Carolrhoda, 1976
Andersen, Hans Christian
Emperor's New Clothes
Illustrated by Virginia L. Burton
Published by Houghton Mifflin, 1949
Andersen, Hans Christian
Princess and the Pea
Illustrated by Paul Galdone
Published by Seabury, 1978
Andersen, Hans Christian
Snow Queen
Translated by R. P. Keigwin
Illustrated by Marcia Brown
Published by Scribner, 1972
Andersen, Hans Christian
Thumbelina
Translated by R. P. Keigwin
Illustrated by Adrienne Adams
Published by Scribner, 1961
Andersen, Hans Christian
Ugly Duckling
Translated by R. P. Keigwin
Illustrated by Adrienne Adams
Published by Scribner, 1965
Anderson, C. W.
Blaze and the Gray Spotted Pony
Illustrated by C. W. Anderson
Published by Macmillan, 1974
Anderson, C. W.
Lonesome Little Colt
Illustrated by C. W. Anderson
Published by Macmillan, 1974
Anderson, Eloise
Carlos Goes to School
Illustrated by Harold Berson
Published by Warne, 1973
Anderson, Lonzo
Day the Hurricane Happened
Illustrated by Ann Grifalconi
Published by Scribner, 1974
Anderson, Lonzo
Halloween Party
Illustrated by Adrienne Adams
Published by Scribner, 1974
Anderson, Lonzo
Izzard
Illustrated by Adrienne Adams
Published by Scribner, 1973
Anderson, Lonzo
Ponies of Mykillengi
Illustrated by Adrienne Adams
Published by Scribner, 1966
Anderson, Lonzo
Two Hundred Rabbits
Illustrated by Adrienne Adams
Published by Viking Press, 1968
Anderson, Paul
Red Fox and the Hungry Tiger
Illustrated by Paul Anderson
Published by A-W, 1962
Andre, Evelyn M.
Things We Like to Do
Illustrated by Evelyn M. Andre
Published by Abingdon, 1968
Andrews, Jan
Fresh Fish ... and Chips
Illustrated by Linda Donnelly
Published by Canadian Women's Educational Press, 1973
Andry, Andrew C. and Suzanne C. Kratka
Hi, New Baby
Illustrated by Thomas Di Grazia
Published by Simon & Schuster, 1970
Angelo, Valenti
Acorn Tree
Illustrated by Valenti Angelo
Published by Viking Press, 1958
Annett, Cora
Dog Who Thought He Was a Boy
Illustrated by W. Lorraine
Published by Houghton Mifflin, 1974
Anno, Mitsumasa
King's Flower
Illustrated by Mitsumasa Anno
Published by Collins-World, 1979
Anno, Mitsumasa
Anno's Alphabet: An Adventure in Imagination
Illustrated by Mitsumasa Anno
Published by T.Y. Crowell, 1975
Anno, Mitsumasa
Anno's Counting Book
Illustrated by Mitsumasa Anno
Published by T.Y. Crowell, 1977
Anno, Mitsumasa
Dr. Anno's Magical Midnight Circus
Translated by Meredith Weatherby
Illustrated by Mitsumasa Anno
Published by Weatherhill, 1972

Bibliography / **173**

Anno, Mitsumasa
Topsy-Turvies: Pictures to Stretch the Imagination
Illustrated by Mitsumasa Anno
Published by Weatherhill, 1970
Anno, Mitsumasa
Upside-Downers: More Pictures to Stretch the Imagination
Translated by M. Wetherby and S. Trumbull
Illustrated by Mitsumasa Anno
Published by Weatherhill, 1971
Anonymous
Baby's Farm Animals
Illustrated
Published by Grosset & Dunlap, 1956
Anonymous
Baby's First Golden Books (4)
Illustrated
Published by Western, 1972
Anonymous
Baby's First Library: Counting
Illustrated
Published by Platt & Munk, (n.d.)
Anonymous
Baby's First Library: ABC
Illustrated
Published by Platt & Munk, (n.d.)
Anonymous
Baby's First Library (4)
Illustrated
Published by Platt & Munk, (n.d.)
Anonymous
Baby's First Whitman Books (3)
Illustrated
Published by Nursery Books, (n.d.)
Anonymous
Board Story Books
Illustrated
Published by Nursery Books, (n.d.)
Anonymous
Board Story Books (Child's Play; My Baby Brother)
Illustrated
Published by Nursery Books, (n.d.)
Anonymous
Brimax Animal Board Books
Illustrated
Published by Nursery Books, (n.d.)
Anonymous
Counting Rhymes Board Book
Illustrated
Published by Grosset & Dunlap, 1970
Anonymous
Dean's Cloth Books
Illustrated
Published by Nursery Books, (n.d.)
Anonymous
Dolly Books (4)
Illustrated
Published by Nursery Books, (n.d.)
Anonymous
Folk Tales from Asia for Children Everywhere (6)
Illustrated
Published by Weatherhill, 1979
Anonymous
Golden Photo Board Books (6)
Illustrated
Published by Nursery Books, (n.d.)
Anonymous
Long Board Books (6)
Illustrated
Published by Grosset & Dunlap, (n.d.)
Anonymous
Mother Goose Board Book
Illustrated
Published by Grosset & Dunlap, 1959
Anonymous
Panorama Folding Board Books (3)
Illustrated
Published by Nursery Books, (n.d.)
Anonymous
Peggy Cloth Books (5)
Illustrated
Published by Nursery Books, (n.d.)
Anonymous
Perma-Life Books (3)
Illustrated
Published by Platt & Munk, 1969
Anonymous
Wipe-Clean Books (4)
Illustrated
Published by Western, 1977
Anonymous
Wipe-Clean Books (5)
Illustrated
Published by Nursery Books, (n.d.)
Arbore, Lily
Princess and the Unicorn
Illustrated by Mary Chagnon
Published by Carolrhoda, 1972
Ardizzone, Edward
Sarah and Simon and No Red Paint
Illustrated by Edward Ardizzone
Published by Delacorte, (n.d.)
Armour, Richard
Adventures of Egbert the Easter Egg
Illustrated
Published by McGraw-Hill, 1965
Armour, Richard
Dozen Dinosaurs
Illustrated by Paul Galdone
Published by McGraw-Hill, 1967
Armour, Richard
Sea Full of Whales

Illustrated by Paul Galdone
Published by McGraw-Hill, 1974
Arnold, Rist.
I Like Birds
Illustrated by Rist. Arnold
Published by Tundra Bks, 1977
Arnosky, Jim
Mud Time and More Nathaniel
Stories
Illustrated by Jim Arnosky
Published by A-W, 1979
Arnstein, Helene S.
Billy and Our New Baby
Illustrated by M. Jane Smyth
Published by Human Sciences Press, 1973
Arthur, Catherine
My Sister's Silent World
Illustrated by Catherine Arthur
Published by Children's Press, (n.d.)
Artis, Vicki Kimmel
Brown Mouse and Vole
Illustrated by Jan Hughes
Published by Putnam, 1975
Aruego, Jose
Look What I Can Do
Illustrated by Jose Aruego
Published by Scribner, 1971
Aruego, Jose
Pilyo the Piranha
Illustrated by Jose Aruego
Published by Macmillan, 1971
Asbjornsen, P.C.
Squire's Bride
Illustrated by Marcia Sewall
Published by Atheneum, 1975
Asbjornsen, P.C.
Three Billy Goats Gruff
Illustrated by Marcia Brown
Published by Harcourt Brace Jovanovich, 1957
Asbjornsen, P.C.
Three Billy Goats Gruff
Illustrated by Paul Galdone
Published by Seabury, 1973
Asch, Frank
Monkey Face
Illustrated by Frank Asch
Published by Parents Magazine Press, 1977
Asch, Frank
Moon Bear
Illustrated by Frank Asch
Published by Scribner, 1978
Asch, Frank
Rebecka
Illustrated by Frank Asch
Published by Harper and Row, 1973

Asch, Frank
Sand Cake
Illustrated by Frank Asch
Published by Parents Magazine Press, 1979
Asch, Frank
Turtle Tale
Illustrated by Frank Asch
Published by Dial, 1979
Atkinson, Mary
Maria Teresa
Illustrated by Christine E. Eber
Published by Lollipop Power, 1979
Averill, Esther
Hotel Cat
Illustrated by Esther Averill
Published by Harper and Row, 1969
Averill, Esther
Jenny's Birthday Book
Illustrated by Esther Averill
Published by Harper and Row, 1954
Ayer, Jacqueline
Little Silk
Illustrated by Jacqueline Ayer
Published by Harcourt Brace Jovanovich, 1970
Ayer, Jacqueline
Wish for Little Sister
Illustrated by Jacqueline Ayer
Published by Harcourt Brace Jovanovich, 1960
Babbitt, Natalie
Something
Illustrated by Natalie Babbitt
Published by Farrar, Straus and Giroux, 1970
Bach, Alice
Grouchy Uncle Otto
Illustrated by Steven Kellogg
Published by Harper and Row, 1977
Bach, Alice
Millicent the Magnificent
Illustrated by Steven Kellogg
Published by Harper and Row, 1978
Bach, Alice
Most Delicious Camping Trip Ever
Illustrated by Steven Kellogg
Published by Harper and Row, 1976
Bach, Alice
Smartest Bear and His Brother Oliver
Illustrated by Steven Kellogg
Published by Harper and Row, 1975
Baker, Betty
Little Runner of the Longhouse
Illustrated by Arnold Lobel
Published by Harper and Row, 1962
Baker, Betty
Pig War

Illustrated by Robert Lopshire
Published by Harper and Row, 1969
Baldwin, Anne
Sunflowers for Tina
Illustrated by Ann Grifalconi
Published by Scholastic, 1970
Bales, Carol A.
Kevin Cloud: Chippewa Boy in the City
Illustrated
Published by Contemporary Books, 1972
Balestrino, Philip
Fat and Skinny
Illustrated by Pam Makie
Published by T.Y. Crowell, 1975
Balestrino, Philip
Skeleton Inside You
Illustrated by Don Bolognese
Published by T.Y. Crowell, 1971
Balet, Jan
Joanjo, a Portuguese Tale
Illustrated by Jan Balet
Published by Delacorte, 1967
Balian, Lorna
Aminal
Illustrated by Lorna Balian
Published by Abingdon, 1972
Balian, Lorna
Bah! Humbug
Illustrated by Lorna Balian
Published by Abingdon, 1977
Balian, Lorna
Humbug Rabbit
Illustrated by Lorna Balian
Published by Abingdon, 1974
Balian, Lorna
Humbug Witch
Illustrated by Lorna Balian
Published by Abingdon, 1965
Balian, Lorna
I Love You, Mary Jane
Illustrated by Lorna Balian
Published by Abingdon, 1967
Balian, Lorna
Sometimes It's Turkey, Sometimes It's Feathers
Illustrated by Lorna Balian
Published by Abingdon, 1973
Balian, Lorna
Sweet Touch
Illustrated by Lorna Balian
Published by Abingdon, 1976
Balian, Lorna
A Sweetheart for Valentine
Illustrated by Lorna Balian
Published by Abingdon, 1979
Balian, Lorna
Where in the World Is Henry?

Illustrated by Lorna Balian
Published by Bradbury Press, 1972
Ballard, Lois
True Book of Reptiles
Illustrated by G. Wilde
Published by Children's Press, 1957
Bancroft, Henrietta
Down Come the Leaves
Illustrated by Nonny Hogrogian
Published by T.Y. Crowell, 1961
Bancroft, Henrietta and Richard G. Van Gelder
Animals in Winter
Illustrated by Gaetano Di Palma
Published by T.Y. Crowell, 1963
Bang, Molly
Grey Lady and the Strawberry Snatcher
Illustrated by Molly Bang
Published by Scholastic, 1980
Bang, Molly
Old Woman and the Red Pumpkin
Illustrated by Molly Bang
Adapted by Betsy Bang
Published by Macmillan, 1975
Banner, Angela
Around the World with Ant and Bee
Illustrated
Published by Watts, 1964
Bannon, Laura
Little People of the Night
Illustrated
Published by Houghton Mifflin, 1973
Barber, Janet
Voyage of Jim
Illustrated by Fritz Wegner
Published by Carolrhoda, 1973
Barberis, France
Would You Like a Parrot?
Illustrated by Franco Barberis
Published by Scroll Press, 1979
Barkin, Carol and Elizabeth James
Are We Still Best Friends?
Illustrated by Heinz Kluetmeier
Published by Raintree, 1975
Barnstone, Willis
Day in the Country
Illustrated by Howard Knotts
Published by Harper and Row, 1971
Barr, Cathrine
Bears In—Bears Out
Illustrated
Published by Walck, 1967
Barr, Cathrine
Horse for Sherry
Illustrated by Cathrine Barr
Published by Walck, 1963

Barr, Cathrine
Sammy Seal of the Circus
Illustrated
Published by Walck, 1955

Barr, Elizabeth K.
Willy and Nilly and the Silly Cat
Illustrated
Published by Valkyrie Press, 1976

Barrett, John
Littlest Mule
Illustrated
Adapted by Jane and Dale Baer
Published by Silver Dollar, 1977

Barrett, John M.
Oscar the Selfish Octopus
Illustrated by Jos. Servello
Published by Human Sciences Press, 1979

Barrett, Judi
I Hate to Take a Bath
Illustrated by Chas. P. Slackman
Published by Scholastic, 1975

Barrett, Judi
Wind Thief
Illustrated by Diane Dawson
Published by Atheneum, 1977

Barrett, Judith
Animals Should Definitely Not Wear Clothing
Illustrated by Ron Barrett
Published by Atheneum, 1974

Barrett, Judith
An Apple a Day
Illustrated by Tim Lewis
Published by Atheneum, 1973

Barrett, Judith
Benjamin's 365 Birthdays
Illustrated by Ron Barrett
Published by Atheneum, 1974

Barrett, Judith
Old MacDonald Had an Apartment House
Illustrated by Ron Barrett
Published by Atheneum, 1969

Barrett, Judith
Peter's Pocket
Illustrated by Julia Noonan
Published by Atheneum, 1974

Barrows, Marjorie
Muggins' Big Balloon
Illustrated
Published by Hale, 1964

Barry, Robert
Ramon and the Pirate Gull
Illustrated
Published by McGraw-Hill, 1971

Barthelme, Donald
Slightly Irregular Fire Engine, or the Hithering...Djinn
Illustrated by Donald Barthelme
Published by Farrar, Straus and Giroux, 1971

Bartlett, Margaret
Clean Brook
Illustrated by Aldren A. Watson
Published by T.Y. Crowell, 1960

Bartlett, Margaret
Where the Brook Begins
Illustrated by Aldren A. Watson
Published by T.Y. Crowell, 1961

Bartoli, Jennifer
Nonna
Illustrated by Joan Drescher
Published by Harvey, 1975

Barton, Byron
Applebet Story
Illustrated by Byron Barton
Published by Viking Press, 1973

Barton, Byron
Buzz, Buzz, Buzz
Illustrated by Byron Barton
Published by Macmillan, 1973

Barton, Byron
Elephant
Illustrated by Byron Barton
Published by Seabury, 1971

Barton, Byron
Harry Is a Scaredy-Cat
Illustrated by Byron Barton
Published by Macmillan, 1974

Barton, Byron
Hester
Illustrated by Byron Barton
Published by Greenwillow, 1975

Barton, Byron
Where's Al?
Illustrated by Byron Barton
Published by Seabury, 1972

Basil, Cynthia
Nailheads and Potato Eyes
Illustrated by Janet McCaffery
Published by Morrow, 1976

Baskin, Tobias et al.
Hosie's Aviary
Illustrated by Leonard Baskin
Published by Viking Press, 1979

Bason, Lillian
Those Foolish Molboes!
Illustrated by Margot Tomes
Published by Coward, 1977

Bate, Lucy
Little Rabbit's Loose Tooth
Illustrated by Diane De Groat
Published by Crown, 1975

Bate, Norman
Who Built the Bridge?

Illustrated by Norman Bate
Published by Scribner, 1954
Battles, Edith
One to Teeter-Totter
Illustrated by Rosalind Fry
Published by A. Whitman, 1973
Baum, Arlene and Joseph Baum
Know What? No, What?
Illustrated
Published by Parents Magazine Press, 1964
Baum, Arlene and Joseph Baum
One Bright Monday Morning
Illustrated
Published by Random, 1962
Baum, Willi
Birds of a Feather
Illustrated by Willi Baum
Published by Awani Press, 1969
Baumann, Hans
Hare's Race
Translated by Elizabeth D. Crawford
Illustrated by Antoni Boratynski
Published by Morrow, 1976
Baumann, Kurt
Joseph, the Border Guard
Illustrated by David McKee
Published by Parents Magazine Press, 1972
Baylor, Byrd
Everybody Needs a Rock
Illustrated by Peter Parnall
Published by Scribner, 1974
Baylor, Byrd
Other Way to Listen
Illustrated by Peter Parnall
Published by Scribner, 1979
Baylor, Byrd
Sometimes I Dance Mountains
Illustrated by Kenneth Longtemps
Published by Scribner, 1973
Baylor, Byrd
They Put on Masks
Illustrated by Jerry Ingram
Published by Scribner, 1974
Baylor, Peter
Plink, Plink, Plink
Illustrated by James Marshall
Published by Houghton Mifflin, 1971
Beach, Stewart
Good Morning, Sun's Up
Illustrated by Yataka Sugita
Published by Scroll Press, (n.d.)
Beatty, Hetty B.
Rebel the Reluctant Racehorse
Illustrated by Joshua Tolford
Published by Houghton Mifflin, 1968
Becker, Edna
Nine Hundred Buckets of Paint

Illustrated by Margaret Becker
Published by Abingdon, (n.d.)
Becker, John
Seven Little Rabbits
Illustrated by Barbara Cooney
Published by Walker, 1973
Beckman, Per.
Looking for Lucas
Illustrated by Per. Beckman
Published by D. White, 1968
Behrens, June
Together
Illustrated by Vince Streano
Published by Children's Press, 1975
Beim, Jerrold
Swimming Hole
Illustrated by Louis Darling
Published by Morrow, 1951
Beim, Lorraine and Jerrold Beim
Two Is a Team
Illustrated by E. Crichlow
Published by Harcourt Brace Jovanovich, 1945
Beisner, Monica
Fantastic Toys
Illustrated by Monica Beisner
Published by Follett, 1974
Belloc, Hilaire
Bad Child's Book of Beasts
Illustrated by Basil T. Blackwood
Published by Knopf, 1965
Belpre, Pura
Ote: A Puerto Rican Folk Tale
Illustrated by Paul Galdone
Published by Pantheon, 1969
Belpre, Pura
Rainbow Colored Horse
Illustrated by Antonio Martorell
Published by Warne, 1978
Belting, Natalia
Indy and Mr. Lincoln
Illustrated by Leonard E. Fisher
Published by Holt, Rinehart and Winston, 1963
Bemelmans, Ludwig
Madeline
Illustrated by Ludwig Bemelmans
Published by Viking Press, 1939
Bemelmans, Ludwig
Madeline and the Bad Hat
Illustrated by Ludwig Bemelmans
Published by Viking Press, 1959
Bemelmans, Ludwig
Madeline and the Gypsies
Illustrated by Ludwig Bemelmans
Published by Viking Press, 1959
Bemelmans, Ludwig
Madeline in London

Illustrated by Ludwig Bemelmans
Published by Viking Press, 1961
Bemelmans, Ludwig
Madeline's Rescue
Illustrated by Ludwig Bemelmans
Published by Viking Press, 1953
Benarde, Anita
Pumpkin Smasher
Illustrated by Anita Benarde
Published by Walker, 1979
Benchley, Nathaniel
Red Fox and His Canoe
Illustrated by Arnold Lobel
Published by Harper and Row, 1964
Benchley, Nathaniel
Small Wolf
Illustrated by Joan Sandin
Published by Harper and Row, 1972
Bendick, Jeanne
Why Can't I?
Illustrated by Jeanne Bendick
Published by McGraw-Hill, 1969
Benjamin, Alan
1000 Monsters
Illustrated by Sal Murdocca
Published by Scholastic, 1979
Bennett, Rainey
Secret Hiding Place
Illustrated by Rainey Bennett
Published by Collins-World, 1960
Bennett, Susan
Underground Cats
Illustrated by Susan Bennett
Published by Macmillan, 1974
Benson-Parrish, Barbara
Families Grow in Different Ways
Illustrated by Karen Fletcher
Published by Before We Are Six, Canada, (n.d.)
Benton, Robert
Little Brother, No More
Illustrated by Robert Benton
Published by Knopf, 1960
Berenstain, Stan and Jan Berenstain
Berenstain Bears' Counting Book
Illustrated by Stan and Jan Berenstain
Published by Random, 1976
Berenstain, Stan and Jan Berenstain
He Bear, She Bear
Illustrated by Stan Berenstain
Published by Random, 1974
Berg, Jean
There's Nothing to Do, So Let Me Be You
Illustrated by Madeline Marabella
Published by Westminster, 1966

Berger, Melvin
Energy from the Sun
Illustrated by Guilio Maestro
Published by T.Y. Crowell, 1976
Berger, Melvin
Storms
Illustrated by Joseph Cellini
Published by Coward, 1970
Berger, Terry
Being Alone, Being Together
Illustrated by Heinz Kluetmeier
Published by Raintree, 1974
Berger, Terry
A Friend Can Help
Illustrated by Heinz Kluetmeier
Published by Raintree, 1974
Berger, Terry
How Does It Feel When Your Parents Get Divorced?
Illustrated by Miriam Shapiro
Published by Messner, 1977
Berger, Terry
I Have Feelings
Illustrated by Howard I. Spivak
Published by Human Sciences Press, 1971
Berger, Terry
New Baby
Illustrated by Heinz Kluetmeier
Published by Raintree, 1975
Bernhard, Marcelle
Jamie's Magic Bullet
Illustrated by Marcelle Bernhard
Published by C.E. Tuttle, 1968
Berson, Harold
Balarin's Goat
Illustrated by Harold Berson
Published by Crown, 1972
Berson, Harold
Boy, the Baker, the Miller and More
Illustrated by Harold Berson
Published by Crown, 1974
Berson, Harold
How the Devil Gets His Due
Illustrated by Harold Berson
Published by Crown, 1972
Berson, Harold
I'm Bored, Ma!
Illustrated by Harold Berson
Published by Crown, 1976
Berson, Harold
Joseph and the Snake
Illustrated by Harold Berson
Published by Macmillan, 1979
Berson, Harold
Kassim's Shoes
Illustrated by Harold Berson
Published by Crown, 1977

Berson, Harold
Larbi and Leila: A Tale of Two Mice
Illustrated by Harold Berson
Published by Seabury, 1974

Berson, Harold
A Moose Is Not a Mouse
Illustrated by Harold Berson
Published by Crown, 1975

Berson, Harold
Rats Who Lived in the Delicatessen
Illustrated by Harold Berson
Published by Crown, 1976

Berson, Harold
Thief Who Hugged a Moonbeam
Illustrated by Harold Berson
Published by Seabury, 1972

Berson, Harold
Why Jackal Won't Speak to Hedgehog
Illustrated by Harold Berson
Published by Seabury, 1969

Beskow, Elsa
Pelle's New Suit
Illustrated by Elsa Beskow
Published by Scholastic, 1974

Beskow, Elsa
Peter's Adventures in Blueberry Land
Translated by Sheila La Farge
Illustrated by Elsa Beskow
Published by Delacorte, 1975

Bethell, Jean
Bath Time
Illustrated
Published by Holt, Rinehart and Winston, 1979

Bettina
Pantaloni
Illustrated by Bettina
Published by Harper and Row, 1957

Bianco, Pamela
Valentine Party
Illustrated by Pamela Bianco
Published by Lippincott, 1955

Bierhorst, John
Ring in the Prairie
Illustrated by Diane and Leo Dillon
Published by Dial, 1976

Biesterveld, Betty
Six Days from Sunday
Illustrated by George Armstrong
Published by Rand McNally, 1973

Binzen, Bill
Carmen
Illustrated by Bill Binzen
Published by Coward, 1970

Binzen, Bill
Miguel's Mountain
Illustrated by Bill Binzen
Published by Coward, 1968

Binzen, Bill
Walk
Illustrated by Bill Binzen
Published by Coward, 1972

Birnbaum, A.
Green Eyes
Illustrated by A. Birnbaum
Published by Western, 1973

Bishop, Claire H.
Georgette
Illustrated by Ursula Landshoff
Published by Coward, 1974

Bishop, Claire H.
Truffle Pig
Illustrated by Kurt Weise
Published by Coward, 1971

Bishop, Claire H.
Twenty-Two Bears
Illustrated by Kurt Wiese
Published by Viking Press, 1964

Bishop, Dorothy
Leonard the Lion and Ramon the Mouse
Illustrated
Published by National Textbook, 1972

Bishop, Dorothy
Tina the Tortoise and Carlos the Rabbit
Illustrated
Published by National Textbook, 1972

Black, Algernon
Woman of the Wood
Illustrated by Evaline Ness
Published by Holt, Rinehart and Winston, 1973

Blaine, Marge
Terrible Thing That Happened at Our House
Illustrated by John Wallner
Published by Parents Magazine Press, 1975

Blegvad, Lenore, Ed.
Hark! Hark! the Dogs Do Bark: Other Rhymes About Dogs
Illustrated by Erik Blegvad
Published by Atheneum, 1976

Blegvad, Lenore, Ed.
Mittens for Kittens and Other Rhymes About Cats
Illustrated by Erik Blegvad
Published by Atheneum, 1974

Bloch, Marie
Ivanko and the Dragon
Illustrated by Yaroslava
Published by Atheneum, 1967

Bloom, Freddy
Boy Who Couldn't Hear
Illustrated by Michael Charlton
Published by Bradbury Press, (n.d.)

Bloome, Enid P.
Dogs Don't Belong on Beds
Illustrated by Rose Sommerschield
Published by Doubleday, 1971
Bodecker, Niels M.
Mushroom Center Disaster
Illustrated by Erik Blegvad
Published by Atheneum, 1974
Boden, Alice
Field of Buttercups
Illustrated by Alice Boden
Published by Walck, 1975
Boegehold, Betty
Small Deer's Magic Tricks
Illustrated by Jacqueline Chwast
Published by Coward, 1977
Boegehold, Betty and Cyndy Szekeres
Here's Pippa Again
Illustrated by Cyndy Szekeres
Published by Knopf, 1975
Boegehold, Betty and Cyndy Szekeres
Pippa Mouse
Illustrated by Cyndy Szekeres
Published by Knopf, 1973
Bograd, Larry
Felix in the Attic
Illustrated by Dirk Zimmer
Published by Harvey House, 1978
Boiko, Claire and Sandra Novick
Left-Over Dragon
Illustrated by Dennis M. Arnold
Published by Children's Press, 1977
Bolliger, Max
Fireflies
Translated by Rosenna Hoover
Illustrated by Jiri Trinka
Published by Atheneum, 1970
Bolliger, Max
Golden Apple
Illustrated by Celestino Piatti
Published by Atheneum, 1970
Bolliger, Max
Wooden Man
Illustrated by Fred Bauer
Published by Seabury, 1974
Bonner, Ann and Roger Bonner
Early Birds...Early Words
Illustrated
Published by Scroll Press, 1973
Bonnie, Carey
Grasshopper to the Rescue
Illustrated by Lady McCrady
Published by Morrow, 1979
Bonsall, Crosby N.
And I Mean It, Stanley
Illustrated by Crosby N. Bonsall
Published by Harper and Row, 1974
Bonsall, Crosby
Case of the Hungry Stranger
Illustrated by Crosby Bonsall
Published by Harper and Row, 1969
Bonsall, Crospy
Case of the Scaredy Cats
Illustrated by Crosby Bonsall
Published by Harper and Row, 1971
Bonsall, Crosby
Day I Had to Play with My Sister
Illustrated by Crosby Bonsall
Published by Harper and Row, 1972
Bonsall, Crosby
It's Mine!
Illustrated by Crosby Bonsall
Published by Harper and Row, 1964
Bonsall, Crosby
Listen, Listen
Illustrated by Ylla
Published by Harper and Row, 1964
Bonsall, Crosby
Mine's the Best
Illustrated by Crosby Bonsall
Published by Harper and Row, 1973
Bonsall, Crosby
Piggle
Illustrated by Crosby Bonsall
Published by Harper and Row, 1973
Bonsall, Crosby
Tell Me Some More
Illustrated by Fritz Siebel
Published by Harper and Row, 1961
Bonsall, Crosby
Twelve Bells for Santa
Illustrated by Crosby Bonsall
Published by Harper and Row, 1977
Bonsall, Crosby
What Spot
Illustrated by Crosby Bonsall
Published by Harper and Row, 1963
Bonsall, Crosby
Who's a Pest?
Illustrated by Crosby Bonsall
Published by Harper and Row, 1962
Bonsall, Crosby
Whose Eye Am I?
Illustrated by Ylla
Published by Harper and Row, 1969
Bontemps, Arna
Mr. Kelso's Lion
Illustrated by Len Ebert
Published by Lippincott, 1970
Bonzon, Paul J.
Runaway Flying Horse
Illustrated by Wm. P. DuBois
Published by Parents Magazine Press, 1976

Booth, Eugene
In the Jungle
Illustrated
Published by Raintree, 1977
Booth, Eugene
Under the Ground
Illustrated
Published by Raintree, 1977
Borack, Barbara
Grandpa
Illustrated by Ben Shecter
Published by Harper and Row, 1967
Borack, Barbara
Someone Small
Illustrated by Anita Lobel
Published by Harper and Row, 1969
Borg, Inga
Parrak, the White Reindeer
Illustrated by Inga Borg
Published by Warne, 1959
Bornstein, Ruth
Indian Bunny
Illustrated by Ruth Bornstein
Published by Scholastic, 1975
Bornstein, Ruth
Little Gorilla
Illustrated by Ruth Bornstein
Published by Seabury, 1976
Borten, Helen
Do You Know What I Know?
Illustrated by Helen Borten
Published by Abelard, 1970
Borten, Helen
Do You See What I See?
Illustrated by Helen Borten
Published by Abelard, 1959
Boschini, Henny and Luciano Boschini
Ship in the Field
Illustrated by Henny & Luciano Boschini
Published by Scroll Press, 1973
Bottner, Barbara
Fun House
Illustrated by Barbara Bottner
Published by Prentice-Hall, 1974
Bottner, Barbara
What Would You Do with a Giant?
Illustrated by Barbara Bottner
Published by Putnam, 1972
Botts, Davi
Hey Diddle Diddle and Other Nonsense Rhymes
Illustrated
Published by Hale, 1956
Bourke, Linda
Ethel's Exceptional Egg
Illustrated by Linda Bourke
Published by Harvey House, 1977
Bourne, Miriam and Anne Bourne
Emilio's Summer Day
Illustrated by Ben Shecter
Published by Harper and Row, 1966
Bourne, Miriam
Four-Ring Three
Illustrated by Cyndy Szekeres
Published by Coward, 1973
Bourne, Miriam
Raccoons Are for Loving
Illustrated by Marian Morton
Published by Random, 1968
Bowen, Elizabeth
Good Tiger
Illustrated by M. Nebel
Published by Knopf, 1965
Bowes, Claire
Man from Inverness
Illustrated by Claire Bowes
Published by Lerner, 1968
Bradbury, Ray
Switch on the Night
Illustrated by Madeleine Gekiere
Published by Pantheon, 1955
Bram, Elizabeth
There Is Someone Standing on My Head
Illustrated by Elizabeth Bram
Published by Dial, 1979
Brandenberg, Franz
Fresh Cider and Pie
Illustrated by Franz Brandenberg
Published by Macmillan, 1973
Brandenberg, Franz
I Wish I Was Sick Too
Illustrated by Aliki
Published by Greenwillow, 1976
Brandenberg, Franz
No School Today!
Illustrated by Aliki
Published by Macmillan, 1975
Brandenberg, Franz
A Robber! A Robber!
Illustrated by Aliki
Published by Greenwillow, 1976
Brandenberg, Franz
Secret for Grandmother's Birthday
Illustrated by Aliki
Published by Greenwillow, 1975
Branley, Franklyn M.
Air Is All Around You
Illustrated by Robert Galster
Published by T.Y. Crowell, 1962
Branley, Franklyn M.
Big Tracks, Little Tracks
Illustrated by Leonard Kessler
Published by T.Y. Crowell, 1960

Branley, Franklyn M.
Flash, Crash and Rumble
Illustrated by Ed Emberley
Published by T.Y. Crowell, 1964

Branley, Franklyn M.
Floating and Sinking
Illustrated by Robert Galster
Published by T.Y. Crowell, 1967

Branley, Franklyn M.
High Sounds, Low Sounds
Illustrated by Paul Galdone
Published by T.Y. Crowell, 1967

Branley, Franklyn M.
Rain and Hail
Illustrated by Helen Borten
Published by T.Y. Crowell, 1963

Branley, Franklyn M.
Roots Are Food Finders
Illustrated by Joseph Low
Published by T.Y. Crowell, 1975

Branley, Franklyn M.
Snow Is Falling
Illustrated by Helen Stone
Published by T.Y. Crowell, 1963

Branley, Franklyn M.
Sunshine Makes the Seasons
Illustrated by Shelley Freshman
Published by T.Y. Crowell, 1974

Branley, Franklyn M.
What Makes Day and Night?
Illustrated by Helen Borten
Published by T.Y. Crowell, 1972

Branley, Franklyn M. and Eleanor K. Vaughn
Mickey's Magnet
Illustrated by Crockett Johnson
Published by T.Y. Crowell, 1956

Breinburg, Petronella
Doctor Shawn
Illustrated by Errol Lloyd
Published by T.Y. Crowell, 1975

Breinburg, Petronella
Shawn Goes to School
Illustrated by Errol Lloyd
Published by T.Y. Crowell, 1974

Breinberg, Petronella
Shawn's Red Bike
Illustrated by Errol Lloyd
Published by T.Y. Crowell, 1976

Brenner, Barbara
Amy's Doll
Illustrated by Sy Katzoff
Published by Knopf, 1963

Brenner, Barbara
Baltimore Orioles
Illustrated by J. Winslow Higgenbottom
Published by Harper and Row, 1974

Brenner, Barbara
Bodies
Illustrated by George Ancona
Published by Dutton, 1973

Brenner, Barbara
Faces (Caras-Span.)
Illustrated by George Ancona
Published by Dutton, 1977

Brenner, Barbara
If You Were an Ant
Illustrated by Fred Brenner
Published by Harper and Row, 1973

Brenner, Barbara
Is It Bigger Than a Sparrow: A Box for Young Birdwatchers
Illustrated by Michael Eagle
Published by Knopf, 1972

Brenner, Barbara
Little One Inch
Illustrated by Fred Brenner
Published by Coward, 1977

Brenner, Barbara
Mr. Tall and Mr. Small
Illustrated
Published by Children's Press, 1966

Brenner, Barbara
Nickey's Sister
Illustrated by John E. Johnson
Published by Knopf, 1966

Brenner, Barbara
Wagon Wheels
Illustrated by Don Bolognese
Published by Harper and Row, 1978

Breoger, Achim
Caterpillar's Story
Illustrated by Katrin Brandt
Published by Scroll Press, 1973

Brewer, Mary
What Floats?
Illustrated by Nancy Inderieden
Published by Children's Press, 1976

Brewer, Mary
Wind Is Air
Illustrated by Nancy Inderieden
Published by Children's Press, 1976

Brick, Anna R.
Eli Lives in Israel
Illustrated by Anna R. Brick
Published by Macmillan, 1964

Bridges, William
Lion Island
Illustrated by Sam Dunton and Emmy Haas
Published by Morrow, 1965

Bridgman, Elizabeth
All the Little Bunnies
Illustrated by Elizabeth Bridgman
Published by Atheneum, 1977

Bridwell, Norman
Clifford's Good Deeds
Illustrated by Norman Bridwell
Published by Scholastic, 1976
Bridwell, Norman
Witch Next Door
Illustrated by Norman Bridwell
Published by Scholastic, 1971
Briggs, Raymond, Ed.
Mother Goose Treasury
Illustrated by Raymond Briggs
Published by Coward, 1966
Briggs, Raymond
The Snowman
Illustrated by Raymond Briggs
Published by Random, 1978
Bright, Robert
Friendly Bear
Illustrated by Robert Bright
Published by Doubleday, 1971
Bright, Robert
Georgie
Illustrated by Robert Bright
Published by Doubleday, 1959
Bright, Robert
My Hopping Bunny
Illustrated by Robert Bright
Published by Doubleday, 1971
Bright, Robert
My Red Umbrella
Illustrated by Robert Bright
Published by Morrow, 1959
Brightman, Alan
Like Me
Illustrated by Alan Brightman
Published by Little, Brown, 1976
Brinckloe, Julie
Gordon's House
Illustrated
Published by Doubleday, 1976
Brinckloe, Julie
Spider Web
Illustrated
Published by Doubleday, 1974
Brisley, Joyce Lankester
Milly-Molly-Mandy Stories
Illustrated by Joyce Lankester Brisley
Published by Walck, 1976
Brooks, Judy
Tim Mouse Visits the Farm
Illustrated by Judy Brooks
Published by Lothrop, 1977
Brooke, Leslie
Johnny Crow's Garden
Illustrated by Leslie Brooke
Published by Warne, 1903
Brooke, Leslie
Ring O' Roses
Illustrated by Leslie Brooke
Published by Warne, 1977
Brooks, Gregory
Monroe's Island
Illustrated by Gregory Brooks
Published by Dutton, 1979
Broomfield, Robert
Baby Animal ABC
Illustrated by Robert Broomfield
Published by Penguin, 1968
Brown, Beatrice C.
Jonathan Bing
Illustrated by Judith G. Brown
Published by Lothrop, 1968
Brown, Beverly
Myth Adventures Kraken, the Sea Monster
Illustrated by Carol Koplan
Published by Brasch, 1978
Brown, David
Someone Always Needs a Policeman
Illustrated by David Brown
Published by Simon & Schuster, 1972
Brown, Judith
Muffin
Illustrated by Judith Brown
Published by Abelard, 1972
Brown, Marcia
All Butterflies: An ABC
Illustrated by Marcia Brown
Published by Scribner, 1974
Brown, Marcia
Bun, a Tale from Russia
Illustrated by Marcia Brown
Published by Harcourt Brace Jovanovich, 1972
Brown, Marcia
Dick Whittington and His Cat
Illustrated by Marcia Brown
Published by Scribner, 1950
Brown, Marcia
Felice
Illustrated by Marcia Brown
Published by Scribner, 1958
Brown, Marcia
Henry-Fisherman
Illustrated by Marcia Brown
Published by Scribner, 1949
Brown, Marcia
How, Hippo!
Illustrated by Marcia Brown
Published by Scribner, 1972
Brown, Marcia
Little Carousel
Illustrated by Marcia Brown
Published by Scribner, 1946
Brown, Marcia
Once a Mouse

Illustrated by Marcia Brown
Published by Scribner, 1961
Brown, Marcia
Puss in Boots
Illustrated by Marcia Brown
Published by Scribner, 1952
Brown, Marcia
Stone Soup
Illustrated by Marcia Brown
Published by Scribner, 1947
Brown, Margaret
Wheel on the Chimney
Illustrated by Margaret Brown
Published by Lippincott, 1954
Brown, Margaret Wise
City Noisy Book
Illustrated by Leonard Weisgard
Published by Harper and Row, 1976
Brown, Margaret Wise
Country Noisy Book
Illustrated by Leonard Weisgard
Published by Harper and Row, 1976
Brown, Margaret Wise
Dead Bird
Illustrated by Remy Charlip
Published by A-W, 1958
Brown, Margaret Wise
The Golden Egg Book
Illustrated by Lilian Obligado
Published by Western, 1976
Brown, Margaret Wise
Good Night, Moon
Illustrated by Clement Hurd
Published by Harper and Row, 1977
Brown, Margaret Wise
Indoor Noisy Book
Illustrated by Leonard Weisgard
Published by Harper and Row, 1976
Brown, Margaret Wise
Little Fur Family
Illustrated by Garth Williams
Published by Harper and Row, 1968
Brown, Margaret Wise
Quiet Noisy Book
Illustrated by Leonard Weisgard
Published by Harper and Row, 1950
Brown, Margaret Wise
Runaway Bunny
Illustrated by Clement Hurd
Published by Morrow, 1954
Brown, Margaret Wise
Shhhhhh....Bang
Illustrated by Robert De Veyrac
Published by Harper and Row, 1943
Brown, Margaret Wise
Sleepy Little Lion
Illustrated by Ylla
Published by Harper and Row, 1979

Brown, Margaret Wise
Train to Timbuctoo
Illustrated by Art Seiden
Published by Western, 1951
Brown, Margaret Wise
Wait Till the Moon Is Full
Illustrated by Garth Williams
Published by Harper and Row, 1948
Brown, Margaret Wise
Where Have You Been?
Illustrated by Barbara Cooney
Published by Hastings House, 1963
Browning, Robert
Pied Piper of Hamelin
Illustrated by Kate Greenaway
Published by Warne, 1889
Browning, Robert
Pied Piper of Hamelin
Illustrated by Liesolette Schwartz
Published by Scroll Press, (n.d.)
Bruchac, Joseph, Told by
Stone Giants and Flying Heads
Illustrated by Kahonhes & Brascoupe
Published by Crossing Press, 1975
Bruchac, Joseph, Told by
Turkey Brothers and Other Tales of the Iroquois
Illustrated by Kahones
Published by Crossing Press, 1975
Bruna, Dick
Another Story to Tell
Illustrated by Dick Bruna
Published by Methuen, (n.d.)
Bruna, Dick
The Apple
Illustrated by Dick Bruna
Published by Methuen, 1975
Bruna, Dick
The Circus
Illustrated by Dick Bruna
Published by Methuen, 1975
Bruna, Dick
Dick Bruna's ABC Frieze
Illustrated by Dick Bruna
Published by Methuen, 1976
Bruna, Dick
Dick Bruna's One-Two-Three Frieze
Illustrated by Dick Bruna
Published by Methuen, 1976
Bruna, Dick
Egg
Illustrated by Dick Bruna
Published by Methuen, 1975
Bruna, Dick
I Can Count
Illustrated by Dick Bruna
Published by Methuen, 1975

Bruna, Dick
I Can Count More
Illustrated by Dick Bruna
Published by Methuen, 1976
Bruna, Dick
The King
Illustrated by Dick Bruna
Published by Methuen, 1975
Bruna, Dick
Miffy
Illustrated by Dick Bruna
Published by Methuen, 1975
Bruna, Dick
My Shirt Is White
Illustrated by Dick Bruna
Published by Methuen, 1975
Bruna, Dick
A Story to Tell
Illustrated by Dick Bruna
Published by Methuen, 1975
Brustlein, Janice
Angelique
Illustrated by Roger Duvoisin
Published by Lothrop, (n.d.)
Bryan, Ashley
Dancing Granny
Illustrated by Ashley Bryan
Published by Atheneum, 1977
Buck, Pearl
Little Fox in the Middle
Illustrated by Robert Jones
Published by Macmillan, 1974
Buckley, Helen E.
Grandmother and I
Illustrated by Paul Galdone
Published by Lothrop, 1969
Buckley, Helen E.
Josie and the Snow
Illustrated by Evaline Ness
Published by Lothrop, 1964
Buckley, Helen E.
Little Boy and the Birthdays
Illustrated by Paul Galdone
Published by Lothrop, 1965
Buckley, Helen E.
Little Pig in the Cupboard
Illustrated by Rob Howard
Published by Lothrop, 1968
Buckley, Helen E.
Wonderful Little Boy
Illustrated by Tony Chen
Published by Lothrop, 1970
Budney, Blossom
After Dark
Illustrated by Tony Chen
Published by Lothrop, 1975
Budney, Blossom
A Kiss Is Round
Illustrated by Vladimir Bobri
Published by Lothrop, 1954
Bulla, Clyde R.
New Boy in Dublin: Story of Ireland
Illustrated by Jo Polseno
Published by T.Y. Crowell, 1969
Bulla, Clyde R.
A Tree Is a Plant
Illustrated by Lois Lingnell
Published by T.Y. Crowell, 1960
Bulla, Clyde R.
Valentine Cat
Illustrated by Leonard Weisgard
Published by T.Y. Crowell, 1959
Bulla, Clyde R.
What Makes a Shadow?
Illustrated by Adrienne Adams
Published by T.Y. Crowell, 1962
Bunny
Aloysius Alligator
Illustrated by Ed Wheelan
Published by Island Press, 1974
Bunny
Tigger: Story of a Mayan Ocelot
Illustrated by Bunny
Published by Island Press, 1974
Bunting, Eve
Barney the Beard
Illustrated by Imero Gobbato
Published by Parents Magazine Press, 1975
Burch, Ropert
Joey's Cat
Illustrated by Don Freeman
Published by Viking Press, 1969
Burn, Doris
Andrew Henry's Meadow
Illustrated by Doris Burn
Published by Coward, 1965
Burningham, John
A B C
Illustrated by John Burningham
Published by Bobbs-Merrill, 1967
Burningham, John
The Baby
Illustrated by John Burningham
Published by T.Y. Crowell, 1975
Burningham, John
The Blanket
Illustrated by John Burningham
Published by T.Y. Crowell, 1976
Burningham, John
Come Away from the Water, Shirley
Illustrated by John Burningham
Published by T.Y. Crowell, 1977
Burningham, John
The Cupboard
Illustrated by John Burningham
Published by T.Y. Crowell, 1976

Burningham, John
The Dog
Illustrated by John Burningham
Published by T.Y. Crowell, 1976
Burningham, John
The Friend
Illustrated by John Burningham
Published by T.Y. Crowell, 1976
Burningham, John
Mr. Gumpy's Motor Car
Illustrated by John Burningham
Published by T.Y. Crowell, 1976
Burningham, John
Mr. Gumpy's Outing
Illustrated by John Burningham
Published by Holt, Rinehart and Winston, 1971
Burningham, John
Rabbit
Illustrated by John Burningham
Published by T.Y. Crowell, 1975
Burningham, John
The School
Illustrated by John Burningham
Published by T.Y. Crowell, 1975
Burningham, John
Seasons
Illustrated by John Burningham
Published by Bobbs-Merrill, 1970
Burningham, John
The Snow
Illustrated by John Burningham
Published by T.Y. Crowell, 1975
Burningham, John
Time to Get Out of the Bath, Shirley
Illustrated by John Burningham
Published by T.Y. Crowell, 1979
Burningham, John
Trubloff, Mouse Who Wanted to Play the Balalaika
Illustrated by John Burningham
Published by Random, 1965
Burton, Virginia L.
Choo Choo
Illustrated by Virginia L. Burton
Published by Houghton Mifflin, (n.d.)
Burton, Virginia L.
Katy and the Big Snow
Illustrated by Virginia L. Burton
Published by Houghton Mifflin, 1943
Burton, Virginia L.
Life Story
Illustrated by Virginia L. Burton
Published by Houghton Mifflin, 1962
Burton, Virginia L.
The Little House
Illustrated by Virginia L. Burton
Published by Houghton Mifflin, 1942

Burton, Virginia L.
Maybelle, the Cable Car
Illustrated by Virginia L. Burton
Published by Houghton Mifflin, 1952
Burton, Virginia L.
Mike Mulligan and His Steam Shovel
Illustrated by Virginia L. Burton
Published by Houghton Mifflin, 1977
Busch, Phyllis S.
Exploring As You Walk in the Meadow
Illustrated by Mary M. Thacher
Published by Lippincott, 1972
Busch, Phyllis S.
Puddles & Ponds: Living Things in Watery Places
Illustrated by Arline Strong
Published by Collins-World, 1969
Busch, Phyllis S.
Walk in the Snow
Illustrated
Published by Lippincott, 1971
Byars, Betsy
Go and Hush the Baby
Illustrated by Emily A. McCully
Published by Viking Press, 1971
Byars, Betsy
Lace Snail
Illustrated by Betsy Byars
Published by Viking Press, 1975
Byfield, Barbara
Haunted Churchbell
Illustrated by Barbara Byfield
Published by Doubleday, 1971
Byfield, Barbara
Haunted Ghost
Illustrated by Barbara Byfield
Published by Doubleday, 1973
Cabassa, Victoria
Trixie and the Tiger
Illustrated by Lillian Obligato
Published by Abelard, 1967
Caines, Jeanette
Abby
Illustrated by Steven Kellogg
Published by Harper and Row, 1973
Caines, Jeanette
Daddy
Illustrated by Ronald Himler
Published by Harper and Row, 1977
Caines, Marilyn
Boomer, $3.00 Dog: Puppy Tale
Illustrated
Published by Exposition, 1976
Caldecott, Randolph
The Milkmaid
Illustrated by Randolph Caldecott
Published by Warne, 1882

Calhoun, Mary
Battle Reuben Robin & Kite Uncle John
Illustrated by Janet McCaffery
Published by Morrow, 1973

Calhoun, Mary
Cross-Country Cat
Illustrated by Erick Ingraham
Published by Morrow, 1979

Calhoun, Mary
Houn' Dog
Illustrated by Roger Duvoisin
Published by Morrow, 1959

Calhoun, Mary
Witch Who Lost Her Shadow
Illustrated by Trinka Hakes Noble
Published by Harper and Row, 1979

Calhoun, Mary
Euphonia and the Flood
Illustrated by Simms Taback
Published by Parents Magazine Press, 1976

Calhoun, Mary
Hungry Leprechaun
Illustrated by Roger Duvoisin
Published by Morrow, 1962

Calhoun, Mary
Runaway Brownie
Illustrated by Janet McCaffery
Published by Morrow, 1967

Calhoun, Mary
Wobble the Witch Cat
Illustrated by Roger Duvoisin
Published by Morrow, 1958

Callahan, Dorothy
Under Christopher's Hat
Illustrated by Carol Byard
Published by Scribner, 1972

Cameron, Polly
Green Machine
Illustrated by Consuelo Joerns
Published by Coward, 1969

Cameron, Polly
I Can't, Said the Ant
Illustrated by Polly Cameron
Published by Coward, 1961

Canepari, Nelly
Mochito: Story of an Ordinary Dog
Illustrated by Jorge Schneider
Published by Blaine-Ethridge, 1975

Caras, Roger A.
Skunk for a Day
Illustrated by Diane Paterson
Published by Dutton, 1976

Carew, Jan
The Third Gift
Illustrated by Leo and Diane Dillon
Published by Little, Brown, 1974

Carini, E.
Take Another Look
Illustrated by E. Carini
Published by Prentice-Hall, 1969

Carle, Eric
Do You Want to Be My Friend?
Illustrated by Eric Carle
Published by T.Y. Crowell, 1971

Carle, Eric
Have You Seen My Cat?
Illustrated by Eric Carle
Published by Watts, 1973

Carle, Eric
I See a Song
Illustrated by Eric Carle
Published by T.Y. Crowell, 1973

Carle, Eric
The Mixed-up Chameleon
Illustrated by Eric Carle
Published by T.Y. Crowell, 1975

Carle, Eric
My Very First Book of Colors
Illustrated by Eric Carle
Published by T.Y. Crowell, 1974

Carle, Eric
My Very First Book of Numbers
Illustrated by Eric Carle
Published by T.Y. Crowell, 1974

Carle, Eric
My Very First Book of Shapes
Illustrated by Eric Carle
Published by T.Y. Crowell, 1974

Carle, Eric
My Very First Book of Words
Illustrated by Eric Carle
Published by T.Y. Crowell, 1974

Carle, Eric
Pancakes! Pancakes!
Illustrated by Eric Carle
Published by Knopf, 1970

Carle, Eric
Rooster Who Set Out to See the World
Illustrated by Eric Carle
Published by Watts, 1972

Carle, Eric
Secret Birthday Message
Illustrated by Eric Carle
Published by T.Y. Crowell, 1972

Carle, Eric
Tiny Seed
Illustrated by Eric Carle
Published by T.Y. Crowell, 1970

Carle, Eric
Very Hungry Caterpillar
Illustrated by Eric Carle
Published by Collins-World, 1969

Carle, Eric
Very Long Tail: A Folding Book
Illustrated by Eric Carle
Published by T.Y. Crowell, 1972
Carle, Eric
Very Long Train: A Folding Book
Illustrated by Eric Carle
Published by T.Y. Crowell, 1972
Carle, Eric
Walter the Baker
Illustrated by Eric Carle
Published by Knopf, 1972
Carley, Wayne
Percy the Parrot Yelled Quiet!
Illustrated by Art Cumings
Published by Garrard, 1974
Carley, Wayne
The Witch Who Forgot
Illustrated by Lou Cunette
Published by Garrard, 1974
Carlson, Bernice
Picture That!
Illustrated by Dolores Marie Rowland
Published by Abingdon, 1977
Carlson, Natalie Savage
Marie Louise and Christophe
Illustrated by Ariane Dewey and Jose Aruego
Published by Scribner, 1974
Carlson, Natalie Savage
Time for the White Egret
Illustrated by Charles Robinson
Published by Scribner, 1979
Carrick, Carol
The Accident
Illustrated by Donald Carrick
Published by Seabury, 1976
Carrick, Carol
Beach Bird
Illustrated by Donald Carrick
Published by Dial, 1973
Carrick, Carol
The Blue Lobster
Illustrated by Donald Carrick
Published by Dial, 1971
Carrick, Carol
Brook
Illustrated by Donald Carrick
Published by Macmillan, 1967
Carrick, Carol
Clearing in the Forest
Illustrated by Donald Carrick
Published by Dial, 1970
Carrick, Carol
Dirt Road
Illustrated by Donald Carrick
Published by Macmillan, 1970
Carrick, Carol
Lost in the Storm
Illustrated by Donald Carrick
Published by Seabury, 1974
Carrick, Carol
Old Mother Witch
Illustrated by Donald Carrick
Published by Seabury, 1975
Carrick, Carol
The Pond
Illustrated by Donald Carrick
Published by Macmillan, 1970
Carrick, Carol
A Rabbit for Easter
Illustrated by Donald Carrick
Published by Greenwillow, 1979
Carrick, Carol
Swamp Spring
Illustrated by Donald Carrick
Published by Macmillan, 1969
Carrick, Carol and Donald Carrick
The Foundling
Illustrated by Donald Carrick
Published by Seabury, 1977
Carrick, Donald
Drip Drop
Illustrated by Donald Carrick
Published by Macmillan, 1973
Carrick, Donald
The Tree
Illustrated by Donald Carrick
Published by Macmillan, 1971
Carroll, Ruth
The Chimp and the Clown
Illustrated by Ruth Carroll
Published by Walck, 1968
Carrick, Malcolm
I Can Squash Elephants: Masai Tale About Monsters
Illustrated
Published by Viking Press, 1978
Carroll, Ruth
Dolphin and the Mermaid
Illustrated by Ruth Carroll
Published by Walck, 1974
Carroll, Ruth
Hullabaloo: The Elephant Dog
Illustrated by Ruth Carroll
Published by Walck, 1975
Carroll, Ruth
Rolling Downhill
Illustrated by Ruth Carroll
Published by Walck, 1973
Carroll, Ruth
What Whiskers Did
Illustrated by Ruth Carroll
Published by Walck, 1965
Carroll, Ruth
Where's the Bunny?
Illustrated by Ruth Carroll
Published by Walck, 1950

Carroll, Ruth and Latrobe
 Carroll
 Managing Hen & Floppy Hound
 Illustrated by Ruth Carroll
 Published by Walck, 1972
Cartwright, Sally
 Sand
 Illustrated by Donald Madden
 Published by Coward, 1975
Cartwright, Sally
 The Tide
 Illustrated by Marilyn Miller
 Published by Coward, 1971
Cartwright, Sally
 Water Is Wet
 Illustrated by Marylin Hafner
 Published by Coward, 1973
Cathon, Laura
 Tot Botot and His Little Flute
 Illustrated by Arnold Lobel
 Published by Macmillan, 1970
Caudill, Rebecca
 Pocketful of Cricket
 Illustrated by Evaline Ness
 Published by Holt, Rinehart and
 Winston, 1964
Caudill, Rebecca and James
 Ayars
 Contrary Jenkins
 Illustrated by Glen Rounds
 Published by Holt, Rinehart and
 Winston, 1969
Censori, Robert
 Shopping Bag Lady
 Illustrated by Robert Censori
 Published by Holiday House, 1977
Cervantes, Esther de Michael and
 Alex Cervantes
 Senora Pepino and Her Bad Luck
 Cats
 Illustrated
 Published by Blaine-Ethridge, 1976
Chaffin, Lillie D.
 Bear Weather
 Illustrated by Helga Aichinger
 Published by Macmillan, 1969
Chaffin, Lilli D.
 Tommy's Big Problem
 Illustrated by Haris Petie
 Published by Lantern Press, (n.d.)
Chalmers, Mary
 Be Good, Harry
 Illustrated by Mary Chalmers
 Published by Harper and Row, 1969
Chang, Kathleen
 Iron Moonhunter
 Illustrated by Kathleen Chang
 Published by Children's Book
 Press—S.F., (n.d.)

Chapman, Kim Westsmith
 Magic Hat
 Illustrated by Kitty Riley Clark
 Published by Lollipop Power, 1976
Chardiet, Bernice
 C Is for Circus
 Illustrated by Brinton Turkle
 Published by Walker, 1971
Chardiet, Bernice
 Juan Bobo & The Pig: Puerto Rican
 Folktale
 Illustrated by Hope Meryman
 Published by Walker, 1973
Charles, Donald
 Busy Beaver's Day
 Illustrated by Donald Charles
 Published by Children's Press, 1972
Charlip, Remy and Lillian Moore
 Hooray for Me!
 Illustrated by Vera Williams
 Published by Parents Magazine Press,
 1975
Charlip, Remy and Burton Supree
 Harlequin & Gift of Many Colors
 Illustrated by Remy Charlip
 Published by Parents Magazine Press,
 1973
Charlip, Remy and Burton Supree
 Mother, Mother, I Feel Sick; Send for
 the Doctor Quick . . .
 Illustrated by Remy Charlip
 Published by Parents Magazine Press,
 1966
Charmatz, Bill
 Cat's Whiskers
 Illustrated by Bill Charmatz
 Published by Macmillan, 1969
Chase, Francine
 Visit to the Hospital
 Illustrated by James Bama
 Published by Grosset & Dunlap,
 1957
Chen, Tony
 Run, Zebra, Run
 Illustrated by Tony Chen
 Published by Lothrop, 1972
Chenery, Janet
 Pickles and Jake
 Illustrated by Lilian Obligado
 Published by Viking Press, 1975
Chenery, Janet
 Toad Hunt
 Illustrated by Ben Shecter
 Published by Harper and Row, 1967
Cheng, Hou-Tien
 The Chinese New Year
 Illustrated
 Published by Holt, Rinehart and
 Winston, 1976

Choate, Judith
Awful Alexander
Illustrated by Steven Kellogg
Published by Doubleday, 1976
Chorao, Kay
The Baby's Lap Book
Illustrated by Kay Chorao
Published by Dutton, 1977
Chorao, Kay
Lester's Overnight
Illustrated by Kay Chorao
Published by Dutton, 1977
Chorao, Kay
Maudie's Umbrella
Illustrated by Kay Chorao
Published by Dutton, 1975
Chorao, Kay
Molly's Moe
Illustrated by Kay Chorao
Published by Seabury, 1976
Christian, Mary Blount
No Dogs Allowed, Jonathan
Illustrated by Don Madden
Published by A-W, 1975
Christian, Mary Blount
The Sand Lot
Illustrated by Dennis Kendrick
Published by Harvey House, 1978
Chroman, Eleanor
It Could Be Worse
Illustrated by Margrit Fiddle
Published by Children's Press, 1972
Chute, Marchette
Around and About
Illustrated by Marchette Chute
Published by Dutton, 1957
Ciardi, John
Monster Den or Look What Happened at My House
Illustrated by Edward Gorey
Published by Lippincott, 1966
Ciardi, John
Scrappy the Pup
Illustrated by Jane Miller
Published by Lippincott, 1960
Ciardi, John
You Know Who
Illustrated by Edward Gorey
Published by Lippincott, 1964
Clark, Ann
In My Mother's House
Illustrated by Velino Herrera
Published by Viking Press, 1941
Cleary, Beverly
Real Hole
Illustrated by Mary Stevens
Published by Morrow, 1960
Cleary, Beverly
Two Dog Biscuits
Illustrated by Mary Stevens
Published by Morrow, 1961
Clifton, Lucille
All Us Come Cross the Water
Illustrated by John Steptoe
Published by Holt, Rinehart and Winston, 1973
Clifton, Lucille
Amifika
Illustrated by Thomas DiGrazia
Published by Dutton, 1977
Clifton, Lucille
Boy Who Didn't Believe in Spring
Illustrated by Brinton Turkle
Published by Dutton, 1973
Clifton, Lucille
Don't You Remember?
Illustrated by Evaline Ness
Published by Dutton, 1973
Clifton, Lucille
Everett Anderson's Friend
Illustrated
Published by Holt, Rinehart and Winston, 1976
Clifton, Lucille
Everett Anderson's Nine Month Long
Illustrated by Ann Grifalconi
Published by Holt, Rinehart and Winston, 1979
Clifton, Lucille
Everett Anderson's 1-2-3
Illustrated by Ann Grifalconi
Published by Holt, Rinehart and Winston, 1977
Clifton, Lucille
Good, Says Jerome
Illustrated by Stephanie Douglas
Published by Dutton, 1973
Clifton, Lucille
My Brother Fine with Me
Illustrated by Moneta Barnett
Published by Holt, Rinehart and Winston, 1975
Clifton, Lucille
Three Wishes
Illustrated by Stephanie Douglas
Published by Viking Press, 1976
Clymer, Eleanor
Horatio
Illustrated by Robert Quackenbush
Published by Atheneum, 1974
Clymer, Eleanor
Horatio's Birthday
Illustrated by Robert Quackenbush
Published by Atheneum, 1976
Clymer, Eleanor
Leave Horatio Alone

Bibliography / 191

Illustrated by Robert Quackenbush
Published by Atheneum, 1974
Clymer, Eleanor
Tiny Little House
Illustrated by Ingrid Fetz
Published by Atheneum, 1964
Coatsworth, Elizabeth
Lonely Maria
Illustrated by Evaline Ness
Published by Pantheon, 1960
Cohen, Barbara
Carp in the Bathtub
Illustrated by Joan Halpern
Published by Lothrop, 1972
Cohen, Miriam
Best Friends
Illustrated by Lillian Hoban
Published by Macmillan, 1971
Cohen, Miriam
New Teacher
Illustrated by Lillian Hoban
Published by Macmillan, 1974
Cohen, Miriam
Will I Have a Friend?
Illustrated by Lillian Hoban
Published by Macmillan, 1971
Coker, Gylbert
Naptime
Illustrated by Gylbert Coker
Published by Delacorte, 1979
Cole, Brock
The King at the Door
Illustrated by Brock Cole
Published by Doubleday, 1979
Cole, Helen
Po'nya, Her Story
Illustrated
Published by Exposition, 1976
Cole, Joanna
A Chick Hatches
Illustrated
Published by Morrow, 1976
Cole, Joanna
My Puppy Is Born
Illustrated by Jerome Wexler
Published by Morrow, 1973
Cole, Joanna
Plants in Winter
Illustrated by Kazue Mizumura
Published by T.Y. Crowell, 1973
Cole, William
I Went to the Animal Fair
Illustrated
Published by Collins-World, 1958
Cole, William, Editor
Oh, What Nonsense
Illustrated by Tomi Ungerer
Published by Viking Press, 1966

Cole, William
What's Good for a 5-Year-Old?
Illustrated by Edward Sorel
Published by Holt, Rinehart and Winston, 1969
Cole, William
What's Good for a 4-Year-Old?
Illustrated by Tomi Ungerer
Published by Holt, Rinehart and Winston, 1967
Cole, William
What's Good for a 3-Year-Old?
Illustrated by Lillian Hoban
Published by Holt, Rinehart and Winston, 1974
Collins, David
Kim Soo and His Tortoise
Illustrated by Alix Cohen
Published by Lion Press, 1971
Colman, Hila
Watch That Watch
Illustrated by Leonard Weisgard
Published by Morrow, 1962
Combs, Patricia
The Magic Pot
Illustrated by Patricia Combs
Published by Lothrop, 1977
Conford, Ellen
Impossible Possum
Illustrated by Rosemary Wells
Published by Little, Brown, 1971
Conger, Lesley
Tops and Bottoms
Illustrated by Imero Gobbato
Published by Scholastic, 1970
Conger, Marion
Who Has Seen the Wind?
Illustrated by Susan Perl
Published by Abingdon, 1959
Conklin, Gladys
I Caught a Lizard
Illustrated by Arthur Marokvia
Published by Holiday House, 1967
Conklin, Gladys
Little Apes
Illustrated by Joseph Cellini
Published by Holiday House, 1970
Conklin, Gladys
Lucky Ladybugs
Illustrated by Glen Rounds
Published by Holiday House, 1968
Conklin, Gladys
Tarantula, the Giant Spider
Illustrated
Published by Holiday House, 1972
Conklin, Gladys
We Like Bugs

Illustrated by Arthur Marokvia
Published by Holiday House, 1962
Conklin, Gladys
When Insects Are Babies
Illustrated by Arthur Marokvia
Published by Holiday House, 1969
Conover, Chris
Six Little Ducks
Illustrated by Chris Conover
Published by T.Y. Crowell, 1976
Constant, Alberta
Motoring Millers
Illustrated by Beth and Joe Krush
Published by T.Y. Crowell, 1969
Cook, Gladys
Big Book of Cats
Illustrated by A. Seiden
Published by Grosset & Dunlap, 1965
Cooke, Ann
Giraffes at Home
Illustrated
Published by T.Y. Crowell, 1972
Cooney, Barbara
Mother Goose in French
Translated by Hugh Latham
Illustrated by Barbara Cooney
Published by T.Y. Crowell, 1964
Cooper, Elizabeth
Fish from Japan
Illustrated by Beth and Joe Krush
Published by Harcourt Brace Jovanovich, 1969
Corey, Dorothy
No Company Was Coming to Samuel's House
Illustrated
Published by Blaine-Ethridge, 1976
Corey, Dorothy
Pepe's Private Christmas
Illustrated by John Wallner
Published by Scholastic, 1979
Corey, Dorothy
You Go Away
Illustrated by Lois Axeman and Caroline Rubin
Published by A. Whitman, 1975
Cornish, Sam
Grandmother's Pictures
Illustrated by Jeanne Johns
Published by Bradbury Press, 1976
Cort, Margaret
Little Oleg
Illustrated by John Cort
Published by Carolrhoda, 1971
Craft, Ruth
Carrie Hepple's Garden
Illustrated by Irene Haas
Published by Atheneum, 1979

Craft, Ruth
Winter Bear
Illustrated by Eric Blegvad
Published by Atheneum, 1975
Craig, M. Jean
The Sand, the Sea and Me
Illustrated by Audrey Newell
Published by Walker, 1972
Crampton, Gertrude
Scuffy the Tugboat
Illustrated by Tibor Gergely
Published by Western, 1973
Crampton, Gertrude
Tootle
Illustrated by Tibor Gergely
Published by Western, 1945
Crawford, Sue Heffernan
Minoo's Family
Illustrated by Frances McGlynn
Published by Before We Are Six (Canada), 1974
Crawston, Vee
Matuk, the Eskimo Boy
Illustrated by Haris Petie
Published by Lantern Press, 1965
Cressey, James
Fourteen Rats and a Rat Catcher
Illustrated by Tamasin Cole
Published by Prentice-Hall, 1977
Cretan, Gladys
Lobo and Brewster
Illustrated by Patricia Combs
Published by Lothrop, 1971
Cretan, Gladys
Messy Sally
Illustrated by Pat G. Porter
Published by Lothrop, 1972
Crews, Donald
Freight Train
Illustrated by Donald Crews
Published by Greenwillow, 1978
Cromie, William J.
Steven and the Green Turtle
Illustrated by Tom Eaton
Published by Harper and Row, 1970
Crowe, Robert L.
Clyde Monster
Illustrated by Kay Chorao
Published by Dutton, 1976
Crowther, Robert
The Most Amazing Hide and Seek Alphabet Book
Illustrated
Published by Viking Press, 1977
Cummings, E.E.
Fairy Tales
Illustrated by John Eaton
Published by Harcourt Brace Jovanovich, 1965

Cutler, Ivor
Elephant Girl
Illustrated by Helen Oxenbury
Published by Morrow, 1976
Dahl, Roald
The Enormous Crocodile
Illustrated by Quentin Blake
Published by Knopf, 1979
Dahl, Roald
Fantastic Mr. Fox
Illustrated by Donald Chaffin
Published by Knopf, 1970
Dalgliesh, Alice
Little Wooden Farmer
Illustrated by Anita Lobel
Published by Macmillan, 1968
Dalgliesh, Alice
Thanksgiving Story
Illustrated by Helen Sewell
Published by Scribner, 1954
Daly, Kathleen
A Child's Book of Birds
Illustrated by Fred Brenner
Published by Doubleday, 1977
Daniels, Guy
Peasants Pea Patch
Translated by Guy Daniels
Illustrated by Robert Quackenbush
Published by Delacorte, 1971
Daniels, Velma Seawell
Kat—the Tale of a Calico Cat
Illustrated
Published by Pelican, 1977
Danish, Barbara
Dragon and the Doctor
Illustrated by Barbara Danish
Published by Feminist Press, 1971
Darling, Lois and Louis Darling
Worms
Illustrated by Lois Darling
Published by Morrow, 1972
Darwin, Leonard
What Makes a Telephone Work?
Illustrated by Leonard Darwin
Published by Little, Brown, 1970
Dauer, Rosamond
Mrs. Piggery Snout
Illustrated by Ib Ohlsson
Published by Harper and Row, 1977
Dauer, Rosamond
My Friend Jasper Jones
Illustrated by Jerry Joyner
Published by Parents Magazine Press, 1977
Daugherty, James
Andy and the Lion
Illustrated by James Daugherty
Published by Viking Press, 1938

D'Aulaire, Ingri and Edgar D'Aulaire
Animals Everywhere
Illustrated by Edgar D'Aulaire
Published by Doubleday, 1954
D'Aulaire, Ingri and Edgar D'Aulaire
Terrible Troll-Bird
Illustrated
Published by Doubleday, 1976
David, Eugene
Crystal Magic
Illustrated by Abner Graboff
Published by Prentice-Hall, 1965
Davis, Daphne
Baby Animal Book
Illustrated by Craig Pineo
Published by Western, 1964
Day, Jennifer W.
What Is a Mammal?
Illustrated by Ann Brewster
Published by Western, 1975
Dayrell, Elphinstone and Blair Lent
Why the Sun and Moon Live in the Sky
Illustrated by Blair Lent
Published by Houghton Mifflin, 1968
Dayton, Mona
Earth and Sky
Illustrated by Roger Duvoisin
Published by Harper and Row, 1969
De Angeli, Marguerite
Book of Nursery and Mother Goose Rhymes
Illustrated by Marguerite De Angeli
Published by Doubleday, 1954
DeBrunhoff, Jean
Babar and Father Christmas
Illustrated by Jean DeBrunhoff
Published by Random, 1949
DeBrunhoff, Jean
Babar and His Children
Translated by Merle Haas
Illustrated by Jean DeBrunhoff
Published by Random, 1954
DeBrunhoff, Jean
Babar and Zephir
Translated by Merle Haas
Illustrated by Jean DeBrunhoff
Published by Random, 1942
DeBrunhoff, Jean
Babar the King
Illustrated by Jean DeBrunhoff
Published by Random, 1937
DeBrunhoff, Jean
Meet Babar and His Family
Illustrated by Jean DeBrunhoff
Published by Random, 1973
DeBrunhoff, Laurent
Babar Comes to America

Illustrated by Laurent DeBrunhoff
Published by Random, 1965
DeBrunhoff, Laurent
Babar Visits Another Planet
Illustrated by Laurent DeBrunhoff
Published by Random, 1972
DeBrunhoff, Laurent
Babar's Birthday Surprise
Illustrated by Laurent DeBrunhoff
Published by Random, 1970
DeBrunhoff, Laurent
Babar's Castle
Translated by Merle Haas
Illustrated by Laurent DeBrunhoff
Published by Random, 1962
DeBrunhoff, Laurent
Babar's Cousin
Translated by Merle Haas
Illustrated by Laurent DeBrunhoff
Published by Random, 1952
DeBrunhoff, Laurent
Babar's French Lessons
Illustrated by Laurent DeBrunhoff
Published by Random, 1963
DeBrunhoff, Laurent
Babar's Moon Trip
Illustrated by Laurent DeBrunhoff
Published by Random, 1969
DeBrunhoff, Laurent
Babar's Spanish Lessons
Illustrated by Laurent DeBrunhoff
Published by Random, 1965
DeBrunhoff, Laurent
Babar's Trunk
Illustrated by Laurent DeBrunhoff
Published by Random, 1969
DeBrunhoff, Laurent
Bonhomme and the Huge Monster
Illustrated by Laurent DeBrunhoff
Published by Pantheon, 1974
De Bruyn, Monica
Six Special Places
Illustrated by Monica De Bruyn
Published by A. Whitman, 1975
De Forest, Charlotte B.
Prancing Pony: Nursery Rhymes from Japan
Illustrated by Kaiko Aida
Published by Weatherhill, 1968
Degen, Bruce
Aunt Possum and the Pumpkin Man
Illustrated by Bruce Degen
Published by Harper and Row, 1977
De Groat, Diane
Alligator's Toothache
Illustrated by Diane De Groat
Published by Crown, 1977

De Grosbois, Louise, et al.
Mommy Works on Dresses
Translated by Caroline Bayard
Illustrated
Published by Canadian Women's Educational Press, 1977
Deguine, Jean-Claude
Emperor Penguins
Illustrated by Kazue Mizumura
Published by Stephen Greene Press, Vermont, 1974
Delafield, Celia
Mrs. Mallard's Ducklings
Illustrated by Leonard Weisgard
Published by Lothrop, 1946
De La Mare, Walter
Warmint
Illustrated by Evaline Ness
Published by Scribner, 1976
Delaney, Ned
One Dragon to Another
Illustrated by Ned Delaney
Published by Houghton Mifflin, 1976
Delaney, Ned
Two Strikes, Four Eyes
Illustrated by Ned Delaney
Published by Houghton Mifflin, 1976
Delaunay, Sonia
Sonia Delaunay's Alphabet
Illustrated by Sonia Delaunay
Published by T.Y. Crowell, 1972
Delton, Judy
Penny-Wise, Fun Foolish
Illustrated by Giulio Maestro
Published by Crown, 1977
Delton, Judy
Rabbit Finds a Way
Illustrated by Joe Lasker
Published by Crown, 1975
Delton, Judy
Three Friends Find Spring
Illustrated by Giulio Maestro
Published by Crown, 1977
Delton, Judy
Two Good Friends
Illustrated by Giulio Maestro
Published by Crown, 1974
Delton, Judy
Two Is Company
Illustrated by Giulio Maestro
Published by Crown, 1976
Dennis, Wesley
Flip
Illustrated by Wesley Dennis
Published by Viking Press, 1941
Dennis, Wesley
Tumble: The Story of a Mustang
Illustrated by Wesley Dennis
Published by Hastings House, 1966

DePaola, Tomie
Big Anthony and the Magic Ring
Illustrated by Tomie DePaola
Published by Harcourt Brace Jovanovich, 1979
DePaola, Tomie
Charlie Needs a Cloak
Illustrated by Tomie DePaola
Published by Prentice-Hall, 1974
DePaola, Tomie
Fight the Night
Illustrated by Tomie DePaola
Published by Lippincott, 1968
DePaola, Tomie
Four Stories for Four Seasons
Illustrated by Tomie DePaola
Published by Prentice-Hall, 1977
DePaola, Tomie
Michael Bird-Boy
Illustrated by Tomie DePaola
Published by Prentice-Hall, 1975
DePaola, Tomie
Nana Upstairs and Nana Downstairs
Illustrated by Tomie DePaola
Published by Putnam, 1973
DePaola, Tomie
Quicksand Book
Illustrated by Tomie DePaola
Published by Holiday House, 1977
DePaola, Tomie
Strega Nona
Illustrated by Tomie DePaola
Published by Prentice-Hall, 1975
DePaola, Tomie
Watch Out for the Chicken Feet in Your Soup
Illustrated by Tomie DePaola
Published by Prentice-Hall, 1974
DePaola, Tomie
When Everyone Was Fast Asleep
Illustrated by Tomie DePaola
Published by Holiday House, 1976
DePoix, Carol
Jo, Flo and Yolanda
Illustrated by Stephanie Sove Ney
Published by Lollipop Power, 1973
DeRegniers, Beatrice
Catch a Little Fox
Illustrated by Brinton Turkle
Published by Seabury, 1968
DeRegniers, Beatrice
How Joe Bear & Sam Mouse Got Together
Illustrated by Brinton Turkle
Published by Parents Magazine Press, 1965
DeRegniers, Beatrice
It Does Not Say Meow
Illustrated by Paul Galdone
Published by Seabury, 1972
DeRegniers, Beatrice
Little Sister & Month Brothers
Illustrated by Margot Tomes
Published by Seabury, 1976
DeRegniers, Beatrice
May I Bring a Friend?
Illustrated by Beni Montresor
Published by Atheneum, 1964
DeRegniers, Beatrice
Snow Party
Illustrated by R. Zimnik
Published by Pantheon, 1959
DeRegniers, Beatrice and Irene Haas
Little House of Your Own
Illustrated by Irene Haas
Published by Harcourt Brace Jovanovich, 1955
DeRegniers, Beatrice and Irene Haas
Something Special
Illustrated by Irene Haas
Published by Harcourt Brace Jovanovich, 1958
DeRegniers, Beatrice and Irene Haas
Was It a Good Trade?
Illustrated by Irene Haas
Published by Harcourt Brace Jovanovich, 1956
DeRegniers, Beatrice and Leona Pierce
Who Likes the Sun
Illustrated by Leona Pierce
Published by Harcourt Brace Jovanovich, 1961
Desbarats, Peter
Gabrielle & Selena
Illustrated by Nancy Grossman
Published by Harcourt Brace Jovanovich, 1968
Devlin, Harry and Wende Devlin
Cranberry Mystery
Illustrated by Harry Devlin
Published by Scholastic, 1979
Devlin, Wende and Harry Devlin
Old Black Witch
Illustrated by Harry Devlin
Published by Parents Magazine Press, 1966
Devlin, Wende and Harry Devlin
Old Witch Rescues Halloween
Illustrated
Published by Garrard, 1976
Dickens, Frank and Harry Devlin
Boffo—the Great Motorcycle Race
Illustrated by Frank Dickens
Published by Scholastic, 1979

Dillon, Ellis
Wise Man on the Mountain
Illustrated by Gaynor Chapman
Published by Atheneum, 1970
Dionetti, Michelle
Thalia Brown and the Blue Jug
Illustrated by James Calvin
Published by A-W, 1979
Dobrin, Arnold
Gilly Gilhooley: A Tale of Ireland
Illustrated by Arnold Dobrin
Published by Crown, 1976
Dobrin, Arnold
Josephine's Imagination
Illustrated by Arnold Dobrin
Published by Scholastic, 1973
Dobrin, Arnold
Little Monk & the Tiger: A Tale of Thailand
Illustrated
Published by Coward, 1965
Dobrin, Arnold
Taro and the Sea Turtles
Illustrated by Arnold Dobrin
Published by Coward, 1966
Domanska, Janina
Din, Dan, Don—It's Christmas
Illustrated
Published by Greenwillow, 1975
Domanska, Janina
King Krakus and the Dragon
Illustrated by Janina Domanska
Published by Greenwillow, 1979
Domanska, Janina
Little Red Hen
Illustrated by Janina Domanska
Published by Macmillan, 1973
Domanska, Janina
Look, There's a Turtle Flying
Illustrated by Janina Domanska
Published by Macmillan, 1973
Domanska, Janina
Spring Is
Illustrated by Janina Domanska
Published by Greenwillow, 1976
Domanska, Janina
Turnip
Illustrated by Janina Domanska
Published by Macmillan, 1969
Domanska, Janina
What Do You See?
Illustrated by Janina Domanska
Published by Macmillan, 1974
Donnison, Polly
William the Dragon
Illustrated by Polly Donnison
Published by Coward, 1973
Dorian, Marguerite
When the Snow Is Blue
Illustrated by Marguerite Dorian
Published by Lothrop, 1959
Dorsky, Blanche
Harry: A True Story
Illustrated by Muriel Batherman
Published by Prentice-Hall, 1977
Dotts, Maryann
I Am Happy
Illustrated by Harriette Hughey
Published by Abingdon, 1971
Dragonwagon, Crescent
Strawberry Dress Escape
Illustrated by Lillian Hoban
Published by Scribner, 1975
Dragonwagon, Crescent
When Light Turns into Night
Illustrated by Robert Parker
Published by Harper and Row, 1975
Dragonwagon, Crescent
Will I Be Okay?
Illustrated by Ben Shecter
Published by Harper and Row, 1977
Dragonwagon, Crescent
Wind Rose
Illustrated by Ronald Himler
Published by Harper and Row, 1976
Dragonwagon, Crescent
Your Owl Friend
Illustrated by Ruth Bornstein
Published by Harper and Row, 1977
DuBois, William Pene
Bear Circus
Illustrated by William Pene DuBois
Published by Viking Press, 1971
DuBois, William Pene
Bear Party
Illustrated by William Pene DuBois
Published by Viking Press, 1963
DuBois, William Pene
Hare and Tortoise
Illustrated by William Pene DuBois
Published by Doubleday, 1972
DuBois, William Pene
Lion
Illustrated by William Pene DuBois
Published by Viking Press, 1956
Duff, Maggie
Jonny and His Drum
Illustrated by Charles Robinson
Published by Walck, 1972
Dugan, William
Sign Book
Illustrated
Published by Western, 1976
Dulieu, Jean
Paulus and the Dragon
Translated by Vivien Visser

Illustrated by Jean Dulieu
Published by Crossing Press, 1977
Dunn, Judy
Little Duck
Illustrated by Phoebe Dunn
Published by Random, 1976
Durham, Mae
Tobei: A Japanese Tale
Illustrated by Mitsu Yashima
Published by Bradbury Press, 1974
Durio, Alice
Cajun Columbus
Illustrated by James Rice
Published by Pelican, 1975
Duvoisin, Roger
Crocodile in the Tree
Illustrated by Roger Duvoisin
Published by Knopf, 1973
Duvoisin, Roger
Easter Treat
Illustrated by Roger Duvoisin
Published by Knopf, 1954
Duvoisin, Roger
Jasmine
Illustrated by Roger Duvoisin
Published by Knopf, 1973
Duvoisin, Roger
Missing Milkman
Illustrated by Roger Duvoisin
Published by Knopf, 1966
Duvoisin, Roger
Our Veronica Goes to Petunia's Farm
Illustrated by Roger Duvoisin
Published by Knopf, 1962
Duvoisin, Roger
Petunia
Illustrated by Roger Duvoisin
Published by Knopf, 1950
Duvoisin, Roger
Snowy and Woody
Illustrated by Roger Duvoisin
Published by Knopf, 1979
Duvoisin, Roger
Spring Snow
Illustrated by Roger Duvoisin
Published by Knopf, 1963
Duvoisin, Roger
Two Lonely Ducks: A Counting Book
Illustrated by Roger Duvoisin
Published by Knopf, 1955
Duvoisin, Roger
Veronica
Illustrated by Roger Duvoisin
Published by Knopf, 1961
Duvoisin, Roger
Veronica and the Birthday Present
Illustrated by Roger Duvoisin
Published by Knopf, 1971

Eastman, Philip D.
Are You My Mother?
Illustrated
Published by Harper and Row, 1961
Eastman, Philip D.
Big Dog, Little Dog: A Bedtime Story
Illustrated
Published by Random, 1973
Eastman, Philip D.
Flap Your Wings
Illustrated
Published by Random, 1969
Eastman, P.P.
Everything Happens to Aaron
Illustrated
Published by Random, 1976
Eastwick, Ivy O.
Seven Little Popovers
Illustrated
Published by Follett, 1979
Eber, Christine Engla
Just Momma and Me
Illustrated
Published by Lollipop Power, 1975
Eberle, Irmegarde
Fawn in the Woods
Illustrated
Published by T.Y. Crowell, 1962
Eberle, Irmegarde and Myron Scott
Robins on the Window Sill
Illustrated
Published by T.Y. Crowell, 1958
Ehrlich, Amy
The Everyday Train
Illustrated by Martha Alexander
Published by Dial, 1977
Ehrlich, Amy
Zeek Silver Moon
Illustrated by Robert Parker
Published by Dial, 1972
Eichenberg, Fritz
Ape in a Cape
Illustrated by Fritz Eichenberg
Published by Harcourt Brace Jovanovich, 1952
Eichenberg, Fritz
Dancing in the Moon: Counting Rhymes
Illustrated by Fritz Eichenberg
Published by Harcourt Brace Jovanovich, (n.d.)
Eichler, Margrit
Martin's Father
Illustrated by Bev Magennis
Published by Lollipop Power, 1971
Einsel, Walter
Did You Ever See?
Illustrated
Published by Scholastic, 1969

Eiseman, Alberta
Candido
Illustrated by Lilian Obligato
Published by Macmillan, 1967
Elisofon, Eliot
Zaire: A Week in Joseph's World
Illustrated by Eliot Elisofon
Published by Macmillan, 1973
Elkin, Benjamin
King Who Could Not Sleep
Illustrated by Victoria Chess
Published by Parents Magazine Press, 1975
Elkin, Benjamin
Loudest Noise in the World
Illustrated by James Daugherty
Published by Viking Press, 1954
Elkin, Benjamin
Six Foolish Fishermen
Illustrated by Bernice Myers
Published by Children's Press, 1957
Elkin, Benjamin
Such Is the Way of the World
Illustrated by Yoko Mitsuhashi
Published by Parents Magazine Press, 1968
Elliott, Harley
The Tiger's Spots
Illustrated
Published by Crossing Press, 1977
Elting, Mary
Water Come, Water Go
Illustrated
Published by Harvey, 1964
Emberley, Barbara
Drummer Hoff
Illustrated by Ed Emberley
Published by Prentice-Hall, 1967
Emberley, Barbara
One Wide River to Cross
Illustrated by Ed Emberley
Published by Prentice-Hall, 1966
Emberley, Barbara
Story of Paul Bunyan
Illustrated by Ed Emberley
Published by Prentice-Hall, 1963
Emberley, Ed
Green Says Go
Illustrated by Ed Emberley
Published by Little, Brown, 1968
Emberley, Ed
Klippity Klop
Illustrated by Ed Emberley
Published by Little, Brown, 1974
Emberley, Ed
Wing on a Flea: Book About Shapes
Illustrated by Ed Emberley
Published by Little, Brown, 1961

Engelbert, Victor
Goats of Agadez
Illustrated by Victor Engelbert
Published by Harcourt Brace Jovanovich, 1973
English, Betty, Ed.
Women at Their Work
Illustrated by Betty English
Published by Dial, 1977
Engvick, William, Ed.
Lullabies and Night Songs
Illustrated by Maurice Sendak
Published by Harper and Row, 1965
Epstein, Sam and Beryl Epstein
Hold Everything
Illustrated by Tomie DePaola
Published by Holiday House, 1973
Epstein, Sam and Beryl Epstein
Pick It Up
Illustrated by Tomie DePaola
Published by Holiday House, 1971
Epstein, Sherrie S.
Penny, the Medicine Maker: Story of Penicillin
Illustrated by Mark Springer
Published by Lerner, 1960
Erickson, Russell
The Snow of Ohreeganau
Illustrated by Joseph Low
Published by Lothrop, 1974
Erickson, Russell
Warton and Morton
Illustrated by Lawrence DiFiori
Published by Lothrop, 1976
Ernst, Kathryn
Danny and His Thumb
Illustrated by Tomie DePaola
Published by Prentice-Hall, 1975
Ernst, Kathryn
Owl's New Cards
Illustrated
Published by Crown, 1977
Estes, Shirley
Robbie's Friend George
Illustrated by Shirley Estes
Published by Carolrhoda, 1972
Ets, Marie Hall
Another Day
Illustrated by Marie Hall Ets
Published by Viking Press, 1953
Ets, Marie Hall
Elephant in a Well
Illustrated by Marie Hall Ets
Published by Penguin, 1973
Ets, Marie Hall
Gilberto and the Wind
Illustrated by Marie Hall Ets
Published by Viking Press, 1963

Ets, Marie Hall
In the Forest
Illustrated by Marie Hall Ets
Published by Viking Press, 1944

Ets, Marie Hall
Jay Bird
Illustrated by Marie Hall Ets
Published by Viking Press, 1974

Ets, Marie Hall
Just Me
Illustrated by Marie Hall Ets
Published by Viking Press, 1965

Ets, Marie Hall
Play with Me
Illustrated by Marie Hall Ets
Published by Viking Press, 1955

Ets, Marie Hall
Talking Without Words
Illustrated by Marie Hall Ets
Published by Viking Press, 1968

Evans, Eva
Sleepy Time
Illustrated by R. Champion
Published by Houghton Mifflin, 1962

Everton, Macduff
El Circo Magico: Finding Magic Circus
Illustrated by Macduff Everton
Published by Carolrhoda, 1979

Faison, Eleanora
Becoming
Illustrated by Cecilia Ercin
Published by Vermont Crossroads, 1979

Fanshawe, Elizabeth
Rachel
Illustrated
Published by Bradbury Press, 1977

Farber, Norma
As I Was Crossing Boston Common
Illustrated by Arnold Lobel
Published by Dutton, 1975

Farber, Norma
I Found Them in the Yellow Pages
Illustrated by Marc Brown
Published by Little, Brown, 1973

Farber, Norma
Where's Gomer?
Illustrated by Wm Pene DuBois
Published by Dutton, 1974

Farjeon, Eleanor
Nursery Rhymes of London Town
Illustrated by MacDonald Gill
Published by Duckworth Press,—N.J., (n.d.)

Fassler, Joan
All Alone with Daddy
Illustrated by Dorothy L. Gregory
Published by Human Sciences Press, 1975

Fassler, Joan
The Boy with a Problem
Illustrated
Published by Human Sciences Press, 1971

Fassler, Joan
Don't Worry, Dear
Illustrated
Published by Human Sciences Press, 1971

Fassler, Joan
Howie Helps Himself
Illustrated by Joe Lasker
Published by A. Whitman, 1975

Fassler, Joan
The Man of the House
Illustrated by Peter Landa
Published by Human Sciences Press, 1979

Fassler, Joan
My Grandpa Died Today
Illustrated
Published by Human Sciences Press, 1971

Fassler, Joan
One Little Girl
Illustrated by Jane M. Smyth
Published by Human Sciences Press, 1969

Fatio, Louise
Happy Lion
Illustrated by Roger Duvoisin
Published by McGraw-Hill, 1954

Fatio, Louise
Hector Penguin
Illustrated by Roger Duvoisin
Published by McGraw-Hill, 1973

Fatio, Louise
Marc and Pixie and the Walls in Mrs. Jones' Garden
Illustrated by Roger Duvoisin
Published by McGraw-Hill, 1975

Fatio, Louise
Red Bantam
Illustrated by Roger Duvoisin
Published by McGraw-Hill, 1963

Fatio, Louise
Three Happy Lions
Illustrated by Roger Duvoisin
Published by McGraw-Hill, 1959

Fay, Hermann
My Sea
Illustrated by Hermann Fay
Published by Rand McNally, 1974

Feelings, Muriel
Jambo Means Hello: Swahili Alphabet Book
Illustrated by Tom Feelings
Published by Dial, 1974

Feelings, Muriel
Moja Means One: Swahili Counting Book
Illustrated by Tom Feelings
Published by Dial, 1971

Felder, Eleanor
X Marks the Spot
Illustrated by Marylin Hafner
Published by Coward, 1972

Felt, Sue
Rosa-Too-Little
Illustrated by Sue Felt
Published by Doubleday, 1950

Fender, Kay
Odette, a Bird in Paris
Illustrated by Phillipe Dumas
Published by Prentice-Hall, 1977

Fennema, Ilona and Georgette Apol
Dirk's Wooden Shoes
Illustrated by Georgette Apol
Published by Harcourt Brace Jovanovich, 1970

Fenton, Edward
Big Yellow Balloon
Illustrated by Ib Ohlsson
Published by Doubleday, 1967

Fenton, Edward
Fierce John
Illustrated by Wm. Pene DuBois
Published by Holt, Rinehart and Winston, 1969

Field, Eugene
Wynken, Blynken and Nod
Illustrated by Barbara Cooney
Published by Hastings House, 1970

Field, Eugene
Wynken, Blynken and Nod
Illustrated by Holly Johnson
Published by Warne, 1973

Fifield, Flora and Nola Langer
Pictures for the Palace
Illustrated
Published by Vanguard, (n.d.)

Fisher, Aileen
Best Little House
Illustrated by Arnold Spilka
Published by T.Y. Crowell, 1966

Fisher, Aileen
Cricket in a Thicket
Illustrated by Feodor Rojankovsky
Published by Scribner, 1963

Fisher, Aileen
Do Bears Have Mothers Too?
Illustrated by Eric Carle
Published by T.Y. Crowell, 1973

Fisher, Aileen
Going Barefoot
Illustrated by Adrienne Adams
Published by T.Y. Crowell, 1960

Fisher, Aileen
I Like Weather
Illustrated by Janina Domanska
Published by T.Y. Crowell, 1963

Fisher, Aileen
In the Middle of the Night
Illustrated by Adrienne Adams
Published by T.Y. Crowell, 1965

Fisher, Aileen
Listen, Rabbit
Illustrated by Symeon Shimin
Published by T.Y. Crowell, 1964

Fisher, Aileen
My Cat Has Eyes of Sapphire Blue
Illustrated by Marie Angel
Published by T.Y. Crowell, 1973

Fisher, Aileen
My Mother and I
Illustrated by Kazue Mizumura
Published by T.Y. Crowell, 1967

Fisher, Aileen
Once We Went on a Picnic
Illustrated by Tony Chen
Published by T.Y. Crowell, 1975

Fisher, Aileen
Sing, Little Mouse
Illustrated by Symeon Shimin
Published by T.Y. Crowell, 1969

Fisher, Aileen
We Went Looking
Illustrated by Marie Angel
Published by T.Y. Crowell, 1968

Fisher, Lucretia
Two Monsters
Illustrated by Thomas Jardine
Published by Stemmer House, 1976

Flack, Marjorie
Angus and the Cat
Illustrated by Marjorie Flack
Published by Doubleday, 1971

Flack, Marjorie
Angus and the Ducks
Illustrated by Marjorie Flack
Published by Doubleday, 1939

Flack, Marjorie
Angus Lost
Illustrated by Marjorie Flack
Published by Doubleday, 1941

Flack, Marjorie
Ask Mr. Bear
Illustrated by Marjorie Flack
Published by Macmillan, 1958

Flack, Marjorie
 Story About Ping
 Illustrated by Kurt Wiese
 Published by Viking Press, 1933
Flack, Marjorie and DuBose Heyward
 Country Bunny and the Little Golden Shoes
 Illustrated by Marjorie Flack
 Published by Houghton Mifflin, 1973
Flanagan, Terry
 A Big Surprise
 Illustrated
 Published by Random, 1974
Floethe, Louise and Richard Floethe
 Islands of Hawaii
 Illustrated by Richard Floethe
 Published by Scribner, 1964
Flora, James
 Great Green Turkey Creek Monster
 Illustrated by James Flora
 Published by Atheneum, 1976
Flora, James
 Sherwood Walks Home
 Illustrated by James Flora
 Published by Harcourt Brace Jovanovich, 1966
Flora, James
 Stewed Goose
 Illustrated by James Flora
 Published by Atheneum, 1973
Flory, Jane
 The Unexpected Grandchildren
 Illustrated by Carolyn Croll
 Published by Houghton Mifflin, 1977
Flory, Jane
 We'll Have a Friend for Lunch
 Illustrated by Carolyn Croll
 Published by Houghton Mifflin, 1975
Fontaine, Theodor
 Sir Ribbeck of Ribbeck of Havelland
 Translated by Elizabeth Shub
 Illustrated by Nonny Hogrogian
 Published by Macmillan, 1969
Foreman, Michael
 Dinosaurs and All That Rubbish
 Illustrated
 Published by T.Y. Crowell, 1973
Foreman, Michael
 Two Giants
 Illustrated by Michael Foreman
 Published by Pantheon, 1967
Foreman, Michael
 War and Peas
 Illustrated
 Published by T.Y. Crowell, 1974
Foster, Doris V.
 Pocketful of Seasons
 Illustrated by Talivaldis Stubis
 Published by Lothrop, 1960
Foster, Doris
 Tell Me, Mr. Owl
 Illustrated by Helen Stone
 Published by Lothrop, 1957
Fournier, Catherine, Ed.
 Coconut Thieves
 Illustrated by Janina Domanska
 Published by Scribner, 1964
Fox, Charles P.
 When Autumn Comes
 Illustrated
 Published by Contemporary Books, 1966
Fox, Siv Cedering
 The Blue Horse and Other Night Poems
 Illustrated by Donald Carrick
 Published by Seabury, 1979
Fox, William W.
 The Amazing Bee
 Illustrated by William W. Fox
 Published by Walck, 1977
Francis, Frank
 Magic Wallpaper
 Illustrated by Frank Francis
 Published by Abelard, 1970
Francis, Frank
 Natasha's New Doll
 Illustrated
 Published by O'Hara, 1974
Francoise
 Big Rain
 Illustrated by Francoise
 Published by Scribner, 1961
Francoise
 Chou Chou
 Illustrated by Francoise
 Published by Scribner, 1958
Francoise
 Minou
 Illustrated by Francoise
 Published by Scribner, 1962
Francoise
 Jeanne-Marie in Gay Paris
 Illustrated by Francoise
 Published by Scribner, 1956
Frasconi, Antonio
 House That Jack Built: Picture Book in Two Languages
 Illustrated by Antonio Frasconi
 Published by Harcourt Brace Jovanovich, 1958
Frasconi, Antonio
 Snow and Sun: South American Folk Rhyme in Two Languages
 Illustrated by Antonio Frasconi

Published by Harcourt Brace
Jovanovich, 1961
Freeman, Don
Beady Bear
Illustrated by Don Freeman
Published by Viking Press, 1954
Freeman, Don
Bearymore
Illustrated by Don Freeman
Published by Viking Press, 1976
Freeman, Don
Chalk Box Story
Illustrated by Don Freeman
Published by Lippincott, 1976
Freeman, Don
Come Again, Pelican
Illustrated by Don Freeman
Published by Viking Press, 1961
Freeman, Don
Corduroy
Illustrated by Don Freeman
Published by Viking Press, 1968
Freeman, Don
Dandelion
Illustrated by Don Freeman
Published by Viking Press, 1964
Freeman, Don
Flash the Dash
Illustrated by Don Freeman
Published by Children's Press, 1973
Freeman, Don
Fly High, Fly Low
Illustrated by Don Freeman
Published by Viking Press, 1957
Freeman, Don
Guard Mouse
Illustrated by Don Freeman
Published by Viking Press, 1974
Freeman, Don
Inspector Peckit
Illustrated by Don Freeman
Published by Viking Press, 1972
Freeman, Don
Mop Top
Illustrated by Don Freeman
Published by Viking Press, 1955
Freeman, Don
Norman the Doorman
Illustrated by Don Freeman
Published by Viking Press, 1959
Freeman, Don
Paper Party
Illustrated by Don Freeman
Published by Viking Press, 1974
Freeman, Don
Penguins, of All People
Illustrated by Don Freeman
Published by Viking Press, 1971

Freeman, Don
Pocket for Corduroy
Illustrated by Don Freeman
Published by Viking Press, 1978
Freeman, Don
A Rainbow of My Own
Illustrated by Don Freeman
Published by Viking Press, 1966
Freeman, Don
Seal and the Slick
Illustrated by Don Freeman
Published by Viking Press, 1974
Freeman, Don
Space Witch
Illustrated by Don Freeman
Published by Viking Press, 1959
Freeman, Don
Tilly Witch
Illustrated by Don Freeman
Published by Viking Press, 1969
Freeman, Don
Turtle and the Dove
Illustrated by Don Freeman
Published by Viking Press, 1964
Freeman, Don
Will's Quill
Illustrated by Don Freeman
Published by Viking Press, 1977
Freeman, Lucy
The Eleven Steps
Illustrated by Julie Brinckloe
Published by Doubleday, 1975
Freeman, Lydia and Don Freeman
Pet of the Met
Illustrated by Don Freeman
Published by Viking Press, 1953
Fregosi, Claudia
A Gift
Illustrated
Published by Prentice-Hall, 1976
Fregosi, Claudia
The Mammoth, the Owl and the Crab
Illustrated by Claudia Fregosi
Published by Macmillan, 1975
Freschet, Berniece
Bernard of Scotland Yard
Illustrated by Gina Freschet
Published by Scribner, 1979
Freschet, Berniece
Happy Dromedary
Illustrated by Glen Rounds
Published by Scribner, 1977
Freschet, Berniece
Old Bullfrog
Illustrated by Roger Duvoisin
Published by Scribner, 1972
Freschet, Berniece
Owl and the Prairie Dog

Illustrated
Published by Scribner, 1969
Freschet, Berniece
Turtle Pond
Illustrated by Donald Carrick
Published by Scribner, 1971
Freschet, Berniece
Web in the Grass
Illustrated by Roger Duvoisin
Published by Scribner, 1972
Friedman, Joy T.
Look Around and Listen
Illustrated by Joy T. Friedman
Published by Grosset & Dunlap, 1976
Friedman, Joy T.
The Eels' Strange Journey
Illustrated by Gail Owens
Published by T.Y. Crowell, 1976
Friedman, Judith
Biting Book
Illustrated by Kees De Kiefte
Published by Prentice-Hall, 1975
Friedrich, Priscilla and Otto Friedrich
The Easter Bunny That Overslept
Illustrated by Adrienne Adams
Published by Lothrop, 1957
Friskey, Margaret
Chicken Little Count-to-Ten
Illustrated by K. Evans
Published by Children's Press, 1946
Froman, Robert
Mushrooms and Molds
Illustrated
Published by T.Y. Crowell, 1972
Fry, C.
Boat That Mooed
Illustrated by Leonard Weisgard
Published by Macmillan, 1965
Fuchs, Erich
Journey to the Moon
Illustrated by Erich Fuchs
Published by Dial, 1970
Fujikawa, Gyo
Gyo Fujikawa's A-Z Picture Book
Illustrated by Gyo Fujikawa
Published by Grosset & Dunlap, 1974
Fujikawa, Gyo
Babies
Illustrated by Gyo Fujikawa
Published by Grosset & Dunlap, 1963
Fujikawa, Gyo
Betty Bear's Birthday
Illustrated by Gyo Fujikawa
Published by Grosset & Dunlap, 1977
Fujikawa, Gyo
Board Books (6)
Illustrated by Gyo Fujikawa
Published by Grosset & Dunlap, 1963

Fujikawa, Gyo
Mother Goose
Illustrated by Gyo Fujikawa
Published by Grosset & Dunlap, 1968
Fujikawa, Gyo
Our Best Friends
Illustrated by Gyo Fujikawa
Published by Grosset & Dunlap, 1977
Fujita, Tamao
The Boy and the Bird
Translated by Koyoko Tucker
Illustrated by Chiyo Ono
Published by John Day, 1972
Funai, Mamoru
Moke and Poki in the Rain Forest
Illustrated
Published by Harper and Row, 1972
Futamata, Eigoro
How Not to Catch a Mouse
Translated by Meredith Weatherby
Illustrated by Eigoro Futamata
Published by Weatherhill, 1972
Gackenbach, Dick
Crackle Gluck and the Sleeping Toad
Illustrated by Dick Gackenbach
Published by Seabury, 1979
Gackenbach, Dick
Do You Love Me?
Illustrated by Dick Gackenbach
Published by Seabury, 1975
Gackenbach, Dick
Harry and the Terrible Whatzit
Illustrated by Dick Gackenbach
Published by Seabury, 1977
Gaeddert, Lou Ann
Gustav, the Gourmet Giant
Illustrated by Steven Kellogg
Published by Dial, 1976
Gaeddert, Lou Ann
Noisy Nancy and Nick
Illustrated by Gioia Fiammenghi
Published by Doubleday, 1970
Gaeddert, Lou Ann
Noisy Nancy Norris
Illustrated by Gioia Fiammenghi
Published by Doubleday, 1971
Gag, Wanda
ABC Bunny
Illustrated by Wanda Gag
Published by Coward, 1933
Gag, Wanda
Millions of Cats
Illustrated by Wanda Gag
Published by Coward, 1928
Galbraith, Kathryn
Spots Are Special
Illustrated
Published by Atheneum, 1976

Galdone, Joanna
Gertrude, the Goose Who Forgot
Illustrated by Paul Galdone
Published by Watts, 1975
Grimm, Brothers
Hansel and Gretel
Translated by Charles Scribner, Jr.
Illustrated by Adrienne Adams
Published by Scribner, 1975
Grimm, Brothers
Hans in Luck
Illustrated by Paul Galdone
Published by Parents Magazine Press, 1980
Galdone, Paul
Henny Penny
Illustrated by Paul Galdone
Published by Seabury, 1968
Galdone, Paul
History of Mother Twaddle & the Achievements of Her Son Jack
Illustrated by Paul Galdone
Published by Seabury, 1974
Galdone, Paul
Horse, Fox and Lion
Illustrated by Paul Galdone
Published by Seabury, 1968
Galdone, Paul
Life of Jack Sprat, His Wife and His Cat
Illustrated by Paul Galdone
Published by McGraw-Hill, 1969
Galdone, Paul
Little Red Hen
Illustrated by Paul Galdone
Published by Seabury, 1973
Galdone, Paul
Little Red Riding Hood
Illustrated by Paul Galdone
Published by McGraw-Hill, 1974
Galdone, Paul
Magic Porridge Pot
Illustrated by Paul Galdone
Published by Seabury, 1976
Galdone, Paul
Monkey and the Crocodile
Illustrated by Paul Galdone
Published by Seabury, 1969
Galdone, Paul
Old Woman and Her Pig
Illustrated by Paul Galdone
Published by McGraw-Hill, 1961
Galdone, Paul
Puss in Boots
Illustrated by Paul Galdone
Published by Seabury, 1976
Galdone, Paul
The Three Bears
Illustrated by Paul Galdone
Published by Seabury, 1972
Galdone, Paul
Three Little Pigs
Illustrated by Paul Galdone
Published by Seabury, 1970
Galdone, Paul
Three Wishes
Illustrated by Paul Galdone
Published by McGraw-Hill, 1961
Galyean, Thelma
Peppy, Patchy and Magic Star
Illustrated by Pat Brown
Published by NELP, Austin, Texas, 1976
Gans, Roma
Birds at Night
Illustrateo by Aliki
Published by T.Y. Crowell, 1976
Gans, Roma
Bird Talk
Illustrated by Jo Polseno
Published by T.Y. Crowell, 1971
Gans, Roma
Caves
Illustrated by Guilio Maestro
Published by T.Y. Crowell, 1977
Gans, Roma
Hummingbirds in the Garden
Illustrated by Grambs Miller
Published by T.Y. Crowell, 1969
Gans, Roma
Icebergs
Illustrated by Bobri
Published by T.Y. Crowell, 1964
Gans, Roma
Oil: The Buried Treasure
Illustrated
Published by T.Y. Crowell, 1975
Gans, Roma
Wonder of Stones
Illustrated by Joan Berg
Published by T.Y. Crowell, 1963
Gantos, Jack
The Perfect Pal
Illustrated by Nicole Rubel
Published by Houghton Mifflin, 1979
Gantos, Jack
Rotten Ralph
Illustrated by Nicole Rubel
Published by Houghton Mifflin, 1976
Gantos, John B.
Sleepy Ronald
Illustrated by Nicole Rubel
Published by Houghton Mifflin, 1976
Ganz, Barbara
Alberto and His Missing Sock

Translated by Augustina S. Del
  Favero
Illustrated by Phyllis Noda
Published by Blaine-Ethridge, 1975
Garcia, Marcia
The Adventures of Connie and Diego
Illustrated by Malaquias Montoya
Published by Children's Book Press,
  S.F., (n.d.)
Garcia, Richard
My Aunt Otilia's Spirits
Illustrated by Roger I. Reyes and
  Robin Cherin
Published by Children's Book Press,
  S.F., (n.d.)
Garelick, May
About Owls
Illustrated by Tony Chen
Published by Scholastic, 1975
Garelick, May
Down to the Beach
Illustrated by Barbara Cooney
Published by Scholastic, 1973
Garelick, May and Barbara Brenner
Tremendous Tree Book
Illustrated by Fred Brenner
Published by Scholastic, 1979
Garrett, Helen
Angelo, the Naughty One
Illustrated by Leo Politi
Published by Penguin, 1970
Garrison, Christian
Little Pieces of the West Wind
Illustrated by Diane Goode
Published by Bradbury Press, 1975
Gaspar, Tomas Rodriguez
Yolanda's Hike
Illustrated by Sue Brown
Published by New Seed Press, 1974
Gauch, Patricia
Christina Katerina and the Box
Illustrated by Doris Burn
Published by Coward, 1971
Gauch, Patricia
Grandpa and Me
Illustrated by Symeon Shimin
Published by Coward, 1972
Gauch, Patricia
Once Upon a Dinkelsbuhl
Illustrated by Tomie DePaola
Published by Putnam, 1977
Gay, Zhenya
Small One
Illustrated by Zhenya Gay
Published by Viking Press, 1958
Gelman, Rita
Hey, Kid
Illustrated by Karol Nicklaus
Published by Watts, 1977

Geoffroy, Bernice
Irene's Idea
Illustrated by Frances McGlynn
Published by Before We Are Six,
  Canada, (n.d.)
George, Jean C.
All Upon a Sidewalk
Illustrated by Don Bolognese
Published by Dutton, 1974
George, Jean C.
The Wentletrap
Illustrated by Symeon Shimin
Published by Dutton, 1977
Georgiou, Constantine
The Clock
Illustrated by Bernard Lipscomb
Published by Harvey House, 1977
Georgiou, Constantine
The Nest
Illustrated by Bethany Tudor
Published by Harvey House, 1972
Gergely, Tibor
Busy Day, Busy People
Illustrated by Tibor Gergely
Published by Random, 1973
Gergely, Tibor
The Parrot Book
Illustrated by Tibor Gergely
Published by Western, 1976
Gerger, Dawn
Beginning Search-A-Word Shapes
Illustrated
Published by Grosset & Dunlap, 1975
Gerler, William, Compiled by
A Pack of Riddles
Illustrated by Guilio Maestro
Published by Dutton, 1975
Gerson, Mary-Joan
Omoteji's Baby Brother
Illustrated by Elzia Moon
Published by Walck, 1974
Gerson, Mary-Joan
Why the Sky Is Far Away
Illustrated by Hope Merryman
Published by Harcourt Brace
  Jovanovich, 1974
Gilbert, Miriam
Rosie: The Oldest Horse in St.
  Augustine
Illustrated by J. Roch
Published by Island Press, 1974
Gilbreath, Alice
Nature's Squirt Guns, Bubble Pipes &
  Fireworks
Illustrated by Jo Polseno
Published by Walck, 1977
Gilbreath, Alice
Nature's Underground Palaces:
  Caves/Caverns

Illustrated by Michael Eagle
Published by Walck, 1978
Ginsburg, Mirra
Chick and the Duckling
Illustrated by Jose Aruego
Published by Macmillan, 1972
Ginsburg, Mirra
How the Sun Was Brought Back to the Sky
Illustrated by Jose Aruego and Ariane Dewey
Published by Macmillan, 1975
Ginsburg, Mirra
Proud Maiden, Tungak and the Sun
Translated by Mirra Ginsburg
Illustrated by Igor Galanin
Published by Macmillan, 1974
Ginsburg, Mirra
Two Greedy Bears
Illustrated by Jose Aruego
Published by Macmillan, 1976
Ginsburg, Mirra
Which Is the Best Place?
Illustrated by Mirra Ginsburg
Adapted by Mirra Ginsburg (from Dudochkin)
Published by Macmillan, 1976
Girion, Barbara
Boy with the Special Face
Illustrated by Heidi Palmer
Published by Abingdon, 1979
Gittings, Elisa
Shape Books
Illustrated by Elisa Gittings
Published by Activity Resources, 1974
Glasgow, Aline
Honschi
Illustrated by Tony Chen
Published by Parents Magazine Press, 1972
Glendinning, Sally
Jimmy and Joe See a Monster
Illustrated by Paul Frame
Published by Garrard, 1972
Glovach, Linda
Hey, Wait for Me—I'm Amelia
Illustrated by Linda Glovach
Published by Prentice-Hall, 1971
Gobhai, Mehlli
Legend of the Orange Princess
Illustrated by Mehlli Gobhai
Published by Holiday House, 1971
Godden, Rumer
Old Woman Who Lived in a Vinegar Bottle
Illustrated by Mairi Hedderwick
Published by Penguin, 1974

Goff, Beth
Where's Daddy? Story of Divorce
Illustrated by Susan Perl
Published by Beacon Press, 1969
Goffstein, M.B.
Across the Sea
Illustrated by M.B. Goffstein
Published by Farrar, Straus and Giroux, 1968
Goffstein, M.B.
Fish for Supper
Illustrated by M.B. Goffstein
Published by Dial, 1976
Goffstein, M.B.
Neighbors
Illustrated by M.B. Goffstein
Published by Harper and Row, 1979
Goffstein, M.B.
Two Piano Tuners
Illustrated by M.B. Goffstein
Published by Farrar, Straus and Giroux, 1970
Goins, Ellen H.
Long Winter Sleep: Story Mammal Hibernation
Illustrated by Ellen H. Goins
Published by Walck, 1978
Goldberg, Martha
Boy Who Loved Horses
Illustrated
Published by Scholastic, 1976
Goldin, Augusta
Salt
Illustrated by Robert Galster
Published by T.Y. Crowell, 1966
Goldin, Augusta
Straight Hair, Curly Hair
Illustrated by Ed Emberley
Published by T.Y. Crowell, 1966
Goldin, Augusta
Sunlit Sea
Illustrated by Paul Galdone
Published by T.Y. Crowell, 1968
Goldin, Augusta
Where Does Your Garden Grow?
Illustrated by Helen Borten
Published by T.Y. Crowell, 1967
Goldman, Louis
Turkey: A Week in Samil's World
Illustrated by Louis Goldman
Published by Macmillan, 1973
Goldman, Louis and Seymour Reit
A Week in Hagar's World: Israel
Illustrated by Louis Goldman
Published by Macmillan, 1969
Goldman, Susan and Caroline Rubin, Eds.
Grandma Is Somebody Special

Illustrated by Susan Goldman
Published by A. Whitman, 1976
Goldreich, Gloria and Esther Goldreich
What Can She Be? A Farmer
Illustrated by Robert Ipcar
Published by Lothrop, 1976
Goldreich, Gloria and Esther Goldreich
What Can She Be? A Geologist
Illustrated by Robert Ipcar
Published by Lothrop, 1976
Goldreich, Gloria and Esther Goldreich
What Can She Be? A Lawyer
Illustrated by Robert Ipcar
Published by Lothrop, 1973
Goldreich, Gloria and Esther Goldreich
What Can She Be? A Newscaster
Illustrated by Robert Ipcar
Published by Lothrop, 1973
Goldreich, Gloria and Esther Goldreich
What Can She Be? A Police Officer
Illustrated by Robert Ipcar
Published by Lothrop, 1975
Goldreich, Gloria and Esther Goldreich
What Can She Be? A Veterinarian
Illustrated by Robert Ipcar
Published by Lothrop, 1972
Goldsmid, Paula
Did You Ever?
Illustrated by Janice Schopler
Published by Lollipop Power, 1971
Goodall, John
Adventures Paddy Pig
Illustrated by John Goodall
Published by Harcourt Brace Jovanovich, 1968
Goodall, John
Creepy Castle
Illustrated by John Goodall
Published by Atheneum, 1975
Goodall, John
Jacko
Illustrated by John Goodall
Published by Harcourt Brace Jovanovich, 1972
Goodall, John
Paddy's Evening Out
Illustrated by John Goodall
Published by Atheneum, 1973
Goodall, John
Midnight Adventures of Kelly, Dot and Esmeralda
Illustrated by John Goodall
Published by Atheneum, 1973

Goodall, John
Naughty Nancy, the Bad Bridesmaid
Illustrated by John Goodall
Published by Atheneum, 1975
Goodall, John
The Surprise Picnic
Illustrated by John Goodall
Published by Atheneum, 1976
Goodenough, Simon
Dinosaurs and Prehistoric Animals
Illustrated
Published by Children's Book Press—S.F., 1979
Goodenow, Earle
Last Camel
Illustrated by Earle Goodenow
Published by Walck, 1968
Goodsell, Jane
Katie's Magic Glasses
Illustrated by Barbara Cooney
Published by Houghton Mifflin, 1965
Goodyear, Carmen
Sheep Book
Illustrated
Published by Lollipop Power, 1972
Gordon, Bernard
Once There Was a Passenger Pigeon
Illustrated
Published by Walck, 1976
Gordon, Esther and Bernard Gordon
There Really Was a Dodo
Illustrated by Lawrence Di Fiori
Published by Walck, 1974
Gordon, Esther and Bernard Gordon
If an Auk Could Talk
Illustrated by Pamela B. Ford
Published by Walck, 1977
Gordon, Shirley
Crystal Is the New Girl
Illustrated by Edward Frascino
Published by Harper and Row, 1976
Gordon, Shirley
Green Hornet Lunchbox
Illustrated by Margaret B. Graham
Published by Houghton Mifflin, 1973
Goudey, Alice
The Day We Saw the Sun Come Up
Illustrated by Adrienne Adams
Published by Scribner, 1961
Gough, Irene
The Golden Lamb
Illustrated by Joy Murray
Published by Lerner, 1968
Grabianski, Janusz
Androcles and the Lion
Illustrated by Janusz Grabianski
Published by Watts, 1970

Graham, Al
Timothy Turtle
Illustrated by Tony Palazzo
Published by Penguin, 1970
Graham, Margaret
Be Nice to Spiders
Illustrated by Margaret Graham
Published by Harper and Row, 1967
Graham, Margaret
Benjy and the Barking Bird
Illustrated by Margaret Graham
Published by Harper and Row, 1971
Graham, Margaret
Benjy's Boat Trip
Illustrated by Margaret Graham
Published by Harper and Row, 1977
Graham, Margaret
Benjy's Dog House
Illustrated by Margaret Graham
Published by Harper and Row, 1973
Grahame, Kenneth
Bertie's Escapade
Illustrated by Ernest R. Shepard
Published by Harper and Row, 1977
Grahame, Kenneth
The River Bank (from: Wind in Willows)
Illustrated by Adrienne Adams
Published by Scribner, 1977
Gramatky, Hardie
Bolivar
Illustrated by Hardie Gramatky
Published by Putnam, 1961
Gramatky, Hardie
Hercules
Illustrated by Hardie Gramatky
Published by Putnam, 1940
Gramatky, Hardie
Homer and the Circus Train
Illustrated by Hardie Gramatky
Published by Putnam, 1957
Gramatky, Hardie
Little Toot
Illustrated by Hardie Gramatky
Published by Putnam, 1939
Grant, Anne
Danbury's Burning
Illustrated by Pat Howell
Published by Walck, 1976
Grant, Sandy
Hey, Look at Me: A City ABC
Illustrated by Larry Mulvehill
Published by Bradbury Press, 1973
Graves, Robert
Big Green Book
Illustrated by Maurice Sendak
Published by Macmillan, 1968

Gray, Genevieve
Keep an Eye on Kevin: Safety Begins at Home
Illustrated by Don Madden
Published by Lothrop, 1973
Gray, Genevieve
Send Wendell
Illustrated by Symeon Shimin
Published by McGraw-Hill, 1974
Grayson, Marion F.
Let's Count and Count Out
Illustrated by Deborah McClintock
Published by Walck, 1975
Green, Mary M.
Everybody Has a House and Everybody Eats
Illustrated by Louis Klein
Published by A-W, 1961
Green, Melinda
Bembel Man's Bakery
Illustrated by Barbara Seuling
Published by Scholastic, 1979
Green, Nancy
Bigger Giant
Illustrated
Published by Follett, 1963
Green, Norma, Retold by
The Hole in the Dike
Illustrated by Eric Carle
Published by T.Y. Crowell, 1974
Green, Phyllis
A New Mother for Martha
Illustrated by Peggy Luks
Published by Human Sciences Press, 1978
Greenberg, Barbara
The Bravest Babysitter
Illustrated by Diane Patterson
Published by Dial, (n.d.)
Greene, Carla
Cowboys: What Do They Do?
Illustrated by Leonard Kessler
Published by Harper and Row, 1972
Greenfield, Eloise
Bubbles
Illustrated by Eric Marlow
Published by Drum and Spear Press, 1972
Greenfield, Eloise
First Pink Light
Illustrated by Moneta Barnett
Published by T.Y. Crowell, 1976
Greenfield, Eloise
Good News
Illustrated by Pat Cummings
Published by Coward, 1977
Greenfield, Eloise
Me and Nessie

Illustrated by Moneta Barnett
Published by T.Y. Crowell, 1975
Greenfield, Eloise
She Come Bringing Me That Little
  Baby Girl
Illustrated by John Steptoe
Published by Lippincott, 1974
Greenwald, Sheila
The Hot Day
Illustrated
Published by Bobbs-Merrill, 1972
Gregor, Arthur S.
Animal Babies
Illustrated by Ylla
Published by Harper and Row, 1976
Gregor, Arthur S.
Little Elephant
Illustrated by Ylla
Published by Harper and Row, 1976
Grender, Iris
You and Your Child Measuring
  Things
Illustrated by Geoffrey Butcher
Published by Knopf, 1976
Gretz, Susanna
Teddy Bears One to Ten
Illustrated by Susanna Gretz
Published by Follett, 1968
Grifalconi, Ann
City Rhythms
Illustrated
Published by Bobbs-Merrill, 1965
Grimm Brothers
The Bear and the Kingbird
Translated by Lore Segal
Illustrated by Chris Conover
Published by Farrar, Strauss and
  Giroux, (n.d.)
Grimm Brothers
Bremen Town Musicians
Illustrated by Paul Galdone
Published by McGraw-Hill, 1968
Grimm Brothers
Briar Rose: Story Sleeping Beauty
Illustrated by Margery Gill
Published by Walck, 1973
Grimm Brothers
Hansel and Gretel
Illustrated by Arnold Lobel
Published by Delacorte, 1971
Grimm Brothers
Little Red Riding Hood
Illustrated by Harriet Pincus
Published by Harcourt Brace
  Jovanovich, 1968
Grimm Brothers
Rumpelstiltskin
Illustrated by Jacqueline Ayer

Published by Harcourt Brace
  Jovanovich, (n.d.)
Grimm Brothers
Seven Ravens
Illustrated by Felix Hoffman
Published by Harcourt Brace
  Jovanovich, 1963
Grimm Brothers
Snow White and Seven Dwarfs
Translated by Randall Jarrell
Illustrated by Nancy E. Burkert
Published by Farrar, Straus and
  Giroux, 1972
Grimm Brothers
The Table, Donkey, and Stick
Illustrated by Paul Galdone
Published by McGraw-Hill, 1976
Grimm Brothers
Thorn Rose
Illustrated by Errol Le Crain
Published by Bradbury Press, (n.d.)
Grimm Brothers
Wolf and Seven Little Kids
Illustrated by Otto Svend and Anne
  Rogers
Published by Larousse, 1977
Grimm, Jacob
Frog Prince
Illustrated by Paul Galdone
Published by McGraw-Hill, 1975
Grimm, Jacob
Shoemaker and the Elves
Illustrated by Adrienne Adams
Published by Scribner, 1960
Grollman, Sharon
More Time to Grow
Illustrated
Published by Beacon Press, 1977
Gross, Alan
Sometimes I Worry
Illustrated
Published by Children's Press, 1979
Gross, Michael
The Fable of the Fig Tree
Illustrated by Mila Lazarevich
Published by Walck, 1975
Gross, Ruth Belov
A Book About Pandas
Illustrated
Published by Scholastic, 1974
Gross, Ruth Belov
A Book About Your Skeleton
Illustrated by Deborah Robison
Published by Hastings House, 1979
Gross, Ruth Belov
Snakes
Illustrated
Published by Scholastic, 1975

Gross, Ruth Belov
What Is That Alligator Saying?
Illustrated by John Hawkinson
Published by Hastings House, 1972
Grossbart, Francine
Big City
Illustrated by Francine Grossbart
Published by Harper and Row, 1966
Gruelle, Johnny
Marcella
Illustrated by Johnny Gruelle
Published by Bobbs-Merrill, 1968
Guggenmos, Josef
Wonder Fish from the Sea
Illustrated by Irmgard Lucht
Published by Parents Magazine Press, 1971
Gulette, Margaret M.
Lost Bellybutton
Illustrated by Leslie Udry
Published by Lollipop Power, 1976
Gunning, Monica
Perico Bonito
Illustrated by Suzanne Plummer
Published by Blaine-Ethridge, (n.d.)
Gunning, Monica
The Two Georges
Illustrated
Published by Blaine-Ethridge, 1976
Gurney, Eric
Eric Gurney's Pop-Up Book of Dogs
Illustrated
Published by Random, 1973
Gwynne, Fred
Chocolate Moose for Dinner
Illustrated
Published by Dutton, 1976
Hader, Berta and Elmer Hader
Little Stone House
Illustrated by Berta and Elmer Hader
Published by Macmillan, 1944
Hader, Berta and Elmer Hader
Lost in the Zoo
Illustrated
Published by Macmillan, 1951
Haley, Gail E.
The Abominable Swampman
Illustrated by Gail E. Haley
Published by Viking Press, 1975
Haley, Gail E.
A Story, A Story
Illustrated by Gail E. Haley
Published by Atheneum, 1976
Hall, Donald
Ox-Cart Man
Illustrated by Barbara Cooney
Published by Warne, 1979
Hall, Donald
Riddle Rat
Illustrated by Mort Gerberg
Published by Warne, 1977
Hallinan, P.K.
Just Being Alone
Illustrated
Published by Children's Press, 1976
Hallinan, P.K.
That's What a Friend Is
Illustrated by P.K. Hallinan
Published by Children's Press, 1977
Hallinan, P.K.
We're Very Good Friends, My Brother and I
Illustrated by P.K. Hallinan
Published by Children's Press, 1973
Hamerstrom, Frances
Walk When the Moon Is Full
Illustrated by Robert Katona
Published by Crossing Press, 1975
Hamilton, Norse and Emily Hamilton
My Name Is Emily
Illustrated by Jenni Oliver
Published by Greenwillow, 1979
Hamm, Jacquie
Crybaby
Illustrated by Jacquie Hamm
Published by Scholastic, 1979
Handforth, Thomas
Mei Li
Illustrated
Published by Doubleday, 1938
Hanlon, Emily
What If a Lion Eats Me & I Fall into a Hippopotamus' Mud Hole
Illustrated by Leigh Grant
Published by Delacorte, 1975
Hanson, Joan
I Don't Like Timmy
Illustrated by Joan Hanson
Published by Carolrhoda, 1972
Hanson, Joan
I Won't Be Afraid
Illustrated by Joan Hanson
Published by Carolrhoda, 1974
Hanson, Joan
Monster's Nose Was Cold
Illustrated by Joan Hanson
Published by Carolrhoda, 1971
Hapgood, Miranda
Martha's Mad Day
Illustrated by Emily A. McCully
Published by Crown, 1977
Hardendorff, Jeanne
The Bed Just So
Illustrated by Lisl Weil
Published by Scholastic, 1976
Hardendorff, Jeanne
Slip! Slop! Gobble!

Illustrated by Emily A. McCully
Published by Lippincott, 1970
Harper, Anita
How We Live
Illustrated by Christine Roche
Published by Harper and Row, 1977
Harper, Anita
How We Work
Illustrated by Christine Roche
Published by Harper and Row, 1977
Harper, Wilhelmina
Gunniwolf
Illustrated by William Wiesner
Published by Dutton, 1967
Harriett
Froggie Went A-Courtin'
Illustrated
Published by Harvey House, 1967
Harris, Audrey
Why Did He Die?
Illustrated by Susan Dalke
Published by Lerner, 1965
Harris, Dorothy J.
House Mouse
Illustrated by Barbara Cooney
Published by Warne, 1973
Harris, Dorothy J.
School Mouse
Illustrated by Chris Conover
Published by Warne, 1977
Harrison, David
Boy with a Drum
Illustrated by Eloise Wilkin
Published by Western, 1971
Harrison, David
Little Turtle's Big Adventure
Illustrated by John P. Miller
Published by Random, 1969
Harrison, David
Monster! Monster!
Illustrated by Rosalind Fry
Published by Western, 1975
Hartelius, Margaret
Birthday Trombone
Illustrated by Margaret Hartelius
Published by Doubleday, 1977
Hartelius, Margaret
The Chicken's Child
Illustrated by Margaret Hartelius
Published by Doubleday, 1975
Hartmann, Larice
Who Will Fly with Butterfly?
Illustrated
Published by Valkyrie Press, 1977
Harvey, Fran
Why Does It Rain?
Illustrated by John and Lucy
  Hawkinson
Published by Harvey House, 1969

Hasler, Eveline
Miranda's Magic
Translated by Elizabeth Shub
Illustrated by Antonella
  Bolliger-Savelli
Published by Macmillan, 1975
Hatch, Shirley
Wind Is to Feel
Illustrated
Published by Coward, 1973
Hautzig, Esther
At Home: A Visit in Four Languages
Illustrated by Aliki
Published by Macmillan, 1968
Hautzig, Esther
In School: Learning in Four
  Languages
Illustrated by Nonny Hogrogian
Published by Macmillan, 1969
Hawes, Judy
Bees and Beelines
Illustrated by Aliki
Published by T.Y. Crowell, 1964
Hawes, Judy
Goats Who Killed the Leopard
Illustrated by Ric Estrada
Published by T.Y. Crowell, 1970
Hawes, Judy
Ladybug, Ladybug, Fly Away
  Home
Illustrated by Ed Emberley
Published by T.Y. Crowell, 1973
Hawes, Judy
My Daddy Longlegs
Illustrated
Published by T.Y. Crowell, 1972
Hawes, Judy
Shrimps
Illustrated by Joseph Low
Published by T.Y. Crowell, 1967
Hawes, Judy
Spring Peepers
Illustrated
Published by T.Y. Crowell, 1975
Hawes, Judy
Watch Honeybees with Me
Illustrated by Helen Stone
Published by T.Y. Crowell, 1964
Hawes, Judy
What I Like About Toads
Illustrated by Ruth and James
  McCrea
Published by T.Y. Crowell, 1969
Hawes, Judy
Why Frogs Are Wet
Illustrated by Don Madden
Published by T.Y. Crowell, 1975
Hawkins, Mark
A Lion Under Her Bed

Illustrated by Jean Vallario
Published by Holt, Rinehart and
Winston, 1979
Hawkinson, Lucy
Dance, Dance, Amy-Chan
Illustrated
Published by A. Whitman, 1964
Hayes, Geoffrey
Bear by Himself
Illustrated by Geoffrey Hayes
Published by Harper and Row,
1976
Haywood, Carolyn
Valentine Fantasy
Illustrated by Victor and Glenys
Ambrus
Published by Morrow, 1976
Hazen, Barbara Shook
The Gorilla Did It
Illustrated by Ray Cruz
Published by Atheneum, 1974
Hazen, Barbara Shook
Me I See
Illustrated by Ati Forberg
Published by Abingdon, 1979
Hazen, Barbara Shook
To Be Me
Illustrated by Frances Hook
Published by Children's Press, 1975
Hazen, Barbara Shook
Two Homes to Live In
Illustrated by Peggy Luks
Published by Human Sciences Press,
1977
Hazen, Barbara Shook
Ups and Downs of Marvin
Illustrated by Richard Cuffari
Published by Atheneum, 1976
Hazen, Barbara Shook
What's Inside?
Illustrated by Richard Erdoes
Published by Lion Press, 1969
Hazen, Barbara Shook
Why Couldn't I Be an Only Kid Like
You, Wigger?
Illustrated by Leigh Grant
Published by Atheneum, 1975
Hazen, Barbara Shook
World, World, What Can I Do?
Illustrated by Margaret Leibold
Published by Abingdon, 1976
Hazen, Nancy
Grownups Cry Too
Illustrated
Published by Lollipop Power, 1973
**Heathers, Anne and Frances
Esteban**
Handful of Surprises
Illustrated by Frances Esteban

Published by Harcourt Brace
Jovanovich, 1961
Hefter, Richard
Strawberry Word Book
Illustrated by Richard Hefter
Published by Larousse, 1974
Hefter, Richard
Things That Go
Illustrated by Richard Hefter
Published by Larousse, 1975
Hefter, Richard
Yes and No: A Book of Opposites
Illustrated by Richard Hefter
Published by Larousse, 1975
Hefter, Richard and Martin Boskof
Great Big Alphabet Picture Book
Illustrated by Richard Hefter
Published by Grosset & Dunlap,
1974
Heide, Florence
Sound of Sunshine, Sound of Rain
Illustrated by Kenneth Longtemps
Published by Parents Magazine Press,
1970
**Heide, Florence and Sylvia Van
Clief**
That's What Friends Are For
Illustrated by Brinton Turkle
Published by Scholastic, 1968
Hellie, Ann
Brian and the Long, Long Scarf
Illustrated by Nan Brooks
Published by Carolrhoda, 1973
Hellsing, Lennart
Pirate Book
Translated by J. Wm. Smith
Illustrated by Poul Stroyer
Published by Delacorte, 1972
Hellsing, Lennart
The Wonderful Pumpkin
Illustrated by Svend Otto
Published by Atheneum, 1977
**Helmering, Doris and John
Helmering**
We're Going to Have a Baby
Illustrated by Robert Cassell
Published by Abingdon, 1979
Herman, Harriet
The Forest Princess
Illustrated by Carole Dwinell
Published by Rainbow Press, 1974
Hertz, Grete Janus
Hi, Daddy, Here I Am
Illustrated by Kirsten Jensinius
Published by Lerner, 1964
Hess, Lilo
Shetland Ponies
Illustrated by Lilo Hess
Published by T.Y. Crowell, 1964

Hickman, Martha Whitmore
I'm Moving
Illustrated by Leigh Grant
Published by Abingdon, 1975
Hickman, Martha Whitmore
My Friend William Moved Away
Illustrated by Bill Myers
Published by Abingdon, 1979
Hill, Elizabeth S.
Evan's Corner
Illustrated by Nancy Grossman
Published by Holt, Rinehart and Winston, 1967
Hillert, Margaret
Little Puff
Illustrated by Sid Jordan
Published by Follett, 1973
Himler, Ann
Waiting for Cherries
Illustrated by Don Bolognese
Published by Harper and Row, 1976
Himler, Ronald
Girl on the Yellow Giraffe
Illustrated
Published by Harper and Row, 1976
Himler, Ronald and Ann Himler
Little Owl, Keeper of the Trees
Illustrated by Ronald Himler
Published by Harper and Row, 1974
Hirsch, Karen
My Sister
Illustrated by Nancy Indereiden
Published by Carolrhoda, 1977
Hirsch, Linda
The Sick Story
Illustrated by John Wallner
Published by Hastings House, 1976
Hirsh, Marilyn
Ben Goes into Business
Illustrated by Marilyn Hirsh
Published by Holiday House, 1973
Hirsh, Marilyn
Could Anything Be Worse?
Illustrated by Marilyn Hirsh
Published by Holiday House, 1974
Hirsh, Marilyn
Potato Pancakes All Around
Illustrated by Marilyn Hirsh
Published by Bonim, 1978
Hirsh, Marilyn
The Rabbi and the 29 Witches
Illustrated by Marilyn Hirsh
Published by Holiday House, 1977
Hirsh, Marilyn
Where Is Yonkela?
Illustrated by Marilyn Hirsh
Published by Crown, 1969
Hitte, Kathryn
Boy, Was I Mad

Illustrated by Mercer Mayer
Published by Parents Magazine Press, 1969
Hoban, Lillian
Mr. Pig and Sonny Too
Illustrated by Lillian Hoban
Published by Harper and Row, (n.d.)
Hoban, Russell
Henry and the Monstrous Din
Illustrated by Lillian Hoban
Published by Harper and Row, 1966
Hoban, Russell
Baby Sister for Frances
Illustrated by Lillian Hoban
Published by Harper and Row, 1976
Hoban, Russell
A Bargain for Frances
Illustrated by Lillian Hoban
Published by Harper and Row, 1970
Hoban, Russell
Bedtime for Frances
Illustrated by Garth Williams
Published by Harper and Row, 1960
Hoban, Russell
Best Friends for Frances
Illustrated by Lillian Hoban
Published by Harper and Row, 1969
Hoban, Russell
Birthday for Frances
Illustrated by Lillian Hoban
Published by Harper and Row, 1976
Hoban, Russell
Bread and Jam for Frances
Illustrated by Lillian Hoban
Published by Harper and Row, 1964
Hoban, Russell
Dinner at Alberta's
Illustrated by James Marshall
Published by T.Y. Crowell, 1975
Hoban, Russell
Egg Thoughts & Other Frances Songs
Illustrated by Lillian Hoban
Published by Harper and Row, 1972
Hoban, Russell
Emmet Otter's Jug-Band Christmas
Illustrated by Lillian Hoban
Published by Scholastic, 1979
Hoban, Russell
Harvey's Hideout
Illustrated by Lillian Hoban
Published by Parents Magazine Press, 1969
Hoban, Russell
Letitia Rabbit's String Song
Illustrated by Mary Chalmers
Published by Coward, 1973
Hoban, Russell
Little Brute Family

Illustrated by Lillian Hoban
Published by Macmillan, 1972
Hoban, Russell
Near Thing for Captain Najork
Illustrated by Quentin Blake
Published by Atheneum, 1976
Hoban, Russell
Nothing to Do
Illustrated by Lillian Hoban
Published by Harper and Row, 1964
Hoban, Russell
Stone Doll of Sister Brute
Illustrated by Lillian Hoban
Published by Macmillan, 1968
Hoban, Russell
Ten What? A Mystery Counting
 Book
Illustrated by Sylvie Selig
Published by Scribner, 1975
Hoban, Russell
Ugly Bird
Illustrated
Published by Macmillan, 1969
Hoban, Russell and Sylvie Selig
Crocodile and Pierrot
Illustrated by Sylvie Selig
Published by Scribner, 1977
Hoban, Tana
Count and See
Illustrated by Tana Hoban
Published by Macmillan, 1972
Hoban, Tana
Dig, Drill, Dump, Fill
Illustrated by Tana Hoban
Published by Greenwillow, 1975
Hoban, Tana
Is It Red? Is It Yellow? Is It Blue?
Illustrated by Tana Hoban
Published by Greenwillow, 1979
Hoban, Tana
Look Again
Illustrated by Tana Hoban
Published by Macmillan, 1971
Hoban, Tana
One Little Kitten
Illustrated by Tana Hoban
Published by Greenwillow, 1979
Hoban, Tana
Over, Under, Through, & Other
 Spatial Concepts
Illustrated by Tana Hoban
Published by Macmillan, 1973
Hoban, Tana
Push-Pull, Empty-Full: Book of
 Opposites
Illustrated by Tana Hoban
Published by Macmillan, 1972
Hoban, Tana
Where Is It?

Illustrated by Tana Hoban
Published by Macmillan, 1974
Hoberman, Mary Ann
Bugs: Poems
Illustrated by Victoria Chess
Published by Viking Press, 1976
Hoberman, Mary Ann
A House Is a House for Me
Illustrated by Betty Fraser
Published by Viking Press, 1979
Hoberman, Mary Ann
I Like Old Clothes
Illustrated by Jacqueline Chwast
Published by Knopf, 1976
Hoberman, Mary Ann
A Little Book of Beasts
Illustrated by Peter Parnall
Published by Simon & Schuster,
 1973
Hoberman, Mary Ann
Looking Book
Illustrated by Jerry Joyner
Published by Knopf, 1973
Hoberman, Mary Ann
Nuts to You & Nuts to Me: Alphabet
 of Poems
Illustrated by Ronni Solbert
Published by Knopf, 1974
Hoberman, Mary Ann
Raucus Auk: Menagerie of Poems
Illustrated by Joseph Low
Published by Viking Press, 1973
Hobzek, Mildred
We Came A-Marching One, Two,
 Three
Illustrated by William Pene DuBois
Published by Scholastic, 1979
Hochschild, Arlie Russell
Coleen, the Question Girl
Illustrated by Gail Ashby
Published by Feminist Press, 1974
Hodges, Elizabeth
Free as a Frog
Illustrated by Paul Giovano Poulos
Published by A-W, 1976
Hodges, Margaret
Wave
Illustrated by B. Lent
Published by Houghton Mifflin, 1964
Hoff, Syd
Danny and the Dinosaur
Illustrated by Syd Hoff
Published by Harper and Row, 1958
Hoff, Syd
Mahatma
Illustrated by Syd Hoff
Published by Putnam, 1969
Hoffman, Beth G.
Red Is for Apples

Illustrated by Don Bolognese
Published by Random, 1966
Hoffman, Rosekrans
Anna Banana
Illustrated by Rosekrans Hoffman
Published by Knopf, 1975
Hogan, Carol G.
Eighteen Cousins
Illustrated by Beverly Komoda
Published by Parents Magazine Press, 1968
Hogner, Nils
The Nosy Colt
Illustrated by Richard Lebenson
Published by Walck, 1973
Hogrogian, Nonny
Apples
Illustrated by Nonny Hogrogian
Published by Macmillan, 1972
Hogrogian, Nonny
Carrot Cake
Illustrated by Nonny Hogrogian
Published by Greenwillow, 1977
Hogrogian, Nonny
The Contest
Illustrated by Nonny Hogrogian
Published by Greenwillow, 1976
Hogrogian, Nonny
One Fine Day
Illustrated by Nonny Hogrogian
Published by Macmillan, 1974
Holl, Adelaide
ABC of Cars, Trucks and Machines
Illustrated by W. Dugan
Published by McGraw-Hill, 1970
Holl, Adelaide
Rain Puddle
Illustrated by Roger Duvoisin
Published by Lothrop, 1965
Holl, Adelaide
Remarkable Egg
Illustrated by Roger Duvoisin
Published by Lothrop, 1968
Holland, Vicki
We Are Having a Baby
Illustrated by Vicki Holland
Published by Scribner, 1972
Holman, Felice
Elizabeth the Treasure Hunter
Illustrated by Eric Blegvad
Published by Macmillan, 1964
Holmes, Efner Tudor
Amy's Goose
Illustrated by Tasha Tudor
Published by T.Y. Crowell, 1977
Holmes, Efner Tudor
The Christmas Cat
Illustrated by Tasha Tudor
Published by T.Y. Crowell, 1976

Holzenthaler, Jean
My Feet Do
Illustrated by George Ancona
Published by Dutton, 1979
Holzenthaler, Jean
My Hands Can
Illustrated by Nancy Tafuri
Published by Dutton, 1979
Hopf, Alice
Carab: The Trapdoor Spider
Illustrated
Published by Putnam, 1970
Hopkins, Lee Bennett
Girls Can Too!
Illustrated by Emily A. McCully
Published by Watts, 1972
Hopkins, Lee Bennett, Ed.
Go to Bed!
Illustrated by Rosekrans Hoffman
Published by Knopf, 1979
Hopkins, Marjorie
Three Visitors
Illustrated by Anne Rockwell
Published by Parents Magazine Press, 1967
Horn, Axel
You Can Be Taller
Illustrated by Myron Ehrenberg
Published by Little, Brown, 1974
Horvath, Betty
Jasper Makes Music
Illustrated by Don Bolognese
Published by Watts, 1967
Horwitz, Elinor L.
When the Sky Is Like Lace
Illustrated by Barbara Cooney
Published by Lippincott, 1975
Hough, Charlotte
Wonky Donkey
Illustrated
Published by Penguin, 1975
Howell, Ruth R.
Everything Changes
Illustrated by Arline Strong
Published by Atheneum, 1968
Howell, Ruth R.
Splash and Flow
Illustrated by Arline Strong
Published by Atheneum, 1973
Huber, Ursula
Nock Family Circus
Illustrated by Celestino Piatti
Published by Atheneum, 1968
Hughes, Shirley
George the Babysitter
Illustrated by Shirley Hughes
Published by Prentice-Hall, 1977

Hughes, Shirley
Moving Molly
Illustrated by Shirley Hughes
Published by Prentice-Hall, 1979

Hughes, Ted
Nessie the Monster
Illustrated
Published by Bobbs-Merrill, 1974

Hume, Lotta Carswell
Favorite Children's Stories/China & Tibet
Illustrated by Lo-Koon Chiu
Published by C.E. Tuttle, 1962

Humphrey, Margo
The River That Gave Gifts
Illustrated by Margo Humphrey
Published by Children's Book Press, S.F., (n.d.)

Huntington, Harriet E.
Let's Look at Insects
Illustrated
Published by Doubleday, 1969

Hurd, Edith
Catfish and the Kidnapped Cat
Illustrated by Clement Hurd
Published by Harper and Row, 1974

Hurd, Edith
Come with Me to Nursery School
Illustrated
Published by Coward, 1970

Hurd, Edith
The Day the Sun Danced
Illustrated by Clement Hurd
Published by Harper and Row, 1966

Hurd, Edith
Last One Home Is a Green Pig
Illustrated by Clement Hurd
Published by Harper and Row, 1974

Hurd, Edith
Look for a Bird
Illustrated by Clement Hurd
Published by Harper and Row, 1977

Hurd, Edith
The Mother Beaver
Illustrated by Clement Hurd
Published by Little, Brown, 1971

Hurd, Edith
The Mother Whale
Illustrated by Clement Hurd
Published by Little, Brown, 1973

Hurd, Edith
Sand Pipers
Illustrated by Lucienne Bloch
Published by T.Y. Crowell, 1961

Hurd, Edith
So-So Cat
Illustrated by Clement Hurd
Published by Harper and Row, 1965

Hurd, Edith
Starfish
Illustrated by Lucienne Bloch
Published by T.Y. Crowell, 1962

Hurd, Edith
What Whale Where?
Illustrated by Clement Hurd
Published by Harper and Row, 1966

Hurd, Edith
Wilson's World
Illustrated by Clement Hurd
Published by Harper and Row, 1971

Hurlimann, Bettina and Paul Nussbaumer
Barry: The Story of a Brave St. Bernard
Translated by Elizabeth D. Crawford
Illustrated by Paul Nussbaumer
Published by Harcourt Brace Jovanovich, 1968

Hurlimann, Ruth
The Cat and the Mouse Who Shared a House
Illustrated
Published by Walck, 1974

Hutchins, Pat
Changes, Changes
Illustrated by Pat Hutchins
Published by Macmillan, 1973

Hutchins, Pat
Clocks and More Clocks
Illustrated by Pat Hutchins
Published by Macmillan, 1973

Hutchins, Pat
Don't Forget the Bacon
Illustrated by Pat Hutchins
Published by Macmillan, 1972

Hutchins, Pat
Goodnight Owl
Illustrated by Pat Hutchins
Published by Macmillan, 1972

Hutchins, Pat
Happy Birthday, Sam
Illustrated by Pat Hutchins
Published by Greenwillow, 1978

Hutchins, Pat
Rosie's Walk
Illustrated by Pat Hutchins
Published by Macmillan, 1968

Hutchins, Pat
Surprise Party
Illustrated by Pat Hutchins
Published by Macmillan, 1969

Hutchins, Pat
Titch
Illustrated by Pat Hutchins
Published by Macmillan, 1971

Hutchins, Pat
Tom and Sam

Illustrated by Pat Hutchins
Published by Macmillan, 1968
Hutchins, Pat
Wind Blew
Illustrated by Pat Hutchins
Published by Macmillan, 1974
Heyduck-Huth, Hilde
In the Village
Illustrated by Hilde Heyduck-Huth
Published by Harcourt Brace
  Jovanovich, 1971
Ichikawa, Satomi
Friends
Illustrated by Satomi Ichikawa
Published by Parents Magazine Press,
  1977
Imanishi, Sukeyuki
Moon and the Fishes
Illustrated by Sukeyuki Imanishi
Published by Japan Pubns., 1973
Ipcar, Dahlov
Biggest Fish in the Sea
Illustrated by Dahlov Ipcar
Published by Viking Press, 1972
Ipcar, Dahlov
Bright Barnyard
Illustrated by Dahlov Ipcar
Published by Knopf, 1966
Ipcar, Dahlov
Bug City
Illustrated by Dahlov Ipcar
Published by Holiday House,
  1975
Ipcar, Dahlov
Calico Jungle
Illustrated by Dahlov Ipcar
Published by Knopf, 1965
Ipcar, Dahlov
Land of Flowers
Illustrated by Dahlov Ipcar
Published by Viking Press, 1974
Ipcar, Dahlov
One Horse Farm
Illustrated by Dahlov Ipcar
Published by Doubleday, 1950
Ipcar, Dahlov
Ten Big Farms
Illustrated by Dahlov Ipcar
Published by Knopf, 1958
Ipcar, Dahlov
Wild Whirlwind
Illustrated by Dahlov Ipcar
Published by Knopf, 1968
Isadora, Rachel
Max
Illustrated by Rachel Isadora
Published by Macmillan, 1976
Isadora, Rachel
Willaby

Illustrated by Rachel Isadora
Published by Macmillan, 1977
Isenbart, Hans-Heinrich
A Foal Is Born
Translated by Catherine Edwards
Illustrated by Hanns-Jorg Anders
Published by Putnam, 1976
Itse, Elizabeth, Compiled by
Hey, Bug! and Other Poems About
  Little Things
Illustrated by Susan C. Smith
Published by McGraw-Hill, 1972
Iverson, Genie
I Want to Be Big
Illustrated by David McPhail
Published by Dutton, 1979
Iwasaki, Chihiro
The Birthday Wish
Illustrated by Chihiro Iwasaki
Published by McGraw-Hill, 1974
Iwasaki, Chihiro
A New Baby Is Coming to My
  House
Illustrated by Chihiro Iwasaki
Published by McGraw-Hill, (n.d.)
Jackson, Kathryn
Tawny Scrawny Lion
Illustrated by Gustav Tenggren
Published by Western, 1952
**Jackson, Kathryn and Byron
  Jackson**
Big Elephant
Illustrated by Feodor Rojankovsky
Published by Western, 1974
**Jackson, Kathryn and Byron
  Jackson**
Saggy Baggy Elephant
Illustrated by Gustav Tenggren
Published by Western, 1975
Jacobs, Francine
Legs of the Moon
Illustrated by Rocco Negri
Published by Coward, 1971
Jacobs, Joseph
Jack and the Beanstalk
Illustrated by Margery Gill
Published by Walck, 1975
Jacobs, Joseph
Jack the Giant-Killer
Illustrated by Fritz Wegner
Published by Walck, 1971
Jacobs, Leland B.
Is Somewhere Always Far
  Away?
Illustrated by John E. Johnson
Published by Holt, Rinehart and
  Winston, 1967
Jacobs, Leland B.
Teeny-Tiny

Illustrated by Leland B. Jacobs
Published by Garrard, 1976
Jameson, Cynthia
Clay Pot Boy
Illustrated by Arnold Lobel
Published by Coward, 1973
Jameson, Cynthia
One for the Price of Two
Illustrated by Anita Lobel
Published by Parents Magazine Press, 1972
Jamieson, Doug
The Last Visit
Illustrated by Francie Kirk
Published by Before We Are Six, Canada, 1975
Janosch
Thieves and the Raven
Translated by Elizabeth Shub
Illustrated by Janosch
Published by Macmillan, 1970
Jarrell, Mary
The Knee Baby
Illustrated by Symeon Shimin
Published by Farrar, Straus and Giroux, 1973
Jarrell, Randall
A Bat Is Born
Illustrated by John Schoenherr
Published by Doubleday, 1978
Jeffers, Susan
All the Pretty Horses
Illustrated by Susan Jeffers
Published by Macmillan, 1974
Jenkins, Jordan
Learning About Love
Illustrated
Published by Children's Press, 1979
Jenkins, Marie
Moon Jelly
Illustrated by Rene Martin
Published by Holiday House, 1969
Jenson, Virginia
Sara and the Door
Illustrated by Ann Strugnell
Published by A-W, 1977
Jeschke, Susan
Devil Did It
Illustrated by Susan Jeschke
Published by Holt, Rinehart and Winston, 1975
Jeschke, Susan
Grandma and the Genji
Illustrated by Susan Jeschke
Published by Holt, Rinehart and Winston, 1977
Jeschke, Susan
Rima and Zeppo
Illustrated
Published by Dutton, 1976
Jewell, Nancy
Bus Ride
Illustrated by Ronald Himler
Published by Harper and Row, 1978
Jewell, Nancy
Calf, Goodnight
Illustrated by Leonard Weisgard
Published by Harper and Row, 1973
Jewell, Nancy
Cheer Up, Pig
Illustrated by Ben Shecter
Published by Harper and Row, 1975
Jewell, Nancy
The Family Under the Moon
Illustrated by Leonard Kessler
Published by Harper and Row, 1976
Jewell, Nancy
Snuggle Bunny
Illustrated by Mary Chalmers
Published by Harper and Row, 1972
Jewell, Nancy
Try and Catch Me
Illustrated by Leonard Weisgard
Published by Harper and Row, 1972
Joerns, Consuelo
The Lost and Found House
Illustrated by Consuelo Joerns
Published by Scholastic, 1979
Johnson, Crockett
Harold and the Purple Crayon
Illustrated by Crockett Johnson
Published by Harper and Row, 1958
Johnson, Crockett
Harold's ABC
Illustrated by Crockett Johnson
Published by Harper and Row, 1963
Johnson, Crockett
Harold's Circus
Illustrated by Crockett Johnson
Published by Harper and Row, 1959
Johnson, Crockett
Harold's Trip to the Sky
Illustrated by Crockett Johnson
Published by Harper and Row, 1957
Johnson, Crockett
A Picture for Harold's Room
Illustrated by Crockett Johnson
Published by Harper and Row, 1960
Johnson, Crockett
Will Spring Be Early or Will Spring Be Late?
Illustrated by Crockett Johnson
Published by T.Y. Crowell, 1959
Johnson, Hannah L.
From Apple Seed to Applesauce
Illustrated by Daniel Dorn, Jr.
Published by Lothrop, 1977

Johnson, Hannah L.
From Seed to Jack-O-Lantern
Illustrated by Daniel Dorn, Jr.
Published by Lothrop, 1974
Johnson, Ryerson
Upstairs and Downstairs
Illustrated by Lisl Weil
Published by T.Y. Crowell, 1962
Johnson, Sylvia A.
Penelope the Tortoise
Translated by Dyan Hammarberg
Illustrated
Published by Carolrhoda, 1976
Johnson, Sylvia A.
Penny and Pete the Lambs
Translated by Dyan Hammarberg
Illustrated
Published by Carolrhoda, 1976
Johnston, Johanna
Sugarplum
Illustrated by Marvin Bileck
Published by Knopf, 1955
Johnston, Tony
Mole and Troll Trim the Tree
Illustrated by Wallace Tripp
Published by Putnam, 1974
Johnston, Tony
Odd Jobs
Illustrated by Tomie DePaola
Published by Putnam, 1977
Jones, Elizabeth
Big Susan
Illustrated by Elizabeth Jones
Published by Macmillan, 1967
Jones, Harold
There and Back Again
Illustrated
Published by Atheneum, 1977
Jones, Hettie
Trees Stand Shining: Poetry of the North American Indian
Illustrated by Hettie Jones
Published by Dial, 1976
Jones, Penelope
I Didn't Want to Be Nice
Illustrated by Rosalie Orlando
Published by Bradbury Press, 1977
Jonsen, George
Favorite Tales Monsters and Trolls
Illustrated by John O'Brien
Published by Random, 1977
Jordon, Helene
How a Seed Grows
Illustrated by Joseph Low
Published by T.Y. Crowell, 1960
Jordon, Helene
Seeds by Wind and Water
Illustrated by Nils Hogner
Published by T.Y. Crowell, 1962
Joslin, Sesyle and John Alcorn
La Fiesta
Illustrated
Published by Harcourt Brace Jovanovich, 1967
Joslin, Sesyle and Leonard Weisgard
Brave Baby Elephant
Illustrated by Leonard Weisgard
Published by Harcourt Brace Jovanovich, 1960
Kahl, Virginia
Baron's Booty
Illustrated by Virginia Kahl
Published by Scribner, 1963
Kahl, Virginia
Duchess Bakes a Cake
Illustrated by Virginia Kahl
Published by Scribner, 1955
Kahl, Virginia
Giants, Indeed!
Illustrated by Virginia Kahl
Published by Scribner, 1974
Kahl, Virginia
Gunhilde and the Halloween Spell
Illustrated by Virginia Kahl
Published by Scribner, 1975
Kahl, Virginia
Habits of the Rabbits
Illustrated by Virginia Kahl
Published by Scribner, 1957
Kahl, Virginia
How Do You Hide a Monster?
Illustrated by Virginia Kahl
Published by Scribner, 1971
Kahl, Virginia
How Many Dragons Are Behind the Door?
Illustrated by Virginia Kahl
Published by Scribner, 1977
Kahl, Virginia
Perfect Pancake
Illustrated by Virginia Kahl
Published by Scribner, 1960
Kahl, Virginia
Plum Pudding for Christmas
Illustrated by Virginia Kahl
Published by Scribner, 1956
Kahl, Virginia
Whose Cat Is That?
Illustrated by Virginia Kahl
Published by Scribner, 1979
Kalan, Robert
Blue Sea
Illustrated by Donald Crews
Published by Greenwillow, 1979
Kalan, Robert
Rain

Illustrated by Donald Crews
Published by Greenwillow, 1978
Kantrowitz, Mildred
Goodbye Kitchen
Illustrated by Mercer Mayer
Published by Parents Magazine Press,
1972
Kantrowitz, Mildred
I Wonder If Herbie's Home Yet
Illustrated by Tony DeLuna
Published by Parents Magazine Press,
1971
Kantrowitz, Mildred
Maxie
Illustrated by Emily A. McCully
Published by Parents Magazine Press,
1970
Kantrowitz, Mildred
When Violet Died
Illustrated by Emily A. McCully
Published by Parents Magazine Press,
1973
Kantrowitz, Mildred
Willy Bear
Illustrated by Nancy Winslow Parker
Published by Parents Magazine Press,
1976
Katz, Bobbi
Nothing But a Dog
Illustrated by Esther Gilman
Published by Feminist Press, 1972
Kaufman, Bob
Watch My Tracks
Illustrated by Debbie Holland
Published by Knopf, 1971
Kaufman, Joe
Baseball Book
Illustrated by Joe Kaufman
Published by Western, 1976
Kaufman, John
Bats in the Dark
Illustrated by John Kaufman
Published by T.Y. Crowell, 1972
Kaufman, John
Flying Reptiles in the Age of
  Dinosaurs
Illustrated
Published by Morrow, 1976
Kay, Helen
A Day in the Life of a Baby
  Gibbon
Illustrated by Symeon Shimin
Published by Abelard, 1972
Keating, Norma
Mister Chu
Illustrated by B. Bryson
Published by Macmillan, 1965
Keats, Ezra Jack
Apt. 3
Illustrated by Ezra Jack Keats
Published by Macmillan, 1971
Keats, Ezra Jack
Dreams
Illustrated by Ezra Jack Keats
Published by Macmillan, 1974
Keats, Ezra Jack
Goggles
Illustrated by Ezra Jack Keats
Published by Macmillan, 1969
Keats, Ezra Jack
Hi, Cat
Illustrated by Ezra Jack Keats
Published by Macmillan, 1972
Keats, Ezra Jack
Jennie's Hat
Illustrated by Ezra Jack Keats
Published by Harper and Row, 1966
Keats, Ezra Jack
Kitten for a Day
Illustrated by Ezra Jack Keats
Published by Watts, 1974
Keats, Ezra Jack
Letter to Amy
Illustrated by Ezra Jack Keats
Published by Harper and Row, 1968
Keats, Ezra Jack
Little Drummer Boy
Illustrated by Ezra Jack Keats
Published by Macmillan, 1968
Keats, Ezra Jack
Louie
Illustrated by Ezra Jack Keats
Published by Greenwillow, 1975
Keats, Ezra Jack
Maggie and the Pirate
Illustrated by Ezra Jack Keats
Published by Scholastic, 1979
Keats, Ezra Jack
Over in the Meadow
Illustrated by Ezra Jack Keats
Published by Scholastic, 1972
Keats, Ezra Jack
Pet Show!
Illustrated by Ezra Jack Keats
Published by Macmillan, 1974
Keats, Ezra Jack
Peter's Chair
Illustrated by Ezra Jack Keats
Published by Harper and Row,
1967
Keats, Ezra Jack
Pssst! Doggie
Illustrated by Ezra Jack Keats
Published by Watts, 1973
Keats, Ezra Jack
Skates
Illustrated by Ezra Jack Keats
Published by Watts, 1973

Keats, Ezra Jack
Snowy Day
Illustrated by Ezra Jack Keats
Published by Viking Press, 1962
Keats, Ezra Jack
Whistle for Willie
Illustrated by Ezra Jack Keats
Published by Viking Press, 1977
Keats, Ezra Jack and Pat Cherr
My Dog Is Lost!
Illustrated by Ezra Jack Keats
Published by T.Y. Crowell, 1960
Keats, Mark
Sancho, Pronto and the Engineer
Translated by Raul Carrera
Illustrated by Alex Cervantes
Published by Blaine-Ethridge, 1976
Keeping, Charles
Nanny Goat and the Fierce Dog
Illustrated by Charles Keeping
Published by Scroll Press, 1974
Keith, Eros
Nancy's Backyard
Illustrated by Eros Keith
Published by Harper and Row, 1973
Keith, Eros
Rrra-a-h
Illustrated by Eros Keith
Published by Bradbury Press, 1969
Keller, Beverly
Pimm's Place
Illustrated by Jacqueline Chwast
Published by Coward, 1979
Kellogg, Steven
Island of the Skog
Illustrated by Steven Kellogg
Published by Dial, 1973
Kellogg, Steven
Much Bigger Than Martin
Illustrated
Published by Dial, 1976
Kellogg, Steven
The Mysterious Tadpole
Illustrated by Steven Kellogg
Published by Dial, 1977
Kellogg, Steven
Mystery Beast of Ostergeest
Illustrated by Steven Kellogg
Published by Dial, 1971
Kellogg, Steven
Mystery of the Missing Red Mitten
Illustrated by Steven Kellogg
Published by Dial, 1974
Kellogg, Steven
Won't Somebody Play with Me?
Illustrated by Steven Kellogg
Published by Dial, 1972

Kennedy, Richard
The Leprechaun's Story
Illustrated by Marcia Sewall
Published by Dutton, 1979
Kennedy, Richard
The Lost Kingdom of Karnica
Illustrated by Uri Shulevitz
Published by Scribner, 1979
Kennedy, Richard
The Mouse God
Illustrated by Stephen Harvard
Published by Little, Brown, 1979
Kenniston, Ken
The Man Who Loved Birds
Illustrated by Ken Kenniston
Published by Harvey House, 1962
Kent, Jack
The Egg Book
Illustrated by Jack Kent
Published by Macmillan, 1975
Kent, Jack
The Fat Cat
Illustrated by Jack Kent
Published by Scholastic, 1972
Kent, Jack
Floyd the Tiniest Elephant
Illustrated by Jack Kent
Published by Doubleday, 1979
Kent, Jack
Jack Kent's Book of Nursery Tales
Illustrated by Jack Kent
Published by Random, 1970
Kepes, Juliet
Five Little Monkeys
Illustrated
Published by Houghton Mifflin, 1952
Kepes, Juliet
Frogs Merry
Illustrated by Juliet Kepes
Published by Pantheon, 1961
Kepes, Juliet
Run, Little Monkeys, Run, Run, Run,
Illustrated by Juliet Kepes
Published by Pantheon, 1974
Kerr, Judith
Mog, the Forgetful Cat
Illustrated by Judith Kerr
Published by Parents Magazine Press, 1972
Kesselman, Wendy
Time for Jody
Illustrated by Gerald Dumas
Published by Harper and Row, 1975
Kesselman, Wendy and Norma Holt
Angelita
Illustrated
Published by Hill and Wang, 1970
Kessler, Ethel
The Day Daddy Stayed Home

Illustrated by Leonard Kessler
Published by Doubleday, 1971
Kessler, Ethel and Leonard Kessler
All for Fall
Illustrated by Leonard Kessler
Published by Parents Magazine Press, 1974
Kessler, Ethel and Leonard Kessler
Big Red Bus
Illustrated
Published by Doubleday, 1964
Kessler, Ethel and Leonard Kessler
Do Baby Bears Sit in Chairs?
Illustrated by Leonard Kessler
Published by Doubleday, (n.d.)
Kijima, Hajime
Little White Hen
Illustrated by Setsuko Hane
Published by Harcourt Brace Jovanovich, 1967
Kilbourne, Frances
Overnight Adventure
Illustrated by Ann Powell
Published by Canadian Women's Educational Press, 1977
Kimishima, Hisako
Lum Fu and the Golden Mountain
Translated by Alvin Tresselt
Illustrated by Dai Hachi Ohta
Published by Parents Magazine Press, 1971
Kimishima, Hisako
The Princess of the Rice Fields
Illustrated by Sumiko Mizushi
Published by Walker, 1970
Kimmel, Margaret M.
Magic in the Mist
Illustrated by Trina S. Hyman
Published by Atheneum, 1974
Kimura, Yasuko
Fergus
Illustrated by Yasuko Kimura
Published by McGraw-Hill, 1976
Kimura, Yasuko
Fergus and the Sea Monster
Illustrated by Yasuko Kimura
Published by McGraw-Hill, 1977
Kindred, Wendy
Lucky Wilma
Illustrated by Wendy Kindred
Published by Dial, 1973
Kingman, Lee
Peter's Long Walk
Illustrated by Barbara Cooney
Published by Doubleday, 1953
Kinney, Jean
What Does the Tide Do?
Illustrated
Published by A-W, 1966
Kipling, Rudyard
Elephant's Child
Illustrated by Leonard Weisgard
Published by Walker, 1970
Kipling, Rudyard
How the Leopard Got His Spots
Illustrated by Leonard Weisgard
Published by Walker, (n.d.)
Kipling, Rudyard
How the Rhinoceros Got His Skin
Illustrated by Leonard Weisgard
Published by Walker, 1974
Kirtland, Susanne
Easy Answers to Hard Questions
Illustrated by Susan Perl
Published by Grosset & Dunlap, 1969
Kishida, Eriko
Lion and the Bird's Nest
Illustrated by Chiyioko Nakatani
Published by T.Y. Crowell, 1973
Klein, Leonore
D Is for Rover
Illustrated by Robert Quackenbush
Published by Harvey House, 1970
Klein, Leonore
Just a Minute: A Book About Time
Illustrated by Leonard Kessler
Published by Harvey House, 1969
Klein, Leonore
Just Like You
Illustrated by Audrey Walters
Published by Harvey House, 1968
Klein, Leonore
Only One Ant
Illustrated by Charles Robinson
Published by Hastings House, 1971
Klein, Leonore
Runaway John
Illustrated by Sunny Warner
Published by Knopf, 1963
Klein, Leonore
What Is an Inch?
Illustrated
Published by Harvey House, 1966
Klein, Norma
Girls Can Be Anything
Illustrated by Roy Doty
Published by Dutton, 1973
Klein, Norma
If I Had My Way
Illustrated by Ray Cruz
Published by Pantheon, 1974
Klein, Norma
A Train for Jane
Illustrated by Miriam Schottland
Published by Feminist Press, 1974

Klein, Norma
  Visiting Pamela
  Illustrated by Kay Chorao
  Published by Dial, 1979
Klimowicz, Barbara
  Ha, Ha, Ha, Henrietta
  Illustrated by Ray Burns
  Published by Abingdon, 1975
Klimowicz, Barbara
  When Shoes Eat Socks
  Illustrated by Gloria Kamen
  Published by Abingdon, 1971
Knight, Clayton
  Big Book of Helicopters
  Illustrated
  Published by Grosset & Dunlap, 1971
Knight, David C.
  Let's Find Out About Mars
  Illustrated by Don Miller
  Published by Watts, 1966
Knight, David C.
  Let's Find Out About Sound
  Illustrated by Ulrich Schramm
  Published by Watts, 1975
Knight, David C.
  Let's Find Out About Telephones
  Illustrated by Don Miller
  Published by Watts, 1967
Knight, David C.
  Let's Find Out About Weather
  Illustrated by Rene Martin
  Published by Watts, 1967
Knight, Hilary
  Firefly in a Fir Tree
  Illustrated by Hilary Knight
  Published by Harper and Row, 1963
Knight, Hilary
  Night Before Christmas
  Illustrated by Hilary Knight
  Published by Harper and Row, 1963
Knight, Hilary
  Where's Wallace?
  Illustrated by Hilary Knight
  Published by Harper and Row, 1964
Knobler, Susan
  The Tadpole and the Frog
  Illustrated
  Published by Harvey House, 1974
Knotts, Howard
  Winter Cat
  Illustrated by Howard Knotts
  Published by Harper and Row, 1972
Kohn, Bernice
  Everything Has a Shape & Everything Has a Size
  Illustrated by Aliki
  Published by Prentice-Hall, 1966

Kohn, Bernice
  Koalas
  Illustrated by Gail Haley
  Published by Prentice-Hall, 1972
Kohn, Bernice
  One Day It Rained Cats and Dogs
  Illustrated by Aliki
  Published by Coward, 1965
Kohn, Bernice
  Raccoons
  Illustrated by John Hamberger
  Published by Prentice-Hall, 1968
Komoda, Beverly
  Simon's Soup
  Illustrated by Beverly Komoda
  Published by Scholastic, 1979
Konner, Alfred
  Clever Coot
  Illustrated by Irmhild and Hilmar Proft
  Published by Carolrhoda, 1971
Konner, Alfred
  Jolli
  Illustrated by Irmhild and Hilmar Proft
  Published by Lerner, (n.d.)
Korschunow, Irina
  Piebald Pup
  Illustrated by Gerhard Oberlander
  Published by Astor-Honor, 1959
Kotzwinkle, William
  Elephant Boy
  Illustrated
  Published by Farrar, Straus and Giroux, 1970
Kotzwinkle, William
  Firemen
  Illustrated by Joe Servello
  Published by Pantheon, 1969
Kotzwinkle, William
  Supreme, Superb, Exalted...One & Only Magic Bldg.
  Illustrated by Joe Servello
  Published by Farrar, Straus and Giroux, 1973
Krahn, Fernando
  April Fools
  Illustrated by Fernando Krahn
  Published by Dutton, 1974
Krahn, Fernando
  The Family Minus
  Illustrated by Fernando Krahn
  Published by Parents Magazine Press, 1977
Krahn, Fernando
  Flying Saucer Full of Spaghetti
  Illustrated by Fernando Krahn
  Published by Dutton, 1970

Krahn, Fernando
Gustavus and Stop
Illustrated by Fernando Krahn
Published by Dutton, (n.d.)
Krahn, Fernando
Little Love Story
Illustrated by Fernando Krahn
Published by Lippincott, 1976
Krahn, Fernando
Sebastian and the Mushroom
Illustrated by Fernando Krahn
Published by Dial, 1976
Krahn, Fernando
The Self-Made Snowman
Illustrated by Fernando Krahn
Published by Lippincott, 1974
Krahn, Fernando
What Is a Man?
Illustrated by Fernando Krahn
Published by Delacorte, 1972
Krahn, Fernando and Maria D. Krahn
The Life of Numbers
Illustrated by Fernando Krahn
Published by Simon & Schuster, 1970
Krasilovsky, Phyllis
The Cow Who Fell in the Canal
Illustrated by Peter Spier
Published by Doubleday, 1972
Krasilovsky, Phyllis
The Man Who Didn't Wash His Dishes
Illustrated by Barbara Cooney
Published by Doubleday, 1950
Krasilovsky, Phyllis
The Man Who Tried to Save Time
Illustrated by Maria Sewell
Published by Doubleday, 1979
Krasilovsky, Phyllis
Scaredy Cat
Illustrated by Ninon
Published by Macmillan, 1959
Krasilovsky, Phyllis
Shy Little Girl
Illustrated by Trina Hyman
Published by Houghton Mifflin, 1970
Krasilovsky, Phyllis
Very Tall Little Girl
Illustrated by Olivia Cole
Published by Doubleday, 1969
Kratz, Marilyn
The Garden Book
Illustrated by June Talarczyk
Published by Denison, (n.d.)
Kraus, Robert
Big Brother
Illustrated by Robert Kraus
Published by Parents Magazine Press, 1973
Kraus, Robert
Boris Bad Enough
Illustrated by Ariane Dewey and Jose Aruego
Published by Dutton , 1976
Kraus, Robert
Bunya the Witch
Illustrated by Mischa Richter
Published by Dutton, 1971
Kraus, Robert
Daddy Long Ears
Illustrated
Published by Simon & Schuster, 1970
Kraus, Robert
Herman the Helper
Illustrated by Ariane Dewey and Jose Aruego
Published by Dutton, 1977
Kraus, Robert
How Spider Saved Halloween
Illustrated by Robert Kraus
Published by Dutton, 1974
Kraus, Robert
Leo the Late Bloomer
Illustrated by Jose Aruego
Published by Dutton, 1971
Kraus, Robert
Littlest Rabbit
Illustrated by Robert Kraus
Published by Scholastic, 1975
Kraus, Robert
Milton the Early Riser
Illustrated by Jose Aruego
Published by Dutton, 1972
Kraus, Robert
Noel the Coward
Illustrated by Ariane Dewey and Jose Aruego
Published by Dutton, 1977
Kraus, Robert
Owliver
Illustrated by Jose Aruego
Published by Dutton, 1974
Kraus, Robert
Three Friends
Illustrated
Published by Dutton, 1975
Kraus, Robert
Trouble with Spider
Illustrated by Robert Kraus
Published by Harper and Row, 1962
Kraus, Robert
Whose Mouse Are You?
Illustrated by Jose Aruego
Published by Macmillan, 1972
Kraus, Robert and Richard Oldden
Pip Squeak, Mouse in Shining Armor
Illustrated by Richard Oldden
Published by Dutton, 1971

Krauss, Ruth
Backward Day
Illustrated by Marc Simont
Published by Harper and Row, 1950

Krauss, Ruth
Big World and Little House
Illustrated by Marc Simont
Published by Harper and Row, 1956

Krauss, Ruth
Birthday Party
Illustrated by Maurice Sendak
Published by Harper and Row, 1957

Krauss, Ruth
Carrot Seed
Illustrated by Crockett Johnson
Published by Harper and Row, 1945

Krauss, Ruth
Everything Under a Mushroom
Illustrated
Published by Scholastic, 1974

Krauss, Ruth
Happy Day
Illustrated by Marc Simont
Published by Harper and Row, 1949

Krauss, Ruth
Hole Is to Dig: First Book of Definitions
Illustrated by Maurice Sendak
Published by Harper and Row, 1952

Krauss, Ruth
I'll Be You and You Be Me
Illustrated by Maurice Sendak
Published by Harper and Row, 1954

Krauss, Ruth
Little Boat Lighter Than a Cork
Illustrated by Esther Gilman
Published by Walker, 1976

Krauss, Ruth
Monkey Day
Illustrated by Phyllis Rowand
Published by Bookstore Press, 1957

Krauss, Ruth
Open House for Butterflies
Illustrated by Maurice Sendak
Published by Harper and Row, 1960

Krauss, Ruth
Very Special House
Illustrated by Maurice Sendak
Published by Harper and Row, 1953

Krauss, Ruth
Is There a Lion in the House?
Illustrated by Charles Robinson
Published by Walck, 1970

Kredenser, Gail
One Dancing Drum
Illustrated by Stanley Mack
Published by Phillips, 1971

Kroll, Steven
Candy Witch
Illustrated by Marilyn Hafner
Published by Holiday House, 1979

Kroll, Steven
Gobbledy Gook
Illustrated by Kelly Oechsli
Published by Holiday House, 1977

Kroll, Steven
Is Milton Missing?
Illustrated by Dick Gackenbach
Published by Holiday House, 1975

Kroll, Steven
That Makes Me Mad!
Illustrated by Hillary Knight
Published by Pantheon, 1976

Kroll, Steven
The Tyrannosaurus Game
Illustrated by Tomie DePaola
Published by Holiday House, 1976

Kruss, James
Three by Three
Illustrated by Eva J. Rubin
Published by Macmillan, 1965

Kumin, Maxine
Mittens in May
Illustrated by E. Gilbert
Published by Putnam, 1962

Kumin, Maxine
When Great Grandmother Was Young
Illustrated by Don Almquist
Published by Putnam, 1971

Kunhardt, Dorthy
Pat the Bunny
Illustrated by Dorthy Kunhardt
Published by Western, 1962

Kurelek, William
Prairie Boy's Winter
Illustrated
Published by Houghton Mifflin, 1973

Kuskin, Karla
A Boy Had a Mother Who Bought Him a Hat
Illustrated
Published by Houghton Mifflin, 1976

Kuskin, Karla
In the Flaky Frosty Morning
Illustrated by Karla Kuskin
Published by Harper and Row, 1969

Kuskin, Karla
James and the Rain
Illustrated
Published by Harper and Row, 1957

Kuskin, Karla
Just Like Everyone Else
Illustrated
Published by Harper and Row, 1959

Kuskin, Karla
Roar and More

Illustrated by Karla Kuskin
Published by Harper and Row, 1956
Kuskin, Karla
Sand and Snow
Illustrated by Karla Kuskin
Published by Harper and Row, 1965
Kuskin, Karla
Walk the Mouse Girls Took
Illustrated by Karla Kuskin
Published by Harper and Row, 1967
Kwitz, Mary
Mouse at Home
Illustrated by Mary Kwitz
Published by Harper and Row, 1966
Kwitz, Mary
When It Rains
Illustrated by Mary Kwitz
Published by Follett, 1974
Lachman, Ruth
Boats
Illustrated by Leonora and Herbert Combes
Published by Western, 1951
La Fontaine, Jean de
Hare and Tortoise
Illustrated by Brian Wildsmith
Published by Watts, 1966
La Fontaine, Jean de
The Lion and the Rat
Illustrated by Brian Wildsmith
Published by Watts, 1963
La Fontaine, Jean de
The North Wind and the Sun
Illustrated by Brian Wildsmith
Published by Watts, 1964
Lane, Carolyn
Voices of Green Willow Pond
Illustrated by Wallace Tripp
Published by Houghton Mifflin, 1972
Lang, Andrew
To Your Good Health
Illustrated
Published by Holiday House, 1973
Langner, Nola
Freddy, My Grandfather
Illustrated by Nola Langner
Published by Scholastic, 1979
Langner, Nola
Go and Shut the Door
Illustrated by Nola Langner
Published by Dial, 1971
Langner, Nola
Rafiki
Illustrated by Nola Langner
Published by Viking Press, 1977
Langstaff, John
Frog Went A-Courtin'
Illustrated by Feodor Rojankovsky
Published by Harcourt Brace Jovanovich, 1955
Langstaff, John and Feodor Rojankovsky
Over in the Meadow
Illustrated by Feodor Rojankovsky
Published by Harcourt Brace Jovanovich, 1967
Langstaff, John
Soldier, Soldier, Won't You Marry Me?
Illustrated by Anita Lobel
Published by Doubleday, 1972
Langstaff, John
The Two Magicians
Illustrated by Fritz Eichenberg
Published by Atheneum, 1973
Langstaff, John and Joe Krush
Ol' Dan Tucker
Illustrated by Joe Krush
Published by Harcourt Brace Jovanovich, 1963
Lapsley, Susan
I Am Adopted
Illustrated by Michael Charlton
Published by Bradbury Press, 1975
Larranga, Robert
King's Shadow
Illustrated by Joe Greenwald
Published by Carolrhoda, 1970
Larranga, Robert
Sniffles
Illustrated by Pat Seitz
Published by Carolrhoda, 1973
Lasker, Joe
He's My Brother
Illustrated by Joe Lasker
Published by A. Whitman, 1974
Lasker, Joe
Mothers Can Do Anything
Illustrated by Joe Lasker
Published by A. Whitman, 1972
Lasky, Kathryn
I Have Four Names for My Grandfather
Illustrated by Christopher G. Knight
Published by Little, Brown, 1976
Lasky, Kathryn
My Island Grandma
Illustrated by Emily A. McCully
Published by Warne, 1979
Lasky, Kathryn and Lucy Floyd
Agatha's Alphabet
Illustrated by Dora Leder
Published by Rand McNally, 1975
Latham, Jean
Wa O'Ka

Illustrated by Pablo Ramirez
Published by Bobbs-Merrill, (n.d.)
Lattimore, Eleanor
Little Pear
Illustrated by Eleanor Lattimore
Published by Harcourt Brace
Jovanovich, 1968
Laurence
Village in Normandy
Illustrated by Laurence
Published by Bobbs-Merrill, 1968
Lawrence, Jacob
Harriet and the Promised Land
Illustrated
Published by Simon & Schuster, 1968
Lawson, Pat
Kuma Is a Maori Girl
Illustrated by Dennis Hodgson
Published by Hastings House, 1967
Leaf, Munro
Noodle
Illustrated by Ludwig Bemelmans
Published by Scholastic, 1969
Leaf, Munro
Safety Can Be Fun
Illustrated by Munro Leaf
Published by Lippincott, 1961
Leaf, Munro
The Story of Ferdinand
Illustrated by Robert Lawson
Published by Viking Press, 1936
Leaf, Munro
Turnabout
Illustrated by Munro Leaf
Published by Lippincott, 1967
Leaf, Munro
Wee Gillis
Illustrated by Robert Lawson
Published by Viking Press, 1938
Leaf, Munro
Who Cares? I Do
Illustrated
Published by Lippincott, 1971
Leaf, Munro
Wishing Pool
Illustrated by Munro Leaf
Published by Lippincott, 1960
Lear, Edward
The Dong with the Luminous
 Nose
Illustrated by Edward Gorey
Published by A-W, 1969
Lear, Edward
The Jumblies
Illustrated by Edward Gorey
Published by Warne, 1907
Leech, Jay and Zane Spencer
Bright Fawn and Me

Illustrated by Glo Coalson
Published by T.Y. Crowell, 1979
Leen, Nina
Taking Pictures
Illustrated
Published by Holt, Rinehart and
Winston, 1977
LeGuin, Ursula K.
Leese Webster
Illustrated by James Brunsman
Published by Atheneum, 1979
Leher, Lore
Letter Goes to Sea
Illustrated by Hetty Krist-Schulz
Published by Harvey House, 1970
Leichman, Seymour
Wicked Wizard and the Wicked Witch
Illustrated by Seymour Leichman
Published by Harcourt Brace
Jovanovich, 1972
Lenski, Lois
Big Little Davy
Illustrated by Lois Lenski
Published by Walck, 1956
Lenski, Lois
I Like Winter
Illustrated by Lois Lenski
Published by Walck, 1950
Lenski, Lois
The Little Auto
Illustrated by Lois Lenski
Published by Walck, 1934
Lenski, Lois
The Little Train
Illustrated by Lois Lenski
Published by Walck, 1940
Lenski, Lois
Now It's Fall
Illustrated by Lois Lenski
Published by Walck, 1948
Lenski, Lois
On a Summer Day
Illustrated by Lois Lenski
Published by Walck, 1953
Lenski, Lois
Papa Small
Illustrated by Lois Lenski
Published by Walck, 1966
Lenski, Lois
Policeman Small
Illustrated by Lois Lenski
Published by Walck, 1962
Lenski, Lois
Spring Is Here
Illustrated by Lois Lenski
Published by Walck, 1945
Lenski, Lois
Suprise for Davy

Illustrated by Lois Lenski
Published by Walck, 1947
Lenthall, Patricia Riley
Carlotta and the Scientist
Illustrated by Patricia Riley Lenthall
Published by Lollipop Power, 1973
Lenzen, Hans
Blue Marble
Illustrated by Marie-Louise Pricken
Published by Abelard, 1969
Leokum, Arkady
More Tell Me Why
Illustrated by Arkady Leokum
Published by Grosset & Dunlap, 1967
Lerner, Marguerite Rush, M.D.
Dear Little Mumps Child
Illustrated by George Overlie
Published by Lerner, 1959
Lerner, Marguerite Rush, M.D.
Michael Gets the Measles
Illustrated by George Overlie
Published by Lerner, 1959
Lerner, Marguerite Rush, M.D.
Twins
Illustrated by Lawrence Spiegel
Published by Lerner, 1961
Lerner, Sharon
Who Will Wake up Spring?
Illustrated by Sharon Lerner
Published by Lerner, (n.d.)
Lester, Helen
Cora Copycat
Illustrated by Helen Lester
Published by Dutton, 1979
Lester, Julius
Knee-high Man
Illustrated by Ralph Pinto
Published by Dial, 1972
Lestima, Dorothy
May Day
Illustrated by Hope Merryman
Published by T.Y. Crowell, 1967
Le-Tan, Pierre
Happy Birthday Oliver!
Illustrated by Pierre Le-Tan
Published by Random, 1979
LeTord, Bijou
A Perfect Place to Be
Illustrated by Bijou LeTord
Published by Parents Magazine Press, 1976
LeTord, Bijou
Picking and Weaving
Illustrated by Bijou LeTord
Published by Scholastic, 1980
Leverich, Kathleen
The Hungry Fox and the Foxy Duck
Illustrated by Paul Galdone

Published by Parents Magazine Press, 1979
Levine, Edna
Lisa and Her Soundless World
Illustrated by Gloria Kamen
Published by Human Sciences Press, 1974
Levinson, Irene
Peter Learns to Crochet
Illustrated by Ketra Sutherland
Published by New Seed Press, 1973
Levitan, Sonia
A Single Speckled Egg
Illustrated by John Larrecq
Published by Parnassus Press, 1976
Levy, Elizabeth
Nice Little Girls
Illustrated by Mordicai Gerstein
Published by Delacorte, 1974
Lewis, Anne
Toss and Catch
Illustrated
Published by Harvey House, 1965
Lewis, Claudia
When I Go to the Moon
Illustrated by Leonard Weisgard
Published by Macmillan, 1973
Lewis, Richard
In a Spring Garden
Illustrated by Ezra Jack Keats
Published by Dial, 1976
Lewis, Richard
The Park
Illustrated
Published by Simon & Schuster, 1968
Lewis, Stephen
Zoo City
Illustrated
Published by Greenwillow, 1976
Lewis, Thomas P.
Dragon Kite
Illustrated by Errol LeCain
Published by Holt, Rinehart and Winston, 1974
Lewis, Thomas P.
Hill of Fire
Illustrated by Joan Sandin
Published by Harper and Row, 1971
Lewke, Susan
The Return of Chato
Illustrated
Published by Aardvark, 1974
Lexau, Joan
Benjie
Illustrated by Don Bolognese
Published by Dial, 1964
Lexau, Joan
Benjie on His Own

Illustrated by Don Bolognese
Published by Dial, 1970
Lexau, Joan
Crocodile and Hen
Illustrated by Joan Sandin
Published by Harper and Row, 1963
Lexau, Joan
Emily and the Clunky Baby and
  Next-Door Dog
Illustrated by Martha Alexander
Published by Dial, 1972
Lexau, Joan
House So Big
Illustrated
Published by Harper and Row, 1968
Lexau, Joan
I'll Tell on You
Illustrated by Gail Owens
Published by Dutton, 1976
Lexau, Joan
Me Day
Illustrated by Robert Weaver
Published by Dial, 1971
Lexau, Joan
The Spider Makes a Web
Illustrated by Arabelle Wheatley
Published by Hastings House, 1979
Leydenfrost, Robert
Did Anyone See My Elephant?
Illustrated
Published by Doubleday, 1977
Leydenfrost, Robert
Other Side of the Mountain
Illustrated by Robert Leydenfrost
Published by Macmillan, 1968
Leydenfrost, Robert
Ten Little Elephants
Illustrated
Published by Doubleday, 1975
Lifton, Betty
Cock and the Ghost Cat
Illustrated by Fuku Akino
Published by Atheneum, 1965
Lifton, Betty
Goodnight, Orange Monster
Illustrated by Cyndy Szekeres
Published by Atheneum, 1972
Lifton, Betty
Mud Snail Son
Illustrated by Fuku Akino
Published by Atheneum, 1971
Lifton, Betty
One-Legged Ghost
Illustrated by Fuku Akino
Published by Atheneum, 1968
Lindley, Alice
Story of the Little Round Man
Illustrated by Angela Sykes
Published by **Warne, 1979**

Link, Martin and Charles Blood
Goat in the Rug
Illustrated by Nancy Parker
Published by Parents Magazine Press,
  1976
Lionni, Leo
Alexander and the Wind-Up Mouse
Illustrated by Leo Lionni
Published by Random,˙1969
Lionni, Leo
Alphabet Tree
Illustrated by Leo Lionni
Published by Pantheon, 1968
Lionni, Leo
Biggest House in the World
Illustrated by Leo Lionni
Published by Viking Press,
  1972
Lionni, Leo
Color of His Own
Illustrated by Leo Lionni
Published by Pantheon, 1976
Lionni, Leo
Fish Is Fish
Illustrated by Leo Lionni
Published by Pantheon, 1970
Lionni, Leo
Frederick
Illustrated by Leo Lionni
Published by Pantheon, 1966
Lionni, Leo
Greentail Mouse
Illustrated by Leo Lionni
Published by Pantheon, 1973
Lionni, Leo
In the Rabbit Garden
Illustrated by Leo Lionni
Published by Pantheon, 1975
Lionni, Leo
Inch by Inch
Illustrated by Leo Lionni
Published by Astor-Honor, 1960
Lionni, Leo
Little Blue and Little Yellow
Illustrated by Leo Lionni
Published by Astor-Honor, 1959
Lionni, Leo
On My Beach There Are Many
  Pebbles
Illustrated by Leo Lionni
Published by Astor-Honor, 1961
Lionni, Leo
Pezzetino
Illustrated by Leo Lionni
Published by Pantheon, 1975
Lionni, Leo
Swimmy
Illustrated by Leo Lionni
Published by Pantheon, 1963

Lionni, Leo
Theodore and the Talking Mushroom
Illustrated by Leo Lionni
Published by Pantheon, 1971
Lionni, Leo
Tico and the Golden Wings
Illustrated by Leo Lionni
Published by Pantheon, 1964
Lipkind, William and Nicolas Mordvinoff
Finders Keepers
Illustrated by Nicolas Mordvinoff
Published by Harcourt Brace Jovanovich, 1973
Lipkind, William and Nicolas Mordvinoff
Little Tiny Rooster
Illustrated by Nicolas Mordvinoff
Published by Harcourt Brace Jovanovich, 1960
Lipkind, William and Nicolas Mordvinoff
Two Reds
Illustrated by Nicolas Mordvinoff
Published by Harcourt Brace Jovanovich, (n.d.)
Lippman, Peter
New at the Zoo
Illustrated
Published by Harper and Row, 1969
Lisker, Sonia
I Can Be
Illustrated
Published by Hastings House, 1972
Lisker, Sonia
Lost
Illustrated by Sonia Lisker
Published by Harcourt Brace Jovanovich, 1975
Lisker, Sonia and Leigh Dean
Two Special Cards
Illustrated by Sonia Lisker
Published by Harcourt Brace Jovanovich, 1976
List, Ilka
Grandma's Beach Surprise
Illustrated
Published by Putnam, 1975
Littledale, Freya, Retold By
Elves and the Shoemaker
Illustrated by Brinton Turkle
Published by Scholastic, 1977
Littledale, Harold
Alexander
Illustrated by Tom Vroman
Published by Parents Magazine Press, 1964
Livermore, Elaine
One to Ten, Count Again

Illustrated by Elaine Livermore
Published by Houghton Mifflin, 1973
Livingston, Myra C. and Erik Blegvad
I'm Hiding
Illustrated by Erik Blegvad
Published by Harcourt Brace Jovanovich, 1961
Llerena, Carlos A.
Sticks, Stones
Illustrated by Carlos A. Llerena
Published by Holt, Rinehart and Winston, 1977
Lobel, Adrianne
Small Sheep in a Pear Tree
Illustrated
Published by Harper and Row, 1977
Lobel, Anita
A Birthday for the Princess
Illustrated by Anita Lobel
Published by Harper and Row, 1973
Lobel, Anita
Potatoes, Potatoes
Illustrated by Anita Lobel
Published by Harper and Row, 1967
Lobel, Anita
Seamstress of Salzburg
Illustrated by Anita Lobel
Published by Harper and Row, 1970
Lobel, Anita
Sven's Bridge
Illustrated by Anita Lobel
Published by Harper and Row, 1965
Lobel, Anita
Troll Music
Illustrated by Anita Lobel
Published by Harper and Row, 1966
Lobel, Anita
Under a Mushroom
Illustrated by Anita Lobel
Published by Harper and Row, 1970
Lobel, Arnold
Days with Frog and Toad
Illustrated by Arnold Lobel
Published by Harper and Row, 1979
Lobel, Arnold
Frog and Toad Together
Illustrated by Arnold Lobel
Published by Harper and Row, 1972
Lobel, Arnold
Giant John
Illustrated by Arnold Lobel
Published by Harper and Row, 1964
Lobel, Arnold
Gregory Griggs and Other Nursery Rhyme People
Illustrated by Arnold Lobel
Published by Greenwillow, 1978

Bibliography / 231

Lobel, Arnold
Holiday for Mister Muster
Illustrated by Arnold Lobel
Published by Harper and Row, 1963

Lobel, Arnold
How the Rooster Saved the Day
Illustrated by Anita Lobel
Published by Greenwillow, 1977

Lobel, Arnold
Lucille
Illustrated by Arnold Lobel
Published by Harper and Row, 1964

Lobel, Arnold
Man Who Took the Indoors Out
Illustrated by Arnold Lobel
Published by Harper and Row, 1974

Lobel, Arnold
Martha, the Movie Mouse
Illustrated by Arnold Lobel
Published by Harper and Row, 1966

Lobel, Arnold
Mouse Soup
Illustrated by Arnold Lobel
Published by Harper and Row, 1977

Lobel, Arnold
On the Day P. Stuyvesant Sailed into Town
Illustrated by Arnold Lobel
Published by Harper and Row, 1971

Lobel, Arnold
Owl at Home
Illustrated by Arnold Lobel
Published by Harper and Row, 1975

Lobel, Arnold
Prince Bertram the Bad
Illustrated by Arnold Lobel
Published by Harper and Row, 1963

Lobel, Arnold
A Treeful of Pigs
Illustrated by Anita Lobel
Published by Greenwillow' 1979

Lobel, Arnold
Zoo for Mister Muster
Illustrated by Arnold Lobel
Published by Harper and Row, (n.d.)

Lofgren, Vif
Wonderful Tree
Illustrated by Vif Lofgren
Published by Delacorte, 1970

Long, Ruthanna
Great Monster Contest
Illustrated by Tim and Greg Hildebrandt
Published by Western, 1977

Lord, Beman
Days of the Week
Illustrated by Walter Erhard
Published by Walck, 1968

Lord, John Vernon
Runaway Roller Skate
Illustrated by John Vernon Lord
Published by Harper and Row, 1977

Lord, John Vernon and Janet Burroway
Giant Jam Sandwich
Illustrated by John Vernon Lord
Published by Houghton Mifflin, 1973

Loree, Kate
Pails and Snails
Illustrated by Audrey Walters
Published by Harvey House, 1967

Loree, Sharron
The Sunshine Family and the Pony
Illustrated by Sharron Loree
Published by Seabury, 1972

Lovelace, Maud
Valentine Box
Illustrated by Ingrid Ietz
Published by T.Y. Crowell, 1966

Low, Alice
David's Windows
Illustrated by Tomie DePaola
Published by Putnam, 1974

Low, Alice
Witches' Holiday
Illustrated by Tony Walton
Published by Pantheon, 1971

Low, Joseph
Boo to a Goose
Illustrated by Joseph Low
Published by Atheneum, 1975

Low, Joseph
Little Though I Be
Illustrated
Published by McGraw-Hill, 1976

Lowrey, Janette S.
Poky Little Puppy
Illustrated by Gustaf Tenggren
Published by Western, 1973

Lowrey, Janette S.
Six Silver Spoons
Illustrated by Robert Quackenbush
Published by Harper and Row, 1971

Lucero, Faustina H.
Little Indians' ABC
Illustrated
Published by Oddo, (n.d.)

Lund, Doris
The Paint-Box Sea
Illustrated by Symeon Shimon
Published by McGraw-Hill, 1972

Lund, Doris
You Ought to See Herbert's House
Illustrated by Steven Kellogg
Published by Watts, 1973

Lustig, Loretta
The Pop-up Book of Trucks
Illustrated
Published by Random, 1974
Lystad, Mary
Halloween Parade
Illustrated by Cyndy Szekeres
Published by Putnam, 1973
Lystad, Mary
That New Boy
Illustrated by Emily A. McCully
Published by Crown, 1973
MacDonald, Betty
Hello, Mrs. Piggle-Wiggle
Illustrated by Hillary Knight
Published by Lippincott, 1957
MacDonald, Golden
Red Light, Green Light
Illustrated by Leonard Weisgard
Published by Doubleday, 1944
McCabe, Inger
Week in Henry's World: El Barrio
Illustrated by Inger McCabe
Published by Macmillan, 1971
McCaffery, Janet
Swamp Witch
Illustrated by Janet McCaffery
Published by Morrow, 1970
McCloskey, Robert
Blueberries for Sal
Illustrated by Robert McCloskey
Published by Viking Press, 1948
McCloskey, Robert
Lentil
Illustrated by Robert McCloskey
Published by Viking Press, 1940
McCloskey, Robert
Make Way for Ducklings
Illustrated by Robert McCloskey
Published by Viking Press, 1941
McCloskey, Robert
One Morning in Maine
Illustrated by Robert McCloskey
Published by Viking Press, 1952
McClung, Robert
Horseshoe Crab
Illustrated by Robert McClung
Published by Morrow, 1967
McClung, Robert
Ladybug
Illustrated by Robert McClung
Published by Morrow, 1966
McClung, Robert
Sea Star
Illustrated by Robert McClung
Published by Morrow, 1975
McCord, David
Every Time I Climb a Tree

Illustrated by Marc Simont
Published by Little, Brown, 1967
McDermott, Beverly
Crystal Apple: A Russion Tale
Illustrated by Beverly McDermott
Published by Viking Press, 1974
McDermott, Beverly
Sedna: An Eskimo Myth
Illustrated by Beverly McDermott
Published by Viking Press, 1975
McDermott, Gerald
Anansi the Spider: A Tale from Ashanti
Illustrated by Gerald McDermott
Published by Holt, Rinehart and Winston, 1977
McDermott, Gerald
Arrow to the Sun: A Pueblo Indian Tale
Illustrated
Published by Viking Press, 1974
McDermott, Gerald
Magic Tree: A Tale from the Congo
Illustrated by Gerald McDermott
Published by Penguin, 1977
McDermott, Gerald
The Stonecutter: A Japanese Folktale
Illustrated by Gerald McDermott
Published by Viking Press, 1975
McGovern, Ann
Black Is Beautiful
Illustrated by Hope Wurmfeld
Published by Scholastic, 1970
McGovern, Ann
Feeling Mad, Sad, Bad, Glad
Illustrated by Hope Wurmfeld
Published by Walker, 1978
McGovern, Ann
Half a Kingdom
Illustrated by Nola Langner
Published by Warne, 1977
McGovern, Ann
Hee Haw
Illustrated by Eric Von Schmidt
Published by Houghton Mifflin, 1969
McGovern, Ann
Little Whale
Illustrated by John Hamberger
Published by Scholastic, 1979
McGovern, Ann
Scram, Kid!
Illustrated by Nola Langner
Published by Viking Press, 1974
McGovern, Ann
Sharks
Illustrated by Murray Tinkleman
Published by Scholastic, 1976
McGovern, Ann
Too Much Noise

Illustrated by Simms Taback
Published by Houghton Mifflin, 1967
McGovern, Ann
The Underwater World of the Coral Reef
Illustrated
Published by Scholastic, 1977
McGovern, Ann
Zoo, Where Are You?
Illustrated by Ezra Jack Keats
Published by Harper and Row, 1964
MacGregor, Ellen
Theodore Turtle
Illustrated by Paul Galdone
Published by Whitlesey House, 1955
McHargue, Georgess
The Mermaid and the Whale
Illustrated by Robert Andrew Parker
Published by Holt, Rinehart and Winston, 1973
McHargue, Georgess
The Private Zoo
Illustrated by Michael Foreman
Published by Viking Press, 1975
McInnes, John
The Ghost Said Boo
Illustrated by Lou Cunette
Published by Garrard, 1974
McInnes, John
Have You Ever Seen a Monster?
Illustrated by Tom Eaton
Published by Garrard, 1974
McInnes, John
How Pedro Got His Name
Illustrated by Edward Malsberg
Published by Garrard, 1974
McInnes, John
Leo Lion Paints It Red
Illustrated by Tom Eaton
Published by Garrard, 1974
McKee, David
The Magician and the Petnapping
Illustrated by David McKee
Published by Houghton Mifflin, 1977
McKee, David
The Magician Who Lost His Magic
Illustrated by David McKee
Published by Abelard, 1970
McKee, David
The Man Who Was Going to Mind the House
Illustrated by David McKee
Published by Abelard, 1973
McKown, Robin
Rakoto and the Drongo Bird
Illustrated
Published by Lothrop, 1966

McLeod, Emilie
One Snail and Me
Illustrated by Walter Lorraine
Published by Little, Brown, 1961
McNaught, Harry
Five Hundred Words to Grow On
Illustrated
Published by Random, 1973
McNaught, Harry
The Truck Book
Illustrated
Published by Random, 1978
McNeer, May
My Friend Mac
Illustrated by Lynd Ward
Published by Houghton Mifflin, 1973
McNeill, Janet
The Mouse and the Mirage
Illustrated by Walter Erhard
Published by Walck, 1966
McNulty, Faith
How to Dig a Hole to the Other Side of the World
Illustrated by Marc Simont
Published by Harper and Row, 1979
McNulty, Faith
Woodchuck
Illustrated by Joan Sandin
Published by Harper and Row, 1974
McPhail, David
Bear's Toothache
Illustrated
Published by Little, Brown, 1972
McTrusty, Ron
Dandelion Year
Illustrated by Ron McTrusty
Published by Harvey House, 1977
Machetanz, Sara and Fred Machetanz
Puppy Named Gih
Illustrated by Fred Machetanz
Published by Scribner, 1957
Mack, Bruce
Jesse's Dream Skirt
Illustrated by Marian Buchanan
Published by Lollipop Power, 1979
Mack, Nancy
I'm Not Going
Illustrated by Heinz Kluetmeier
Published by Raintree, 1976
Mack, Nancy
Tracy
Illustrated by Heinz Kluetmeier
Published by Raintree, 1976
Mack, Stan
Ten Bears in My Bed: A Goodnight Countdown
Illustrated by Stan Mack
Published by Pantheon, 1974

Maestro, Betsy
Harriet Goes to the Circus
Illustrated by Guilio Maestro
Published by Crown, 1977

Maestro, Betsy
In My Boat
Illustrated by Guilio Maestro
Published by T.Y. Crowell, 1976

Maestro, Betsy
On the Go: A Book of Adjectives
Illustrated by Guilio Maestro
Published by Crown, 1979

Maestro, Betty
Where Is My Friend? A Word
  Concept Book
Illustrated by Guilio Maestro
Published by Crown, 1976

Maestro, Betsy
A Wise Monkey Tale
Illustrated by Guilio Maestro
Published by Crown, 1975

Maestro, Guilio
The Remarkable Plant in Apartment 4
Illustrated by Guilio Maestro
Published by Bradbury Press, 1973

Maestro, Guilio
Tortoise's Tug of War
Illustrated by Guilio Maestro
Published by Bradbury Press, 1971

Mahan, Joan
Art, the Altogether Aged Aardvark
Illustrated
Published by Aurora, (n.d.)

Mahy, Margaret
The Boy Who Was Followed Home
Illustrated by Steven Kellogg
Published by Watts, 1975

Mahy, Margaret
Lion in the Meadow
Illustrated by Jenny Williams
Published by Watts, 1969

Maley, Anne
Have You Seen My Mother?
Illustrated by Yutaka Sugita
Published by Carolrhoda, 1975

Mallett, Anne
Here Comes Tagalong
Illustrated by Stephen Kellogg
Published by Parents Magazine Press, 1971

Mandry, Kathy
How to Grow a Jelly Glass Farm
Illustrated by Joe Toto
Published by Pantheon, 1974

Mandry, Kathy and Joe Toto
How to Make Elephant Bread
Illustrated by Joe Toto
Published by Pantheon, 1971

Manes, Stephen
Mule in the Mail
Illustrated by Mary Chalmers
Published by Coward, 1979

Mann, Peggy
King Lawrence, the Alarm Clock
Illustrated by Ray Cruz
Published by Doubleday, 1976

Manning, James, Jr.
Zach, the Unusual Donkey
Illustrated by James Manning, Jr.
Published by Exposition, 1977

Manushkin, Fran
Swinging and Swinging
Illustrated by Thomas DiGrazia
Published by Harper and Row, 1976

Margolis, Richard
Wish Again, Big Bear
Illustrated by Robert Lopshire
Published by Macmillan, 1972

Mari, Iela and Enzo Mari
The Apple and the Moth
Illustrated by Iela Mari
Published by Pantheon, 1970

Mari, Iela and Enzo Mari
The Chicken and the Egg
Illustrated by Iela Mari
Published by Pantheon, 1970

Mariana
Miss Flora McFlimsy's May Day
Illustrated by Mariana
Published by Lothrop, 1969

Mariana
Miss Flora McFlimsy's Valentine
Illustrated by Mariana
Published by Lothrop, 1961

Mark, Susan E.
Please, Michael, That's My Daddy's
  Chair
Illustrated by Winnie Mertens
Published by Canadian Women's
  Educational Press, (n.d.)

Marshall, James
George and Martha
Illustrated by James Marshall
Published by Houghton Mifflin, 1972

Marshall, James
The Guest
Illustrated by James Marshall
Published by Houghton Mifflin, 1975

Marshall, James
Portly McSwine
Illustrated by James Marshall
Published by Houghton Mifflin, 1979

Marshall, James
Willis
Illustrated by James Marshall
Published by Houghton Mifflin, 1974

Marshall, James
Yummers
Illustrated by James Marshall
Published by Houghton Mifflin, 1973
Martel, Cruz
Yagua Days
Illustrated by Jerry Pinkney
Published by Dial, 1976
Martin, Patricia Miles
The Little Brown Hen
Illustrated by Harper Johnson
Published by T.Y. Crowell, 1960
Martin, Patricia Miles
The Dog and the Boat Boy
Illustrated by Earl Thollander
Published by Putnam, 1969
Martin, Patricia Miles
Raccoon and Mrs. McGinnis
Illustrated by Leonard Weisgard
Published by Putnam, 1961
Martin, Patricia Miles
Rice Bowl Pet
Illustrated by Ezra Jack Keats
Published by T.Y. Crowell, 1962
Martin, Patricia Miles
Rolling the Cheese
Illustrated by Alton Raible
Published by Atheneum, 1966
Martin, Sarah
Old Mother Hubbard and Her Dog
Translated by Virginia A. Jensen
Illustrated by Ib S. Olsen
Published by Coward, 1976
Martin, Susan
The Adventures of Sapo
Illustrated by Susan Martin
Published by Aardvark, 1974
Masey, Mary Lou and Frieda Forman
Teddy and the Moon
Illustrated by Helen Basilevsky
Published by Harvey House, 1972
Massie, Diane Redfield
Briar Rose and the Golden Eggs
Illustrated by Diane Redfield Massie
Published by Parents Magazine Press, 1973
Massie, Diane Redfield
Chameleon Was a Spy
Illustrated by Diane Redfield Massie
Published by T.Y. Crowell, 1979
Massie, Diane Redfield
Dazzle
Illustrated by Diane Redfield Massie
Published by Parents Magazine Press, 1969
Massie, Diane Redfield
Monstrous Glisson Glop
Illustrated by Diane Redfield Massie
Published by Parents Magazine Press, 1970
Massie, Diane Redfield
Walter Was a Frog
Illustrated by Diane Redfield Massie
Published by Simon & Schuster, 1970
Mathis, Sharon
The Hundred Penny Box
Illustrated by Leo and Diane Dillon
Published by Viking Press, 1975
Matsuno, Masako
Taro and the Bamboo Shoot
Illustrated by Yasuo Segawa
Published by Pantheon, 1974
Matsutani, Miyoko
Crane Maiden
Illustrated by Chihiro Iwasaki
Published by Parents Magazine Press, 1968
Mattmuller, Felix
We Want a Little Sister
Illustrated by Marcus Schneider
Published by Lerner, (n.d.)
Maury, Inez
My Mother and I Are Growing Strong
Translated by Anna Munoz
Illustrated by Sandy Speidel
Published by New Seed Press, 1978
Maury, Inez
My Mother the Mail Carrier
Translated by Nora Alemany
Illustrated by Lady McCrady
Published by Feminist Press, (n.d.)
May, Julian
Before the Indians
Illustrated by Symeon Shimin
Published by Holiday House, 1969
May, Julian
Horses: How They Came to Be
Illustrated by Lorence Bjorklund
Published by Holiday House, 1968
May, Julian
Why People Are Different Colors
Illustrated by Symeon Shimin
Published by Holiday House, 1971
Mayer, Marianna and Mercer Mayer
Me and My Flying Machine
Illustrated by Marianna and Mercer Mayer
Published by Parents Magazine Press, 1971
Mayer, Mercer
Ah-Choo
Illustrated by Mercer Mayer
Published by Dial Press, 1977
Mayer, Mercer
Bubble Bubble

Illustrated by Mercer Mayer
Published by Astor-Honor, 1968
Mayer, Mercer
Four Frogs in a Box
Illustrated by Mercer Mayer
Published by Dial, 1976
Mayer, Mercer
Frog Goes to Dinner
Illustrated by Mercer Mayer
Published by Dial Press, 1974
Mayer, Mercer
Frog on His Own
Illustrated by Mercer Mayer
Published by Dial, 1973
Mayer, Mercer
Frog, Where Are You?
Illustrated by Mercer Mayer
Published by Dial, 1969
Mayer, Mercer
The Great Cat Chase
Illustrated by Mercer Mayer
Published by Scholastic, 1975
Mayer, Mercer
Hiccup
Illustrated by Mercer Mayer
Published by Dial, (n.d.)
Mayer, Mercer
If I Had...
Illustrated by Mercer Mayer
Published by Dial, 1968
Mayer, Mercer
Just For You
Illustrated by Mercer Mayer
Published by Western, 1975
Mayer, Mercer
Oops
Illustrated by Mercer Mayer
Published by Dial, 1977
Mayer, Mercer
Queen Always Wanted to Dance
Illustrated by Mercer Mayer
Published by Simon & Schuster, 1971
Mayer, Mercer
Silly Story
Illustrated by Mercer Mayer
Published by Parents Magazine Press, 1972
Mayer, Mercer
Terrible Troll
Illustrated by Mercer Mayer
Published by Dial, 1968
Mayer, Mercer
There's a Nightmare in My Closet
Illustrated by Mercer Mayer
Published by Dial, 1968
Mayer, Mercer
Two Moral Tales
Illustrated by Mercer Mayer
Published by Scholastic, 1974

Mayer, Mercer
What Do You Do with a Kangaroo?
Illustrated by Mercer Mayer
Published by Scholastic, 1973
Mayer, Mercer
You're the Scaredy-Cat
Illustrated by Mercer Mayer
Published by Parents Magazine Press, 1974
Mayer, Mercer and Marianna Mayer
A Boy, a Dog, a Frog, and a Friend
Illustrated by Mercer Mayer
Published by Dial Press, 1971
Mayer, Mercer and Marianna Mayer
Mine
Illustrated by Mercer Mayer
Published by Simon & Schuster, 1970
Mayer, Mercer ano Marianna Mayer
One Frog Too Many
Illustrated by Mercer Mayer
Published by Dial, 1977
Mayers, Patrick
Just One More Block
Illustrated by Lucy Hawkinson
Published by A. Whitman, 1970
Meeks, Esther K.
Curious Cow
Illustrated by Mel Pekarsky
Published by Scholastic, 1973
Memling, Carl
Hi, All You Rabbits
Illustrated by Myra McGee
Published by Parents Magazine Press, 1970
Memling, Carl
What's in the Dark?
Illustrated by John E. Johnson
Published by Parents Magazine Press, 1971
Meriwether , L.
Don't Ride the Bus on Monday: The Rosa Parks Story
Illustrated
Published by Prentice-Hall, 1973
Merriam , Eve
Bam! Zam! Zoom!
Illustrated
Published by Walker, 1972
Merriam , Eve
Boys and Girls, Girls and Boys
Illustrated by Harriet Sherman
Published by Holt, Rinehart & Winston, 1972
Merriam, Eve
Gaggle of Geese
Illustrated by Paul Galdone
Published by Knopf, 1960
Merriam, Eve
Good Night to Annie

Illustrated by John Wallner
Published by Scholastic, 1979
Merriam, Eve
Mommies at Work
Illustrated by Beni Montresor
Published by Knopf, 1961
Merriam, Eve
That Noodle-Head Epaminondas
Illustrated by Trina S. Hyman
Published by Follett, 1968
Merriam, Eve
What Can You Do with a Pocket?
Illustrated by Harriet Simon
Published by Knopf, 1964
Merrill, Jean
Travels of Marco
Illustrated by Ronni Solbert
Published by Knopf, 1965
Merrill, Jean and Frances G. Scott
Here I Come...Ready or Not
Illustrated
Published by A. Whitman, 1970
Mertens, Winnie
My Feet Roll
Illustrated by Winnie Mertens
Published by Before We Are Six (Canada), 1977
Meyer, Elizabeth C.
Blue China Pitcher
Illustrated
Published by Abingdon, 1974
Miles, Betty
Day of Spring
Illustrated by Marjorie Aurbach
Published by Knopf, 1970
Miles, Betty
Day of Winter
Illustrated by Remy Charlip
Published by Knopf, 1961
Miles, Betty
A House for Everyone
Illustrated by Jo Lowery
Published by Knopf, 1958
Miles, Miska
Apricot ABC
Illustrated by Peter Parnall
Published by Little, Brown, 1969
Miles, Miska
Nobody's Cat
Illustrated by John Schoenherr
Published by Little, Brown, 1969
Miles, Miska
Small Rabbit
Illustrated by Jim Arnosky
Published by Little, Brown, 1977
Miles, Miska
Wharf Rat

Illustrated by John Schoenherr
Published by Little, Brown, 1972
Milgram, Mary
Brothers Are All the Same
Illustrated
Published by Dutton, 1978
Miller, Albert G.
Pop-up Hide & Seek: A Child's First Counting Book
Illustrated
Published by Random, 1966
Miller, Arthur
Jane's Blanket
Illustrated by Emily A. McCully
Published by Viking Press, 1972
Miller, Edna
Mousekin's Woodland Sleepers
Illustrated by Edna Miller
Published by Prentice-Hall, 1977
Miller, Minrie T.
Grandma's Tiny Kitty
Illustrated
Published by Mojave Books, (n.d.)
Milne, A. A.
House at Pooh Corner
Illustrated by Ernest H. Shepard
Published by Dutton, 1961
Milne, A. A.
Now We Are Six
Illustrated by Ernest H. Shepard
Published by Dutton, 1961
Milne, A.A.
When We Were Very Young
Illustrated by Ernest H. Shepard
Published by Dutton, 1961
Milne, A.A.
Winnie the Pooh
Illustrated by Ernest H. Shepard
Published by Dutton, 1974
Milord, Sue and Jerry Milord
Maggie and the Goodbye Gift
Illustrated by Jerry Milord
Published by Lothrop, 1979
Minarik, Else H.
Cat and Dog
Illustrated by Fritz Siebel
Published by Harper and Row, 1960
Minarik, Else H.
Little Bear
Illustrated by Maurice Sendak
Published by Harper and Row, 1957
Minarik, Else H.
The Little Giant Girl and the Elf Boy
Illustrated by Garth Williams
Published by Harper and Row, 1963
Mizumura, Kazue
Blue Whale
Illustrated by Kazue Mizumura
Published by T.Y. Crowell, 1971

Mizumura, Kazue
Flower Moon Snow: A Book of Haiku
Illustrated by Kazue Mizumura
Published by T.Y. Crowell, 1977

Mizumura, Kazue
I See the Winds
Illustrated by Kazue Mizumura
Published by T.Y. Crowell, 1966

Mizumura, Kazue
If I Built a Village
Illustrated by Kazue Mizumura
Published by T.Y. Crowell, 1971

Mizumura, Kazue
If I Were a Cricket
Illustrated by Kazue Mizumura
Published by T.Y. Crowell, 1973

Mizumura, Kazue
If I Were a Mother
Illustrated by Kazue Mizumura
Published by T.Y. Crowell, 1968

Mizumura, Kazue
Opossum
Illustrated by Kazue Mizumura
Published by T.Y. Crowell, 1974

Modell, Frank
Tooley! Tooley!
Illustrated by Frank Modell
Published by Greenwillow, 1979

Moeri, Louise
How the Rabbit Stole the Moon
Illustrated by Marc T. Brown
Published by Houghton Mifflin, 1977

Moffett, Martha
A Flower Pot Is Not a Hat
Illustrated by Susan Perl
Published by Dutton, 1972

Molarsky, Osmond
Right Thumb, Left Thumb
Illustrated by John E. Johnson
Published by A-W, 1969

Moncure, Jane B.
Wait, Says His Father
Illustrated by Helen E. Endres
Published by Child's World, 1975

Monjo, F.N.
Drinking Gourd
Illustrated by Fred Brenner
Published by Harper and Row, 1969

Montgomery, Constance and Raymond Montgomery
Vermont Farm and the Sun
Illustrated by Dennis Curran
Published by Vermont Crossroads, 1979

Montgomery, Constance and Raymond Montgomery
Vermont Road Builder
Illustrated by Larry Barns
Published by Vermont Crossroads, 1979

Montgomery, Constance
Vermont School Bus Ride
Illustrated by Larry Barns
Published by Vermont Crossroads, 1979

Moody, Elizabeth
Patty Cake
Illustrated
Published by Quadrangle, 1974

Moore, Clement
The Night Before Christmas
Illustrated by Leonard Weisgard
Published by Grosset & Dunlap, 1949

Moore, John Travers
All Along the Way
Illustrated by Nancy Inderieden
Published by Carolrhoda, 1973

Moore, Lilian
The Little Raccoon and No Trouble at All
Illustrated by Gioia Fiammenghi
Published by McGraw-Hill, 1972

Moore, Lilian
Papa Albert
Illustrated by Gioia Fiammenghi
Published by Atheneum, 1964

Moore, Nancy and Edward Leight
Miss Harriet Hippopotamus and the Most Wonderful
Illustrated by Ermintrude
Published by Vanguard, (n.d.)

Mooser, Stephen
The Ghost with Halloween Hiccups
Illustrated by Tomie DePaola
Published by Watts, 1977

Morgan, Shirley
Rain, Rain Don't Go Away
Illustrated by Edward Ardizzone
Published by Dutton, 1972

Morris, Robert
Seahorse
Illustrated by Arnold Lobel
Published by Harper and Row, 1972

Morrison, Bill
Squeeze a Sneeze
Illustrated by Bill Morrison
Published by Houghton Mifflin, 1977

Mosel, Arlene
Funny Little Woman
Illustrated by Blair Lent
Published by Dutton, 1972

Mosel, Arlene
Tikki Tikki Tembo
Illustrated by Blair Lent
Published by Holt, Rinehart & Winston, 1968

Moss, Geoffrey
Arthur's Artichoke
Illustrated by Geoffrey Moss
Published by Dial Press, 1970
Munari, Bruno
ABC
Illustrated by Bruno Munari
Published by Collins-World, 1960
Munari, Bruno
Bruno Munari's Zoo
Illustrated by Bruno Munari
Published by Collins-World, 1963
Murschetz, Luis
A Hamster's Journey
Translated by Harry Allard
Illustrated by Luis Murschetz
Published by Prentice-Hall, 1976
Murschetz, Luis
Mister Mole
Translated by Diane Martin
Illustrated by Luis Murschetz
Published by Prentice-Hall, 1976
Musgrove, Margaret W.
Ashanti To Zulu: African Traditions
Illustrated by Leo and Diane Dillon
Published by Dial, 1976
Myers, Amy
I Know a Monster
Illustrated by Amy Myers
Published by A-W, 1979
Myers, Bernice
Apple War
Illustrated by Bernice Myers
Published by Parents Magazine Press, 1973
Myller, Lois
No! No!
Illustrated by Cyndy Szekeres
Published by Simon & Schuster, 1971
Nakatani, Chiyoko
My Day on the Farm
Illustrated by Chiyoko Nakatani
Published by T.Y. Crowell, 1977
Nakatani, Chiyoko
My Teddy Bear
Illustrated by Chiyoko Nakatani
Published by T.Y. Crowell, 1975
Nakatani, Chiyoko
The Zoo in My Garden
Illustrated by Chiyoko Nakatani
Published by T.Y. Crowell, 1973
Nash, Ogden
Animal Garden
Illustrated by Hillary Knight
Published by Lippincott, 1965
Nash, Ogden
The Cruise of the Aardvark
Illustrated by Wendy Watson
Published by Lippincott, 1967
Nash, Ogden
Custard the Dragon and the Wicked Knight
Illustrated by Linell Nash
Published by Little, Brown, 1961
Nasson, Valentina
The Chosen Baby
Translated by Glo Coalson
Illustrated
Published by Lippincott, 1977
Ness, Evaline
Amelia Mixed the Mustard and Other Poems
Illustrated by Evaline Ness
Published by Scribner, 1975
Ness, Evaline
Do You Have the Time, Lydia?
Illustrated
Published by Dutton , 1971
Ness, Evaline
Sam Bangs and Moonshine
Illustrated by Evaline Ness
Published by Holt, Rinehart and Winston, 1966
Ness, Evaline
Tom Tit Tot
Illustrated by Evaline Ness
Published by Scribner, 1965
Ness, Evaline
Yeck Eck
Illustrated by Evaline Ness
Published by Dutton, 1974
Neumann, Rudolph
The Bad Bear
Translated by Jack Prelutsky
Illustrated by Eva J. Rubin
Published by Macmillan, 1967
Newberry, Clare T.
Barkis
Illustrated by Clare T. Newberry
Published by Harper and Row, 1938
Newberry, Clare T.
Kitten's ABC
Illustrated by Clare T. Newberry
Published by Harper and Row, 1965
Newberry, Clare T.
Marshmallow
Illustrated by Clare T. Newberry
Published by Harper and Row, 1942
Newberry, Clare T.
Mittens
Illustrated by Clare T. Newberry
Published by Harper and Row, 1936
Newberry, Clare T.
Smudge
Illustrated by Clare T. Newberry
Published by Harper and Row, 1948

Newberry, Clare T.
T-Bone the Baby-Sitter
Illustrated by Clare T. Newberry
Published by Harper and Row, 1950

Newfield, Marcia
Six Rags Apiece
Illustrated by Nola Langner
Published by Warne, 1976

Nicoll, Helen
Meg and Mog
Illustrated by Jan Pienkowski
Published by Atheneum, 1973

Nicholson, Geraldine
Adventures of Muku
Illustrated
Published by Dillon, 1975

Nicholson, William
Clever Bill
Illustrated by William Nicholson
Published by Farrar, Straus and Giroux, 1977

Nicklaus, Carol
Can You Find What's Missing?
Illustrated by Carol Nicklaus
Published by Random, 1974

Nicklaus, Carol
What's That Noise?
Illustrated by Carol Nicklaus
Published by Platt Munk, 1975

Nic Leodhas, Sorche
All in the Morning Early
Illustrated by Evaline Ness
Published by Holt, Rinehart and Winston, 1963

Nic Leodhas, Sorche
Always Room for One More
Illustrated by Nonny Hogrogian
Published by Holt, Rinehart and Winston, 1965

Niklewiczowa, Maria
Sparrow's Magic
Translated by Alvin Tresselt
Illustrated by Fuyuji Yamanaka
Published by Parents Magazine Press, 1970

Niland, Deborah
ABC of Monsters
Illustrated by Deborah Niland
Published by McGraw-Hill, 1978

Nodset, Joan
Go Away, Dog
Illustrated by Crosby Bonsall
Published by Harper and Row, 1963

Nodset, Joan and Fritz Siebel
Who Took the Farmer's Hat?
Illustrated by Fritz Siebel
Published by Harper and Row, 1963

Nolan, Dennis
Monster Bubbles: A Counting Book
Illustrated
Published by Prentice-Hall, 1976

Nolan, Madeena Spray
My Daddy Don't Go to Work
Illustrated by Jim Lamarche
Published by Carolrhoda, 1979

Oakley, Graham
The Church Cat Abroad
Illustrated by Graham Oakley
Published by Atheneum, 1973

Oakley, Graham
The Church Mice Adrift
Illustrated by Graham Oakley
Published by Atheneum, 1976

Oakley, Graham
The Church Mice and the Moon
Illustrated by Graham Oakley
Published by Atheneum, 1974

Oakley, Graham
The Church Mice at Bay
Illustrated by Graham Oakley
Published by Atheneum, 1979

Oakley, Graham
The Church Mice Spread Their Wings
Illustrated by Graham Oakley
Published by Atheneum, 1975

Oakley, Graham
The Church Mouse
Illustrated by Graham Oakley
Published by Atheneum, 1972

O'Brien, John
Grouch and the Tower and Other Sillies
Illustrated by John O'Brien
Published by Harper and Row, 1977

Ogle, Lucille and Tine Thoburn
I Hear Sounds in a Children's World
Illustrated by Eloise Wilkin
Published by McGraw-Hill, 1971

Ogle, Lucille
I Spy with My Little Eye
Illustrated by Joe Kaufman
Published by McGraw-Hill, 1970

Oliver, Jane
Pierre the Muskrat
Illustrated
Published by Walck, 1972

Olsen, Ib Spang
The Boy in the Moon
Translated by Virginia Allen Jensen
Illustrated by Ib Spang Olsen
Published by Parents Magazine Press, 1977

O'Neill, Mary
Hailstones and Halibut Bones
Illustrated by Leonard Weisgard
Published by Doubleday, (n.d.)

Oppenheim, Joanne
Have You Seen Trees?
Illustrated
Published by A-W, 1967
Oppenheim, Joanne
On the Other Side of the River
Illustrated by Aliki
Published by Watts, 1972
Orange, Anne
Flower Book
Illustrated by Sharon Lerner
Published by Lerner, 1975
Orange, Anne
Leaf Book
Illustrated by Sharon Lerner
Published by Lerner, 1975
Orgel, Doris
Merry Merry Fibruary
Illustrated by Arnold Lobel
Published by Parents Magazine Press, 1977
Ormondroyd, Edward
Broderick
Illustrated by John M. Larrecq
Published by Parnassus Press, 1969
Ormondroyd, Edward
Theodore
Illustrated by John M. Larrecq
Published by Parnassus Press, 1969
Ormondroyd, Edward
Theodore's Rival
Illustrated by John M. Larrecq
Published by Parnassus Press, 1971
Otto, Svend
Taxi Dog
Illustrated by Svend Otto
Published by Scholastic, 1979
Ottum, Bob and Joanne Wood
Santa's Beard Is Soft and Warm
Illustrated by Rod Ruth
Published by Western, 1974
Overbeck, Cynthia
Butterfly Book
Illustrated by Sharon Lerner
Published by Lerner, 1976
Overbeck, Cynthia
Curly the Piglet
Translated by Dyan Hammarberg
Illustrated
Published by Carolrhoda, 1976
Overbeck, Cynthia
Fish Book
Illustrated by Sharon Lerner
Published by Lerner, 1976
Overbeck, Cynthia
Fruit Book
Illustrated by Sharon Lerner
Published by Lerner, 1975

Overbeck, Cynthia
Vegetable Book
Illustrated by Sharon Lerner
Published by Lerner, 1975
Overlie, George
The Tallest Tree
Illustrated by George Overlie
Published by Lerner, 1965
Oxenbury, Helen
Helen Oxenbury's ABC of Things
Illustrated by Helen Oxenbury
Published by Watts, 1972
Oxenbury, Helen
Numbers of Things
Illustrated by Helen Oxenbury
Published by Watts, 1968
Oxenbury, Helen
Pig Tale
Illustrated by Helen Oxenbury
Published by Morrow, 1973
Paek, Min
Aekyung's Dream
Illustrated by Min Paek
Published by Children's Book Press, S.F., (n.d.)
Palazzo, Tony
The Biggest and the Littlest Animals
Illustrated by Tony Palazzo
Published by Lion Press, 1973
Palmer, Candida
A Ride on High
Illustrated by Tom H. Hall
Published by Lippincott, 1966
Palmer, Helen M.
A Fish Out of Water
Translated by Carlos Rivera
Illustrated
Published by Random, 1967
Papas, Theodore
Story of Mister Nero
Illustrated
Published by Coward, 1966
Parish, Peggy
Amelia Bedelia
Illustrated by Fritz Siebel
Published by Harper and Row, 1963
Parish, Peggy
Amelia Bedelia and the Suprise Shower
Illustrated by Fritz Siebel
Published by Harper and Row, 1966
Parish, Peggy
Dinosaur Time
Illustrated by Arnold Lobel
Published by Harper and Row, 1974
Parish, Peggy
Little Indian

Illustrated by John E. Johnson
Published by Simon & Schuster, 1968
Parish, Peggy
Ootah's Lucky Day
Illustrated by Mamoru Funai
Published by Harper and Row, 1970
Parish, Peggy
Snapping Turtle's All Wrong Day
Illustrated by John E. Johnson
Published by Simon & Schuster, 1970
Parish, Peggy
Thank You, Amelia Bedelia
Illustrated by Fritz Siebel
Published by Harper and Row, 1964
Parish, Peggy
Too Many Rabbits
Illustrated by Leonard Kessler
Published by Scholastic, 1976
Parker, Nancy W.
Love from Uncle Clyde
Illustrated by Nancy W. Parker
Published by Dodd, Mead, 1977
Parkin, Rex
Red Carpet
Illustrated by Rex Parkin
Published by Macmillan, 1967
Parnall, Peter
The Great Fish
Illustrated by Peter Parnall
Published by Doubleday, 1973
Parry, Marian
King of the Fish
Illustrated by Marian Parry
Published by Macmillan, 1977
Parsons, Ellen
Rainy Day Together
Illustrated by Lillian Hoban
Published by Harper and Row, 1971
Parsons, Virginia
The Horse Book
Translated by Rene Sanchez
Illustrated by Virginia Parsons
Published by Western, 1968
Pasternak, Carol and Allen Sutterfield
Stone Soup
Illustrated by Hedy Campbell
Published by Canadian Women's Educational Press, (n.d.)
Paterson, A.B.
Waltzing Matilda
Illustrated
Published by Holt, Rinehart and Winston, 1972
Paterson, Diane
The Biggest Snowstorm Ever
Illustrated by Diane Paterson
Published by Dial, 1974

Paterson, Diane
Eat!
Illustrated by Diane Paterson
Published by Dial, 1975
Paterson, Diane
Smile for Auntie
Illustrated by Diane Paterson
Published by Dial, 1976
Payne, Emmy
Katy No-Pocket
Illustrated by H.A. Rey
Published by Houghton Mifflin, 1969
Pearson, Susan
Izzie
Illustrated by Robert A. Parker
Published by Dial, 1975
Pearson, Susan
Monnie Hates Lydia
Illustrated by Diane Paterson
Published by Dial, 1975
Pearson, Susan
That's Enough for One Day, J.P.
Illustrated by Kay Chorao
Published by Dial, 1977
Peck, Richard
Monster Night at Grandma's House
Illustrated by Don Freeman
Published by Viking Press, 1977
Peet, Bill
Big Bad Bruce
Illustrated by Bill Peet
Published by Houghton Mifflin, 1977
Peet, Bill
The Caboose Who Got Loose
Illustrated by Bill Peet
Published by Houghton Mifflin, 1971
Peet, Bill
Cowardly Clyde
Illustrated by Bill Peet
Published by Houghton Mifflin, 1979
Peet, Bill
Farewell to Shady Glade
Illustrated by Bill Peet
Published by Houghton Mifflin, 1966
Peet, Bill
Gnats of Knotty Pine
Illustrated by Bill Peet
Published by Houghton Mifflin, 1975
Peet, Bill
Hubert's Hair Raising Adventure
Illustrated
Published by Houghton Mifflin, 1959
Peet, Bill
Huge Harold
Illustrated
Published by Houghton Mifflin, 1961
Peet, Bill
Merle the High Flying Squirrel

Illustrated by Bill Peet
Published by Houghton Mifflin, 1974
Peet, Bill
Chester, the Worldly Pig
Illustrated
Published by Houghton Mifflin, 1965
Peet, Bill
Kermit the Hermit
Illustrated
Published by Houghton Mifflin, 1965
Peet, Bill
Pinkish, Purplish, Bluish Egg
Illustrated by Bill Peet
Published by Houghton Mifflin, 1963
Peet, Bill
Randy's Dandy Lions
Illustrated by Bill Peet
Published by Houghton Mifflin, 1964
Peet, Bill
Smoky
Illustrated by Bill Peet
Published by Houghton Mifflin, 1962
Peet, Bill
The Spooky Tail of Prewitt Peacock
Illustrated by Bill Peet
Published by Houghton Mifflin, 1973
Peet, Bill
Wump World
Illustrated by Bill Peet
Published by Houghton Mifflin, 1970
Penney, Richard L.
Penguins Are Coming
Illustrated by Tom Eaton
Published by Harper and Row, 1969
Peppe, Rodney
Odd One Out
Illustrated
Published by Viking Press, 1974
Peppe, Rodney
Cat and Mouse
Illustrated by Rodney Peppe
Published by Holt, Rinehart and Winston, (n.d.)
Perkins, Al
Ear Book
Illustrated by Bill O'Brian
Published by Random, 1968
Perkins, Al
Hand, Hand, Fingers, Thumb
Illustrated by Eric Gurney
Published by Random, 1969
Perkins, Al
Nose Book
Illustrated by Roy McKie
Published by Random, 1970
Perrault, Charles
Cinderella
Illustrated by Marcia Brown
Published by Scribner, 1954

Perrault, Charles
Little Red Riding Hood
Illustrated by William Stobbs
Published by Walck, 1973
Perrine, Mary
Salt Boy
Illustrated by Leonard Weisgard
Published by Houghton Mifflin, 1973
Perry, Elizabeth
The Waltzing Tiger and Other Animal Verses
Illustrated by Mary C. Young
Published by Exposition Press, 1976
Perry, Patricia and Marietta Lynch
Mommy and Daddy Are Divorced
Illustrated by Marietta Lynch and Patricia Perry
Published by Dial, 1978
Peter, John
What Time Is It?
Illustrated
Published by Grosset & Dunlap, 1968
Petersham, Maud and Miska Petersham
The Box with Red Wheels
Illustrated by Miska Petersham
Published by Macmillan, 1949
Petersham, Maud and Miska Petersham
Circus Baby
Illustrated by Miska Petersham
Published by Macmillan, 1950
Petersham, Maud and Miska Petersham
Rooster Crows
Illustrated by Miska Petersham
Published by Macmillan, 1945
Peterson, Esther Allen
Frederick's Alligator
Illustrated by Susanna Natti
Published by Crown, 1979
Peterson, Hans
Erik and the Christmas Horse
Illustrated by Ilon Wikland
Published by Lothrop, 1970
Peterson, Jeanne
I Have a Sister: My Sister Is Deaf
Illustrated by Deborah Ray
Published by Harper and Row, 1977
Peterson, Jeanne Whitehouse
This Is That
Illustrated by Deborah Ray
Published by Harper and Row, 1979
Peterson, John
The Littles
Illustrated by Roberta C. Clark
Published by Scholastic, 1970

Peterson, John
The Littles' Suprise Party
Illustrated by Roberta C. Clark
Published by Scholastic, 1974
Petie, Haris
Billions of Bugs
Illustrated by Haris Petie
Published by Prentice-Hall, 1975
Petrides, Heidrun
Hans and Peter
Illustrated by Heidrun Petrides
Published by Harcourt Brace Jovanovich, 1963
Phillips, Charles Fox
Red Raspberry Crunch
Illustrated by Charles Fox Phillips
Published by Walck, 1978
Phleger, Frederick
Red Tag Comes Back
Illustrated by Arnold Lobel
Published by Harper and Row, (n.d.)
Piatti, Celestino
Celestino Piatti's Animal ABC
Illustrated by Celestino Piatti
Published by Atheneum, 1966
Piatti, Celestino
Happy Owls
Illustrated by Celestino Piatti
Published by Atheneum, 1964
Pienkowski, Jan
Colors
Illustrated by Jan Pienkowski
Published by Harvey House, 1977
Pienkowski, Jan
Numbers
Illustrated by Jan Pienkowski
Published by Harvey House, 1975
Pienkowski, Jan
Shapes
Illustrated by Jan Pienkowski
Published by Harvey House, 1975
Pienkowski, Jan
Sizes
Illustrated by Jan Pienkowski
Published by Harvey House, 1975
Pincus, Harriet
Minna and Pippin
Illustrated by Harriet Pincus
Published by Farrar, Straus and Giroux, 1972
Pine, Tillie and Joseph Levine
The Incas Knew
Illustrated by Ann Grifalconi
Published by McGraw-Hill, 1968
Pine, Tillie and Joseph Levine
Measurements and How We Use Them
Illustrated by Harriet Sherman
Published by McGraw-Hill, 1974

Pine, Tillie and Joseph Levine
The Polynesians Knew
Illustrated by Marilyn Hirsh
Published by McGraw-Hill, 1974
Pinkwater, Manus
Around Fred's Bed
Illustrated by Robert Mertens
Published by Prentice Hall, 1976
Pinkwater, Manus
Big Orange Splot
Illustrated by Manus Pinkwater
Published by Hastings House, 1977
Pinkwater, Manus
The Blue Thing
Illustrated by Manus Pinkwater
Published by Prentice-Hall, 1977
Pinkwater, Manus
Fat Elliot and the Gorilla
Illustrated by Manus Pinkwater
Published by Scholastic, 1974
Pinkwater, Manus
Terrible Roar
Illustrated by Manus Pinkwater
Published by Knopf, 1970
Pinkwater, Manus
The Three Big Hogs
Illustrated by Manus Pinkwater
Published by Seabury, 1975
Pinkwater, Manus
Wuggie Norple Story
Illustrated by Tomie DePaola
Published by Scholastic, 1980
Piper, Watty
The Little Engine That Could
Illustrated
Published by Platt & Munk, 1954
Pitt, Valerie
Let's Find Out About Streets
Illustrated by Sheila Granda
Published by Watts, 1969
Plath, Sylvia
Bed Book
Illustrated by Emily A. McCully
Published by Harper and Row, 1976
Politi, Leo
Butterflies Come
Illustrated by Leo Politi
Published by Scribner, 1957
Politi, Leo
Emmet
Illustrated by Leo Politi
Published by Scribner, 1971
Politi, Leo
Lito and the Clown
Illustrated by Leo Politi
Published by Scribner, 1964
Politi, Leo
Little Leo

Illustrated by Leo Politi
Published by Scribner, 1951
Politi, Leo
Moy Moy
Illustrated by Leo Politi
Published by Scribner, 1960
Politi, Leo
The Nicest Gift
Illustrated by Leo Politi
Published by Scribner, 1973
Politi, Leo
Pedro, Angel of Olvera Street
Illustrated by Leo Politi
Published by Scribner, 1946
Politi, Leo
Song of the Swallows
Illustrated by Leo Politi
Published by Scribner, 1949
Polushkin, Maria
Bubba and Babba
Illustrated by Diane De Groat
Published by Crown, 1976
Polushkin, Maria
The Little Hen and the Giant
Illustrated by Yuri Salzman
Published by Harper and Row, 1977
Polushkin, Maria
Who Said Meow?
Illustrated by Giulio Maestro
Published by Crown, 1975
Pomerantz, Charlotte
Ballad of the Long-Tailed Rat
Illustrated by Marian Parry
Published by Macmillan, 1975
Pomerantz, Charlotte
The Piggy in the Puddle
Illustrated by James Marshall
Published by Macmillan, 1974
Pope, Billy
Let's Build a House
Illustrated
Published by Taylor, 1975
Pope, Billy
Let's Go to the Supermarket
Illustrated by Billy Pope
Published by Taylor, 1975
Pope, Billy
Let's Visit a Rubber Company
Illustrated
Published by Taylor, 1971
Pope, Billy
Let's Visit a Silver Company
Illustrated
Published by Taylor, 1971
Pope, Billy
Let's Visit the Newspaper
Illustrated
Published by Taylor, 1975

Pope, Billy
Let's Visit the Railroad
Illustrated
Published by Taylor, 1971
Postma, Lidia
The Stolen Mirror
Illustrated by Lidia Postma
Published by McGraw-Hill, 1976
Poston, Elizabeth
Baby's Song Book
Illustrated by William Stobbs
Published by T.Y. Crowell, 1972
Potter, Beatrix
The Sly Old Cat
Illustrated by Beatrix Potter
Published by Warne, 1972
Potter, Beatrix
Tailor of Gloucester
Illustrated by Beatrix Potter
Published by Warne, 1968
Potter, Beatrix
Tale of Johnny Townmouse
Illustrated by Beatrix Potter
Published by Warne, 1918
Potter, Beatrix
Tale of Mrs. Tiggy Winkle
Illustrated by Beatrix Potter
Published by Warne, 1905
Potter, Beatrix
Tale of Mrs. Tittlemouse
Illustrated by Beatrix Potter
Published by Warne, 1910
Potter, Beatrix
Tale of Peter Rabbit
Illustrated by Beatrix Potter
Published by Warne, 1903
Potter, Beatrix
Tale of Timmy Tiptoes
Illustrated by Beatrix Potter
Published by Warne, 1911
Potter, Beatrix
Tale of Tuppenny
Illustrated by Marie Angel
Published by Warne, 1973
Potter, Beatrix
Tale of Two Bad Mice
Illustrated by Beatrix Potter
Published by Warne, 1904
Potter, Marian
Little Red Caboose
Illustrated by Tibor Gergely
Published by Western, 1953
Powell, Ann
Strange Street
Illustrated by Ann Powell
Published by Kids Can Press (Canada), 1975

Powell, Meredith and Gail Yokubinas
What to Be?
Illustrated by Richard Mlodock
Published by Children's Press, 1972

Prather, Ray
New Neighbors
Illustrated
Published by McGraw-Hill, 1974

Prather, Ray
No Trespassing
Illustrated by Ray Prather
Published by Macmillan, 1974

Pratt, Ellen
Amy and the Cloud Basket
Illustrated by Lisa Russell
Published by Lollipop Power, 1975

Prelutsky, Jack
Terrible Tiger
Illustrated by Arnold Lobel
Published by Macmillan, 1970

Preston, Edna Mitchell
One Dark Night
Illustrated by Kurt Werth
Published by Viking Press, 1969

Preston, Edna Mitchell
Popcorn and Ma Goodness
Illustrated by Robert A. Parker
Published by Viking Press, 1969

Preston, Edna Mitchell
Temper Tantrum Book
Illustrated by Rainey Bennett
Published by Viking Press, 1969

Preston, Edna Mitchell and Barbara Cooney
Squawk to the Moon, Little Goose
Illustrated by Barbara Cooney
Published by Penguin, 1976

Price, Roger
Last Little Dragon
Illustrated by Mamoru Funai
Published by Harper and Row, 1969

Prieto, Mariana
When the Monkeys Wore Sombreros
Illustrated by Robert Quackenbush
Published by Harvey House, 1969

Pringle, Laurence
Water Plants
Illustrated by Kazue Mizumura
Published by T.Y. Crowell, 1975

Provensen, Alice and Martin Provensen
A Book of Seasons
Illustrated by Alice & Martin Provensen
Published by Random, 1975

Provensen, Alice and Martin Provensen
My Little Hen
Illustrated by Alice & Martin Provensen
Published by Random, 1973

Provensen, Alice and Martin Provensen
Our Animals Friends at Maple Hill Farm
Illustrated
Published by Random, 1974

Pursell, Margaret Sanford
Polly, the Guinea Pig
Illustrated
Published by Carolrhoda, 1977

Quackenbush, Robert
Along Came the Model T
Illustrated by Robert Quackenbush
Published by Scholastic, 1980

Quackenbush, Robert
Clementine
Illustrated by Robert Quackenbush
Published by Lippincott, 1974

Quackenbush, Robert
Go Tell Aunt Rhody
Illustrated by Aliki
Published by Macmillan, 1974

Quackenbush, Robert
The Most Welcome Visitor
Illustrated by Robert Quackenbush
Published by Dutton, 1979

Quackenbush, Robert
Old MacDonald Had a Farm
Illustrated
Published by Lippincott, 1972

Quackenbush, Robert
Pop! Goes the Weasel...N.Y. in 1776 and Today
Illustrated by Robert Quackenbush
Published by Lippincott, 1976

Quigley, Lillian
Blind Men and the Elephant
Illustrated by Janice Holland
Published by Scribner, 1959

Rabinowitz, Sandy
The Red Horse and the Bluebird
Illustrated by Sandy Rabinowitz
Published by Harper and Row, 1975

Rabinowitz, Sandy
What's Happening to Daisy?
Illustrated
Published by Harper and Row, 1977

Radford, Ruby
Mary McLeod Bethune
Illustrated by Lydia Rosier
Published by Putnam, 1973

Rand, Ann and A. Birnbaum
Did a Bear Just Walk There?
Illustrated by A. Birnbaum

Published by Harcourt Brace
  Jovanovich, 1966
Rand, Ann and Paul Rand
  Listen! Listen!
  Illustrated by Paul Rand
  Published by Harcourt Brace
  Jovanovich, 1970
Rand, Ann and Paul Rand
  I Know a Lot of Things
  Illustrated by Paul Rand
  Published by Harcourt Brace
  Jovanovich, 1956
Randall, Blossom E.
  Fun for Chris
  Illustrated by Eunice Smith
  Published by A. Whitman, 1956
Ransome, Arthur
  Fool of the World and the Flying Ship
  Illustrated by Uri Shulevitz
  Published by Farrar, Straus and Giroux, 1968
Raskin, Ellen
  And It Rained
  Illustrated by Ellen Raskin
  Published by Atheneum, 1969
Raskin, Ellen
  Franklin Stein
  Illustrated by Ellen Raskin
  Published by Atheneum, 1972
Raskin, Ellen
  Ghost in a Four Room Apartment
  Illustrated by Ellen Raskin
  Published by Atheneum, 1969
Raskin, Ellen
  Moose, Goose and Little Nobody
  Illustrated
  Published by Parents Magazine Press, 1974
Raskin, Ellen
  Nothing Ever Happens on My Block
  Illustrated by Ellen Raskin
  Published by Atheneum, 1966
Raskin, Ellen
  Spectacles
  Illustrated by Ellen Raskin
  Published by Atheneum, 1969
Raskin, Ellen
  Twenty-Two, Twenty-Three
  Illustrated
  Published by Atheneum, 1976
Raskin, Ellen
  Who, Said Sue, Said Whoo?
  Illustrated by Ellen Raskin
  Published by Atheneum, 1973
Rayner, Mary
  Garth Pig and the Ice Cream Lady
  Illustrated
  Published by Atheneum, 1977

Raynor, Dorka
  This Is My Father and Me
  Illustrated by Dorka Raynor
  Published by A. Whitman, 1973
Razzi, James
  Don't Open This Box
  Illustrated by James Razzi
  Published by Parents Magazine Press, 1973
Reavin, Sam
  Hurray for Captain Jane
  Illustrated by Emily A. McCully
  Published by Parents Magazine Press, 1971
Reesink, Maryke and Georgette Apol
  Two Windmills
  Illustrated by Georgette Apol
  Published by Harcourt Brace Jovanovich, 1967
Reich, Hanns, Ed.
  Laughing Camera for Children
  Illustrated
  Published by Hill & Wang, 1971
Reiss, John J.
  Colors
  Illustrated by John J. Reiss
  Published by Bradbury Press, 1969
Reiss, John J.
  Numbers
  Illustrated by John J. Reiss
  Published by Bradbury Press, 1971
Reiss, John J.
  Shapes
  Illustrated
  Published by Bradbury Press, 1974
Ressner, Phil
  August Explains
  Illustrated by Crosby Bonsall
  Published by Harper and Row, 1963
Ressner, Philip
  Dudley Pippin
  Illustrated by Arnold Lobel
  Published by Harper and Row, 1963
Reuter, Margaret
  My Mother Is Blind
  Illustrated
  Published by Children's Press, 1979
Rey, H.A.
  Anybody at Home?
  Illustrated
  Published by Houghton Mifflin, (n.d.)
Rey, H.A.
  Feed the Animals
  Illustrated
  Published by Houghton Mifflin, (n.d.)
Rey, H.A.
  Cecily G. and Nine Monkeys
  Illustrated by H.A. Rey
  Published by Houghton Mifflin, 1977

Rey, H.A.
Curious George
Illustrated by H.A. Rey
Published by Houghton Mifflin, 1941

Rey, H.A.
See the Circus
Illustrated by H.A. Rey
Published by Houghton Mifflin, 1956

Rey, H.A.
Where's My Baby?
Illustrated
Published by Houghton Mifflin, 1956

Rey, Margaret and H.A. Rey
Billy's Picture
Illustrated by H.A. Rey
Published by Harper and Row, 1948

Rey, Margaret and H.A. Rey
Pretzel
Illustrated by H.A. Rey
Published by Harper and Row, 1944

Rey, Margaret and H.A. Rey
Spotty
Illustrated by H.A. Rey
Published by Harper and Row, 1945

Reyther, Becky
My Mother Is the Most Beautiful Woman in the World
Illustrated by Ruth Gannett
Published by Lothrop, 1945

Ricciuti, Edward
Animal for Alan
Illustrated by Tom Eaton
Published by Harper and Row, 1970

Ricciuti, Edward
Catch a Whale by the Tail
Illustrated by Geoffrey Moss
Published by Harper and Row, 1969

Rice, Eve
New Blue Shoes
Illustrated by Eve Rice
Published by Macmillan, 1975

Rice, Eve
Oh Lewis!
Illustrated by Eve Rice
Published by Macmillan, 1974

Rice, Eve
Sam Who Never Forgets
Illustrated
Published by Greenwillow, 1977

Rice, Eve
What Sadie Sang
Illustrated
Published by Greenwillow, 1976

Rice, James
Cajun Alphabet
Illustrated by James Rice
Published by Pelican, 1976

Rice, James
Gaston Goes to Mardi Gras
Illustrated by James Rice
Published by Pelican, 1979

Rice, James
Gaston Goes to Texas
Illustrated by James Rice
Published by Pelican, 1979

Rice, James
Gaston, the Green-Nosed Alligator
Illustrated by James Rice
Published by Pelican, 1974

Rich, Gibson
Firegirl
Illustrated by Charlotte P. Farley
Published by Feminist Press, 1972

Ridiman, Bob
What Is a Shadow?
Illustrated by Bob Ridiman
Published by Parents Magazine Press, 1973

Ridout, Ronald and Michael Holt
The Life Cycle Book of Frogs
Illustrated
Published by Grosset & Dunlap, 1974

Ringi, Kjell
The Sun and the Cloud
Illustrated
Published by Harper and Row, 1971

Rimanelli, Giose and Paul Pinsleur
Poems Make Pictures; Pictures Make Poems
Illustrated by Ronni Solbert
Published by Pantheon, 1972

Rinkoff, Barbara
Guess What Rocks Do
Illustrated by Leslie Morrill
Published by Lothrop, 1975

Rinkoff, Barbara
Guess What Trees Do
Illustrated by Beatrice Darwin
Published by Lothrop, 1974

Rinkoff, Barbara
No Pushing-No Ducking: Safety in the Water
Illustrated by Roy Doty
Published by Lothrop, 1974

Risom, Ole
I Am a Kitten
Illustrated by Jan Pfloog
Published by Western, 1970

Roa, Annia
Peter Pelican
Illustrated by William Henry
Published by Island Press, 1974

Roach, Marilynne
The Mouse and the Song
Illustrated by Joseph Low
Published by Parents Magazine Press, 1974

Robbins, Ruth
Babushka and the Three Kings
Illustrated by Nicholas Sidjakov
Published by Parnassus Press, 1960

Roberts, Elizabeth
Jumping Jackdaws! Here Comes Simon
Illustrated by Prudence Seward
Published by Rand McNally, 1975

Roberts, Thom
Pirates in the Dark
Illustrated by Harold Berson
Published by Crown, 1973

Robinson, Adjai
Femi and Old Grandaddie
Illustrated by Jerry Pinkney
Published by Coward, 1972

Robles, Al
Looking for Ifugao Mountain
Illustrated by Jim Dong
Published by Children's Book Press, S.F., (n.d.)

Roche, A.K.
Clever Turtle
Illustrated by A.K. Roche
Published by Prentice-Hall, 1969

Roche, A.K.
Onion Maidens
Illustrated by A.K. Roche
Published by Prentice-Hall, 1968

Roche, A.K.
Pumpkin Heads
Illustrated by A.K. Roche
Published by Prentice-Hall, 1968

Rockwell, Anne
The Awful Mess
Illustrated by Anne Rockwell
Published by Parents Magazine Press, 1973

Rockwell, Anne
Buster and the Bogeyman
Illustrated by Anne Rockwell
Published by Scholastic, 1978

Rockwell, Anne
Dancing Stars: An Iroquois Legend
Illustrated
Published by T.Y. Crowell, 1972

Rockwell, Anne
Gollywhopper Egg
Illustrated
Published by Macmillan, 1974

Rockwell, Anne
Machines
Illustrated by Harlow Rockwell
Published by Macmillan, 1972

Rockwell, Anne
Monkey's Whiskers: A Brazilian Folktale
Illustrated by Anne Rockwell
Published by Parents Magazine Press, 1971

Rockwell, Anne
Poor Goose
Illustrated
Published by T.Y. Crowell, 1976

Rockwell, Anne
Tool Box
Illustrated by Harlow Rockwell
Published by Macmillan, 1974

Rockwell, Anne
When the Drum Sang
Illustrated by Anne Rockwell
Published by Parents Magazine Press, 1970

Rockwell, Anne
The Wolf Who Had a Wonderful Dream: A French Folktale
Illustrated
Published by T.Y. Crowell, 1973

Rockwell, Anne and Harlow Rockwell
Head to Toe
Illustrated
Published by Doubleday, 1973

Rockwell, Anne and Harlow Rockwell
Toad
Illustrated
Published by Doubleday, 1972

Rockwell, Anne and Harlow Rockwell
Thruway
Illustrated by Anne and Harlow Rockwell
Published by Macmillan, 1972

Rockwell, Harlow
My Dentist
Illustrated by Harlow Rockwell
Published by Greenwillow, 1975

Rockwell, Harlow
My Doctor
Illustrated by Harlow Rockwell
Published by Macmillan, 1973

Rockwell, Harlow
My Nursery School
Illustrated
Published by Greenwillow, 1976

Rockwell, Thomas
How to Eat Fried Worms
Illustrated by Emily A. McCully
Published by Watts, 1973

Rockwood, Joyce
To Spoil the Sun
Illustrated
Published by Holt, Rinehart and Winston, 1976

Rogers, Helen Spelman
Morris and His Brave Lion
Illustrated by Glo Coalson
Published by McGraw-Hill, 1975

Rogers, Pamela
David and His Grandfather
Illustrated by Janet Duchesne
Published by Penguin, 1975

Rohmer, Harriet
The Headless Pirate: Costa Rica
Illustrated by Ray Rios
Adapted by Harriet Rohmer
Published by Children's Book Press, S.F., (n.d.)

Rohmer, Harriet
How We Came to the Fifth World: Aztec Myth
Illustrated by Graciela Carrillo De Lopez
Adapted by Harriet Rohmer and Mary Anchondo
Published by Children's Book Press, S.F., (n.d.)

Rohmer, Harriet
The Little Horse of Seven Colors: Folktale of Nicaragua
Illustrated by Roger I. Reyes
Adapted by Harriet Rohmer and Mary Anchondo
Published by Children's Book Press, S.F., (n.d.)

Rohmer, Harriet
The Magic Boys: Guatemala
Illustrated by Patricia Rodriguez
Adapted by Harriet Rohmer and Mary Anchondo
Published by Children's Book Press, S.F., (n.d.)

Rohmer, Harriet
The Mighty God Viracocha: Myth From Peru and Bolivia
Illustrated by Richard Montez and Mike Rios
Adapted by Harriet Rohmer and Mary Anchondo
Published by Children's Book Press, S.F., (n.d.)

Rohmer, Harriet
Skyworld Woman: Philippines
Illustrated by Roger I. Reyes
Adapted by Harriet Rohmer and Mary Anchondo
Published by Children's Book Press, S.F., (n.d.)

Rohmer, Harriet
Atariba and Niguayona: Puerto Rico
Illustrated by Consuelo Mendez Castillo
Adapted by Harriet Rohmer and Mary Anchondo
Published by Children's Book Press, S.F., (n.d.)

Rohmer, Harriet
Cuna Song: Panama
Illustrated by Irene Perez
Adapted by Harriet Rohmer and Jesus Guerrero Rea
Published by Children's Book Press, S.F., (n.d.)

Rohmer, Harriet
Land of Icy Death: Chile
Illustrated by Xavier Viramontes
Adapted by Harriet Rohmer and Jesus Guerrero Rea
Published by Children's Book Press, S.F., (n.d.)

Rohmer, Harriet
The Treasure of Guatavita: Colombia
Illustrated by Carlos Loarca
Adapted by Harriet Rohmer & Jesus Guerrero Rea
Published by Children's Book Press, S.F., (n.d.)

Rojankovsky, Feodor
Animals in the Zoo
Illustrated by Feodor Rojankovsky
Published by Knopf, 1962

Rojankovsky, Feodor
Animals on the Farm
Illustrated by Feodor Rojankovsky
Published by Knopf, 1967

Rojankovsky, Feodor
The Great Big Wild Animal Book
Illustrated by Feodor Rojankovsky
Published by Western, 1976

Rojankovsky, Feodor
Tall Book of Mother Goose
Illustrated by Feodor Rojankovsky
Published by Harper and Row, 1942

Rojankovsky, Feodor
The Tall Book of Nursery Tales
Illustrated by Feodor Rojankovsky
Published by Harper and Row, 1944

Rose, Anne-Retold by
Akimba and the Magic Cow
Illustrated by Hope Merryman
Published by Scholastic, 1979

Rose, Anne
How Does a Czar Eat Potatoes?
Illustrated by Janosch
Published by Lothrop, 1973

Rose, Gerald
The Tiger-Skin Rug
Illustrated by Gerald Rose
Published by Prentice-Hall, 1979

Rose, Joseph
Inchy, Pinchy & Winchy & Seth & Littlefish
Illustrated
Published by Exposition, 1977

Rosen, Winifred
Marvin's Manhole
Illustrated by Rosemary Wells
Published by Dial, 1970

Rosenbaum, Eileen
Ronnie
Illustrated
Published by Parents Magazine Press, 1969

Rosenfeld, Sam
Drop of Water
Illustrated by Helen Basilevsky
Published by Harvey House, 1970

Roser, Wiltrud
Everything About Easter Rabbits
Translated by Eva L. Mayer
Illustrated by Wiltrud Roser
Published by T.Y. Crowell, 1973

Ross
Easy Book of Grand Prix Racing
Illustrated
Published by Harvey House, 1975

Rossetti, Christina
What Is Pink?
Illustrated by Jose Aruego
Published by Macmillan, 1971

Rothman, Joel
I Can Be Anything You Can Be
Illustrated by Susan Perl
Published by Scroll Press, 1973

Rothman, Joel
Night Lights
Illustrated by Joe Lasker
Published by A. Whitman, 1972

Roughsey, Dick
Giant Devil-Dingo
Illustrated by Dick Roughsey
Published by Macmillan, 1975

Rounds, Glen
Once We Had a Horse
Illustrated
Published by Holiday House, 1971

Rowand, Phyllis
It Is Night
Illustrated
Published by Harper and Row, 1953

Rowland, Florence W.
Little Sponge Fisherman
Illustrated
Published by Putnam, 1969

Roy, Ron
Old Tiger, New Tiger
Illustrated by Pat Bargielski
Published by Abingdon, 1979

Rozek, Evalyn
Tinker's Rescue
Illustrated by Holly Daley
Published by Carolrhoda, 1975

Ruben, Patricia
Apples to Zippers: An Alphabet Book
Illustrated
Published by Doubleday, 1976

Rubin, Caroline, Ed.
Grandparents Around the World
Illustrated by Dorka Raynor
Published by A. Whitman, 1977

Ruffins, Reynold
My Brother Never Feeds the Cat
Illustrated by Reynold Ruffins
Published by Scribner, 1979

Rush, Sara
Hucket-A-Bucket Down the Street
Illustrated by Harold K. Lamson
Published by Lerner, 1965

Russ, Lavinia
Alec's Sand Castle
Illustrated by James Stevenson
Published by Harper and Row, 1972

Russell, Solveig P.
The Crusty Ones: A First Look at Crustaceans
Illustrated by Lawrence DiFiori
Published by Walck, 1974

Russell, Solveig P.
Lines and Shapes
Illustrated by Arnold Spilka
Published by Walck, 1965

Russell, Solveig P.
Motherly Smith and Brother Bimbo
Illustrated by Susan Perl
Published by Abingdon, 1971

Russell, Solveig P.
Size, Distance, Weight: A First Look at Measuring
Illustrated by Margot Tomes
Published by Walck, 1968

Russell, Solveig P.
What Good Is a Tail?
Illustrated
Published by Bobbs-Merrill, 1962

Russell, Solveig P.
What's the Time, Starling?...Nature's Clocks
Illustrated by Lynne Cherry
Published by Walck, 1977

Ryan, Cheli D.
Hildilid's Night
Illustrated by Arnold Lobel
Published by Macmillan, 1971

Ryder, Joanne
Fog in the Meadow

Illustrated by Gail Owens
Published by Harper and Row, 1979
Ryder, Joanne
  A Wet and Sandy Day
  Illustrated by Donald Carrick
  Published by Harper and Row, 1977
St. George, Judith
  By George, Bloomers!
  Illustrated by Margot Tomes
  Published by Coward, 1976
Sakade, Florence, Ed.
  Japanese Children's Favorite Stories
  Illustrated by Yoshio Kurosaki
  Published by Chas. Tuttle, 1958
Salten, Felix
  Bambi
  Illustrated
  Published by Grosset & Dunlap, 1969
Samuel, Yoshiko Y.
  Twelve Years, Twelve Animals
  Illustrated by Margo Locke
  Published by Abingdon, 1972
Sandberg, Inger
  Come on Out, Daddy
  Illustrated by Lasse Sandberg
  Published by Delacorte, 1971
Sandberg, Inger
  Let's Play Desert
  Illustrated by Lasse Sandberg
  Published by Delacorte, 1974
Sandburg, Carl
  Wedding Procession of the Rag Doll...Broom Handle
  Illustrated by Harriet Pincus
  Published by Harcourt Brace Jovanovich, 1950
Sarah, Becky
  Fanshen, the Magic Bear
  Illustrated by Dana Smith
  Published by New Seed Press, (n.d.)
Sasaki, Tazu
  The Golden Thread: Japanese Stories for Children
  Translated by Fanny Mayer
  Illustrated by Tazu Sasaki
  Published by C.E. Tuttle, (n.d.)
Sattler, Helen R.
  Train Whistles: A Language in Code
  Illustrated
  Published by Lothrop, 1977
Sauer, Julia L.
  Mike's House
  Illustrated by Don Freeman
  Published by Viking Press, 1954
Saul, Wendy
  Butcher, Baker, Cabinet Maker: Women at Work

Illustrated by Abigail Heyman
Published by T.Y. Crowell, 1978
Sauro, Regina
  The Too-Long Trunk
  Illustrated by Haris Petie
  Published by Lantern Press, 1964
Savelli-Bollinger, Antonella
  The Knitted Cat
  Illustrated
  Published by Macmillan, 1972
Savelli-Bollinger, Antonella
  Mouse and the Knitted Cat
  Illustrated
  Adapted by Elizabeth Shub
  Published by Macmillan, 1974
Sawyer, Ruth
  Journey Cake, Ho
  Illustrated by Robert McCloskey
  Published by Viking Press, 1953
Say, Allen
  Feast of Lanterns
  Illustrated by Allen Say
  Published by Harper and Row, 1976
Scapa
  The Magic Pencil
  Illustrated by Scapa
  Published by Scribner, 1977
Scarry, Richard
  Richard Scarry's ABC Word Book
  Illustrated by Richard Scarry
  Published by Random, 1971
Scarry, Richard
  Richard Scarry's Best Counting Book Ever
  Illustrated by Richard Scarry
  Published by Random, 1975
Scarry, Richard
  Richard Scarry's Best Word Book Ever
  Illustrated by Richard Scarry
  Published by Western, 1963
Scarry, Richard
  Richard Scarry's Busiest People Ever
  Illustrated by Richard Scarry
  Published by Random, 1976
Scarry, Richard
  Richard Scarry's Hop Aboard, Here We Go
  Illustrated by Richard Scarry
  Published by Western, 1972
Schaleben-Lewis, Joy
  The Dentist and Me
  Illustrated by Murray Weiss
  Published by Raintree, 1977
Schaeppi, Mary
  Tale of the Magic Bread
  Illustrated by Gisela Werner
  Published by Scroll Press, 1970

Scheer, Julian
 Rain Makes Applesauce
 Illustrated by Marvin Bileck
 Published by Holiday House, 1964
Scheer, Julian
 Upside Down Day
 Illustrated by Kelly Oechsli
 Published by Holiday House, 1968
Schertle, Alice
 The Gorilla in the Hall
 Illustrated by Paul Galdone
 Published by Lothrop, 1977
Schick, Eleanor
 City Green
 Illustrated by Eleanor Schick
 Published by Macmillan, 1974
Schick, Eleanor
 City in the Summer
 Illustrated by Eleanor Schick
 Published by Macmillan, 1969
Schick, Eleanor
 City in the Winter
 Illustrated by Eleanor Schick
 Published by Macmillan, 1970
Schick, Eleanor
 I'm Going to the Ocean
 Illustrated by Eleanor Schick
 Published by Macmillan, 1966
Schick, Eleanor
 Jeanie Goes Riding
 Illustrated by Eleanor Schick
 Published by Macmillan, 1968
Schick, Eleanor
 Making Friends
 Illustrated by Eleanor Schick
 Published by Macmillan, 1969
Schick, Eleanor
 Peggy's New Brother
 Illustrated by Eleanor Schick
 Published by Macmillan, 1970
Schick, Eleanor
 Peter and Mr. Brandon
 Illustrated by Donald Carrick
 Published by Macmillan, 1973
Schlein, Miriam
 The Girl Who Would Rather Climb Trees
 Illustrated by Judith Gwyn Brown
 Published by Harcourt Brace Jovanovich, 1975
Schlein, Miriam
 Heavy Is a Hippopotamus
 Illustrated
 Published by A-W, 1954
Schlein, Miriam
 How Do You Travel?
 Illustrated by Paul Galdone
 Published by Abingdon, 1954

Schlein, Miriam
 My House
 Illustrated by Joe Lasker
 Published by A-W, 1971
Schlein, Miriam
 The Rabbit's World
 Illustrated by Peter Parnall
 Published by Scholastic, 1973
Schlein, Miriam
 Shapes
 Illustrated
 Published by A-W, 1952
Schlein, Miriam
 What's Wrong with Being a Skunk?
 Illustrated by Ray Cruz
 Published by Scholastic, 1974
Schneider, Gerlinde
 Uncle Harry
 Illustrated
 Published by Macmillan, 1972
Schroder, William
 Pea Soup and Sea Serpents
 Illustrated by William Schroder
 Published by Lothrop, 1977
Schuchman, Joan
 Two Places to Sleep
 Illustrated by Jim Lamarche
 Published by Carolrhoda, 1979
Schwartz, Charles and Elizabeth Schwartz
 Cottontail Rabbit
 Illustrated by Charles Schwartz
 Published by Holiday House, 1957
Schwartz, Charles and Elizabeth Schwartz
 When Water Animals Are Babies
 Illustrated by Charles Schwartz
 Published by Holiday House, 1970
Schweitzer, Byrd B.
 Amigo
 Illustrated by Garth Williams
 Published by Macmillan, 1963
Schweitzer, Byrd
 One Small Blue Bead
 Illustrated by Symeon Shimin
 Published by Macmillan, 1965
Schweninger, Ann
 A Dance for Three
 Illustrated by Ann Schweninger
 Published by Dial, 1979
Schweninger, Ann
 The Hunt for Rabbit's Galosh
 Illustrated by Kay Chorao
 Published by Doubleday, 1976
Schweninger, Ann, Ed.
 The Man in the Moon as He Sails the Sky
 Illustrated by Ann Schweninger
 Published by Dodd, Mead, 1979

Scott, Ann Herbert
Big Cowboy Western
Illustrated by Richard W. Lewis
Published by Lothrop, 1956
Scott, Ann Herbert
On Mother's Lap
Illustrated by Glo Coalson
Published by McGraw-Hill, 1972
Scott, N.H.
Sam
Illustrated by Symeon Shimon
Published by McGraw-Hill, 1967
Sears, Paul McCutcheon
Downy Woodpecker
Illustrated by Barbara Latham
Published by Holiday House, 1953
Seeger, Pete and Charles Seeger
The Foolish Frog
Illustrated
Published by Macmillan, 1973
Segal, Lore
All the Way Home
Illustrated by James Marshall
Published by Farrar, Straus and Giroux, 1973
Segal, Lore
Tell Me a Mitzi
Illustrated by Harriet Pincus
Published by Farrar, Straus and Giroux, 1970
Segal, Lore
Tell Me a Trudy
Illustrated by Rosemary Wells
Published by Farrar, Straus and Giroux, 1977
Seidler, Rosalie
Panda Cake
Illustrated by Rosalie Seidler
Published by Scholastic, 1979
Selden, George
Sparrow Socks
Illustrated by Peter Lippman
Published by Harper and Row, 1965
Selsam, Millicent E.
All Kinds of Babies
Illustrated by Symeon Shimin
Published by Scholastic, 1969
Selsam, Millicent E.
Animals of the Sea
Illustrated by John Hamberger
Published by Scholastic, 1976
Selsam, Millicent E.
Benny's Animals and How He Put Them in Order
Illustrated by Arnold Lobel
Published by Harper and Row, 1966
Selsam, Millicent E.
Egg to Chick
Illustrated by Barbara Wolff
Published by Harper and Row, 1970
Selsam, Millicent E.
How Animals Sleep
Illustrated
Published by Scholastic, 1969
Selsam, Millicent E.
How Puppies Grow
Illustrated by Esther Bubley
Published by Scholastic, 1972
Selsam, Millicent E.
Is This a Baby Dinosaur?...Science Picture Puzzles
Illustrated
Published by Harper and Row, 1972
Selsam, Millicent E.
Let's Get Turtles
Illustrated by Arnold Lobel
Published by Harper and Row, 1965
Selsam, Millicent E.
More Potatoes!
Illustrated by Ben Shecter
Published by Harper and Row, 1972
Selsam, Millicent E.
Popcorn
Illustrated by Jerome Wexler
Published by Morrow, 1976
Selsam, Millicent E.
Seeds and More Seeds
Illustrated by Tomi Ungerer
Published by Harper and Row, 1959
Selsam, Millicent E.
Terry and the Caterpillars
Illustrated
Published by Harper and Row, 1969
Selsam, Millicent E.
When an Animal Grows
Illustrated by John Kaufman
Published by Harper and Row, 1966
Selsam, Millicent E. and Joyce Hunt
A First Look at Mammals
Illustrated by Harriet Springer
Published by Scholastic, 1976
Selsam, Millicent E. and Joyce Hunt
A First Look at Snakes, Lizards and Other Reptiles
Illustrated by Harriet Springer
Published by Scholastic, 1976
Sendak, Maurice
Alligators All Around
Illustrated by Maurice Sendak
Published by Harper and Row, 1962
Sendak, Maurice
Chicken Soup with Rice: A Book of Months
Illustrated by Maurice Sendak
Published by Harper and Row, 1962
Sendak, Maurice
One Was Johnny

Illustrated by Maurice Sendak
Published by Harper and Row, 1962
Sendak, Maurice
Pierre
Illustrated by Maurice Sendak
Published by Harper and Row, 1962
Sendak, Maurice
Sign on Rosie's Door
Illustrated by Maurice Sendak
Published by Harper and Row, 1960
Sendak, Maurice
Very Far Away
Illustrated by Maurice Sendak
Published by Harper and Row, 1957
Sendak, Maurice
Where the Wild Things Are
Illustrated by Maurice Sendak
Published by Harper and Row, 1963
Sendak, Maurice and Matthew Margolis
Some Swell Pup
Illustrated by Maurice Sendak
Published by Farrar, Straus and Giroux, 1976
Serfozo, Mary
Welcome, Roberto!
Illustrated
Published by Follett, 1969
Serraillier, Ian
Suppose You Met a Witch
Illustrated by Ed Emberley
Published by Little, Brown, 1973
Seuling, Barbara
The Great Big Elephant and the Very Small Elephant
Illustrated by Barbara Seuling
Published by Crown, 1977
Seuling, Barbara
Teeny Tiny Woman: An Old English Ghost Tale
Illustrated by Barbara Seuling
Published by Viking Press, 1976
Seuss, Dr.
And to Think That I Saw It on Mulberry Street
Illustrated by Dr. Seuss
Published by Vanguard Press, 1937
Seuss, Dr.
Bartholomew and the Oobleck
Illustrated by Dr. Seuss
Published by Random, 1949
Seuss, Dr.
The Cat in the Hat
Illustrated by Dr. Seuss
Published by Random, 1957
Seuss, Dr.
Five Hundred Hats of Bartholomew Cubbins
Illustrated by Dr. Seuss
Published by Hale, 1938
Seuss, Dr.
Green Eggs and Ham
Illustrated by Dr. Seuss
Published by Random, 1960
Seuss, Dr.
Horton Hears a Who
Illustrated by Dr. Seuss
Published by Random, 1954
Seuss, Dr.
Lorax
Illustrated by Dr. Seuss
Published by Random, 1971
Seuss, Dr.
Thidwick, The Big-Hearted Moose
Illustrated by Dr. Seuss
Published by Random, 1948
Sewall, Marcia
The Wee, Wee Mannie and the Big, Big Coo
Illustrated by Marcia Sewall
Published by Little, Brown, 1977
Shanks, Ann Z.
About Garbage and Stuff
Illustrated by Ann Z. Shanks
Published by Viking Press, 1973
Shapp, Charles and Martha Shapp
Let's Find Out About Snakes
Illustrated by Rene Martin
Published by Watts, 1968
Shapp, Charles and Martha Shapp
Let's Find Out About the Moon
Illustrated by Yukio Tashiro
Published by Watts, 1975
Shapp, Charles and Martha Shapp
Let's Find Out About the Sun
Illustrated by Stephanie Later
Published by Watts, 1975
Shapp, Charles and Martha Shapp
Let's Find Out About Trees: Arbor Day
Illustrated by Allan Eitzen
Published by Watts, 1970
Shapp, Charles and Martha Shapp
Let's Find Out About Water
Illustrated by Carol Nicklaus
Published by Watts, 1975
Shapp, Charles and Martha Shapp
Let's Find Out About What Electricity Does
Illustrated by Leonard Shortall
Published by Watts, 1975
Sharmat, Majorie W.
Burton and Dudley
Illustrated by Barbara Cooney
Published by Holiday House, 1975

Sharmat, Marjorie W.
Edgemont
Illustrated by Cyndy Szekeres
Published by Coward, 1976

Sharmat, Marjorie W.
Gladys Told Me to Meet Her Here
Illustrated by Edward Frascino
Published by Harper and Row, 1970

Sharmat, Marjorie W.
Goodnight, Andrew; Goodnight, Craig
Illustrated by Mary Chalmers
Published by Harper and Row, 1969

Sharmat, Marjorie W.
I Don't Care
Illustrated by Lillian Hoban
Published by Macmillan, 1977

Sharmat, Marjorie W.
I Want Mama
Illustrated by Emily A. McCully
Published by Harper and Row, 1974

Sharmat, Marjorie W.
I'm Not Oscar's Friend Anymore
Illustrated
Published by Dutton, 1975

Sharmat, Marjorie W.
I'm Terrific
Illustrated by Kay Chorao
Published by Holiday House, 1977

Sharmat, Marjorie W.
Mooch the Messy
Illustrated by Ben Shecter
Published by Harper and Row, 1976

Sharmat, Marjorie W.
Morris Brookside, a Dog
Illustrated by Ronald Himler
Published by Holiday House, 1973

Sharmat, Marjorie W.
Mr. Jameson and Mr. Phillips
Illustrated
Published by Harper and Row, 1979

Sharmat, Marjorie W.
Octavia Told Me a Secret
Illustrated by Roseanne Litzinger
Published by Scholastic, 1979

Sharmat, Marjorie W.
Rex
Illustrated by Emily A. McCully
Published by Harper and Row, 1967

Sharmat, Marjorie W.
Say Hello, Vanessa
Illustrated by Lillian Hoban
Published by Holiday House, 1979

Sharmat, Marjorie W.
Sophie and Gussie
Illustrated by Lillian Hoban
Published by Macmillan, 1976

Sharmat, Marjorie W.
The 329th Friend
Illustrated by Cyndy Szekeres
Published by Scholastic, 1979

Sharmat, Marjorie W.
Walter the Wolf
Illustrated by Kelly Oechsil
Published by Holiday House, 1975

Sharmat, Mitchell
Gregory the Terrible Eater
Illustrated by Ariane Dewey and Jose Aruego
Published by Scholastic, 1980

Shaw, Charles G.
It Looked Like Spilt Milk
Illustrated by Charles G. Shaw
Published by Harper and Row, 1947

Shaw, Evelyn
A Fish Out of School
Illustrated by Ralph Carpentier
Published by Harper and Row, 1970

Shaw, Evelyn
Octopus
Illustrated by Ralph Carpentier
Published by Harper and Row, 1971

Shaw, Richard
The Kitten in the Pumpkin Patch
Illustrated by Jacqueline Kahane
Published by Warne, 1973

Shay, Arthur
What Happens When You Go to the Hospital
Illustrated by Arthur Shay
Published by Contemporary Books, 1969

Shecter, Ben
Conrad's Castle
Illustrated by Ben Shecter
Published by Harper and Row, 1967

Shecter, Ben
Hester the Jester
Illustrated
Published by Harper and Row, 1977

Shecter, Ben
Hiding Game
Illustrated by Ben Shecter
Published by Parents Magazine Press, 1977

Shecter, Ben
Molly Patch and Her Animal Friends
Illustrated by Ben Shecter
Published by Harper and Row, 1975

Shecter, Ben
Partouche Plants a Seed
Illustrated by Ben Shecter
Published by Harper and Row, 1966

Shecter, Ben
A Summer Secret
Illustrated by Ben Shecter
Published by Harper and Row, 1977

Shecter, Ben
The Toughest and Meanest Kid on the Block
Illustrated by Ben Shecter
Published by Putnam, 1973

Sheldon, Aure
Of Cobblers and Kings
Illustrated by Don Leake
Published by Scholastic, 1979

Sherman, Ivan
I Am a Giant
Illustrated by Ivan Sherman
Published by Harcourt Brace Jovanovich, 1975

Sherman, Ivan
I Do Not Like It When My Friend Comes to Visit
Illustrated
Published by Harcourt Brace Jovanovich, 1973

Sherman, Ivan
Robert and the Magic String
Illustrated by Ivan Sherman
Published by Harcourt Brace Jovanovich, 1973

Shimin, Symeon
A Special Birthday
Illustrated by Symeon Shimin
Published by McGraw-Hill, 1976

Shortall, Leonard
Andy, the Dog Walker
Illustrated by Leonard Shortall
Published by Morrow, 1968

Shortall, Leonard
One Way: A Trip with Traffic Signs
Illustrated by Leonard Shortall
Published by Prentice-Hall, 1975

Showers, Paul
A Baby Starts to Grow
Illustrated by Rosalind Fry
Published by T.Y. Crowell, 1969

Showers, Paul
Book of Scary Things
Illustrated by Susan Perl
Published by Doubleday, 1977

Showers, Paul
Drop of Blood
Illustrated by Don Madden
Published by T.Y. Crowell, 1972

Showers, Paul
Find Out by Touching
Illustrated by Robert Galster
Published by T.Y. Crowell, 1961

Showers, Paul
Follow Your Nose
Illustrated by Paul Galdone
Published by T.Y. Crowell, 1963

Showers, Paul
Hear Your Heart
Illustrated by Joseph Low
Published by T.Y. Crowell, 1975

Showers, Paul
How Many Teeth?
Illustrated by Paul Galdone
Published by T.Y. Crowell, 1976

Showers, Paul
How You Talk
Illustrated by Robert Galster
Published by T.Y. Crowell, 1967

Showers, Paul
In the Night
Illustrated by Ezra Jack Keats
Published by T.Y. Crowell, 1961

Showers, Paul
Listening Walk
Illustrated by Aliki
Published by T.Y. Crowell, 1961

Showers, Paul
Look at Your Eyes
Illustrated by Paul Galdone
Published by T.Y. Crowell, 1962

Showers, Paul
Sleep Is for Everyone
Illustrated by Wendy Watson
Published by T.Y. Crowell, 1974

Showers, Paul
Where Does the Garbage Go?
Illustrated by Loretta Lustig
Published by T.Y. Crowell, 1974

Showers, Paul
Your Skin and Mine
Illustrated by Paul Galdone
Published by T.Y. Crowell, 1965

Shulevitz, Uri
Dawn
Illustrated by Uri Shulevitz
Published by Farrar, Straus and Giroux, 1974

Shulevitz, Uri
The Magician
Illustrated by Uri Shulevitz
Published by Macmillan, 1973

Shulevitz , Uri
Oh, What a Noise!
Illustrated by Uri Shulevitz
Published by Macmillan, 1971

Shulevitz, Uri
One Monday Morning
Illustrated by Uri Shulevitz
Published by Scribner, 1967

Shulevitz, Uri
Rain Rain Rivers
Illustrated by Uri Shulevitz
Published by Farrar, Straus and Giroux, 1969

Shulevitz, Uri
Soldier and the Tsar in the Forest
Illustrated by Uri Shulevitz
Published by Farrar, Straus and Giroux, 1972

Shulevitz, Uri
The Treasure
Illustrated by Uri Shulevitz
Published by Farrar, Straus and Giroux, 1978

Shura, Mary
Mary's Marvelous Mouse
Illustrated by Adrienne Adams
Published by Knopf, 1962

Silverstein, Shel
Giving Tree
Illustrated by Shel Silverstein
Published by Harper and Row, 1964

Silverstein, Shel
Missing Piece
Illustrated by Shel Silverstein
Published by Harper and Row, 1976

Silverstein, Shel
Where the Sidewalk Ends
Illustrated by Shel Silverstein
Published by Harper and Row, 1974

Simon, Norma
All Kinds of Families
Illustrated by Joe Lasker
Published by A. Whitman, 1975

Simon, Norma
I Know What I Like
Illustrated by Dora Leder
Published by A. Whitman, 1971

Simon, Norma
I Was So Mad!
Illustrated by Dora Leder
Published by A. Whitman, 1974

Simon, Norma
What Do I Do?
Illustrated by Joe Lasker
Published by A. Whitman, 1969

Simon, Norma
What Do I Say?
Illustrated by Joe Lasker
Published by A. Whitman, 1967

Simon, Seymour
About Your Heart
Illustrated by Angeline Culfogienis
Published by Harper and Row, 1975

Simon, Seymour
Finding Out with Your Senses
Illustrated by Emily A. McCully
Published by McGraw-Hill, 1971

Simon, Seymour
A Tree on Your Street
Illustrated by Betty Fraser
Published by Holiday House, 1973

Singer, Marilyn
The Dog Who Insisted He Wasn't
Illustrated
Published by Dutton, 1976

Singer, Yvonne
Sara and the Apartment Building
Illustrated by Ann Powell
Published by Kids Can Press (Canada), 1976

Sislowitz, Marcel
Look! How Your Eyes See
Illustrated by Jim Arnosky
Published by Coward, 1977

Sivulich, Sandra
I'm Going on a Bear Hunt
Illustrated by Glen Rounds
Published by Dutton, 1973

Skaar, Grace
What Do the Animals Say?
Illustrated by Grace Skaar
Published by Scholastic, 1973

Skolsky, Mindy W.
Whistling Teakettle and Other Stories About Hannah
Illustrated by K. Weinhaus
Published by Harper and Row, 1977

Skorpen, Liesel M.
All the Lassies
Illustrated by Bruce M. Scott
Published by Dial, 1970

Skorpen, Liesel M.
Bird
Illustrated by Joan Sandin
Published by Harper and Row, 1976

Skorpen, Liesel M.
Elizabeth
Illustrated by Martha Alexander
Published by Harper and Row, 1970

Skorpen, Liesel M.
Mandy's Grandmother
Illustrated by Martha Alexander
Published by Dial Press, 1974

Skorpen, Liesel M.
Michael
Illustrated by Joan Sandin
Published by Harper and Row, 1975

Skorpen, Liesel M.
Old Arthur
Illustrated by Wallace Tripp
Published by Harper and Row, 1972

Skorpen, Liesel M.
Outside My Window
Illustrated by Mercer Mayer
Published by Harper and Row, 1968

Skorpen, Liesel M.
We Were Tired of Living in a House
Illustrated by Doris Burn
Published by Coward, 1969

Skurzynski, Gloria
Martin by Himself
Illustrated by Lynn Munsinger
Published by Houghton Mifflin, 1979
Skurzynski, Gloria
Two Fools and a Faker
Illustrated by William Papas
Published by Lothrop, 1977
Sleator, William
The Angry Moon
Illustrated by Blair Lent
Published by Little, Brown, 1970
Slepian, Jan and Ann Seidler
The Hungry Thing
Illustrated by Richard Martin
Published by Scholastic, 1972
Slobodkin, Louis
Clear the Track
Illustrated by Louis Slobodkin
Published by Macmillan, 1967
Slobodkin, Louis
Good Place to Hide
Illustrated
Published by Macmillan, 1961
Slobodkin, Louis
The Late Cuckoo
Illustrated by Louis Slobodkin
Published by Vanguard Press, 1962
Slobodkin, Louis
Magic Michael
Illustrated by Louis Slobodkin
Published by Macmillan, 1944
Slobodkin, Louis
Moon Blossom and the Golden Penny
Illustrated by Louis Slobodkin
Published by Vanguard Press, 1963
Slobodkin, Louis
Polka Dot Goat
Illustrated by Louis Slobodkin
Published by Macmillan, 1964
Slobodkin, Louis
Read About the Policeman
Illustrated by Louis Slobodkin
Published by Watts, 1966
Slobodkin, Louis
Trick or Treat
Illustrated by Louis Slobodkin
Published by Macmillan, 1972
Slobodkin, Louis
Yasu and the Strangers
Illustrated by Louis Slobodkin
Published by Macmillan, 1965
Slobodkina, Esphyr
Caps for Sale
Illustrated
Published by A-W, 1947
Small, Ernest and Blair Lent
Baba Yaga
Illustrated
Published by Houghton Mifflin, 1966
Smaridge, Norah
Only Silly People Waste
Illustrated by Mary Carrithers
Published by Abingdon, 1973
Smith, Elwood
The See & Hear & Smell & Taste & Touch Book
Illustrated by Elwood Smith
Published by O'Hara, 1973
Smith, Garry and Vesta Smith
Poco
Illustrated by Fred Crump
Published by Blaine Etheridge, 1975
Smith, Howard E.
Play with the Wind
Illustrated by Jacqueline Chivast
Published by McGraw-Hill, 1972
Smith, Lucia B.
A Special Kind of Sister
Illustrated by Chuck Hall
Published by Holt, Rinehart and Winston, 1979
Smith, Virginia
Not Here and Never Was
Illustrated by Virginia Smith
Published by Harvey House, 1968
Smith, William J.
It Rains—It Shines
Illustrated by Shelly Lichterman
Published by Harvey House, 1967
Smith, William J.
Laughing Time
Illustrated by Juliet Kepes
Published by Little, Brown, 1955
Snyder, Zilpha K.
The Princess and the Giants
Illustrated by Beatrice Darwin
Published by Atheneum, 1973
Sobol, Harriet
Jeff's Hospital Book
Illustrated by Patricia Agre
Published by Walck, 1975
Softly, Barbara
A Yellow-Lemon Elephant Called Trunk
Illustrated by Tony Veale
Published by Harvey House, 1976
Sonneborn, Ruth A.
Friday Night Is Papa Night
Illustrated by Emily A. McCully
Published by Viking Press, 1970
Sonneborn, Ruth A.
I Love Gram
Illustrated by Leo Carty
Published by Viking Press, 1971
Sonneborn, Ruth A.
Someone Is Eating the Sun

Illustrated by Eric Gurney
Published by Random House, 1974
Soule, Jean C.
Never Tease a Weasel
Illustrated by Denman Hampson
Published by Parents Magazine Press, 1964
Soule, Jean C. and Nancy J. Soule
Scuttle, the Stowaway Mouse
Illustrated by Barbara Remington
Published by Parents Magazine Press, 1969
Spier, Peter
Crash, Bang, Boom
Illustrated by Peter Spier
Published by Doubleday, 1972
Spier, Peter
Fast-Slow, High-Low: A Book of Opposites
Illustrated by Peter Spier
Published by Doubleday, 1972
Spier, Peter
Fox Went Out on a Chilly Night
Illustrated by Peter Spier
Published by Doubleday, 1961
Spier, Peter
Gobble, Growl, Grunt
Illustrated by Peter Spier
Published by Doubleday, 1971
Spier, Peter
Oh, Were They Ever Happy!
Illustrated by Peter Spier
Published by Doubleday, 1978
Stamaty, Mark
Minnie Maloney and Macaroni
Illustrated
Published by Dial, 1976
Stanek, Muriel
Left, Right, Left, Right
Illustrated by Lucy Hawkinson
Published by A. Whitman, 1969
Stanton, Elizabeth and Henry Stanton
Sometimes I Like to Cry
Illustrated by Richard Leyden
Published by A. Whitman, 1978
Steadman, Ralph
The Bridge
Illustrated by Ralph Steadman
Published by Collins-World, 1975
Steedman, Julie
Emergency Room: An ABC Tour
Illustrated by Julie Steedman
Published by Windy Hill Press, 1975
Steel, Flora Annie
Tattercoats
Illustrated
Published by Bradbury Press, 1976

Steig, William
The Amazing Bone
Illustrated
Published by Farrar, Straus and Giroux, 1976
Steig, William
Amos and Boris
Illustrated by William Steig
Published by Farrar, Straus and Giroux, 1977
Steig, William
Bad Island
Illustrated by William Steig
Published by Simon & Schuster, 1969
Steig, William
Caleb and Kate
Illustrated by William Steig
Published by Farrar, Straus and Giroux, 1977
Steig, William
Farmer Palmer's Wagon Ride
Illustrated by William Steig
Published by Farrar, Straus and Giroux, 1974
Steig, William
Roland the Minstrel Pig
Illustrated
Published by Harper and Row, 1968
Steig, William
Sylvester and the Magic Pebble
Illustrated by William Steig
Published by Simon & Schuster, 1969
Stein, Sara Bonnett
About Dying
Illustrated
Published by Walker, 1974
Stein, Sara Bonnett
About Handicaps
Illustrated
Published by Walker, 1974
Stein, Sara Bonnett
About Phobias
Illustrated by Erika Stone
Published by Walker, 1979
Stein, Sara Bonnett
The Adopted One
Illustrated by Erika Stone
Published by Walker, 1979
Stein, Sara Bonnett
A Hospital Story
Illustrated
Published by Walker, 1974
Stein, Sara Bonnett
On Divorce
Illustrated by Erika Stone
Published by Walker, 1979
Stein, Sara Bonnett
That New Baby

Illustrated
Published by Walker, 1974
Steiner, Charlotte
Listen to My Seashell
Illustrated
Published by Knopf, 1968
Steiner, Charlotte
Ten in a Family
Illustrated by Charlotte Steiner
Published by Knopf, 1960
Steiner, Jorg
The Bear Who Wanted to Be a Bear
Illustrated by Jorg Miller
Published by Atheneum, 1976
Stephens, Henry Louis
A Frog He Would A-Wooing Go
Illustrated by Henry Louis Stephens
Published by Walker, 1967
Stephens, William M.
Islands
Illustrated by Lydia Rosier
Published by Holiday House, 1974
Stephens, William M. and Peggy Stephens
Flamingo: Bird of Flame
Illustrated by Matthew Kalmenoff
Published by Holiday House, 1972
Stephens, William M. and Peggy Stephens
Hermit Crab
Illustrated by Christine Sapieha
Published by Holiday House, 1969
Stephens, William M. and Peggy Stephens
Octopus
Illustrated by Anthony D'Attilio
Published by Holiday House, 1968
Steptoe, John
Birthday
Illustrated by John Steptoe
Published by Holt, Rinehart and Winston, 1972
Steptoe, John
My Special Best Words
Illustrated by John Steptoe
Published by Viking Press, 1974
Steptoe, John
Stevie
Illustrated by John Steptoe
Published by Harper and Row, 1969
Sternberg, Martha
Japan: A Week in Daisuke's World
Illustrated by Minoru Aoki
Published by Macmillan, 1973
Stevens, Carla
Hooray for Pig!
Illustrated by Rainey Bennett
Published by Seabury, 1974

Stevens, Cat
Teaser and the Firecat
Illustrated
Published by Scholastic, 1974
Stevens, Leonard
The Trucks That Haul by Night
Illustrated
Published by T.Y. Crowell, 1966
Stevens, Margaret
When Grandpa Died
Illustrated by Margaret Stevens
Published by Children's Press, 1979
Stevenson, Drew
Ballad of Penelope Lou...and Me
Illustrated by Marcia Sewall
Published by Crossing Press, 1979
Stevenson, James
Could Be Worse!
Illustrated by James Stevenson
Published by Greenwillow, 1977
Stevenson, James
Monty
Illustrated by James Stevenson
Published by Greenwillow, 1979
Stevenson, James
Wilfred the Rat
Illustrated
Published by Greenwillow, 1977
Stevenson, Maria
Bufo: A Toad-Un Crapaud
Illustrated
Published by Tundra Bks, 1977
Stewart-Kellerhals, Heather
Muktu, the Backward Muskox
Illustrated by Karen Muntean
Published by Press Gang Publishers, (Canada), 1978
Stewart, R. and D. Madden
The Daddy Book
Illustrated
Published by McGraw-Hill, 1972
Stokes, Jack
Let's Be Nature's Friend
Illustrated by Jack Stokes
Published by Walck, 1977
Stokes, Jack
Let's Catch a Fish
Illustrated by Jack Stokes
Published by Walck, 1974
Stone, A. Harris
Last Free Bird
Illustrated by Sheila Heins
Published by Prentice-Hall, 1967
Stone, Jon
The Monster at the End of the Book
Illustrated by Mike Smolin
Published by Western, 1976

Stren, Patti
  Hug Me
  Illustrated
  Published by Harper and Row, 1977
Suba, Susanne
  Monkeys and the Pedlar
  Illustrated
  Published by Viking Press, 1970
Sugita, Yutaka
  Blackie, the Bird Who Could
  Illustrated
  Published by McGraw-Hill, 1975
Sugita, Yutaka
  The Flower Family
  Illustrated
  Published by McGraw-Hill, 1975
Sugita, Yutaka
  Helena, the Unhappy Hippopotamus
  Illustrated
  Published by McGraw-Hill, 1974
Sugita, Yutaka
  My Friend, Little John
  Illustrated by Yutaka Sugita
  Published by McGraw-Hill, 1973
Suhl, Yuri
  Simon Boom Gives a Wedding
  Illustrated by Margot Zemach
  Published by Scholastic, 1972
Sukus, Jan
  My Toolbox Book
  Illustrated by Patti Boyd
  Published by Western, 1977
Sullivan, George
  Plants to Grow Indoors
  Illustrated by Bill Barss
  Published by Follett, (n.d.)
Supraner, Robyn
  Giggly-Wiggly Snicketty-Snick
  Illustrated by Stan Tusan
  Published by Scholastic, 1979
Supraner, Robyn
  It's Not Fair!
  Illustrated by Randall Enos
  Published by Warne, 1976
Surowiecki, Sandra Lucas
  Joshua's Day
  Illustrated by Patricia Riley Lenthall
  Published by Lollipop Power, 1972
Suteyev, A.
  Mushroom in the Rain
  Illustrated by Jose Aruego
  Adapted by Mirra Ginsberg
  Published by Macmillan, 1974
Suteyev, Vladimir
  Three Kittens
  Illustrated by Giulio Maestro
  Adapted by Mirra Ginsberg
  Published by Crown, 1973

Suteyev, Vladimir
  What Kind of Bird Is That?
  Illustrated by Giulio Maestro
  Adapted by Mirra Ginsberg
  Published by Crown, 1973
Sutherland, Margaret
  Hello, I'm Karen
  Illustrated by Jane Paton
  Published by Coward, 1976
Sutton,
  Big Book of Wild Animals
  Illustrated
  Published by Grosset & Dunlap, (n.d.)
Svendsen, Carol
  Hulda
  Illustrated by Julius Svendsen
  Published by Houghton Mifflin, 1974
Swallow, Su
  Cars, Trucks and Trains
  Illustrated by Michael & Ann Ricketts
  Published by Grosset & Dunlap, 1974
Swift, Hildegarde and Lynd Ward
  Little Red Lighthouse and Great Gray Bridge
  Illustrated by Lynd Ward
  Published by Harcourt Brace Jovanovich, 1942
Tallon, Robert
  Little Cloud
  Illustrated by Robert Tallon
  Published by Parents Magazine Press, 1979
Tallon, Robert
  Fish Story
  Illustrated by Robert Tallon
  Published by Holt, Rinehart and Winston, 1977
Tallon, Robert
  Worm Story
  Illustrated by Robert Tallon
  Published by Holt, Rinehart and Winston, 1978
Tallon, Robert
  Zoophabets
  Illustrated
  Published by Bobbs-Merrill, 1971
Taniguchi, Kazuko
  Mary Monster, Mischief Maker
  Illustrated
  Published by McGraw-Hill, 1976
Taylor, Barbara
  I Climb Mountains
  Illustrated by Barbara Yacono
  Published by Canadian Women's Educational Press, 1975
Taylor, Mark
  Henry the Castaway
  Illustrated by Graham Booth
  Published by Atheneum, (n.d.)

Taylor, Mark
  Henry Explores the Jungle
  Illustrated by Graham Booth
  Published by Atheneum, 1968
Taylor, Mark
  Henry the Explorer
  Illustrated by Graham Booth
  Published by Atheneum, 1966
Teague, Kathleen
  What Happened to Hector?
  Illustrated by Ric Del Rossi
  Published by Garrard, 1974
Tensen, Ruth
  Come to the City
  Illustrated
  Published by Contemporary Books, 1951
Terris, Susan
  Amanda the Panda and the Redhead
  Illustrated
  Published by Doubleday, 1975
Tester, Sylvia R.
  Feeling Angry
  Illustrated by Peg R. Haag
  Published by Children's Press, 1976
Thaler, Mike
  There's a Hippopotamus Under My Bed
  Illustrated
  Published by Watts, 1977
Thaler, Mike
  What Can a Hippopotamus Be?
  Illustrated by Robert Grossman
  Published by Parents Magazine Press, 1975
Thayer, Jane
  Andy and the Wild Worm
  Illustrated by Beatrice Darwin
  Published by Morrow, 1973
Thayer, Jane
  Gus and the Baby Ghost
  Illustrated by Seymour Fleishman
  Published by Morrow, 1972
Thayer, Jane
  The Popcorn Dragon
  Illustrated by Seymour
  Published by Morrow, 1953
Thayer, Jane
  The Puppy Who Wanted a Boy
  Illustrated by Seymour Fleishman
  Published by Morrow, 1958
Thayer, Jane
  Quiet on Account of the Dinosaur
  Illustrated by Seymour Fleishman
  Published by Morrow, 1964
Thayer, Jane
  Rockets Don't Go to Chicago, Andy
  Illustrated by Meg Wohlberg
  Published by Morrow, 1967

Thayer, Jane
  Andy and the Runaway Horse
  Illustrated by Meg Wohlberg
  Published by Morrow, 1963
Thayer, Marjorie
  The Valentine Box
  Illustrated by Marjorie Burgeson
  Published by Children's Press, 1977
Thomas, Dawn
  Mira! Mira!
  Illustrated by Harold L. James
  Published by Lippincott, 1970
Thomas, Ianthe
  Hi, Mrs. Mallory
  Illustrated by Ann Toulmin-Rothe
  Published by Harper and Row, 1979
Thomas, Ianthe
  Lordy, Aunt Hattie
  Illustrated by Thomas DiGrazia
  Published by Harper and Row, 1973
Thomas, Ianthe
  Walk Home Tired, Billy Jenkins
  Illustrated by Thomas DiGrazia
  Published by Harper and Row, 1974
Thomas, Jane Resh
  Elizabeth Catches a Fish
  Illustrated by Joseph Duffy
  Published by Seabury, 1977
Thomas, Marlo
  Free To Be...You and Me
  Illustrated
  Published by McGraw-Hill, 1974
Thomas, Patricia
  Stand Back, Said the Elephant, I'm Going to Sneeze
  Illustrated by Wallace Tripp
  Published by Lothrop, 1971
Thomas, Patricia
  There Are Rocks in My Socks Said the Ox to the Fox
  Illustrated by Mordecai Gerstein
  Published by Lothrop, 1979
Thompson, Brenda and Rosemary Giesen
  Bones and Skeletons
  Illustrated by Carole Viner and Rosemary Giesen
  Published by Lerner, 1977
Thompson, Jean
  I'm Going to Run Away
  Illustrated by Bill Meyers
  Published by Abingdon, 1975
Thompson, Vivian
  Sad Day, Glad Day
  Illustrated by Lilian Obligado
  Published by Scholastic, 1970
Thurman, Judith
  I'd Like to Try a Monster's Eye

264 / They're Never Too Young for Books

Illustrated by Reina Rubel
Published by Atheneum, 1977
Tichenor, Tom
Smart Bear
Illustrated by Margo Locke
Published by Abingdon, 1970
Tison, Annette and Talus Tayler
Inside and Outside
Illustrated
Published by Collins-World, 1972
Titus, Eve
Anatole
Illustrated by Paul Galdone
Published by McGraw-Hill, 1956
Tobias, Tobi
At the Beach
Illustrated by Gloria Singer
Published by Walck, 1978
Tobias, Tobi
Chasing the Goblins Away
Illustrated by Victor Ambrus
Published by Warne, 1977
Tobias, Tobi
Easy or Hard? That's a Good Question
Illustrated by Gene Sharp
Published by Children's Press, 1977
Tobias, Tobi
Liquid or Solid? That's a Good Question
Illustrated by Gene Sharp
Published by Children's Press, 1977
Tobias, Tobi
Moving Day
Illustrated by William P. DuBois
Published by Knopf, 1976
Tobias, Tobi
Quiet or Noisy? That's a Good Question
Illustrated by Sharon Elzaurdia
Published by Children's Press, 1977
Tobias, Tobi
The Quitting Deal
Illustrated by Trina S. Hyman
Published by Viking Press, 1975
Tobias, Tobi
Where Does It Come From? That's a Good Question
Illustrated
Published by Children's Press, 1979
Tolstoy, Alexei
Great Big Enormous Turnip
Illustrated by Helen Oxenbury
Published by Watts, 1969
Tompert, Ann
The Clever Princess
Illustrated by Patricia Riley Lenthall
Published by Lollipop Power, 1977

Tompert, Ann
Little Fox Goes to the End of the World
Illustrated by John Wallner
Published by Crown, 1976
Toothaker, Roy
Wild Goose Chase
Illustrated by Tom Dunnington
Published by Prentice-Hall, 1975
Towle, Faith M.
Magic Cooking Pot
Illustrated
Published by Houghton Mifflin, 1974
Toye, William
How Summer Came to Canada
Illustrated by Elizabeth Cleaver
Published by Walck, 1969
Toye, William
Mt. Goats of Temlaham
Illustrated by Elizabeth Cleaver
Published by Walck, 1969
Toyet, Khanh
The Little Weaver of Thai-Yen Village
Translated by Khanh Toyet
Illustrated by Nancy Hom
Published by Children's Book Press, S.F., (n.d.)
Tresselt, Alvin R.
Autumn Harvest
Illustrated by Roger Duvoisin
Published by Lothrop, 1951
Tresselt, Alvin R.
Beaver Pond
Illustrated by Roger Duvoisin
Published by Lothrop, 1970
Tresselt, Alvin R.
Bonnie Bess the Weathervane Horse
Illustrated by Eric Blegvad
Published by Parents Magazine Press, 1970
Tresselt, Alvin R.
The Dead Tree
Illustrated by Charles Robinson
Published by Parents Magazine Press, 1972
Tresselt, Alvin R.
Follow the Wind
Illustrated by Roger Duvoisin
Published by Lothrop, 1950
Tresselt, Alvin R.
Frog in the Well
Illustrated by Roger Duvoisin
Published by Lothrop, 1958
Tresselt, Alvin R.
Hide and Seek Fog
Illustrated by Roger Duvoisin
Published by Lothrop, 1965

Bibliography / **265**

Tresselt, Alvin R.
I Saw the Sea Come In
Illustrated by Roger Duvoisin
Published by Lothrop, 1954

Tresselt, Alvin R.
It's Time Now
Illustrated by Roger Duvoisin
Published by Lothrop, 1969

Tresselt, Alvin R.
Mitten
Illustrated by Yaroslava Mills
Published by Lothrop, 1964

Tresselt, Alvin R.
Rain Drop Splash
Illustrated by Leonard Weisgard
Published by Lothrop, 1946

Tresselt, Alvin R.
Smallest Elephant in the World
Illustrated by Milton Glaser
Published by Knopf, 1959

Tresselt, Alvin R.
What Did You Leave Behind?
Illustrated by Roger Duvoisin
Published by Lothrop, 1978

Tresselt, Alvin R.
White Snow, Bright Snow
Illustrated by Roger Duvoisin
Published by Lothrop, 1947

Tresselt, Alvin R.
World in the Candy Egg
Illustrated by Roger Duvoisin
Published by Lothrop, 1967

Trez, Denise and Alain Trez
Smallest Pirate
Illustrated by Denise and Alain Trez
Published by Viking Press, 1970

Tripp, Wallace
Granfa' Grig Had a Pig...New from Mother Goose
Illustrated by Wallace Tripp
Published by Little, Brown, 1976

Tripp, Wallace
Great Big Ugly Man Came up and Tied His Horse to Me
Illustrated by Wallace Tripp
Published by Little, Brown, 1974

Tripp, Wallace
Sir Toby Jingle's Beastly Journey
Illustrated by Wallace Tripp
Published by Coward, 1976

Trofimuk, Ann
Babushka and the Pig
Illustrated by Jerry Pinkney
Published by Houghton Mifflin, 1969

Trotta, John
Hello, This Is a Shape Book
Illustrated
Published by Random, 1972

Truse, Kenneth
Benny's Magic Baking Pan
Illustrated by Bill Morrison
Published by Garrard, 1974

Tucker, Nicholas
Mother Goose Abroad
Translated by Nicholas Tucker
Illustrated by Trevor Stubley
Published by T.Y. Crowell, 1975

Tudor, Tasha
A Is for Annabelle
Illustrated by Tasha Tudor
Published by Walck, 1954

Tudor, Tasha
Around the Year
Illustrated by Tasha Tudor
Published by Walck, 1957

Tudor, Tasha
Corgiville Fair
Illustrated by Tasha Tudor
Published by T.Y. Crowell, 1977

Tudor, Tasha
The County Fair
Illustrated by Tasha Tudor
Published by Walck, 1964

Tudor, Tasha
The Dolls' Christmas
Illustrated by Tasha Tudor
Published by Walck, 1970

Tudor, Tasha
Mother Goose
Illustrated by Tasha Tudor
Published by Walck, 1944

Tudor, Tasha
A Tale for Easter
Illustrated by Tasha Tudor
Published by Walck, 1941

Turin, Adela and Nella Bosnia
Arthur and Clementine
Translated by Lisa Appignanesi
Illustrated
Published by Two Continents, 1977

Turkle, Brinton
Deep in the Forest
Illustrated by Brinton Turkle
Published by Dutton, 1976

Turkle, Brinton
It's Only Arnold
Illustrated by Brinton Turkle
Published by Penguin, 1975

Turkle, Brinton
Thy Friend, Obadiah
Illustrated by Brinton Turkle
Published by Viking Press, 1969

Turkle, Brinton
Obadiah, the Bold
Illustrated by Brinton Turkle
Published by Viking Press, 1965

Turkle, Brinton
Sky Dog
Illustrated by Brinton Turkle
Published by Viking Press, 1969
Turksa, Krystyna
Magician of Cracow
Illustrated
Published by Greenwillow, 1975
Turksa, Krystyna
The Woodcutter's Duck
Illustrated by Krystyna Turksa
Published by Macmillan, 1973
Tworkov, Jack
The Camel Who Took a Walk
Illustrated by Roger Duvoisin
Published by Dutton, 1951
Uchida, Yoshiko
The Birthday Visitor
Illustrated by Charles Robinson
Published by Scribner, 1975
Uchida, Yoshiko
Forever Christmas Tree
Illustrated by Kazue Mizumura
Published by Scribner, 1963
Uchida, Yoshiko
Sumi and the Goat and the Tokyo Express
Illustrated by Kazue Mizumura
Published by Scribner, 1969
Udry, Janice
Emily's Autumn
Illustrated by Eric Blegvad
Published by A. Whitman, 1969
Udry, Janice
Let's Be Enemies
Illustrated by Maurice Sendak
Published by Harper and Row, 1961
Udry, Janice
Mary Ann's Mud Day
Illustrated by Martha Alexander
Published by Harper and Row, 1967
Udry, Janice
Mary Jo's Grandmother
Illustrated by Eleanor Mill
Published by A. Whitman, 1970
Udry, Janice
Moon Jumpers
Illustrated by Maurice Sendak
Published by Harper and Row, (n.d.)
Udry, Janice
A Tree Is Nice
Illustrated by Marc Simont
Published by Harper and Row, 1965
Udry, Janice
What Mary Jo Shared
Illustrated by Eleanor Mill
Published by A. Whitman, 1966
Ueno, Noriko
Elephant Buttons
Illustrated by Noriko Ueno
Published by Harper and Row, 1973
Ungerer, Tomi
Allumette
Illustrated by Tomi Ungerer
Published by Parents Magazine Press, 1974
Ungerer, Tomi
The Beast of Monsieur Racine
Illustrated by Tomi Ungerer
Published by Farrar, Straus and Giroux, 1971
Ungerer, Tomi
Crictor
Illustrated by Tomi Ungerer
Published by Harper and Row, 1958
Ungerer, Tomi
Hat
Illustrated by Tomi Ungerer
Published by Parents Magazine Press, 1970
Ungerer, Tomi
Moon Man
Illustrated by Tomi Ungerer
Published by Harper and Row, 1967
Ungerer, Tomi
One, Two, Where's My Shoe?
Illustrated by Tomi Ungerer
Published by Harper and Row, 1964
Ungerer, Tomi
Orlando, the Brave Vulture
Illustrated by Tomi Ungerer
Published by Harper and Row, 1966
Ungerer, Tomi
Snail, Where Are You?
Illustrated by Tomi Ungerer
Published by Harper and Row, 1962
Ungerer, Tomi
Three Robbers
Illustrated by Tomi Ungerer
Published by Atheneum, 1975
Ungerer, Tomi
Zeralda's Ogre
Illustrated by Tomi Ungerer
Published by Harper and Row, 1967
Ushinsky, Constantin
How a Shirt Grew in the Field
Illustrated by Marguerita and Yaroslava Rudolph
Published by McGraw-Hill, 1967
Van Horn, William
Twitchtoe the Beastfinder
Illustrated by William Van Horn
Published by Atheneum, 1978
Van Leeuwen, Jean
Too Hot for Ice Cream
Illustrated by Martha Alexander
Published by Dial, 1974

Van Tuyle, Jean
The Day the Zoo Caught the Flu
Illustrated
Published by Harvey House, 1979
Van Woerkom, Dorothy
Alexandra, the Rock Eater
Illustrated by Rosekrans Hoffman
Published by Knopf, 1978
Van Woerkom, Dorothy
The Queen Who Couldn't Bake
  Gingerbread
Illustrated by Paul Galdone
Published by Knopf, 1975
Van Woerkom, Dorothy
The Rat, the Ox and the Zodiac
Illustrated by Errol LeCain
Published by Crown, 1976
Varga, Judy
The Battle of the Wind Gods
Illustrated by Judy Varga
Published by Morrow, 1974
Varga, Judy
Janko's Wish
Illustrated by Judy Varga
Published by Morrow, 1969
Varga, Judy
Magic Wall
Illustrated by Judy Varga
Published by Morrow, 1970
Vaughan, Jennifer
Fish and Mammals
Illustrated by Esme Eve
Published by Grosset & Dunlap, 1974
Velthuijs, Max
The Painter and the Bird
Translated by R. Broehel
Illustrated by Max Velthuijs
Published by A. Whitman, 1975
Venable, Alan
The Checker Players
Illustrated by Byron Barton
Published by Lippincott, 1973
Viorst, Judith
Alexander and the Terrible...Very Bad
  Day
Illustrated
Published by Atheneum, 1976
Viorst, Judith
I'll Fix Anthony
Illustrated by Arnold Lobel
Published by Harper and Row, 1969
Viorst, Judith
My Mama Says...
Illustrated by Kay Chorao
Published by Atheneum, 1973
Viorst, Judith
The Tenth Good Thing About
  Barney

Illustrated by Eric Blegvad
Published by Atheneum, 1975
Viorst, Judith
Try It Again, Sam: Safety When You
  Walk
Illustrated by Paul Galdone
Published by Lothrop, 1970
Vogel, Margret-Ilse
Dodo Every Day
Illustrated
Published by Harper and Row, 1977
Vogel, Ilse-Margret
The Don't Be Scared Book: Scares,
  Remedies and Pics
Illustrated by Ilse-Margret Vogel
Published by Atheneum, 1974
Vogel, Ilse-Margret
One Is No Fun, But Twenty Is
  Plenty
Illustrated by Ilse-Margret Vogel
Published by Atheneum, 1972
Vollaud Edition
Mother Goose
Illustrated by Frederick Richardson
Published by Hubbard Press, 1971
Waber, Bernard
Anteater Named Arthur
Illustrated by Bernard Waber
Published by Houghton Mifflin, 1967
Waber, Bernard
Firefly Named Torchy
Illustrated by Bernard Waber
Published by Houghton Mifflin, 1970
Waber, Bernard
House on East Eighty-Eighth Street
Illustrated by Bernard Waber
Published by Houghton Mifflin, 1962
Waber, Bernard
I Was All Thumbs
Illustrated by Bernard Waber
Published by Houghton Mifflin, 1975
Waber, Bernard
Ira Sleeps Over
Illustrated by Bernard Waber
Published by Houghton Mifflin, 1972
Waber, Bernard
Lovable Lyle
Illustrated by Bernard Waber
Published by Houghton Mifflin, 1969
Waber, Bernard
Lyle and the Birthday Party
Illustrated by Bernard Waber
Published by Houghton Mifflin, 1973
Waber, Bernard
Lyle Finds His Mother
Illustrated by Bernard Waber
Published by Houghton Mifflin, 1974
Waber, Bernard
Mice on My Mind

Illustrated by Bernard Waber
Published by Houghton Mifflin, 1977
Waber, Bernard
Nobody Is Perfick
Illustrated by Bernard Waber
Published by Houghton Mifflin, 1971
Waber, Bernard
Rich Cat, Poor Cat
Illustrated by Bernard Waber
Published by Scholastic, 1970
Waber, Bernard
Rose for Mr. Bloom
Illustrated by Bernard Waber
Published by Houghton Mifflin, 1968
Waber, Bernard
You Look Ridiculous Said the Rhino to the Hippo
Illustrated by Bernard Waber
Published by Houghton Mifflin, 1966
Wade, Anne
A Promise Is for Keeping
Illustrated
Published by Children's Press, 1979
Wagner, Jenny
The Bunyip of Berkeley's Creek
Illustrated by Ron Brooks
Published by Bradbury Press, 1977
Wagner, Jenny
John Brown, Rose and the Midnight Cat
Illustrated by Ron Brooks
Published by Bradbury Press, 1978
Wahl, Jan
Carrot Nose
Illustrated by James Marshall
Published by Farrar, Straus and Giroux, 1976
Wahl, Jan
Doctor Rabbit's Foundling
Illustrated by Cyndy Szekeres
Published by Pantheon, 1977
Wahl, Jan
Frankenstein's Dog
Illustrated by Kay Chorao
Published by Prentice-Hall, 1977
Wahl, Jan
Grandmother Told Me
Illustrated by Mercer Mayer
Published by Little, Brown, 1972
Wahl, Jan
Pleasant Fieldmouse's Halloween Party
Illustrated by Wallace Tripp
Published by Putnam, 1974
Wahl, Jan
Margaret's Birthday
Illustrated by Mercer Mayer
Published by Scholastic, 1971

Wahl, Jan
Wolf of My Own
Illustrated by Lillian Hoban
Published by Macmillan, 1969
Wahl, Jan and Hans Christian Andersen
The Woman with Eggs
Illustrated by Ray Cruz
Adapted by Jan Wahl
Published by Crown, 1974
Walker, Barbara K.
Pigs and Pirates: A Greek Tale
Illustrated by Harold Berson
Published by D. White, 1969
Wallace, Daisy, Ed.
Ghost Poems
Illustrated by Tomie DePaola
Published by Holiday House, 1979
Wallace, Daisy, Ed.
Monster Poems
Illustrated by Kay Chorao
Published by Holiday House, 1976
Wallace, Daisy, Ed.
Witch Poems
Illustrated by Trina Schart Hyman
Published by Holiday House, 1976
Walter, Greg
A Box to Begin With
Illustrated by James Heugh
Published by Harvey House, 1978
Walther, Tom
A Spider Might
Illustrated by Tom Walther
Published by Scribner, 1978
Wannamaker, Bruce
What Causes It
Illustrated
Published by Children's Press, 1977
Warburg, Sandol S.
Curl Up Small
Illustrated by T. Hyman
Published by Houghton Mifflin, 1964
Warburg, Sandol S.
From Ambledee to Zumbledee
Illustrated by Walter Lorraine
Published by Houghton Mifflin, 1968
Warburg, Sandol S.
Growing Time
Illustrated by Leonard Weisgard
Published by Houghton Mifflin, 1969
Ward, Lynd
Biggest Bear
Illustrated by Lynd Ward
Published by Houghton Mifflin, 1952
Ward, Lynd
The Silver Pony
Illustrated by Lynd Ward
Published by Houghton Mifflin, 1973

Warriner, Hope
  Sights and Sounds of the City
  Illustrated by Jill Jordon
  Published by Blaine-Ethridge, 1976
Watson, Aldren A.
  My Garden Grows
  Illustrated by Aldren A. Watson
  Published by Viking Press, 1962
Watson, Clyde
  Father Fox's Pennyrhymes
  Illustrated by Wendy Watson
  Published by T.Y. Crowell, 1971
Watson, Clyde
  Hickory Stick Rag
  Illustrated by Wendy Watson
  Published by T.Y. Crowell, 1976
Watson, Clyde
  Tom Fox and the Apple Pie
  Illustrated by Wendy Watson
  Published by T.Y. Crowell, 1972
Watson, Jane
  Animal Dictionary
  Illustrated by Feodor Rojankovsky
  Published by Western, 1960
Watson, Jane
  My Body—How It Works
  Illustrated by Hilde Hoffman
  Published by Western, 1972
Watson, Nancy D.
  Sugar on Snow
  Illustrated by Aldren A. Watson
  Published by Viking Press, 1964
Watson, Nancy D.
  When Is Tomorrow?
  Illustrated by Aldren A. Watson
  Published by Knopf, 1955
Watson, Pauline
  Days with Daddy
  Illustrated by Joanne Scribner
  Published by Prentice-Hall, 1977
Watson, Wendy
  Lollipop
  Illustrated by Wendy Watson
  Published by T.Y. Crowell, 1976
Watts, Bernadette
  David's Waiting Day
  Illustrated by Bernadette Watts
  Published by Prentice-Hall, 1977
Watts, Mabel
  The Basket That Flew over the Mountain
  Illustrated by Harris Petie
  Published by Lantern Press, (n.d.)
Watts, Mabel
  The Elephant That Became a Ferry Boat
  Illustrated
  Published by Lantern Press, 1971

Watts, Majorie-Ann
  Crocodile Medicine
  Illustrated by Majorie-Ann Watts
  Published by Warne, 1978
Waxman, Stephanie
  What Is a Girl? What Is a Boy?
  Illustrated by Stephanie Waxman and Dennis Hicks
  Published by Peace Press, 1976
Weaver, Martin and Virginia Weaver
  Lambs
  Illustrated by Martin Weaver
  Published by Knopf, 1970
Weber, Alfons, M.D.
  Elizabeth Gets Well
  Illustrated by Jacqueline Blass
  Published by T.Y. Crowell, 1970
Webber, Irma
  Up Above and Down Below
  Illustrated
  Published by A-W, 1943
Webster, David
  Let's Find Out About Mosquitos
  Illustrated by Arbelle Wheatley
  Published by Watts, 1974
Webster, Vera
  From One Seed
  Illustrated by Manabu Saito
  Published by Walck, 1977
Weihs, Erika
  Count the Cats
  Illustrated
  Published by Doubleday, 1976
Weil, Lisl
  Candy Egg Bunny
  Illustrated by Lisl Weil
  Published by Holiday House, 1975
Weil, Lisl
  The Funny Old Bag
  Illustrated by Lisl Weil
  Published by Parents Magazine Press, 1974
Weil, Lisl
  Golden Spinning Wheel
  Illustrated by Lisl Weil
  Published by Macmillan, 1969
Weil, Lisl
  Hopping Knapsack
  Illustrated by Lisl Weil
  Published by Macmillan, 1970
Weil, Lisl
  I Wish, I Wish
  Illustrated by Lisl Weil
  Published by Houghton Mifflin, 1957
Weil, Lisl
  Melissa
  Illustrated by Lisl Weil
  Published by Macmillan, 1966

Weil, Lisl
Melissa's Friend Fabrizzio
Illustrated by Lisl Weil
Published by Macmillan, 1967

Weil, Lisl
Ralphi Rhino
Illustrated by Lisl Weil
Published by Walker, 1974

Weil, Lisl
Walt and Pepper
Illustrated by Lisl Weil
Published by Parents Magazine Press, 1974

Weisgard, Leonard
My First Picture Book
Illustrated by Leonard Weisgard
Published by Grosset & Dunlap, 1964

Weisgard, Leonard
Whose Little Bird Am I?
Illustrated by Leonard Weisgard
Published by Warne, 1965

Welber, Robert
Frog, Frog, Frog
Illustrated by Deborah Ray
Published by Pantheon, 1971

Welber, Robert
Goodbye, Hello
Illustrated by Cyndy Szekeres
Published by Pantheon, 1974

Welber, Robert
Train
Illustrated by Deborah Ray
Published by Pantheon, 1972

Wellman, Alice W.
Small Boy Chuku
Illustrated by Richard Cuffari
Published by Houghton Mifflin, 1973

Wellman, Alice W.
Tatu and the Honey Bird
Illustrated
Published by Putnam, 1972

Wells, Rosemary
Abdul
Illustrated by Rosemary Wells
Published by Dial, 1975

Wells, Rosemary
Benjamin and Tulip
Illustrated by Rosemary Wells
Published by Dial, 1973

Wells, Rosemary
Don't Spill It Again, James
Illustrated by Rosemary Wells
Published by Dial, 1977

Wells, Rosemary
Max's First Word/New Suit/Ride/Toys (4)
Illustrated by Rosemary Wells
Published by Dial, 1979

Wells, Rosemary
Noisy Nora
Illustrated by Rosemary Wells
Published by Dial, 1973

Wells, Rosemary
Stanley and Rhoda
Illustrated by Rosemary Wells
Published by Dial, 1979

Wells, Rosemary
Unfortunately Harriet
Illustrated by Rosemary Wells
Published by Dial, 1972

Wersba, Barbara
Amanda Dreaming
Illustrated by Mercer Mayer
Published by Atheneum, 1973

Werth, Kurt
Lazy Jack
Illustrated by Kurt Werth
Published by Viking Press, 1970

Werth, Kurt and Mabel Watts
Molly and the Giant
Illustrated by Kurt Werth
Published by Parents Magazine Press, 1973

Westbrook, Dante
Daxius
Illustrated by Dewey Crumpler
Published by Children's Book Press, S.F., (n.d.)

Westerberg, Christine
The Cap That Mother Made
Illustrated
Published by Prentice-Hall, 1977

Wezel, Peter
Good Bird
Illustrated by Peter Wezel
Published by Harper and Row, 1966

White, E.B.
Charlotte's Web
Illustrated by Garth Williams
Published by Harper and Row, 1952

White, E.B.
Stuart Little
Illustrated by Garth Williams
Published by Harper and Row, 1945

Whitman, Walt
Overhead the Sun: Lines from Walt Whitman
Illustrated by Antonio Frasconi
Published by Farrar, Straus and Giroux, 1969

Whitney, Alex
Once a Bright Red Tiger
Illustrated by Charles Robinson
Published by Walck, 1973

Whitney, Alma
Just Awful

Illustrated by Lillian Hoban
Published by A-W, 1971
Whitney, David
Let's Find Out About Milk
Illustrated by Gloria Gaulke
Published by Watts, 1967
Whitney, Thomas
Vasilisa the Beautiful
Illustrated by Nonny Hogrogian
Published by Macmillan, 1970
Wiesenthal, Eleanor and Ted Wiesenthal
Let's Find Out About Eskimos
Illustrated by Allan Eitzen
Published by Watts, 1969
Wiesenthal, Eleanor and Ted Wiesenthal
Let's Find Out About Rivers
Illustrated by Gerry Contreras
Published by Watts, 1971
Wiesner, William
Little Sarah and Her Johnny-Cake
Illustrated by William Wiesner
Published by Walck, 1974
Wiesner, William
Turnabout
Illustrated by William Wiesner
Published by Seabury, 1972
Wild, Robin and Jocelyn Wild
Dunmousie Monsters
Illustrated by Jocelyn Wild
Published by Coward, 1975
Wildsmith, Brian
Brian Wildsmith's ABC
Illustrated by Brian Wildsmith
Published by Watts, 1963
Wildsmith, Brian
Brian Wildsmith's Birds
Illustrated by Brian Wildsmith
Published by Watts, 1967
Wildsmith, Brian
Brian Wildsmith's Circus
Illustrated by Brian Wildsmith
Published by Watts, 1968
Wildsmith, Brian
Brian Wildsmith's Fishes
Illustrated by Brian Wildsmith
Published by Watts, 1968
Wildsmith, Brian
Brian Wildsmith's Mother Goose
Illustrated by Brian Wildsmith
Published by Watts, 1965
Wildsmith, Brian
Brian Wildsmith's One, Two, Threes
Illustrated by Brian Wildsmith
Published by Watts, (n.d.)
Wildsmith, Brian
Brian Wildsmith's Wild Animals
Illustrated by Brian Wildsmith
Published by Watts, 1967
Wildsmith, Brian
Python's Party
Illustrated by Brian Wildsmith
Published by Watts, 1975
Wildsmith, Brian
Squirrels
Illustrated by Brian Wildsmith
Published by Watts, 1975
Wilkins, Mary E. and Ellin Greens
Pumpkin Giant
Illustrated by Trina Hyman
Published by Lothrop, 1970
Willard, Nancy
Papa's Panda
Illustrated by Lillian Hoban
Published by Harcourt Brace Jovanovich, 1979
Williams, Barbara
Albert's Toothache
Illustrated by Kay Chorao
Published by Dutton, 1977
Williams, Barbara
Gary and the Very Terrible Monster
Illustrated by Lois Axeman
Published by Children's Press, 1973
Williams, Barbara
If He's My Brother
Illustrated by Tomie DePaola
Published by Harvey House, 1976
Williams, Barbara
Kevin's Grandma
Illustrated by Kay Chorao
Published by Dutton, 1975
Williams, Barbara
Someday, Said Mitchell
Illustrated by Kay Chorao
Published by Dutton, 1976
Williams, Garth
Baby Farm Animals
Illustrated
Published by Western, 1959
Williams, Garth
Rabbits' Wedding
Illustrated by Garth Williams
Published by Harper and Row, 1958
Williams, Herb
Little Red Hen
Illustrated by Herb Williams
Published by Prentice-Hall, 1969
Williams, Jay
Bag Full of Nothing
Illustrated by Tom O'Sullivan
Published by Parents Magazine Press, 1974
Williams, Jay
The City Witch and the Country Witch

Illustrated by Ed Renfro
Published by Macmillan, 1979
Williams, Jay
Everyone Knows What a Dragon
  Looks Like
Illustrated by Mercer Mayer
Published by Scholastic, 1976
Williams, Jay
Forgetful Fred
Illustrated by Friso Henstra
Published by Parents Magazine Press,
  1974
Williams, Jay
Petronella
Illustrated by Friso Henstra
Published by Parents Magazine Press,
  1973
Williams, Jay
Pettifur
Illustrated by Hilary Knight
Published by Scholastic, 1977
Williams, Jay
Practical Princess
Illustrated by Friso Henstra
Published by Parents Magazine Press,
  1969
Williams, Jay
Silver Whistle
Illustrated by Friso Henstra
Published by Parents Magazine Press,
  1971
Williams, Jay
The Suprising Things Maui
  Did
Illustrated by Charles Mikolaycak
Published by Scholastic, 1979
Williams, Letty
The Tiger
Translated by Doris Chaves
Illustrated by Herb Williams
Published by Prentice-Hall, 1970
Williamson, Jane
The Trouble with Alark
Illustrated by Jane Williamson
Published by Farrar, Straus and
  Giroux, 1975
Wills, Jonathan
The Travels of Magnus Pole
Illustrated by Jonathan Wills
Published by Houghton Mifflin,
  1975
Wilson, Beth P.
Martin Luther King, Jr.
Illustrated by Floyd Sowell
Published by Putnam, 1971
Wilson, Gahan
The Bang Bang Family
Illustrated by Gahan Wilson
Published by Scribner, 1974

Wilson, Jean
Animals of Warmer Lands
Illustrated
Published by A-W, 1969
Wilson, Jean
The Weather
Illustrated
Published by A-W, 1969
Wilson, Lionel
The Mule Who Refused to Budge
Illustrated by Harold Berson
Published by Crown, 1975
Winn, Marie
Fisherman Who Needed a Knife: Why
  People Need Money
Illustrated by John E. Johnson
Published by Simon & Schuster,
  1970
Winn, Marie
Man Who Made Tops: Why People Do
  Different Work
Illustrated by John E. Johnson
Published by Simon & Schuster, 1970
Winthrop, Elizabeth
Potbellied Possums
Illustrated by Barbara McClintock
Published by Holiday House, 1977
Winthrop, Elizabeth
That's Mine
Illustrated by Emily A. McCully
Published by Holiday House, 1977
Wise, William
Giant Snakes and Other Amazing
  Reptiles
Illustrated
Published by Putnam, 1970
Wise, William
Monsters of the Middle Ages
Illustrated by Tomie DePaola
Published by Putnam, 1971
Wise, William
Monsters of North America
Illustrated by Ben Stahl
Published by Putnam, 1977
Wiseman, Bernard
Little New Kangaroo
Illustrated by Robert Lopshire
Published by Macmillan, 1973
Wiseman, Bernard
Morris the Moose
Illustrated by Bernard Wiseman
Published by Harper and Row, 1959
Withers, Carl A.
Tale of the Black Cat
Illustrated by Alan E. Cober
Published by Holt, Rinehart and
  Winston, 1966
Withers, Carl
Wild Ducks and the Goose

Illustrated by Alan E. Cober
Published by Holt, Rinehart and
  Winston, 1968
Witte, Pat and Eve Witte
Look Look Book
Illustrated by Jerry Smath
Published by Western, 1961
Witte, Pat and Eve Witte
Touch Me Book
Illustrated by Harlow Rockwell
Published by Western, 1961
Witte, Pat and Eve Witte
Who Lives Here?
Illustrated by Aliki
Published by Western, 1961
Wittels, Harriet and Joan Greisman
Things I Hate!
Illustrated by Jerry McConnel
Published by Human Sciences Press,
  1973
Wittman, Sally
A Special Trade
Illustrated by Karen Gundersheimer
Published by Harper and Row, 1978
Wolcott, Patty
The Marvelous Mud Washing
  Machine
Illustrated by Richard Brown
Published by A-W, 1974
Wolde, Gunilla
Betsy and the Chicken Pox
Illustrated by Gunilla Wolde
Published by Random House, 1976
Wolde, Gunilla
Betsy's Baby Brother
Illustrated by Gunilla Wolde
Published by Random House, 1975
Wolde, Gunilla
Betsy's First Day at Nursery School
Illustrated by Gunilla Wolde
Published by Random House, 1976
Wolde, Gunilla
Tommy and Sarah Dress Up
Illustrated by Gunilla Wolde
Published by Houghton Mifflin, 1972
Wolde, Gunilla
Tommy Goes to the Doctor
Illustrated by Gunilla Wolde
Published by Houghton Mifflin, 1972
Woldin, Beth Weiner
Benjamin's Perfect Solution
Illustrated by Beth Weiner Woldin
Published by Warne, 1979
Woldin, Beth Weiner
Ellie to the Rescue
Illustrated by Beth Weiner Woldin
Published by Warne, 1979
Wolf, Pearl
Gorilla Baby: The Story of Patty Cake
Illustrated
Published by Scholastic, 1975
Wolff, Angelicka
Mom, I Broke My Arm
Illustrated by Leo Glueckselig
Published by Lion Press, 1969
Wolff, Angelicka
Mom! I Need Glasses
Illustrated by Dorothy Hill
Published by Lion Press, 1971
Wolkstein, Diane
A Cool Ride in the Sky
Illustrated by Paul Galdone
Published by Knopf, 1973
Wolkstein, Diane
The Magic Orange Tree and Other
  Haitian Folktales
Illustrated by Elsa Henriquez
Published by Knopf, 1978
Wolkstein, Diane
Squirrel's Song
Illustrated by Lillian Hoban
Published by Knopf, 1976
Wong, Herbert
My Goldfish
Illustrated by Arvis Stewart
Published by A-W, 1969
**Wong, Herbert and Matthew F.
  Vessel**
My Lady Bug
Illustrated by Marie Nonnast
  Bohlen
Published by A-W, 1969
**Wong, Herbert and Matthew F.
  Vessel**
Our Tree
Illustrated by Kenneth Longtemps
Published by A-W, 1969
Wong, Kate
Don't Put the Vinegar in the
  Copper
Illustrated by Stephanie Lowe
Published by Children's Book Press,
  S.F., (n.d.)
Wood, Angela
Kids Can Count
Illustrated by Angela Wood
Published by Kids Can Press
  (Canada), 1976
Woolley, Catherine
I Like Trains
Illustrated by George Fonseca
Published by Harper and Row, 1965
Wright, Ethel
Saturday Walk
Illustrated by Richard Rose
Published by A-W, 1954
Wright, Blanche Fisher
The Real Mother Goose

Illustrated by Blanche Fisher Wright
Published by Rand McNally, 1965
Wright, Dare
Edith and the Little Bear Lend a Hand
Illustrated by Dare Wright
Published by Random House, 1972
Wright, Dare
The Lonely Doll
Illustrated by Dare Wright
Published by Doubleday, 1966
Wright, Mildred W.
Henri Goes to the Mardi Gras
Illustrated by Syd Hoff
Published by Putnam, 1971
Wyndham, Robert, Ed.
Chinese Mother Goose Rhymes
Illustrated by Edward Young
Published by Collins-World, 1968
Wynne-Jones, Tim
Madeline and Ermadello
Illustrated by Lindsey Hallam
Published by Canadian Women's Educational Press, 1977
Yarbrough, Camille
Cornrows
Illustrated by Carole Byard
Published by Coward, 1979
Yaroslava
Tusya and the Pot of Gold
Illustrated
Published by Atheneum, 1971
Yashima, Taro
Crow Boy
Illustrated by Taro Yashima
Published by Viking Press, 1955
Yashima, Taro
Momo's Kitten
Illustrated by Taro Yashima
Published by Viking Press, 1961
Yashima, Taro
Seashore Story
Illustrated by Taro Yashima
Published by Viking Press, 1967
Yashima, Taro
Umbrella
Illustrated by Taro Yashima
Published by Viking Press, 1958
Yashima, Taro
Village Tree
Illustrated by Taro Yashima
Published by Viking Press, 1953
Yellow Robe, Rosebud
Tonweya and the Eagles and Other Lakota Indian Tales-Retold
Illustrated by Jerry Pinkney
Published by Dial, 1979
Yeoman, John
Bear's Winter Picnic
Illustrated by Quentin Blake
Published by Macmillan, 1971
Yeoman, John
Beatrice and Vanessa
Illustrated by Quentin Blake
Published by Macmillan, 1975
Yeoman, John
Mouse Trouble
Illustrated by Quentin Blake
Published by Macmillan, 1973
Yeoman, John
Sixes and Sevens
Illustrated by Quentin Blake
Published by Macmillan, 1974
Yeoman, John
The Young Performing Horse
Illustrated by Quentin Blake
Published by Scholastic, 1979
Ylla
Two Little Bears
Illustrated by Ylla
Published by Harper and Row, 1954
Yolen, Jane
Little Spotted Fish
Illustrated by Friso Henstra
Published by Seabury, 1975
Yolen, Jane
Milkweed Days
Illustrated by Gabriel Amadeus Cooney
Published by T.Y. Crowell, 1976
Yolen, Jane
No Bath Tonight
Illustrated by Nancy Winslow Parker
Published by T.Y. Crowell, 1979
Yolen, Jane
The Rainbow Rider
Illustrated by Michael Foreman
Published by T.Y. Crowell, 1974
Yolen, Jane
The Seeing Stick
Illustrated by Mel Furukawa
Published by T.Y. Crowell, 1977
Yolen, Jane
The Simple Prince
Illustrated by Jack Kent
Published by Parents Magazine Press, 1979
Yolen, Jane and Tomie DePaola
The Giants' Farm
Illustrated by Tomie DePaola
Published by Seabury, 1977
Yoo, Grace
Two Korean Brothers: A Story of Hungbu and Nolbu
Illustrated
Published by Far Eastern Research Center, 1970

Yorinks, Arthur
Sid and Sol
Illustrated by Richard Egielski
Published by Farrar, Straus and Giroux, 1977

Young, Miriam
Beware the Polar Bear: Safety on the Ice
Illustrated by Robert Quackenbush
Published by Lothrop, 1970

Young, Miriam
If I Drove a Tractor
Illustrated by Robert Quackenbush
Published by Lothrop, 1973

Young, Miriam
If I Drove a Train
Illustrated by Robert Quackenbush
Published by Lothrop, 1972

Young, Miriam
If I Drove a Truck
Illustrated by Robert Quackenbush
Published by Lothrop, 1967

Young, Miriam
If I Rode a Dinosaur
Illustrated by Robert Quackenbush
Published by Lothrop, 1974

Young, Miriam
Jellybeans for Breakfast
Illustrated by Beverly Komoda
Published by Parents Magazine Press, 1968

Young, Miriam
Miss Suzy's Easter Suprise
Illustrated by Arnold Lobel
Published by Parents Magazine Press, 1972

Yulya
Bears Are Sleeping
Illustrated by Nonny Hogrogian
Published by Scribner, 1967

Zacharias, Thomas
But Where Is the Green Parrot?
Illustrated by Wanda Zacharias
Published by Delacorte, 1968

Zaffo, George
Big Book of Fire Engines
Illustrated by George Zaffo
Published by Grosset & Dunlap, 1970

Zaffo, George
Big Book of Real Boats and Ships
Illustrated by George Zaffo
Published by Grosset & Dunlap, 1972

Zakhoder, Boris
Rosachok: A Russian Story
Illustrated by Yaroslava Mills
Published by Lothrop, 1970

Zalben, Jane B.
Basil and Hillary
Illustrated by Jane B. Zalben
Published by Macmillan, 1975

Zalben, Jane
Cecilia's Older Brother
Illustrated
Published by Macmillan, 1973

Zalben, Jane
Lyle and Humus
Illustrated by Jane Zalben
Published by Macmillan, 1974

Zemach, Harve
Judge: An Untrue Tale
Illustrated by Margot Zemach
Published by Farrar, Straus and Giroux, 1969

Zemach, Harve
Mommy, Buy Me a China Doll
Illustrated by Margot Zemach
Published by Farrar, Straus and Giroux, 1975

Zemach, Harve and Kathe Zemach
Princess and Froggie
Illustrated by Margot Zemach
Published by Farrar, Straus and Giroux, 1975

Zemach, Harve and Margot Zemach
Salt: A Russian Tale
Illustrated by Margot Zemach
Published by Farrar, Straus and Giroux, 1976

Zemach, Kathe
The Beautiful Rat
Illustrated by Kathe Zemach
Published by Scholastic, 1979

Zemach, Margot
Hush Little Baby
Illustrated by Margot Zemach
Published by Dutton, 1976

Zemach, Margot
It Could Always Be Worse: A Yiddish Folktale
Illustrated by Margot Zemach
Published by Farrar, Straus and Giroux, 1977

Zemach, Margot
Little Tiny Woman
Illustrated by Margot Zemach
Published by Bobbs-Merrill, 1965

Zemach, Margot
To Hilda for Helping
Illustrated by Margot Zemach
Published by Farrar, Straus and Giroux, 1977

Zetlan, Marvin
Clumsy Octopus
Illustrated
Published by Harvey House, 1962

Ziegler, Sandra
All of Grandmother's Clocks: About Time
Illustrated by Helen Simon
Published by Children's Press, 1977

Ziljlstra, Tjerk
Benny and His Goose or the Royal Game of the Goose
Illustrated by Ivo DeWeerd
Published by McGraw-Hill, 1975

Zim, Herbert
What's Inside of Me?
Illustrated by Herschel Wartik
Published by Morrow, 1952

Zimelman, Nathan
Walls Are to Be Walked
Illustrated by Donald Carrick
Published by Dutton, 1977

Zimmerman, Arnold
Fafnerl, the Ice Dragon
Illustrated by Arnold Zimmerman
Published by Crossing Press, 1973

Zimmerman, Arnold
Troll Island
Illustrated by Arnold Zimmerman
Published by Crossing Press, 1977

Zimmerman, Naoma
Baby Animals
Illustrated
Published by Rand McNally, 1945

Zindel, Paul
I Love My Mother
Illustrated by John Melo
Published by Harper and Row, 1975

Ziner, Feenie and Paul Galdone
Counting Carnival
Illustrated by Paul Galdone
Published by Coward, 1962

Zion, Gene
All Falling Down
Illustrated by Margaret B. Graham
Published by Harper and Row, 1951

Zion, Gene
Dear Garbage Man
Illustrated by Margaret B. Graham
Published by Harper and Row, 1957

Zion, Gene
Harry and the Lady Next Door
Illustrated by Margaret B. Graham
Published by Harper and Row, 1960

Zion, Gene
Harry by the Sea
Illustrated by Margaret B. Graham
Published by Harper and Row, 1965

Zion, Gene
Harry, the Dirty Dog
Illustrated by Margaret B. Graham
Published by Harper and Row, 1956

Zion, Gene
Meanest Squirrel I Ever Met
Illustrated by Margaret B. Graham
Published by Scribner, 1962

Zion, Gene
No Roses for Harry
Illustrated by Margaret B. Graham
Published by Harper and Row, 1975

Zion, Gene
Plant Sitter
Illustrated by Margaret B. Graham
Published by Harper and Row, 1959

Zicn, Gene
Really Spring
Illustrated by Margaret B. Graham
Published by Harper and Row, 1956

Zion, Gene
Sugar Mouse Cake
Illustrated by Margaret B. Graham
Published by Scribner, 1964

Zion, Gene
The Summer Snowman
Illustrated by Margaret B. Graham
Published by Harper and Row, 1955

Zistel, Era
Thistle
Illustrated
Published by Random House, 1967

Zoll, Max
Animal Babies
Illustrated by Hanns Reich
Published by Hill and Wang, 1971

Zolotow, Charlotte
Big Brother
Illustrated by Mary Chalmers
Published by Harper and Row, 1960

Zolotow, Charlotte
Big Sister and Little Sister
Illustrated by Martha Alexander
Published by Harper and Row, 1966

Zolotow, Charlotte
The Bunny Who Found Easter
Illustrated by Betty F. Peterson
Published by Parnassus Press, 1959

Zolotow, Charlotte
Do You Know What I'll Do?
Illustrated by Garth Williams
Published by Harper and Row, 1958

Zolotow, Charlotte
A Father Like That
Illustrated by Ben Shecter
Published by Harper and Row, 1971

Zolotow, Charlotte
The Hating Book
Illustrated by Ben Shecter
Published by Harper and Row, 1969

Zolotow, Charlotte
Hold My Hand

Illustrated by Thomas DiGrazia
Published by Harper and Row, 1972
Zolotow, Charlotte
I Have a Horse of My Own
Illustrated by Yoko Mitsuhaski
Published by Abelard, 1964
Zolotow, Charlotte
If It Weren't for You
Illustrated by Ben Shecter
Published by Harper and Row, 1966
Zolotow, Charlotte
Janey
Illustrated by Ronald Himler
Published by Harper and Row, 1973
Zolotow, Charlotte
May I Visit?
Illustrated by Erik Blegvad
Published by Harper and Row, 1976
Zolotow, Charlotte
Mister Rabbit and the Lovely Present
Illustrated by Maurice Sendak
Published by Harper and Row, 1962
Zolotow, Charlotte
My Friend John
Illustrated by Ben Shecter
Published by Harper and Row, 1968
Zolotow, Charlotte
My Grandson Lew
Illustrated
Published by Harper and Row, 1974
Zolotow, Charlotte
New Friend
Illustrated by Arvis L. Stewart
Published by Abelard, 1968
Zolotow, Charlotte
Over and Over
Illustrated by Garth Williams
Published by Harper and Row, 1957
Zolotow, Charlotte
Park Book
Illustrated by H.A. Rey
Published by Harper and Row, 1944
Zolotow, Charlotte
The Quarreling Book
Illustrated by Arnold Lobel
Published by Harper and Row, 1963
Zolotow, Charlotte
The Sky Was Blue
Illustrated by Garth Williams
Published by Harper and Row, 1963
Zolotow, Charlotte
Sleepy Book
Illustrated by Vladimir Bobri
Published by Lothrop, 1958

Zolotow, Charlotte
Someday
Illustrated by Arnold Lobel
Published by Harper and Row, 1965
Zolotow, Charlotte
Someone New
Illustrated by Erik Blegvad
Published by Harper and Row, 1978
Zolotow, Charlotte
Storm Book
Illustrated by Margaret B. Graham
Published by Harper and Row, 1952
Zolotow, Charlotte
Summer Is
Illustrated by J. Archer
Published by Abelard, 1967
Zolotow, Charlotte
The Summer Night
Illustrated
Published by Harper and Row, 1974
Zolotow, Charlotte
Three Funny Friends
Illustrated by Mary Chalmers
Published by Harper and Row, 1961
Zolotow, Charlotte
Tiger Called Thomas
Illustrated by Kurt Werth
Published by Lothrop, 1963
Zolotow, Charlotte
Unfriendly Book
Illustrated by William Pene Du Bois
Published by Harper and Row, 1975
Zolotow, Charlotte
Wake Up and Good Night
Illustrated by Leonard Weisgard
Published by Harper and Row, 1971
Zolotow, Charlotte
When I Have a Little Girl
Illustrated by Hilary Knight
Published by Harper and Row, 1965
Zolotow, Charlotte
When I Have a Son
Illustrated by Hilary Knight
Published by Harper and Row, 1967
Zolotow, Charlotte
When the Wind Stops
Illustrated by Howard Knotts
Published by Harper and Row, 1975
Zolotow, Charlotte
William's Doll
Illustrated by William Pene DuBois
Published by Harper and Row, 1972
Zweifel, Frances W.
Bony
Illustrated by Whitney Darrow
Published by Harper and Row, 1977

Publishers Index

A-W Pubs., Inc.
95 Madison Ave.
New York, NY 10016
Aardvark
526 W. 112th St.
New York, NY 10025
Abelard
Abelard-Schuman, Ltd.
Harper & Row Pubs., Inc.
Scranton, PA 18512
Abingdon Press
201 Eighth Ave., S.
Nashville, TN 37202
Activity Resources Co., Inc.
P.O. Box 4875
20655 Hathaway Ave.
Hayward, CA 94541
Astor-Honor, Inc.
48 E. 43rd St.
New York, NY 10017
Atheneum Pubs.
Book Warehouse, Inc.
Vreeland Ave., Boro of Totowa
Paterson, NJ 07512
Awani Press
P.O. Box 881
Fredericksburg, TX 78624
Beacon Press, Inc.
25 Beacon St.
Boston, MA 02108
Before We Are Six (Canada)
15 King Street North
Waterloo, Ontario
Canada
Blaine-Ethridge Books
13977 Penrod St.
Detroit, MI 48223
Bobbs-Merrill Co., Inc.
A Thomas Audel Co.
4300 W. 62nd St.
Indianapolis, IN 46206
Bonim
79 Delancey St.
New York, NY 10002
Bookstore Press
Box 191
RFD 1
Freeport, ME 04032
Bradbury Press
E.P. Dutton & Co., Inc.
201 Park Ave. S.
New York, NY 10003

Brasch
Brasch & Mulliner
227 W. B St.
Ontario, CA 91791
Canadian Women's Educational Press
Suite 305
280 Bloor St., W.
Toronto, Ontario
Canada
Carolrhoda Books, Inc.
241 First Ave., N.
Minneapolis, MN 55401
C.E. Tuttle Co., Inc.
28 S. Main St.
Rutland, VT 05701
Children's Books Press
1461 Ninth Ave.
San Francisco, CA 94122
Children's Press, Inc.
1224 W. Van Buren St.
Chicago, IL 60607
Child's World
Children's Press, Inc.
1224 W. Van Buren St.
Chicago, IL 60607
Collins-World Pub. Co.
2080 W. 117th St.
Cleveland, OH 44111
Contemporary Books
180 N. Michigan Ave.
Chicago, IL 60601
Coward
Coward, McCann & Geoghegan, Inc.
390 Murray Hill Pkwy.
East Rutherford, NJ 07073
Crossing Press
R.D. 3
Trumansburg, NY 14886
Crown Pubs., Inc.
1 Park Ave
New York, NY 10016
D. White
White, David, Co.
14 Vanderventer Ave.
Port Washington, NY 11050
Delacorte Press
Dial Press
1 Dag Hammarskjold Plaza
245 E. 47th St.
New York, NY 10017
Denison, T.S. & Co., Inc.
5100 W. 82nd St.
Minneapolis, MN 55437

Dial Press
1 Dag Hammarskjold Plaza
245 E. 47th St.
New York, NY 10017
Dillon Press
500 S. Third St.
Minneapolis, MN 55415
Doubleday & Co.
501 Franklin Ave.
Garden City, NY 11530
Drum & Spear Press
1371 Fairmont St., N.W.
Washington, DC 20009
Dutton, E.P. & Co.
201 Park Ave., S.
New York, NY 10003
Exposition Press, Inc.
900 S. Oyster Bay Rd.
Hicksville, NY 11801
Farrar, Straus & Giroux, Inc.
19 Union Square
New York, NY 10003
Far Eastern Research Center
P.O. Box 31151
Washington, DC 20031
Feminist Press
SUNY/College at Old Westbury
Box 334
Old Westbury, NY 11568
Follett Pub. Co.
1010 W. Washington Blvd.
Chicago, IL 60607
Garrard Pub. Co.
1607 N. Market St.
Champaign, IL 61820
Greenwillow
William Morrow & Co., Inc.
Wilmor Warehouse
6 Henderson Dr.
West Caldwell, NJ 07006
Hale, E.M. & Co.
128 W. River St.
Chippewa Falls, WI 54729
Harcourt, Brace & Jovanovich
757 Third Ave.
New York, NY 10017
Harper and Row Pubs., Inc.
Scranton, PA 18512
Harvey House
E.M. Hale & Co.
128 W. River St.
Chippewa Falls, WI 54729
Hastings House Pubs., Inc.
10 E. 40th St.
New York, NY 10016
Hill and Wang
Farrar, Straus & Giroux, Inc.

19 Union Square, W.
New York, NY 10003
Holiday House, Inc.
18 E. 53rd St.
New York, NY 10022
Holt, Rinehart & Winston, Inc.
383 Madison Ave.
New York, NY 10017
Houghton Mifflin Co.
2 Park St.
Boston, MA 02107
Human Sciences Press
72 Fifth Ave.
New York, NY 10011
Island Press
175 Bahia Via
Fort Myers Beach, FL 33931
Japan Pubns.
Japan Pubns. Trading Center, Inc.
200 Clearbrook Rd.
Elmsford, NY 10523
John Day Co., Inc.
10 E. 53rd St.
New York, NY 10022
Kids Can Press (Canada)
Box 5974
Station A
Toronto, Ontario
Canada
Knopf, Alfred
Random House, Inc.
400 Hahn Rd.
Westminster, MD 21157
Lantern Press, Inc.
354 Hussey Rd.
Mount Vernon, NY 10552
Larousse & Co., Inc.
572 Fifth Ave.
New York, NY 10036
Lerner Publications Co.
241 First Ave., N.
Minneapolis, MN 55401
Lion Press
Sayre Publishing, Inc.
111 E. 39th St.
New York, NY 10016
Lippincott, J.B. Co.
East Washington Sq.
Philadelphia, PA 19105
Little, Brown, & Co.
200 West St.
Waltham, MA 02154
Lollipop Power, Inc.
P.O. Box 1171
Chapel Hill, NC 27514
Lothrop
Lothrop, Lee & Shepard Co.
William Morrow & Co., Inc.

Wilmor Warehouse
6 Henderson Dr.
West Caldwell, NJ 07006
MacMillan Pub. Co., Inc.
Riverside, NJ 08075
McGraw-Hill Book Co.
1221 Ave. of the Americas
New York, NY 10036
Messner
Messner, Julian, Inc.
Gulf & Western Corp./Simon &
   Schuster Div.
1221 Ave. of the Americas
New York, NY 10036
Methuen, Inc.
572 Fifth Ave.
New York, NY 10036
Mojave Books
7040 Darby Ave.
Reseda, CA 91335
Morrow
Morrow, William & Co.,
   Inc.
Wilmor Warehouse
6 Henderson Dr.
West Caldwell, NJ 07006
NELP
National Educational Laboratory
   Pubs., Inc.
813 Airport Blvd.
Austin, TX 78702
National Textbook
8259 Niles Center Rd.
Skokie, IL 60076
Nursery Books
4430 School Way
Castro Valley, CA 94546
Oddo Pub., Inc.
Storybook Acres
Box 68
Fayetteville, GA 30214
O'Hara
O'Hara, J. Philip, Inc., Pubs.
Book Trading Ltd.
559 W. 26th St.
New York, NY 10001
Pantheon
Random House, Inc.
457 Hahn Rd.
Westminster, MD 21157
Parents Magazine Press
52 Vanderbilt Ave.
New York, NY 10017
Parnassus Press
4080 Halleck St.
Emeryville, CA 94608
Peace Press, Inc.
3828 Willat Ave.
Culver City, CA 90230

Pelican Pub. Co., Inc.
630 Burmaster St.
Gretna, LA 70053
Penguin Books, Inc.
625 Madison Ave.
New York, NY 10022
Platt & Munk Pubs.
Questor Educational Products
1055 Bronx River Ave.
Bronx, NY 10472
Plays, Inc.
8 Arlington St.
Boston, MA 02116
Prentice-Hall, Inc.
Englewood Cliffs, NJ 07632
Press Gang Publishers (Canada)
603 Powell St.
Vancouver, B.C.
Canada
Putnam
Putnam's, G.P., Sons
390 Murray Hill Pkwy.
East Rutherford, NJ 07073
Quadrangle
Harper & Row, Keystone
   Industrial Park
Quadrangle/The New York
   Times Co.
Scranton, PA 18512
Raintree
MacDonald-Raintree, Inc.
Raintree Children's Books
205 W. Highland Ave.
Milwaukee, WI 53203
Rand McNally & Co.
P.O. Box 7600
Chicago, IL 60680
Random
Random House, Inc.
457 Hahn Rd.
Westminster, MD 21157
Scholastic
Scholastic Book Services
906 Sylvan Ave.
Englewood Cliffs, NJ 07632
Scribner
Scribner's, Charles, Sons
Vreeland Ave.
Totowa, NJ 07512
Scroll Press
129 E. 49th St.
New York, NY 10028
Seabury Press, Inc.
Somers, CT 06071
Silver Dollar
Silver Dollar City, MO 65616
Simon & Schuster, Inc.
1230 Ave. of the Americas
New York, NY 10020

Stemmer House Pubs., Inc.
2627 Caves Rd.
Owings Mills, MD 21117
Stephen Greene Press
P.O. Box 1000
Fessenden Rd., Indian Flat
Brattleboro, VT 05301
Sterling Pub. Co.
2 Park Ave.
New York, NY 10016
Taplinger Pub. Co., Inc.
200 Park Ave.
New York, NY 10003
Tundra Books
Scribner
597 5th Ave.
New York, NY 10017
Two Continents Pub., Inc.
5 S. Union St.
Lawrence, MA 01843
Valkyrie Press, Inc.
2125 First Ave., S.
St. Petersburg, FL 33712
Vanguard Press, Inc.
424 Madison Ave.
New York, NY 10017
Vermont Crossroads Press
P.O. Box 333
Waitsfield, VT 05673
Viking Press, Inc.
625 Madison Ave.
New York, NY 10022
Walck
David McKay Co., Inc.
750 Third Ave.
New York, NY 10017
Walker & Co.
720 Fifth Ave.
New York, NY 10019
Warne
Warne, Frederick, & Co., Inc.
101 Fifth Ave.
New York, NY 10003
Watts
Watts, Franklin, Inc., Pubs.
Grolier Inc.
730 Fifth Ave.
New York, NY 10019
Weatherhill
Charles E. Tuttle, Co., Inc.
28 S. Main St.
Rutland, VT 05701
Western Pub. Co., Inc.
Dept. M
1220 Mound Ave.
Racine, WI 53404
Westminster
Westminster Press, R.R. Donnelly & Sons
South Plant
Rt. 32 W.
Crawfordsville, IN 47933
Whitman, Albert, & Co.
560 W. Lake St.
Chicago, IL 60606
Windy Hill Press
1003 Turkey Run Rd.
McLean, VA 22101

DATE DUE